ACKNOWLEDGEMENTS

We are grateful for the help and support of many people:

The staff of the information desk of the John Steinbeck Library of Salinas, California
for helping us track down bibliographical information.

Ellen Bob of Bob and Bob Books in Palo Alto, California for suggesting resources.

Randee Friedman of Sounds Write Productions, Inc., in San Diego, California,
the Jewish music maven, for helping us find music resources.

Joel Eglash of Transcontinental Music, Inc., for graciously sharing his knowledge
of contemporary Jewish music.

Nachama Skolnik Moskowitz, Principal of the Minneapolis Jewish Day School,
for generously sharing with us the *tefilah* curricula she wrote for her school,
and for allowing us to use some of her activity ideas.

Rabbi Eve Ben-Ora of Temple Micah, Denver, for her wonderful suggestions and careful editing.

All of our friends who provided moral support and encouragement.

Audrey Friedman Marcus and Rabbi Raymond A. Zwerin of A.R.E. Publishing, Inc.,
for supporting and encouraging our Jewish educational writing.

Steve Brodsky for continuing the wonderful traditions of A.R.E. Publishing, Inc.
while bringing new ideas and directions to this project.

CONTENTS

INTRODUCTION

TEFILAH

There is little that matches the power and beauty of Jews gathered together in worship. While we can pray individually, structured Jewish worship is a driving force that can bring a community together.

We come together knowing that throughout the world other Jews also gather to share the worship experience. And prayer links us not only to Jewish communities in present time, but also to generations past and future. When we recite the *Sh'ma*, the *Aleinu*, the *Kaddish*, or other prayers, we merge with Jews in other places and at other times who have recited the same words.

Prayer connects us with other Jews, but most importantly, prayer connects us to God. It is the primary means of communication between human beings and God. Through prayer we express our appreciation and gratitude, our frustrations, and our inmost yearnings.

Tefilah is a most complex subject. Teaching the mechanics of reading Hebrew is straightforward, but teaching an understanding of and appreciation for the liturgy is not. Teaching the order of the service, the history of specific prayers and their meanings, can be done step by step, but teaching our students to pray with feeling and intent is a different sort of challenge. We can pass on a plethora of information, demonstrate how to pray, and provide a variety of worship experiences, but, ultimately, each individual determines the impact that such knowledge has on his or her approach to praying.

To put it in terms that are often used to describe liturgy, we can teach the *keva* — the fixed material — but we cannot teach *kavanah*, the feeling. And yet, how we teach the *keva* can significantly influence the students' *kavanah* when praying. If teachers spend most of the time teaching rote pronunciation of the prayers, and very little time on their meaning, then we give students the wrong message of what is most important.

In order for students to begin to develop *kavanah* when praying, we must teach not only how to read the prayers and what they mean, but also the melodies and choreography associated with each phase of the worship service. We must teach not only the mechanics of prayer, but also the underlying spirit and soul of what prayer can do for the Jew who prays.

Even if we are able to do all this, we cannot guarantee that students will develop a sense of *kavanah*. But we will have laid the foundations for this development. The material in *Teaching Tefilah* is designed to help teachers, educators, rabbis, and cantors meet this challenge.

ABOUT THIS BOOK

CONTENTS

Parts I through IV of *Teaching Tefilah* contain fifteen chapters, each dealing with a section of the worship service or a topic related to prayer. Part V, new in this expanded revised edition, contains six new essays reflecting on recent trends in Jewish worship. (See introduction to part V, p. 125).

Each of the first fifteen chapters begins with an Overview which consists of an historical background of the prayer or topic (including sources), important themes, and how that prayer is utilized in the worship service. Following the Overview are Insights from the Tradition, which include quotations about the prayer or topic, as well as other material from secondary sources which help to illuminate or add to our appreciation. While these Insights are not crucial for understanding the prayer or topic, they will greatly enrich the learning process. The Activities, which follow the Insights, are divided into five sections. Within each section the activities are listed according to grade level. We have placed each activity at the grade level where we believe it will be most effective. Certainly, some of the activities may be modified for use in other grade levels , especially in Day School settings. We have used the following divisions: K-2 (early elementary), 3-5 (upper elementary), 6-8 (intermediate), and 9 and up (secondary and adult). Many of the activities are appropriate for more than one level and are so marked. Some of the K-2 activities are also appropriate for preschoolers.

The five sections of activities are:

Text and Context: These activities teach the themes, historical background, and use of the prayer or topic, as well as its place in Jewish liturgy. A variety of teaching strategies is employed.

Arts: This section includes activities in the areas of music, dance, drama, visual arts, and creative writing.

Beyond the Text: Activities in this section use the text as a "jumping off" point to explore issues and ideas which are contained in the prayer, but which go beyond its parameters.

Hebrew: Key words and phrases from the prayer or topic serve as the focal point of these activities, which are designed to enrich the students' understanding of the Hebrew text.

Family: These activities can be used for family programs in the school. Many can be adapted for families to do at home, or for all-school programs.

Each chapter ends with a Bibliography of books, audio recordings, and other resource materials that have been cited in the chapter or which are of particular relevance to the theme. A source is listed for all audiovisual materials. See the listing of audiovisual distributors at the end of the book for contact information.

Also provided is a Glossary of Hebrew terms which appear in the text. These are defined when they are first used; often thereafter, the Hebrew term is used exclusively. The goal is for the teacher to develop a Hebrew liturgy vocabulary, which can be passed along to the students.

The end of the book contains a Bibliography of *siddurim*, comprehensive secondary sources on Jewish liturgy, and other materials, some utilized in this book, which the teacher may also find useful.

WHO CAN USE THIS BOOK

Teaching Tefilah is both a resource book and a teacher's guide. The material herein is primarily for use by teachers in grades K-12. It can be used effectively in a variety of setings.

In Day Schools and Religious Schools, *Teaching Tefilah* can be the basis for a *tefilah* curriculum or serve as a supplement to programs which are already in place.

Participants in and leaders of Junior Congregations will discover that using *Teaching Tefilah* will greatly enhance their worship experiences.

This book can serve as a resource for individuals and groups wishing to become more familiar with Jewish liturgy, e.g., B'nai Mitzvah students, adult study groups, or Havurot.

Teaching Tefilah may also be used as the basis for a weekend retreat or summer camp program.

Substitute teachers will benefit by having ready-made teaching ideas upon which they can draw in last minute situations.

Rabbis and others who lead worship services will find *Teaching Tefilah* an invaluable resource for teaching and learning about prayer. The new chapters included in this Revised Edition will be of particular interest to those seeking to invigorate their synagogue's prayer experience.

And finally, non-Jews who wish to learn more about the history and practice of Jewish liturgy will also find this a useful resource.

PROCEDURE FOR TEACHING TEFILAH

When beginning to teach a course or unit on *tefilah*, the teacher should first clarify the goals and objectives. These goals and objectives may be part of the curriculum given to the teacher, or may need to be created by the teacher in consultation with the Director of Education. The types of activities the teacher chooses will in large measure reflect the goals and objectives.

It is also important that the teacher become familiar with the *siddur* of the synagogue or school. Being aware of the *tefilah* experiences of the students and community will help guide the teacher to prepare lessons that support and enrich those experiences. In turn, those experiences can support the class curriculum. It would also be beneficial to discuss with the rabbi or Director of Education any particular sensitivities and concerns that should be addressed when teaching the course.

In preparing to teach a prayer or topic, it is suggested that the teacher first read the Overview and Insights, and then examine the instructional activities, choosing those that best suit the teaching objectives and the grade level of the students. The teacher should then decide what, if any, additional information or resources will be necessary to enhance the lesson.

In conjunction with learning about *tefilah*, students need opportunities to pray. We strongly suggest that a regular *tefilah* experience be established if one is not already in place. The service can be held either in the sanctuary, the classroom, or another appropriate area. While it is important that students be exposed to worship in the sanctuary, they should also understand that prayer can take place anywhere.

We also suggest incorporating teaching about *tefilah* within the worship experience itself. If the school or camp has regular *tefilah* or the synagogue has Junior Congregation, these provide opportunities for the students to demonstrate and share what they have learned.

To provide continuity to a *tefilah* course, the teacher may wish to consider one of the following year-long projects. The students can create a loose-leaf *siddur*, adding to it each week. Each page should include the prayer or topic being taught and provide space for the students' creative expression. This would be an ideal way to summarize and conclude each lesson. Alternatively, the students can create a *tefilah* journal in which they record personal reactions to the course material and *tefilah* experiences. Each week, the teacher should suggest one or more questions or topics for the students to write about.

IN CONCLUSION

Tefilah is one of the most challenging topics for the classroom teacher. As the students learn about the prayers, their meaning, significance, and context in the liturgy, we hope they will also develop a love and appreciation for *tefilah* which will deepen their spiritual awareness, strengthen their ties to the Jewish people, and connect them to the Divine.

CHAPTER ONE:
AVODAH: JEWISH WORSHIP

OVERVIEW

In the Torah, two of the primary methods of communication between God and human beings are prayer and sacrifice. While prayer is significant, sacrifices seem to take precedence in the biblical tradition. The most common sacrificial offerings were animals, but grain and other produce were also offered. In fact, the first sacrifices recorded in the Torah were offered by Cain ("fruit of the soil") and Abel ("the choicest of the firstborn of his flock") (Genesis 4).

Sacrifices were often made at various local shrines, such as Beth El, Shiloh, Beersheva, Hebron, and Gibeon. Many of these had been Canaanite shrines which the Hebrews took over upon settling in the land.

Sacrifices, such as animals (often the firstborn) or produce (such as the firstfruits), were a way of showing gratitude to God for the blessings one received. Sacrifices also demonstrated one's submission to God Who controlled nature, and they served as recognition/acknowledgement of God's power.

Human sacrifice, however, which was practiced by some ancient cultures, is rejected by the biblical tradition. The Torah specifically forbids offering a child to Molech (Leviticus 18:21 and 20:2-5), and the account of Abraham's binding of Isaac and God's intervention would suggest that human beings were never to be offered up (Genesis 22).

The building of the *Beit HaMikdash* (Temple) in the middle of the tenth century in Jerusalem by King Solomon impacted the religious life of the people, although local shrines were not completely displaced.

The Temple ritual was conducted by the priests, the *Kohen Gadol* (High Priest) assisted by the *Levi'im* (secondary priests). Sacrifices were offered thrice daily, with special additional sacrifices offered on Shabbat and holidays. "The essential element of the daily Temple service was the offering of the *tamid* (continual) sacrifice of two lambs, one in the morning, with which the service began, and one in the afternoon, with which it concluded" (*Encyclopaedia Judaica*, vol. 15, col. 974).

Individuals were permitted to bring offerings between these two sacrifices. They included: *n'davah* (freewill offering), *olah* (burnt offering), *sh'lamim* (peace offerings), *todah* (thanksgiving offering), *minchah* (meal offering), *chata'ot* (sin offerings), and *asham* (guilt offering).

Everyone, of course, could not participate personally at the sacrificial service. Instead, during the late biblical period, the general populace was represented at the sacrifices through a system known as *Ma'amadot* (standing groups). The country was divided into twenty-four areas, with representatives from each area traveling to Jerusalem for a week at a time two times each year. Abraham Millgram points out that at the very time when these representatives were at the *Beit HaMikdash*, "those who remained at home also gathered in their local synagogues . . . and recited the psalms that were chanted at the Temple service." (*Jewish Worship*, p. 78)

In addition to the psalms, which were always part of the ritual at the *Beit HaMikdash*, a liturgy developed to accompany the offerings. Among the biblical passages read were the Ten Commandments and the three paragraphs of the *Sh'ma*. Toward the end of the Second Temple period (first century of the Common Era), prayers composed by the rabbis, including *Ahavah Rabbah, Emet V'yatziv, R'tzei,* and *Sim Shalom,* also became a part of the ritual. Whether these prayers originated in the *Beit HaMikdash* and were then transferred to the synagogue (which was beginning to develop, see Chapter 13) or vice versa is difficult to determine. In any case, apart from the Ten Commandments, all other parts of the liturgy of the *Beit HaMikdash* have been preserved in the *siddur* and used in the synagogue. (For the reason the Ten Commandments were eliminated from the worship service, see Chapter 6.)

The synagogue not only adopted the liturgy of the *Beit HaMikdash,* but the structure of worship as well. The morning service, Shacharit, parallels the morning offering; the afternoon service, Minchah, parallels the afternoon offering. Ma'ariv, the evening service, may have derived from the practice of burning the fat and organs at the *Beit HaMikdash* in the evening. As this was not a required sacrifice, there was debate among the sages of the Talmud whether the evening service was mandatory. Rabban Gamliel's ruling that it was required was accepted as the definitive ruling; thus, there were three required daily services. The Musaf service, the additional service on Shabbat and holidays, parallels the additional offering on these days in the *Beit HaMikdash.*

The destruction of the second *Beit HaMikdash* in 70 c.e. by the Romans effectively ended sacrifices as a form of Jewish worship. The rabbis, led by Yochanan ben Zakkai, ruled that Torah (study), *avodah* (prayer), and *g'milut chasadim* (the performance of good deeds) were acceptable substitutes, equally as efficacious as the sacrifices. The term *avodah,* which referred to the service at the *Beit HaMikdash* as well as to a particular offering, was reinterpreted to refer to "the service of the heart" — prayer (*Ta'anit* 2a).

However, the rabbis believed that the *Beit HaMikdash* would one day be rebuilt and the sacrificial cult reinstituted. Prayers reflecting these beliefs were included in the early liturgy of the synagogue and are part of Orthodox *siddurim.* *Kohanim* and *Levi'im* were given a special role in the synagogue service, receiving the first and second calls to bless the Torah (*aliyot*) respectively.

In addition, *Kohanim* were given the privilege of reciting the priestly benediction (*duchen*) during the *Amidah,* a tradition that is still practiced in traditional synagogues.

There are those who are actively preparing for the rebuilding of a third *Beit HaMikdash.* The Temple Institute in Jerusalem oversees research about the "materials, measurements, and forms of the ninety-three sacred Temple vessels" and has begun "construction of these golden, silver, and copper treasures and Priestly garments" (*Guide to the Treasures of the Temple Exhibition*, p. 3).

Reform Judaism rejected the idea of the rebuilding of the *Beit HaMikdash* and the reinstitution of the sacrificial cult; therefore, prayers reflecting these themes were either eliminated entirely from its liturgy or significantly altered to eliminate these ideas. Reconstructionism has also eliminated these prayers from its liturgy. The Conservative liturgy has changed references to the rebuilding of the *Beit HaMikdash* in the future to reminiscences about the *Beit HaMikdash* in the past.

While sacrifices were primary, prayer was also a significant form of communication between God and human beings in the Tanach. Abraham, responding to God's declaration of a covenant, "built an altar to God and invoked God's name" (Genesis 12:8). When Abimelech and his family had been afflicted by God because he had taken Sarah, thinking she was Abraham's sister, "Abraham prayed to God and God healed Abimelech and his wife and his slaves so that they bore children" (Genesis 20:17).

Many biblical prayers are spontaneous pleas to God, the words of which are sometimes included in the text. When Rebekah is barren, Isaac pleads with God on her behalf, but the Torah does not contain his prayer. On the other hand, when Hannah is barren, she offers an eloquent prayer which is contained in I Samuel 2. Another example of prayer is the Song of the Sea (Exodus 15) which the Israelites sang to God upon crossing the Sea of Reeds. And the Book of Psalms is a collection of 150 prayers, many of which were part of the ritual at the *Beit HaMikdash.*

During the period of the *Beit HaMikdash,* but even more so after its destruction, prayer became the primary means of worshiping God. Even before the liturgy was fully developed, the rabbis wrestled with many issues related to prayer. For example, they warned against uttering a vain prayer. "One who cries out [to God] over what is past: it is a vain prayer. If one's wife was pregnant and he said: 'May it be Your will that my wife shall bear a male,' it is a vain prayer. If one was returning from a journey and heard sounds of lamentation in the city and said: 'May it be Your will that they not be in my house,' it is a vain prayer" (*Brachot* 54a).

The rabbis were also concerned about the efficacy of prayer. "R. Meir used to say: 'Two people take to their beds suffering equally from the same illness, or two people are before a criminal court to be judged for the same offense. However, one gets out of bed and the other does not, one escapes death and the other does not. Why does one get up and the other not? Why does one escape death and the other not? Because one prayed and was answered, while the other prayed, but was not answered. Why was one answered and the other not? One prayed with a whole heart and was therefore answered, the other did not pray with a whole heart and was not answered.' R. Eliezer said: 'The one was praying before the final sentence had been pronounced, the other after the final sentence had been pronounced'" (*Rosh HaShanah* 18a).

The rabbis believed that God heard our prayers and answered them. If we human beings could not understand the answer, or could not accept that the answer was just, then it was because human understanding is limited. Prayer remains a theological challenge in our day, particularly in light of the Holocaust. If ever it seemed that prayers should have been answered, it would have been then.

While we cannot know how prayer works, why God seems to answer some prayers and not others (or answers some prayers in the negative), or even if God answers prayers at all, we need to have some understanding of what prayer is.

Prayers of petition are only one type of prayer; there are also prayers of praise and thanksgiving, as well as those in which we ask for God's forgiveness. The majority of prayers in our liturgy are prayers of praise. Even petitionary prayers, such as

the thirteen intermediate *brachot* of the weekday *Amidah*, include the traditional phrase of praise: "*Baruch Atah Adonai*" (Blessed are you, *Adonai*).

We have already seen that the rabbis placed limits on petitionary prayer by prohibiting vain prayer. They also recognized that sometimes a person's prayer might reflect his or her own interest, but not the best interest of the community.

The Palestinian Talmud (*Yoma* V, 3, 42c) contains a report about the prayers which the High Priest recited in the *Beit HaMikdash* on Yom Kippur. He prayed for material and spiritual blessings to be enjoyed by Israel in the new year, and then he asked God *not* to pay attention to prayers of the wayfarers! This request seems strange indeed.

Rabbi Jacob Petuchowski (*Understanding Jewish Prayer*, p. 38) explains the rationale behind the High Priest's unusual prayer. It seems that the wayfarers would ask God to withhold rain in favor of good weather during their journey. The rest of the Jewish community, which depended largely on agriculture, required the timely fall of rain for its very survival. In this context it is clear that the wayfarers' prayers are inappropriate, because they reflect the self-interest of only a small proportion of the population and disregard the best interests of the vast majority. Furthermore, while we are required to pray, God does not need our prayers. Rather, prayer must be viewed as a form of discipline and of self-reflection. Prayer is for our benefit, regardless of whether or not God hears it or responds to it.

This concept is particularly important because Judaism has always stressed that prayers must be linked to action. The prophets often attacked the Temple cult (Isaiah 1:12-15 for example) and rituals such as fasting (Isaiah 58) that the people observed while acting unjustly. The same criticism can be applied to prayers of those who behave unethically. The rabbis considered such a prayer *Chilul HaShem*, a desecration of God's name.

Prayer was not supposed to be escapism from the world, but an opportunity to reflect on the world and our responsibility to it. The Torah passages included in the daily *Birchot HaShachar* remind us of many of our ethical obligations (see Chapter 4). *Pirke Avot*, a collection of sayings and ethical teachings in the Mishnah, is included in most *siddurim*, and traditionally is studied between Pesach and Shavuot on Shabbat afternoons. At best, prayer serves to remind and motivate Jews to fulfill their ritual and ethical *mitzvot* (obligations).

Another issue about prayer which concerned the rabbis was the tension between *keva* (the fixed text of a prayer) and *kavanah* (the intention, devotion, concentration, or focus with which one prayed). The rabbis were at first strongly opposed to writing down prayers; they were considered to be part of the oral tradition (see Chapter 2).

An early discussion about fixed prayer concerning the *mitzvah* of reciting a *brachah* before eating bread is contained in the Talmud (*Brachot* 40a). "Rabbi Meir says: 'If a person sees a loaf of bread and says, "What a fine loaf of bread this is! Bless God who created it," the person has fulfilled the *mitzvah* . . . ' R. Yosi says, 'If a person changes the formula coined by the rabbis, the person has not fulfilled the *mitzvah*.'"

Eventually, those who insisted on a fixed liturgy prevailed. Nevertheless, the rabbis emphasized the importance of praying with *kavanah*. "If one makes prayer a fixed task, it is not a supplication" (*Brachot* 4:4), the Mishnah warns. "One who prays must direct one's heart to heaven" (*Brachot* 31a), the Talmud adds. Just reciting the words, or racing through the liturgy to finish quickly was not considered appropriate; rather, one had to concentrate and be able to pray with devotion and feeling. Some of the sages are reported to have waited an hour from the time they entered the synagogue before praying, in order to get into the right frame of mind (*Brachot* 5:1).

INSIGHTS FROM THE TRADITION

A. Abraham Millgram points out that after the *Beit HaMikdash* was destroyed, the rabbis looked to the teachings about sacrifices for ethical lessons. For example, the meal offering was to be of fine flour mingled with oil to teach that our daily life "should be mingled with the ethical teachings of the Torah." Similarly, when a bird was offered, the crop (gullet) and feathers were removed (whereas animals were normally offered whole) "because the bird flies and eats food which is not its master's, while the domesticated animal is reared on the master's crib." Therefore, we learn that one who worships must be clean from the stains of violence (*Jewish Worship*, p. 54).

B. The medieval Jewish philosopher Moses Maimonides (Rambam) did not accept the sacrificial cult as an appropriate way to worship God. He explained that it was a compromise, instituted by God because it was clear that the Hebrew people was used to such a form of worship and was not yet ready to give it up. By limiting the sacrifices to a certain place (the *Beit HaMikdash*) and certain times, the people were beginning the process that would eventually lead to giving up sacrifice altogether, as they were able to do after the destruction of the second Temple (*Guide for the Perplexed*, Part III, Chapter XXXII).

C. The following *midrash* helped the people deal with the destruction of the *Beit HaMikdash*, suggesting alternatives to the sacrifices which, among other things, had been integral for atonement of sins: "Once, as Rabbi Yochanan ben Zakkai was coming from Jerusalem, Rabbi Joshua followed him and saw the Temple in ruins. 'Woe to us,' Rabbi Joshua cried, 'that this place where Israel atoned for its sins is in ruins.' Rabbi Yochanan replied, 'My son, do not be grieved, for we have another atonement as effective as this: acts of loving-kindness'" (*Avot d'Rabbi Natan* 4).

D. According to the Talmud (*Brachot* 26b), Abraham, Isaac, and Jacob each instituted one of the daily worship services (see Chapter 7). "R. Yosi ben Chanina taught: 'Abraham instituted the morning *Tefilah*, as it says, "And Abraham got up early in the morning to the place where he had stood," and *standing* means *Tefilah*. Isaac instituted the afternoon *Tefilah*, as it says, "And Isaac went out to mediate in the field at dusk," and *meditation* only means *Tefilah* . . . Jacob instituted the evening *Tefilah*, as it says, "And he lighted upon the place," and *lighted upon* only means prayer.'"

E. Some of the Hebrew words relating to sacrifices offer insights into their significance. For example, the word *korban* (sacrifice) is from the root *koof, resh, bet,* which means "to draw near." A sacrifice was a way of drawing near to God. The verb *l'ha'alot,* to sacrifice (usually a burnt offering) is from the root *ayin, lamed, hey,* which in this form means "to bring up." The Hebrew word to pray, *l'hitpallel,* is from the root *pey, lamed, lamed,* which means "to judge oneself."

ACTIVITIES

TEXT AND CONTEXT

1. Ask students to identify the places where they would go to see the following: a baseball game (stadium, arena) and a movie or play (theater). Explain that people gather in certain places to do things together. Ask the students where they gather to pray (synagogue). Point out that although they can pray anywhere, there are special places where Jews come together for worship. Tell the students that before there were individual synagogues, Jews would gather in only one large place in Jerusalem — the *Beit HaMikdash.* Discuss what it would be like if all Jews in your city came together in one place to pray. (K-2)

2. Read to your students *God's Paintbrush* by Sasso, *God Said Amen* by Sasso, *Because Nothing Looks Like God* by Kushner and Kushner, or *Where Does God Live?* by Gold and Perlman. Use these books to begin discussing God with your students and God's relationship to prayer. (K-2)

3. Ask the students if they have ever heard of the word "sacrifice." What does it mean? Have the students ever sacrificed (given up) anything? What would be the hardest thing for them to give up? How does it feel to sacrifice something that belongs to you? Explain how sacrifices were used in ancient Jewish ritual. (K-5)

4. One of the purposes of sacrifice in ancient Israel was to show gratitude to God. Ask the students how they show gratitude. List their

＊ +to their parents

responses on the board. Distribute *siddurim* to the students and ask them to find a prayer that shows gratitude to God. (3-5)

5. It is important that students understand the relationship between prayer and action. Play the following game. Gather the students in a circle. Briefly discuss the relationship between prayer and action. Begin the game by saying, "Prayer leads to action when I say a prayer for someone who is ill and then visit the person." Each student then completes the sentence, "Prayer leads to action when I . . . " A student who is stumped drops out of the game. Play continues until only one person is left. (3-8)

6. According to the rabbis, Abraham, Isaac, and Jacob were responsible for creating the three daily worship services (see Insight D). Divide the students into three groups and assign each group to read one of the biblical passages which is the basis for this tradition: Genesis 19: 27, Genesis 24: 63, Genesis 28: 11. Each group then prepares a short presentation based on the text. (6-8)

7. Briefly discuss with the students the role of the *Kohanim* and *Levi'im* in the *Beit HaMikdash* in Jerusalem. Be sure to point out that these positions were hereditary; one could be a priest only if one's father was a priest (there were no female priests) or if one was a firstborn son who was not redeemed from the priesthood via the ritual of *Pidyon HaBen.* Furthermore, only priests could perform the sacrifices and certain other rituals. Ask the students how this compares with the roles of rabbi and cantor. Students may wish to interview the rabbi and cantor. (6 and up)

8. What if the *Beit HaMikdash* had not been destroyed by the Romans in the year 70 C.E.? After presenting a brief historical background to the students about the destruction of the *Beit HaMikdash* and the consequent cessation of sacrifices, ask the students to pretend that the destruction of the Temple did not occur. What would have been different in Jewish history? What would have been different in Jewish worship? Would we still be offering sacrifices or would we have stopped that practice at a later time? Share with your students that even before the *Beit HaMikdash* was destroyed, some of the prophets expressed criticism of the sacrificial rituals. The prophets were particularly concerned that people would offer sacrifices without changing their behavior. See the following passages: Isaiah 57:14-58:14, Micah 6:1-8. (9 and up)

ARTS

9. One of the purposes of prayer and sacrifice was to show gratitude to God. Direct the students to write a thank-you note for something for which they are grateful. You may wish to read these thank-you notes as part of a worship service. (K-2)

10. The Ten Commandments were read as part of the service in the *Beit HaMikdash* in Jerusalem. To show the importance of this passage, create Ten Commandment plaques. Cut pieces of poster board into tablet shapes. Cover with marbleized paper available in craft shops. Using markers with a chisel point, have the students write the initial word or words of each commandment. Alternatively, use self-hardening clay, which the students shape into tablets and then carve in the first ten letters of the Hebrew alphabet. (K-5)

11. Learn the song "Ten Commandments." Resource: *Bible People Songs* by Klepper and Salkin. (K-3)

12. Listen to the song "*V'asu Li Mikdash*" from *Sounds of Creation/Sounds of Freedom*. Explain to the students that the *Mikdash* (or *Mishkan*/Tabernacle) was the portable sanctuary at which worship took place while the Jewish people was in the wilderness. It is the forerunner of the *Beit HaMikdash*. After listening to the song, ask the students to generate other words that they would use to describe a place in which they would want to worship. (3-8)

13. Use chalk pastels to illustrate the *midrash* which credits each patriarch with establishing one of the prayer services (see Insight D). The pictures should reflect the time of day appropriate to each Patriarch. (3-5)

14. Direct students to make a diorama of the *Beit HaMikdash* in Jerusalem. Drawings upon which to base the dioramas can be found in *Encyclopaedia Judaica* ("Temple" entry). (6 and up)

15. Direct your students to do first person historical accounts of the building of the *Beit HaMikdash* in Jerusalem. To help them understand the building process, invite an architect to speak to the class. Students will also need to do research and can present their material in one of the following formats: television news show, newspaper article, personal diary. (9 and up)

BEYOND THE TEXT

16. Read to your students the description of the building of the sacrificial altar in Exodus 27:1. Ask the students if they know what a cubit is. From the context they should be able to figure out that it is a unit of measure. Explain that a cubit was a unit of measurement long before feet, yards, and meters. A cubit is the distance from one's elbow to the tip of one's fingers. Allow the students to measure items in the classroom, using their arms as cubit measures. (K-2)

17. Tell your students the story of Cain and Abel (Genesis 4:1-16). Discuss the offerings that the brothers brought before God. Why did they bring offerings? Why was one accepted and the other not accepted? What did each bring? Explain the idea of sacrifice as illustrated by the story. You might want to extend this activity by reading to your students *Cain and Abel: Finding the Fruits of Peace* by Sasso. (K-5)

18. Invite a member of 4-H to speak about raising animals. He or she should speak particularly about what it is like to raise an animal and then have to give it up to be sold and slaughtered. Teacher should make the connection to offering an animal as a sacrifice. (3-8)

19. The Overview includes two examples from the Talmud of vain prayers. Share these examples with your students. Ask the students what makes a prayer "vain." Can they give other examples?

What is the difference between a vain prayer and an acceptable prayer? Divide students into groups and direct each group to create a skit which is about not using a vain prayer. (6-8)

20. While the *Beit HaMikdash* was destroyed more than 1900 years ago, the place in Jerusalem where it once stood is still important, not only for Jews, but for Moslems as well. For Jews, one of the supporting walls of the Temple Mount has become a focal point of prayer, called the *Kotel HaMa'aravi* (Western Wall). A mosque, the Dome of the Rock, stands on the Temple Mount. Ask the students to pretend that as a Jewish worshiper standing near the *Kotel*, they are at the mosque above. What might the worshiper feel like? Would Moslems praying at the mosque looking at the Jews at the *Kotel* below feel the same way? It is traditional to write a prayer on a slip of paper (a *k'vitel*) and place it in the Wall. Direct students to write prayers in response to this imagined experience. (6 and up)

21. Will the *Beit HaMikdash* ever be rebuilt? Should it? While some Jews believe that the *Beit HaMikdash* will be rebuilt at the end of days, this idea has been rejected by many others. In Jerusalem, a group is preparing for the possible rebuilding of the *Beit HaMikdash* by researching the various ritual objects necessary for the *Beit HaMikdash* to function properly (see Overview). Hold a mock congregational meeting to discuss a proposal to donate money to this group. Assign various roles to the students (rabbi, cantor, synagogue president, etc.) and be sure that there are students on both sides of the issue. Questions to discuss: Should the Temple be rebuilt? Who would be priests? Who would decide this? Would all Jews be able to participate in this institution? What would be the role of women? (9 and up)

22. Hasidic Judaism has placed particular emphasis on *kavanah* during prayer. Research the origins of Hasidism using a variety of sources. What set Hasidim apart from the majority of Jews of their day? In what ways does Hasidism continue to emphasize *kavanah*? If there is a local Chabad house, you may wish to visit as a class, or

invite a guest speaker. Resources: "Hasidism" in *Encyclopaedia Judaica*, Vol. 7, cols. 1390-1432; *Hasidic Prayer* by Jacobs; *God in All Moments: Mystical and Practical Spiritual Wisdom from Hasidic Masters* edited and translated by Rose. (9 and up)

23. View with the students the film *Raiders of the Lost Ark*. In this movie there is a speculation about the location of the lost Ark of the Covenant, which once was kept in the *Beit HaMikdash*. What do the students think might have happened to the Ark? Is it important to know what happened to it? If one found it, how would one prove that it was the real thing? (9 and up)

HEBREW

24. Introduce your students to the words *"keva"* and *"kavanah."* Examples of *keva*: Sh'ma, Kiddush, Kaddish, etc. Examples of *kavanah*: prayer for someone to get well, thanking God for a new baby, asking God for strength, any personal prayer, etc. Prepare index cards with examples of each type of prayer on them. Each student in turn chooses a card, reads it aloud, and places it in the appropriate column. Point out that we should strive also to pray all fixed prayers with *kavanah*. (3-8)

25. Teach the students the Hebrew names of the daily worship services: Shacharit (morning), Minchah (afternoon), and Ma'ariv (evening), as well as the Musaf (additional) held on Shabbat and festivals. Distribute a sheet of paper to each student. Student divides it into fourths, labeling each section with one of the above words. In each space they draw a picture that symbolizes the particular service or time of day. (3-8)

26. Write the phrases *Beit HaMikdash* (Temple — literally, house of holiness), *Beit HaSefer* (school — literally, house of the book), and *Beit HaKnesset* (synagogue — literally, house of gathering) on the board. Ask students to identify any words they know, and give clues about the others until they are able to identify all of them. Point out that *Beit HaKnesset* literally means house of assembly, and that the word *HaMikdash* has the same root as the words *kadosh*, *Kiddush*, and *Kaddish*, all of which have to do with holiness. To extend the activity listen to the song "Holy Place" from the recording *And You Shall Be a Blessing* by Debbie Friedman. (6-8)

27. Read from a traditional *siddur* a passage about sacrifices, such as *R'tzei* — the fifth *brachah* of the Shabbat *Amidah*. Identify key words which pertain to sacrifices (*avodah, isheh*). Compare this *brachah* to the version found in a non-traditional *siddur* such as *Gates of Prayer* (Reform) or *Kol Haneshamah* (Reconstructionist). (6 and up)

FAMILY

28. Since the destruction of the *Beit HaMikdash* in Jerusalem, the table in the home has symbolically taken the place of the sacrificial altar. The table should always be a special Jewish gathering place. Help families create formal and informal rituals to make mealtime special. For example, families may want to begin every meal by reciting *HaMotzi* and conclude with the *Birkat HaMazon* or other appropriate blessing after eating. Suggest Jewish topics for discussion at meal times. A different family member might be responsible for finding and presenting an interesting Jewish fact or story at each meal.

29. Use *Pirke Avot* as the focus of a family program. Select passages that you find most meaningful, and present them in a variety of formats. For example, one passage could be taught as a song, another could be discussed, another could be interpreted through art. After families have had the opportunity to participate in each activity, ask them to choose one of the sayings that they find most meaningful. Families should make a poster of this maxim and devise a plan of action for implementing it in their lives.

RESOURCES

BOOKS

Encyclopaedia Judaica. Jerusalem: Keter Publishing House Jerusalem Ltd., 1972.

Guide to the Treasures of the Temple Exhibition. Jerusalem: The Temple Institute, n.d.

Gold, August and Matthew J. Perlman. *Where Does God Live?* Woodstock, VT: Skylight Paths Publishing, 2001.

Jacobs, Louis. *Hasidic Prayer*. New York: Schocken Books, 1987.

Kushner, Lawrence and Karen Kushner. *Because Nothing Looks Like God*. Woodstock, VT: Jewish Lights Publishing, 2000.

Millgram, Abraham. *Jewish Worship*. Philadelphia, PA: The Jewish Publication Society of America, 1971.

Petuchowski, Jakob J. *Understanding Jewish Prayer*. New York: Ktav Publishing House, Inc. 1972.

Rose, Or. *God in All Moments: Mystical and Practical Spiritual Wisdom from Hasidic Masters*. Woodstock, VT: Jewish Lights Publishing, 2003.

Sasso, Sandy Eisenberg. *Cain and Abel: Finding the Fruits of Peace*. Woodstock, VT: Jewish Lights Publishing, 2001.

_____. *God's Paintbrush*. Woodstock, VT: Jewish Lights Publishing, 1992.

_____. *God Said Amen*. Woodstock, VT: Jewish Lights Publishing, 2000.

AUDIOVISUAL

Friedman, Debbie. *And You Shall Be a Blessing*. San Diego, CA: Sounds Write Productions, Inc., 1989. Compact disc. Available from A.R.E. Publishing, Inc.

Klepper, Jeff, and Jeff Salkin. *Bible People Songs*. 1981. Audiocassette/songbook set. Available from A.R.E. Publishing, Inc.

Raiders of the Lost Ark. 1981, 115 minutes, rated PG. DVD or videocassette. Available from video stores.

Sounds of Creation/Sounds of Freedom. San Diego, CA: Sounds Write Productions, Inc., 1991. Compact disc and/or songbook. Available from A.R.E. Publishing, Inc.

CHAPTER TWO:
THE SIDDUR

OVERVIEW

The *siddur* (prayer book) reflects the historical development of Jewish liturgy. According to Abraham Millgram, "The religious classic that has been closest to the heart of the Jews is the Jewish book of common prayer, known as the *siddur*" (*Jewish Worship*, p. 3). He continues: "The collective experience of the Jewish people was slowly and painstakingly distilled and deposited in the *siddur* . . . It is not only a handbook for Jewish prayer, but also a faithful record of Jewish thoughts, ideals, hopes, and anxieties during the many centuries of its growth" (Ibid., p. 5). Indeed, the *siddur* contains material from Tanach, Talmud, and Midrash, and from the medieval and (in many cases) modern periods of Jewish history.

The order of the prayer service was originally part of Judaism's oral tradition. In fact, the Talmud contains prohibitions against writing down the liturgy (and other oral teachings). "R. Judah b. Nachmani said, 'The words which are written [Tanach] you may not say by heart, and the words transmitted orally you may not recite from writing'" (*Gittin* 60b). *Tosefta Shabbat* 13:4 goes even further: "Those who write down prayers commit as grave a sin as those who burn the Torah."

The basic order of the liturgy was established primarily by Rabban Gamliel II during the Rabbinic period, shortly after the destruction of the Second Temple. He served as head of the Sanhedrin at Yavneh in the early second century. He established the order of the *brachot* of the weekday *Amidah*, and formulated the wording

for its individual prayers. Where more than one version of a particular *brachah* existed, he selected the version to be used.

Nevertheless, because it was an oral tradition, the liturgy remained fluid for many centuries, with many communities introducing their own prayers and variations. Over time, therefore, the liturgy became more complex, and varied significantly in different communities. There was often confusion about which prayers were required, the wording of some prayers, and the order in which they were to be recited. Evelyn Garfiel points out that "sectarianism was sure to develop unless they could share a common *Prayer Book*" (*Service of the Heart*, p. 34).

Responding to these challenges, R. Yehuda Gaon (eighth century) wrote a responsum (answer to a question of Jewish law) permitting the *shaliach tzibur* (prayer leader) to use a written text on Yom Kippur, when the service is long and elaborate. In this responsum, he acknowledges the existence of prayer books, but does not condone their use for the general public.

By the ninth century, it was common for the *shaliach tzibur* in many communities to use a written text for all services. These texts often represented private efforts to delineate the liturgy. They varied greatly from each other, not only due to local *minhag* (custom), but also to scribal errors.

Because of these discrepancies, the rabbis of ninth century Spain appealed to the highest rabbinic authority of the day, Rav Amram, the head of the Babylonian academy at Sura, to give them a correct order for the worship service. His responsum, entitled "*Seder Tefillot*" (Order of the Prayers), is considered to be the first *siddur*. The word "*siddur*" literally means "order" or "arrangement," and is short for *seder t'fillot*. While this responsum had its greatest impact in Spain, it also influenced the development of the *siddur* in other communities.

Rav Amram's *siddur* was primarily directed toward the *shaliach tzibur*. One of his successors, Rav Saadia Gaon (882-942), authored the first *siddur* directed to the worshiper. The prayers were logically grouped and classified, facilitating access for everyone. Saadia included contemporary liturgical poems, as well as an extensive commentary.

While Saadia's *siddur* greatly influenced prayerbooks throughout the Jewish world of his day, it primarily reflected liturgical traditions and Sephardic customs. The first definitive Ashkenazi *siddur* was compiled by Rabbi Simcha ben Shmuel, a student of Rashi, in the eleventh century. Because he lived in Vitry, France, this *siddur* became known as *Machzor Vitry*, the Cycle of Prayers of Vitry. (While the term "*machzor*" now refers to the High Holy Day *siddur*, its basic meaning — cycle of prayers — meant that it could be used for the festivals, Shabbat, and daily liturgy as well.) The *Machzor Vitry* soon became the official liturgy of French Jewry and the basis of virtually all other Ashkenazic liturgies.

There are a number of differences between the Sephardic and Ashkenazic liturgy. On Yom Kippur, for example, the Ashkenazic tradition includes many *piyyutim* (liturgical poems) by Eleazar Kalir, an eighth century liturgical poet of the land of Israel, whereas the Sephardic tradition tends toward the *piyyutim* of Solomon ibn Gabirol, Judah Halevi, and other medieval Spanish poets. Ashkenazic Jews recite two *brachot* when putting on tefillin, one for each piece, while Sephardic Jews recite only the first *brachah*.

In a Sephardic service, the *Bar'chu* is recited not only at the beginning, but also near the conclusion, so that one who entered late could say it. Whereas *Hallel* (see Chapter 12) is recited at Shacharit by Ashkenazic Jews, it is also recited at Ma'ariv by Sephardic Jews.

The order of the prayers sometimes differs. For example, in the Ashkenazic tradition *Hodu* (See Chapter 5) is recited after *Baruch She'amar*,

while in the Sephardic tradition it is recited before it.

The most noticeable differences between the Ashkenazic and Sephardic rituals are the melodies used for chanting the liturgy, as well as the Torah and Haftarah.

However, the traditions sometimes borrowed from one another. The *Un'taneh Tokef* of the High Holy Day liturgy is attributed to rabbi Amnon of Mayence, Germany, and thus originated in the Ashkenazic tradition, but has been adopted into the Sephardic ritual. *Kabbalat Shabbat*, which originated in the Sephardic community of Safed in the sixteenth century, has been incorporated into the Ashkenazic *siddur*.

There are also liturgical variations within each tradition, especially Sephardic Judaism. As Jews left Spain during the Middle Ages, they settled in many countries including Portugal, Morocco, Italy, and Holland. Each community put its unique imprint on the liturgy based on influences from the communities around them and their own differing experiences.

The first printed *siddur* was apparently published about 1475 on a secret printing press in Montalban, Spain by Juan de Lucena, for the crypto-Jews (Jews who had to practice Judaism secretly) of the Iberian Peninsula. In 1486, the Soncino Press printed the first *siddur* for use by Italian Jewry. The first Ashkenazic *siddur* was published in 1512 in Prague.

The early sixteenth century also marked the first time that the High Holy Day liturgy was published in a separate volume. Although the basic core of the liturgy is the same throughout the year, the many special additions for the holidays, especially the medieval *piyyutim*, led to the creation of a separate book out of practical necessity.

The first translation of the *siddur* into Italian was made in the sixteenth century, although the Italian words were written in Hebrew characters. Later in the sixteenth century, *siddurim* with Yiddish and Spanish translations were published.

The first *siddur* with English translation, *Evening Service for Rosh-Hashanah and Yom Kippur*, was published without attribution in New York in 1761. The translation is, however, ascribed to

Isaac Pinto, who also did the translations for *Prayers for Sabbath, Rosh-Hashanah and Yom Kippur* in 1766.

Siddurim which contained translations were not without controversy. For most of Jewish history, Hebrew has been the universal language of prayer. While one may pray in any language, and many rabbis stress the importance of understanding prayers, Hebrew is the preferred language of Jewish worship. Nevertheless, throughout history, Jews have prayed in the vernacular. Some of the most significant liturgical works, including the *Kaddish, Kol Nidrei,* and *Ha Lachma Anya* from the Pesach Haggadah, are recited in Aramaic, the common tongue of the Jewish communities in Palestine and Babylonia for many centuries.

According to rabbi Jeffrey Cohen, "The use of the vernacular in prayer seems to have been especially favored by the Sephardi communities in the East, and was probably introduced soon after the Exile from Spain in 1492 . . . The Ashkenazim, on the other hand, resisted until much later such a concession to ignorance of Hebrew" (*Blessed Are You*, p. 78. Reprinted by permission of the publisher, Jason Aronson Inc., Northvale, NJ ©1993).

Today, most Orthodox services are conducted entirely in Hebrew, while Reform, Reconstructionist, and Conservative services usually include prayers in both the Hebrew and the vernacular.

Advocates of the continued use of Hebrew prayer, even where many worshipers do not understand Hebrew, offer a number of reasons: Hebrew is the closest thing to a universal Jewish language. Jews can walk into a synagogue anywhere in the world and will feel at home if the prayers are in Hebrew. Hebrew is the original language of most of the prayers. Their meaning is often lost in translations. Especially is this true with respect to the poetic language of prayer. Hebrew is also the language of most of the Tanach and of modern Israel. Rabbi Hayim Halevy Donin claims that "the severance of the organic bond with the Hebrew language by a Jewish community historically has led to the total assimilation and ultimate disappearance of that community" (*To Pray as a Jew*, p. 17).

There are many traditional *siddurim*. Among the most popular are *Rinnat Yisrael, The Complete ArtScroll Siddur,* and *Ha-Siddur Ha-Shalem: Daily Prayer Book.*

Rinnat Yisrael, published in Israel, is entirely in Hebrew, without an English translation. It is used in many synagogues in Israel and some in the Diaspora. It is one of the only traditional *siddurim* with services for Yom HaAtzma'ut (Israel Independence Day) and Yom Yerushalayim (Jerusalem Day).

The Complete ArtScroll Siddur not only has an English translation of the Hebrew text, but an extensive English commentary. It has been used by an increasing number of traditional congregations since its publication in 1984.

Ha-Siddur Ha-Shalem: Daily Prayer Book contains an English translation by Philip Birnbaum. First published in 1949, it has been used widely in Orthodox congregations in North America in the second half of the twentieth century.

Reform Judaism's first *siddur* was the Hamburg Temple Prayerbook (*Seder Ha'Avodah*) published in 1819. It featured an abridged text of many prayers, the substitution of German for the Hebrew in some instances, as well as the elimination of references to ideas that were alien to nineteenth century Reform ideology (the concept of a person as Messiah, the rebuilding of the *Beit HaMikdash,* and the reestablishment of a Jewish national entity in the land of Israel). In addition, unlike traditional *siddurim,* it opened from left to right.

In the United States, a variety of *siddurim* were published beginning in the 1850's. Among the earliest were the Reform *Minhag America,* compiled by Isaac Mayer Wise, and *Olat Tamid,* compiled by David Einhorn. The first official Reform *siddur* for American Jewry was *The Union Prayer Book for Jewish Worship,* published by the Central Conference of American Rabbis (CCAR) in 1895. This *siddur* was revised a number of times, including a major revision in 1940, to reflect changes in Reform Jewish worship — more Hebrew, restoring certain prayers that had been eliminated, etc. In 1975, the CCAR published *Gates of Prayer: The New Union Prayer Book,* which reflected further changes including support of Zionism and the State of Israel. The CCAR is creating a new *siddur, Mishkan Tefilah,* which is scheduled for publication in 2005.

Conservative Judaism published its first American *siddur, Festival Prayer Book,* in 1927, and its first Shabbat *siddur, Sabbath and Festival Prayer Book,* in 1946. The latter reflected continuity with Jewish tradition and respect for the traditional Hebrew text. Modifications were made to some prayers. For example, in the Musaf service, references to animal sacrifices were changed from expressing hope for restoration in the future to acknowledgment of such practice in the past. A new Conservative prayer book, *Siddur Sim Shalom,* was published in 1985. It is more comprehensive than any previous Conservative *siddur,* with services for Shabbat, weekdays, festivals, and home rituals. It also offers a variety of options and alternatives reflecting differing practice among Conservative congregations.

The Reconstructionist movement produced its first official *siddur, Sabbath Prayer Book,* in 1953. Many traditional prayers were eliminated or changed because of theological difficulties. References to Jews as the chosen people were eliminated from the *Aleinu* and the *brachah* before the Torah reading. A new Reconstructionist *siddur* for *erev* Shabbat, *Kol Haneshamah,* was published in 1989; its companion volume for Shabbat morning appeared in 1994. *Kol Haneshamah* restores certain Hebrew texts which had been omitted for non-theological reasons from the first Reconstructionist *siddur.* It includes transliterations of prayers commonly recited by the congregation, as well as a commentary. Its translation is gender neutral. It contains a significant number of alternative readings for each section of the *siddur.*

Kol Haneshamah is the first *siddur* produced by one of the major movements that uses gender sensitive language. For some, this has addressed a major concern. The traditional liturgy and most English translations reflect a masculine bias — human beings as a whole are often called "man" or "mankind," God is referred to as "Lord" and "He." While apologists claim that it is only a matter of semantics, feminists maintain that such usage impacts how people view God.

The Hebrew text presents even more challenges because in Hebrew nouns, adjectives, and verbal forms are either masculine or feminine. Some feminists have rewritten many of the prayers, changing, for example, *"Baruch Atah Adonai"* to *"Bruchah At Shechinah."* However, many feminists argue that gender sensitive language is only one aspect of the greater issue of a God who is thought of as male and who, in the Tanach and the *siddur,* is portrayed in a dominant, hierarchical relationship with human beings (see Chapter 3). One of the first gender sensitive *siddurim* was *Vetaher Libenu,* produced in the 1970s by Congregation Beth El of Sudbury, Massachusetts.

It is not unusual for congregations to create their own *siddurim* or individual worship services, the better to reflect the specific liturgical preferences of that community. Usually, such a prayer book is created by a committee of members working with the rabbi and/or cantor, which studies the liturgy, selects prayers, and/or writes innovative prayers and translations.

INSIGHTS FROM THE TRADITION

A. In the introduction to his *siddur,* Rav Saadia Gaon explained that during his travels he had observed that the liturgy was often marred by omissions, additions, and abridgments. This observation prompted him "to collect and arrange the established prayers, praises, and benedictions so that the original form should be restored. But as to the omissions and additions, I shall point out which are contrary to the fundamentals of prayers and which are not; the former I prohibit; the latter I permit though they have no foundation in tradition." (In Millgram, *Jewish Worship,* p. 387)

B. Although women were excluded from the traditional worship service throughout much of Jewish history, a special type of prayer book containing *T'chinot* (or *tkhines,* in Yiddish), women's devotional prayers, emerged. Judith Plaskow writes: "The *tkhines* by and large convey a spirituality structured by private events and experiences

... *tkhines* are written in the Yiddish vernacular and speak in the singular, each woman addressing God in her own name. The subjects of many of the *tkhines* are private rituals or moments: women's three special commandments — lighting the Sabbath candles, taking the *challah* dough, and ritual immersion; Rosh Hodesh, the celebration of the new moon on which women were exempted from work; important biological events in women's lives like pregnancy and childbirth; visiting the graves of the dead, and personal or family problems and occasions." (*Standing Again at Sinai*, p. 48).

C. While virtually all contemporary *siddurim* are devoid of pictures, some of the early *siddurim* were elaborately illuminated. After the invention of the printing press, woodcuts often replaced these illuminations. These, too, soon ceased, reflecting a concern for violating the commandment against making graven images of God. Of the liturgical texts, only the Haggadah is elaborately illustrated.

D. The *siddur* plays a crucial role in Judaism's effort to sanctify the ordinary. Abraham Millgram observes: "The daily routines of the Jew, his yearly cycles, and the milestones of his life from infancy to death are all accounted for in the *siddur*. It enters into the Jew's living experiences on every level. By means of suitable benedictions and prayers, the *siddur* infuses the Jew's daily activities with an element of sanctity. Such routine acts as eating and drinking, rising in the morning and retiring at night, dressing and washing one's hands are all within the purview of the *siddur*." (*Jewish Worship*, p. 6)

E. While the Talmud was the primary target of Christian censors, the *siddur* was also subject to its share of censorship. Among the prayers censored were the *Aleinu* and *Kol Nidrei* (see Chapters 9 and 12). The Jewish community sometimes responded to such efforts by censoring its own liturgy so as not to offend the Christian majority. The most controversial line of the traditional *Aleinu* remains absent from the prayer in most *siddurim* (see Chapter 9).

F. In his introduction to the *siddur*, Philip Birnbaum wrote: "The *siddur* is the most popular book in Jewish life. No book so completely unites the dispersed people of Israel. If any single volume can tell us what it means to be a Jew, it is the *siddur* which embodies the visions and aspirations, the sorrows and joys of many generations." (*Ha-siddur Ha-Shalem*, p. ix. Reprinted by permission of the publishers, Hebrew Publishing Company, P.O. Box 157, Rockaway Beach, NY 11693. Copyright © 1977. All rights reserved.)

ACTIVITIES

TEXT AND CONTEXT

1. Prior to class, arrange a bookshelf with a variety of books, specifically including a number of *siddurim*. Tell the students to examine the books for a few minutes. Ask: How could the students sort these books? (For example, size, color, illustrated or not illustrated, English only or Hebrew and English, etc.) Explain to the students that one way to sort the books is by what is inside them, for example, storybooks, cookbooks, books of information, etc. Ask the students to identify special Jewish books. Define the word "*siddur*" as the Hebrew term for a prayer book. Tell the students to pick out from among the books those that are *siddurim*. Ask: How did they know it was a *siddur*? What are some of the special characteristics of *siddurim*? (K-2)

2. Obtain *siddurim* from a variety of Jewish communities in different countries. Examine them with the students, noting the similarities and differences. Point out that one of the things that connects Jews all over the world to each other is Hebrew. (K-5)

3. Teach your students basic *siddur* etiquette. Use a large wall chart or the blackboard. Explain that the Jewish people has always treasured books, and certain books, such as the *siddur* and the Tanach, have been especially valued. We treat these books in special ways. Ask students if they have seen, or if they are aware of, how these books are specially treated, writing the responses on the chart or board. Be sure that the following are included on the list: not putting these books on the floor, kissing the books if they are dropped and after using them, not leaving these books open when not in use, burying these books when they can no longer be used. Explain to the students that we treat the books in these ways because they contain the name of God. (K-5)

4. Ask students to write down from memory a familiar story such as "Goldilocks and the Three Bears" or "Little Red Riding Hood." (Alternatively, bring in a few different versions of the same story.) Share the different versions of the story and discuss why there are differences between them. Explain to the students that before there was a *siddur*, prayers were passed down by word of mouth. Ask students if they think that the prayers would have been the same in different places, and if not, why not. Explain that in response to growing differences, the leaders of the community wrote to Rav Amram, one of the leading authorities of the day, asking him for an official order and wording of the prayers. His response, given over 1100 years ago, became the earliest *siddur*. (3-5)

5. Learn the geography of the *siddur* used in your synagogue or school. Provide each student with a copy of the *siddur*. Ask students to find specific parts of the service or prayers. Students should discover that using the table of contents helps them to find what they need quickly. As a class, prepare a "*Siddur* Scavenger Hunt," with each student creating one or more questions. Compile the clues and have the entire class, another class, or parents do the search. (6 and up)

6. Bring to class *siddurim* reflecting the Reform, Reconstructionist, Conservative, and Orthodox traditions. Have students compare them to one another. How are they similar? How are they different? Assign groups of students to investigate specific prayers or services and report to the rest of the class. A variation on this activity would be to choose a particular movement and compare its *siddurim* over several generations. Questions

to consider: How have they changed? Are there differences in language, terminology, or attitudes to various Jewish traditions, the use of Hebrew and/or the vernacular? (6 and up)

7. It is possible to learn a lot about a book from its table of contents. With the students examine the table of contents in a variety of *siddurim*. What are the similarities and differences? What services are included in each? What holiday liturgy is included? Are there any special readings from Jewish texts? It might be helpful to make a chart comparing the tables of contents. (9 and up)

8. Discuss with your students the issue of gender sensitive language. What are some examples of gendered language in prayer (using He for God; using man for all human beings)? Why are some people offended by such language and others not offended? How does this language evoke imagery that might limit how we view God? Give the students a text from a non-gender sensitive *siddur* and direct them to rewrite it, making it gender sensitive. Alternatively, have students compare gender sensitive and non-gender sensitive texts of the same prayer. You may also wish to invite a guest speaker to address this issue. (9 and up)

ARTS

9. Create a cover for a student *siddur*. Use crayons or markers on construction paper or cloth with felt appliqué. (K-2)

10. Make a bookmark for your *siddur*. Take strips of burlap and decorate with yarn stitchery. Or use poster board strips which the students decorate and which are then laminated. (K-5)

11. Design a postage stamp honoring the Jewish idea that books are treasures or that Jews are the People of the Book. (3-5)

12. Create a map for a trip through the *siddur*, using the parts of the *siddur* as places. After students are familiar with the structure of the

siddur, give them materials (paper, markers, etc.) with which to create a map. (3-8)

13. While *siddurim* today are not illustrated because of the concern of creating a graven image, medieval *siddurim* were often elaborately decorated. An example of an initial-word panel from a *siddur* can be found in *Encyclopaedia Judaica*, vol. 11, across from columns 875-876. Using this as an example, have students create an initial-word panel for a prayer of their choice. Display on a bulletin board. (6-8)

14. Examine the titles of a variety of *siddurim*. Determine how the titles were chosen and what the source was of the title (this is usually explained in the introduction of the *siddur*). Brainstorm other possible titles for *siddurim*. Have each student choose one of these titles and design a cover using the title. (6-8)

15. Draw a cartoon or comic strip which expresses a humorous view of a person trying to follow along in the *siddur*. This could become the basis for promoting an adult education class about becoming familiar with the *siddur*. (7 and up)

16. Create a photo exhibit of Jews at prayer. Where permitted or proper, and with the permission of the rabbi or ritual committee, take pictures during various worship services. Be sure to use a variety of worship settings (indoors and outdoors, formal and informal, home and synagogue). Choose some of the pictures and make a display. (9 and up)

17. To sensitize the students to gender issues, have them create collages. Provide newspapers and magazines from which the students cut out words and images that reflect the following categories: male, female, gender free. Students divide their background paper into three sections, with these headings, and place the appropriate words and images in each to create the collage. To contextualize this activity, use it as a follow-up to Activity #8 above. (9 and up)

BEYOND THE TEXT

18. Bring to class examples of special Jewish books such as a *siddur*, *Machzor*, Tanach, Haggadah, etc. Discuss what each book is and how it is used. Ask students how the books are similar to and different from books that they have at home. (K-5)

19. Expand Activity #18 by having students create a bulletin board display of these treasured Jewish books. Each student should create the front cover of one of these books. On a separate card, they write a short explanation of what the book is and how and when it is used. Display the cards along with the covers. (K-5)

20. Tell your students to imagine that the *siddur* could speak. What would it tell them? Students write the dialogue between themselves and the *siddur* in the form of a letter, interview, or story. (3-5)

21. Ask the students what would be the same at synagogues in Jerusalem, Moscow, Paris, Sydney, and Buenos Aires. Direct the conversation to a discussion of the centrality of Hebrew to Jewish worship. Brainstorm reasons for the importance of Hebrew. Divide the class into groups to create an advertising campaign for the importance of Hebrew. Each group should choose a different medium to present its advertisement (videotape, audiotape, live performance, poster, brochure, etc.). (3-8)

22. In the Overview there is mention that the first printed *siddur* was apparently published secretly for crypto-Jews in Spain. Briefly explain to the class about the crypto-Jews (also called Marranos), and have the students create short skits relating to the printing of the first *siddur*. Some issues to consider: Is it worth the risk? How does having a printed *siddur* help sustain Jewish identity? What must be done to fool the authorities? Resources: *Jews of Spain: A History of the Sephardic Experience* by Gerber; *The Mezuzah in the Madonna's Foot: Marranos and Other Secret Jews — A Woman Discovers Her Spiritual Heritage* by Alexy. (6-8)

23. Prior to class, prepare a list of important Jewish books, including: *siddur*, Tanach, Haggadah, Talmud, *Machzor, Midrash, Shulchan Aruch, Guide for the Perplexed*, and *Zohar*. After making sure students understand what each of these books is, ask them individually to rank order the books, based upon their importance for the survival of Judaism. Come together as a class and create a consensus of the five most important books for Judaism's survival. (6 and up)

24. To extend the issue of gender sensitivity (Activity #17), bring to class a variety of books used in classes of the school. Direct the students to look through the books for examples of gender insensitivity in both the pictures and text. What changes should be made? Are there any books that should not be used? Is this censorship, or is it simply being fair? Summarize your findings and present to the principal, Director of Education, rabbi, or school committee. (9 and up)

25. Tell the students that they are the ritual committee of a new synagogue and must recommend a *siddur* for use at services. Begin by brainstorming issues that must be considered when making such a decision, such as: amount of Hebrew, use of creative liturgy, gender sensitive language, ideology, ease of use, etc. Select from this list six criteria that are most significant. Assign each student or pair of students to evaluate one of the *siddurim* based on these criteria and report to the class. After all the reports, the class should try to reach a consensus. (9 and up)

HEBREW

26. Introduce to your students a variety of Hebrew terms with the root *samech*, *dalet*, *resh*, such as *siddur* (prayer book), *Seder* (Pesach service), and *sedra* (weekly Torah portion). Ask the students if they can determine how these terms are related to each other. Introduce the root meaning of "order." Discuss how each term reflects a specific order. (3-8)

27. List on the board in Hebrew the basic rubrics of the *siddur*: Shacharit, Minchah, Ma'ariv, Musaf, *Kabbalat Shabbat, Kriat HaTorah, Birchot HaShachar*, etc. Explain each term to the students. Write each term on a 4" x 6" card. Divide students into teams. Read the term and define. Points are given for correct reading and proper identification. (5 and up)

FAMILY

28. Create a personal *siddur* for the families of your congregation or school. Gather the families together and have them rotate among stations to begin creating the *siddur*. Among the possible stations are making a cover and choosing a name, creating an *erev* Shabbat home liturgy, writing bedtime prayers, and making a calendar of important days (holidays, birthdays, anniversaries) in the coming year. If the *siddur* is looseleaf, then families can add to it during the year with home rituals for each holiday and other important occasions. These can be prepared by the children at school, or sent home with directions to be completed by the families.

29. Hold a Hebrew literacy campaign. This might include a Hebrew marathon during which adults learn the letters and vowels in a day or two days, a monthly column in the synagogue bulletin, workshops introducing Hebrew vocabulary related to a specific topic, Hebrew word of the week as part of the religious school curriculum. Celebrate the culmination of this project with a Hebrew fair. Resource: *Aleph Isn't Tough: An Introduction to Hebrew for Adults* by Motzkin.

RESOURCES

BOOKS

Alexy, Trudi. *The Mezuzah in the Madonna's Foot: Marranos and Other Secret Jews — A Woman Discovers Her Spiritual Heritage*. San Francisco: Harper SanFrancisco, 1994.

Cohen, Jeffrey. *Blessed Are You: A Comprehensive Guide to Jewish Prayer*. Northvale, NJ: Jason Aronson, Inc., 1993.

Donin, Hayim Halevy. *To Pray as a Jew: A Guide to the Prayer Book and the Synagogue Service*. New York: Basic Books, 1980.

Encyclopaedia Judaica. Jerusalem: Keter Publishing House Jerusalem Ltd., 1972.

Garfiel, Evelyn. *Service of the Heart: A Guide to the Jewish Prayer Book*. Northvale, NJ: Jason Aronson Inc., 1999.

Gerber, Jane S. *Jews of Spain: A History of the Sephardic Experience*. New York: Free Press, 1994.

Millgram, Abraham. *Jewish Worship*. Philadelphia, PA: The Jewish Publication Society of America, 1971.

Motzkin, Linda. *Aleph Isn't Tough: An Introduction to Hebrew for Adults*. New York: UAHC Press, 2000.

Plaskow, Judith. *Standing Again at Sinai: Judaism From a Feminist Perspective*. San Francisco: Harper-Collins Publishers, 1990.

Note: *Siddurim* are listed in a separate section in the general Bibliography, pp. 189-198.

CHAPTER THREE: BRACHOT

OVERVIEW

The Talmud teaches that "A person is forbidden to enjoy any of the pleasures of the world without first reciting praise to God" (*Brachot* 35a). In order to assure that we do not take the world for granted, Jews recite *brachot*, blessings.

A special formula, attributed to the sages of the Great Assembly (assumed to be second century B.C.E.), introduces each *brachah*: "*Baruch Atah Adonai Eloheinu Melech HaOlam* — Blessed are You, *Adonai* our God, Ruler of the Universe." While this formula is of rabbinic origin, parts of it are found in the Tanach. Psalm 119:12 begins "*Baruch Atah Adonai,*" and I Chronicles 29:10 reads in part, "*Baruch Atah Adonai, Elohei Yisrael Avinu* — Blessed are You *Adonai,* God of Israel our father.*" This formula contains three elements: a statement of blessing, God's name, and the affirmation of God's sovereignty.

A *brachah* which is recited for the performance of a *mitzvah* contains the additional phrase: "*Asher Kidshanu B'mitzvotav V'tzivanu* — Who has made us holy with *mitzvot* and commanded us . . . "

According to Maimonides, there are three types of *brachot*:

a. *Birchot HaNehenin* — *brachot* of enjoyment said before eating or experiencing a pleasure connected to one of the five senses. Among these *brachot* are:

HaMotzi	eating bread
P'ri HaGafen	drinking wine
P'ri HaEitz	eating fruit of trees
P'ri HaAdamah	eating fruit of the earth
Minei M'zonot	eating cakes or cookies
Shehakol Nih'yeh Bidvaro	eating food other than the above
Minei V'samim	smelling spices
Oseh Ma'aseh V'reishit	seeing lightning, shooting stars, and other natural phenomena
Shenatan Meichochmato L'vasar Vadam	seeing a scholar
Birkat HaMazon	after eating a meal

(For a more extensive list, see *The Authorised Daily Prayer Book* by Hertz, p. 984ff.)

b. *Birchot HaMitzvot* — *brachot* recited before the performance of a *mitzvah.* Examples of this type of *brachah* include *brachot* said for lighting Shabbat, holiday, and Chanukah candles; washing one's hands; blowing the shofar; sitting in the *sukkah;* and reciting *Hallel.*

c. *Birchot Hoda'ah* — *brachot* which express gratitude to God, with praise and/or petition, in order to remind us of God's presence in our world. Among the *brachot* in this category are the *Birchot HaShachar* (see Chapter 4), the *brachot* of the *Amidah* (see Chapter 7), *Birkat HaGomayl* (see Chapter 8), and the *Shehecheyanu.*

Sometimes two or more *brachot* are grouped together to make one longer *brachah.* In such a case, each *brachah* ends with the phrase "*Baruch Atah Adonai . . . *" The first *brachah,* but not the subsequent ones, begins with the phrase "*Baruch Atah Adonai . . . *" Examples of such *brachot* are the traditional *brachah* after the Haftarah (which is comprised of four *brachot*), the *Birkat HaMazon*, and the *brachot* before the *Sh'ma*.

While *brachot* are traditionally said in Hebrew, they can be recited in any language. They are usually recited prior to the pertinent act; no pause should occur between the *brachah* and the act.

Brachot should be recited aloud, although if one says them silently, it is acceptable. A person who responds "Amen" to the *brachah* of another also fulfills the obligation for reciting the *brachah* (*Brachot* 1:13).

Rabbi Meir said that a person should recite 100 *brachot* daily. Although this appears to be a lot, one who follows the tradition of praying three times a day and also reciting the appropriate *brachot* before and after eating would easily have recited at least 100 *brachot*.

INSIGHTS FROM THE TRADITION

A. The word *brachah* has the root *bet, resh, chaf*. Another word with the same root is *berech*, meaning knee, reflecting the connection between praying while kneeling or bending one's knees (see Chapter 9). In addition, the word *b'reichah*, meaning pool or pond, has the same root.

B. While one normally recites *brachot* before the act, there are a few exceptions, the most notable being the *brachah* for lighting Shabbat candles. Since Shabbat begins once the *brachah* is recited, and lighting a fire is prohibited on Shabbat, the candles are lit first and then the *brachah* is recited. It is traditional to cover one's eyes while reciting the *brachah*, and to look upon the candles only after the *brachah* has been recited, as if to pretend that the candles had not been lit prior to the blessing. Other examples of the act preceding the *brachah* are washing one's hands and immersing in a *mikvah*. (*Pesachin* 7b)

C. *Brachot* which are recited for the performance of *mitzvot* begin by addressing God in the second person ("Blessed are You"), but then move into the third person ("Who has made us holy with

mitzvot"). Max Kadushin points out that this characteristic is also found in other prayers such as "*Emet V'yatziv*" (*The Rabbinic Mind*, p. 266). Kadushin explains the "religious genius" of combining these two forms of address which represent two different levels of relationship to God. Addressing God in the second person illustrates "that the relationship to God is felt as to someone who is near, who listens, whom you can face directly. It is a warm, personal relationship" (Ibid.). It establishes a direct, intimate relationship between the worshiper and God. Moving to the third person then allows one to speak of God without addressing God directly.

D. The Torah is the source of all *mitzvot*. However, not all *mitzvot* are explicitly written in the Torah. One such *mitzvah* is the lighting of Chanukah candles. In the Talmud there is a discussion regarding the basis for the blessing. Can we say "*Asher Kidshanu . . .*" (Who has commanded us) concerning the Chanukah candles, for clearly there is no explicit commandment in the Torah. The Talmud cites Deuteronomy 17:11, "You shall not turn aside from the verdict they announce," interpreting the "they" as referring to the rabbis of the Talmud. This verse is then used as the basis for authorizing rabbinic additions to the biblical *mitzvot*. (*Sukkah* 46a)

E. One *brachah* that omits the explicit reference to God's kingship in its opening phrase is the first *brachah* of the *Amidah*, the *Avot*. According to a tradition, the concept of God's kingship is implied in the phrase "God of Abraham," because Abraham was the first to recognize God's sovereignty. (*Tosafot* to *Brachot* 40b)

F. The *Shehecheyanu* is a familiar *brachah* recited on the first day of holidays. According to tradition, it should be recited on a variety of other occasions as well. These include: When one hears good news or witnesses it in person and is the only person who benefits, when one builds or buys a house or purchases new garments, when one eats fruit for the first time in a season, and when one sees a friend one hasn't seen for thirty days or more.

G. There is a widespread misconception among non-Jews, and even some Jews, that saying a *brachah* over food makes it kosher. Food is either kosher or not kosher based upon the dietary laws. Even the *brachah* recited by the *shochet* before slaughtering an animal is said only to affirm that the slaughtering is being done to fulfill a *mitzvah* and does not affect whether the meat is kosher. The purpose of reciting a blessing before eating is to recognize God as the ultimate source of sustenance and does not affect whether or not the food is kosher.

H. Joel Lurie Grishaver, in his book *And You Shall Be a Blessing*, suggests these two metaphors for reciting *brachot*: "Saying a *brakhah* is like shining a spotlight. When we say a *brakhah*, we focus our attention on an experience or an action, and in the process we turn the potentially mundane into an encounter with the holy. It is a *brakhah* that metamorphizes the lighting of a light into the conjuring of a holy time. It is a *brakhah* that makes the consumption of calories an acknowledgment of God's creative powers and God's loving concern for humankind. Through *brakhot*, such possibly mundane acts as tying shoes, eating something bitter, and even shaking a collection of branches in the air all become opportunities to come closer to God.

"Saying a *brakhah* is like looking in a mirror. Each and every *brakhah*-saying experience is a moment of self-analysis. *Brakhot* are first (and perhaps foremost) a statement of radical appreciation, an acknowledgment of God's actions. But, they also generate an important side-effect. When these are examined through the conceptual lens of our creation in 'God's Image,' that which we are praising God for being emerges as that which we will strive to become. Each time we acknowledge that God feeds, or God clothes, or God comforts, or God saves, or God lifts up, we are setting patterns for our own ethical actions: feeding, clothing, comforting, saving, and lifting up." (*And You Shall Be a Blessing*, p. 119. Reprinted by permission of the publisher, Jason Aronson Inc., Northvale, NJ. © 1993.)

I. The phrase which begins many *brachot*, "*Baruch Atah Adonai Eloheinu Melech HaOlam*," is considered by some to be sexist. Alternative versions sometimes replace *Baruch Atah* with *B'ruchah At* (the feminine version of "Blessed are You"), and *Adonai Eloheinu* with *Shechinah* (the Divine Presence, a female term referring to God), and *Melech HaOlam* with *M'kor HaChayim* (source of life).

J. Judith Plaskow has written the following on the issue of what she calls "The Image of God as Dominating Other": "It is not simply male metaphors for God that need to be broken, however, but also the larger picture of who God is. Were feminist objections to Jewish God-language confined to the issue of gender, the manipulation of pronouns and creation of female imagery would fairly easily resolve the difficulties described. In fact, though, experiments with changing liturgical language by adding female metaphors only call attention to larger problems in the underlying conception of the God who is male. Thus, while feminist criticisms of traditional language begin with gender, they come to focus on the deeper issue of images of God's power as dominance. Such images are connected to God's maleness insofar as they mirror male social roles, but the use of gender neutral or even female language does not itself guarantee that images of dominance have been addressed." (*Standing Again at Sinai*, p. 128)

ACTIVITIES

TEXT AND CONTEXT

1. Create for the students a five senses display. To do this, set up five learning centers in the room, one for each sense. At each station have a model or picture of the part of the body which represents the sense (i.e., a nose for smell), a tape recorder, and items involved in the *brachah*. On the tape identify the sense being used, the item involved, and recite or sing the *brachah* in Hebrew followed by the English translation. For example: "On Rosh HaShanah, we hear the sound of the shofar. We say, *Baruch Atah Adonai . . . Lishmoa Kol*

Shofar — Blessed are You . . . Who command-ed us to hear the sound of the shofar." (K-2)

2. Follow up Activity #1 by reviewing each of the items and the sense used. Ask the students if they use more than one sense with any of the items (smelling and tasting the wine, touching the *Kiddush* cup, etc.). Make a chart with the different senses at the top of each column to record responses. (K-2)

3. Try a new approach to the story of Noah's Ark. As you tell the story to the students (using a flannel board or puppets), identify and recite *brachot* which dovetail into the telling of the story. For example, when Noah goes to cut down the wood for the ark, he might have recited the *brachah* for smelling fragrant wood or bark: *Baruch . . . Borei Atzei V'samim* — Blessed are You . . . who creates fragrant woods. When the rains come and there is thunder, Noah could have said: *Baruch . . . Shekocho Ug'vurato Malei Olam* — Blessed are You . . . Whose strength and might fill the world. When Noah sees lightning, he might have said: *Baruch . . . Oseh Ma'asei V'reishit* — Blessed are You . . . Who does the workings of creation. When Noah sees the rainbow: *Baruch . . . Zocheir HaBrit V'ne'eman Bivrito V'kayam B'ma'amaro* — Blessed are You . . . Who remembers the covenant and is faithful to the covenant and to the promise. (K-5)

4. Create a game to help students identify the appropriate *brachah* for each item or situation. Write (in Hebrew or English) the *brachot* you wish to review on a large piece of tag board. Prepare pictures from magazines (or draw them) of various items that are appropriate for the *brachot*. Each student turns over one of the pictures and places it under the appropriate *brachah*. (3-5)

5. Ask the students to recall when they have heard *brachot* recited, being specific (before drinking wine, lighting candles, reading from the Torah, etc.). List responses on the board. Why are blessings recited in these instances? Attempt to elicit from the students the three types of *brachot*

identified in the Overview: *Birchot HaNehenin* (blessings of enjoyment), *Birchot HaMitzvot* (blessings of *mitzvot*); *Birchot Hoda'ah* (blessings of gratitude). (3-8)

6. Take your students on a guided fantasy during which they experience various phenomena of nature for which one recites a *brachah* (seeing the ocean, hearing thunder, smelling fragrant blossoms, etc.). Be sure to recite each *brachah* at the appropriate point in the fantasy. Resource: *The First Jewish Catalog* by Siegel, Strassfeld, and Strassfeld, pp. 150-152. (6 and up)

7. The Overview mentions the tradition of reciting 100 *brachot* a day. Challenge your students to create a list that reaches this goal. Remind the students to include the *brachot* one would recite in each of the daily services and before and after eating meals. (6 and up)

8. Discuss with your students how reciting *brachot* changes what we do. How does reciting a *brachah* elevate something ordinary into something special? Resource: *And You Shall Be a Blessing* by Grishaver, Chapter 8. (9 and up)

9. Teach the students the *brachot* one recites when hearing good news, and on hearing bad news, such as a death. Why are the *brachot* different? Why do we say a *brachah* when we hear bad news? Ask students to recall situations when they might have felt the need to say one of these *brachot*. Do any of the students feel it is not possible to recite a *brachah* for bad news? (9 and up)

ARTS

10. Listen to the song "We Say Shehecheyanu" by Kol B'Seder. Create a bulletin board with the word "*Shehecheyanu*" in large letters. Students draw pictures and write or dictate words or phrases which show what they are thankful for. Resource: *Songs for Growin'* by Kol B'Seder. (K-2)

11. Teach the students the *brachah* for the spices recited at Havdalah: *Baruch . . . Borei Minei V'samim* — Blessed are You . . . Creator of various spices.

Students make a spice picture. Provide each student with an outline drawing of a spice box and a variety of whole spices (cinnamon stick, cloves, allspice, nutmeg, etc.). Students use the spices like mosaic tiles to fill in the spice box. (K-2)

12. Make an illustrated wall mural of various *brachot*. Students can work either individually or in pairs. Each student chooses or is assigned a *brachah*. Students write it in Hebrew and/or English on the mural and then make an illustration which reflects the *brachah*. (3-5)

13. Students write a cinquain (a five line poem with a set pattern) about *brachot*.
　　Line one: A noun
　　Line two: Two adjectives
　　Line three: Three verbs ending in "ing"
　　Line four: Four adjectives
　　Line five: A synonym for the noun in line one
Line one should be the word *brachah* or blessing. Students write and then share their poems. (3-5)

14. Do paper bag dramatics with your students. Divide the class into groups of three or four. Each group receives a paper bag with one item that requires a *brachah* (*Kiddush* cup, Havdalah candle, shofar, etc.) and a number of unrelated objects. Students are to create and present a skit which utilizes all objects in the bag and which includes the recitation of the *brachah* for the ritual object. (6-8)

15. Create the ritual objects for Havdalah and teach the students the *brachah* for each item. To make Havdalah candles, provide for each student candle wicking for three candles and three sheets of beeswax. Cut the candle wicking to the length of the beeswax (long side). Carefully roll the beeswax around the wicking. Braid the three strands together to form a Havdalah candle. To make a spice box, provide each student with a small container or box. Decorate the outside with glued-on decorations or colored markers. Poke small holes in the top or lid. Fill with whole sweet spices. To make a *Kiddush* cup, provide each student with a plastic goblet and permanent markers. Students decorate the goblet on the outside, leaving about a one inch margin at the top free of decoration. Teach the songs "*Shavua Tov,* May You Have a Good Week" by Kol B'Seder and "*Birchot Havdalah*" by Debbie Friedman. Hold a Havdalah ceremony using the ritual objects and the songs. Resources: *Songs for Growin'* by Kol B'Seder; *The World of Your Dreams* by Debbie Friedman. (6 and up)

16. Introduce to the students traditional *brachot* of thanksgiving such as the *Birkat HaGomeil* or the *Shehecheyanu*. Ask students to recall a situation in which they were very thankful. Would one of these blessings have been appropriate to recite then? Have students write their own *brachah* of thanksgiving to fit the situation. (9 and up)

BEYOND THE TEXT

17. Arrange students in a circle. Each in turn completes the following phrase: "When I recite a *brachah*, I feel . . . " Repeat the activity using the phrase: "Saying a *brachah* means . . . " (K-5)

18. Collect pictures (or take pictures) of individuals engaging in an activity which involves reciting a *brachah*. Mount these pictures on construction paper with room for a caption underneath. Each student dictates or writes a caption for one of the pictures. Students share these in a show-and-tell format or as part of a bulletin board display. (K-5)

19. Before class, write on a piece of poster board the *brachah* for seeing a rainbow. Add an illustration if you wish. Display this poster at the front of the classroom. Listen to the song "The Rainbow Covenant" by Robert Solomon on the recording *Sounds of Creation/Sounds of Freedom* or "The Rainbow Blessing" by Debbie Friedman on the recording *Debbie Friedman Live at the Del*. After listening to the song, ask the students why it is important to recite a *brachah* when seeing a rainbow. Is there a connection between the *brachah* and God's promise to Noah? Read through the *brachah* together. You may also wish to make rainbow cookies. Take sugar cookie dough and divide into four or five equal parts.

Using food coloring, color each part differently. Each student receives a small piece of each color dough and creates his/her own rainbow. Bake according to recipe directions. (3-5)

20. With the students, prepare a survey about people's behavior vis-a-vis *brachot*. Generate questions which deal with when, what, where, and why people recite *brachot*. Have the students prepare questionnaires that can be administered to family members, friends, and synagogue members. Compile the results and discuss. (3-8)

21. Saying a *brachah* changes an action, moving it from the ordinary to the special. With your class, make a video demonstrating this idea. First, take videos of students doing a variety of regular activities, such as washing their hands, drinking juice, eating, seeing the ocean, smelling something fragrant, etc. Next, change each scene so that the appropriate *brachah* is said in relationship to the act. View the entire video with the class and discuss the difference between the segments. (3-8)

22. Students are to create a public relations campaign to encourage people to incorporate *brachot* into their lives, including holiday, Shabbat, and daily observance. Divide the students into small groups. Each group selects a *brachah* and decides upon a medium such as television, radio, print advertisements, or the synagogue's web site. Students should learn about the *brachot* they have chosen and generate a list of reasons for why people should recite each *brachah*. Students should incorporate at least one of the reasons into their advertisement. (6 and up)

23. In making the covenant with Abraham, God tells him, "Be a blessing" (Genesis 12:2). Discuss with your students what it means to be a blessing. What are some things people can do in order to be blessings? What can students do to be a blessing to their families? to their friends? to their synagogue? to their community? (6-8)

24. Extend Activity #23 by creating with your students a bulletin board display with the title

"And You Shall Be a Blessing." Brainstorm a list of individuals whose lives have been, or are, blessings. Each student chooses one person and creates a thumbnail sketch, emphasizing the reasons that the person's life is or was a blessing. (The person need not be famous, but can be a family or community member.) Obtain a picture or photograph or have the student draw the person and hang it on the bulletin board along with the thumbnail sketch. You may also wish to listen to the song "*L'chi Lach*" by Debbie Friedman. Resource: *And You Shall be a Blessing* by Debbie Friedman. (6-8)

25. Invite the rabbi or other knowledgeable person to lead a study session on a section of tractate *Brachot* of the Talmud. (9 and up)

26. The phrase *Baruch Atah Adonai . . .* is considered to be problematic by some because it is gendered (see Insights I and J). Hold a debate among the students as to whether the phrase might be changed and, if so, how. You may wish to assign students to a particular position so that all students of one gender are not together. Resources: *Standing Again at Sinai* by Plaskow, Chapter 4; "A Minyan of Opinions on 'Kingship' as a Metaphor of Prayer" in *Reconstructionism Today*, Autumn, 1993; *The Book of Blessings* by Falk. (9 and up)

HEBREW

27. Play lotto using the *brachot*. Each student receives a card with a variety of pictures related to a particular *brachah*. As the teacher recites each *brachah*, students mark the appropriate picture. To make it more challenging, when a student has completed a row he/she recites the *brachah* corresponding to each picture. (3 and up)

28. The Hebrew root of *brachah* (*bet, resh, chaf*) occurs in many forms. Direct students to examine a variety of *brachot* and to identify all words with this root. List these on the board and discuss the meaning of each. Point out that the word "*berech*" (meaning knee) has the same root, and explain the connection between knee and blessing (people used to kneel when saying a blessing and some bend their knees to reflect this tradition). (6 and up)

29. Hold a "*Brachot*-athon." Students should designate a *tzedakah* recipient, then gather pledges from family and friends based on the number of *brachot* they plan to recite in a day. As a class, choose a day to hold the event. Each student records the number of *brachot* recited and collects the pledges. (6 and up)

FAMILY

30. Hold a workshop to introduce Havdalah to families. Provide opportunities for each family to create its own candle, spice box, and *Kiddush* cup (see Activity #15). You will also want to teach the ritual, including the songs, and explain the philosophy of Havdalah as marking a separation of the holy Shabbat from the ordinary days of the week. You may also want to give each family an opportunity to create its own Havdalah ritual.

31. As an ongoing project in your school, have a "*brachah* of the week" which families are asked to recite at the appropriate times. Send home a sheet each week with the *brachah* in Hebrew, English, and transliteration; an explanation of when and how the *brachah* is recited; and suggestions for how to enrich the experience. Begin with some of the common *brachot* (Shabbat candles, *HaMotzi*) and then include others. Encourage families to continue to recite each *brachah* at its appropriate occasion and to add a new *brachah* each week.

For a variety of activities pertaining to the *Birkat HaMazon*, see *Teaching Mitzvot: Concepts, Values, and Activities,* Revised Edition by Kadden and Kadden, pp. 60-62.

RESOURCES

BOOKS AND PERIODICALS

Eisenstein, Ira, et al. A Minyan of Opinions on "Kingship" as a Metaphor of Prayer. *Reconstructionism Today*, Autumn 1993: 11-15.

Falk, Marcia. *The Book of Blessings*. Boston, MA: Beacon Press, 1999.

Grishaver, Joel Lurie. *And You Shall Be a Blessing: An Unfolding of the Six Words that Begin Every Brakhah*. Northvale, NJ: Jason Aronson Inc., 1993.

Hertz, Joseph H. *The Authorised Daily Prayer Book*, Revised Edition. New York: Bloch Publishing Company, 1975.

Kadden, Barbara Binder, and Bruce Kadden. *Teaching Mitzvot: Concepts, Values, and Activities*, Revised Edition. Denver, CO: A.R.E. Publishing, Inc., 2003.

Kadushin, Max. *The Rabbinic Mind*. New York: Bloch Publishing Company, 1972.

Plaskow, Judith. *Standing Again at Sinai: Judaism From a Feminist Perspective*. San Francisco, CA: Harper-Collins Publishers, 1990.

Siegel, Richard; Michael Strassfeld; and Sharon Strassfeld, eds. *The First Jewish Catalog*. Philadelphia, PA: The Jewish Publication Society of America, 1973.

AUDIOVISUAL

Friedman, Debbie. *And You Shall Be a Blessing*. San Diego, CA: Sounds Write Productions, Inc., 1989. Compact disc. Available from A.R.E. Publishing, Inc.

———. *Debbie Friedman Live at the Del*. San Diego, CA: Sounds Write Productions, Inc., 1990. Compact disc. Available from A.R.E. Publishing, Inc.

———. *The World of Your Dreams*. San Diego, CA: Sounds Write Productions, Inc., 1993. Compact disc and songbook. Available from A.R.E. Publishing, Inc.

Kol B'Seder. *Songs for Growin'*. New York: Transcontinental Music Publications, 2001. Compact disc and songbook. Available from A.R.E. Publishing, Inc.

Sounds of Creation/Sounds of Freedom. San Diego, CA: Sounds Write Productions, Inc., 1991. Compact disc and/or songbook. Available from A.R.E. Publishing, Inc.

CHAPTER FOUR:
BIRCHOT HASHACHAR

OVERVIEW

The first part of the daily morning service is called *Birchot HaShachar*, The Morning Blessings. While these *brachot* were originally to be read at home (and still are by many Jews), they are now also read in the synagogue, with a few additions. Since neither the order nor the contents of *Birchot HaShachar* are fixed by *halachah*, these vary, even among Orthodox *siddurim*.

Upon entering the synagogue, it is customary to recite *Mah Tovu* (How goodly are your tents, O Jacob, your dwelling places, O Israel), which consists of Numbers 24:5, Psalms 5:8, 26:8; 95:6 and 69:14. These verses are sometimes chanted by the *shaliach tzibur* ("messenger of the congregation," i.e., prayer leader) or by the congregation. The first phrase, "How goodly are your tents, O Jacob, your dwelling places, O Israel" is interpreted to refer to synagogues and schools (*Sanhedrin* 105b). The rest of *Mah Tovu* refers to the worship of God through prayer. Readings and *brachot* for putting on the *tallit* and *tefillin* follow in some *siddurim* (see chapter 14).

Next are the hymns *Yigdal* and *Adon Olam*. Daniel ben Judah, a fourteenth century poet of Rome, composed *Yigdal*, based upon the thirteen principles of faith of Maimonides. The author of *Adon Olam* is unknown, although some attribute it to the eleventh century Spanish poet Solomon ibn Gabirol. (In the Sephardic, Italian, and Yemenite rituals, *Yigdal* concludes Ma'ariv on *erev* Shabbat and *Adon Olam* concludes Shacharit on Shabbat.)

Worshipers then read the *brachah* for washing

BIRCHOT HASHACHAR
(Morning Blessings)

Mah Tovu (Numbers 24:5, Psalms 5:8, 26:8, 95:6, 69:14)

Tallit (For putting on the prayer shawl)

Tefillin (For putting on the phylacteries)

Adon Olam (Eternal God)

Yigdal (Exalted and praised by the living God)

Asher Yatzar (For health)

Brachot for Torah Study

Torah Study passages:

    Numbers 6:24-26

    Mishnah Peah 1:1

    Talmud *Shabbat* 127a

Elohai N'shama (For the gift of a pure soul)

Birchot HaShachar (Fifteen morning *brachot*)

Vihi Ratzon (Who bestows lovingkindness on Israel)

Y'hi Ratzon (For protection)

Ribon Kol HaOlamim (Master of all worlds)

Readings about Sacrifices

    Numbers 28:1-8

    Leviticus 1:11

    Mishnah Zevachim 5

Rabbi Ishmael's thirteen rules for interpreting Torah

Kaddish d'Rabbanan (Rabbinical Kaddish)

Psalm 30

Kaddish Yatom (Mourner's Kaddish)

one's hands. Just as the priests in the *Beit HaMik-dash* began the daily services with washing their hands (Exodus 30:20), so do Jews before addressing God. The *brachah* does not literally refer to washing one's hands, but to *netilat yadayim*, lifting up one's hands, i.e., consecrating them. Traditionally, Jews recite this *brachah* immediately upon arising.

A *brachah* thanking God for physical health follows. This *brachah*, which is found in *Brachot* 60b, specifically makes mention of the bodily orifices which enable us to function.

The next section of *Birchot HaShachar* allows the Jew to fulfill the obligation for daily Torah study. The importance of study in Judaism is illustrated by its place in the liturgy. Three *brachot* introduce this section; they reflect the preferences of three rabbis (*Brachot* 11b).

Three passages are included for study: from the Tanach, Numbers 6:24-26, the priestly benediction; from the Mishnah, *Peah* 1:1, which lists *mitzvot* which do not have a required minimum (including Torah study); and from the Talmud, *Shabbat* 127a, which lists *mitzvot* one can enjoy in this world while receiving a reward in the world to come. This selection concludes with the phrase "the study of Torah is equal to them all because it leads to them all." These passages are not essential, as there are others in the liturgy which would fulfill the *mitzvah* of Torah study. But in order not to delay fulfilling the requirement, these passages are read immediately following the *brachot*.

The liturgy continues with the prayer *Elohai N'shamah*, which affirms that God has created us with a pure soul (*Brachot* 60a). According to a tradition, sleep constitutes one-sixtieth of death; when one awakens each morning, it is as if one's soul has been restored to the body. In some *siddurim*, this *brachah* follows the *brachah* for thanking God for physical health.

A series of 15 *brachot* follows (all but the fourteenth are in *Brachot* 60b). These reflect the activities one does in the morning from waking up, arising, getting dressed, etc., to going about one's daily affairs. Also included are three controversial *brachot* in which a male Jew thanks God for "not making me a heathen," "not making me a slave," and "not making me a woman." All three are based upon the fact that non-Israelites, slaves, and women are not commanded to observe all of the *mitzvot*. According to the Talmud, greater is the reward of one who is commanded to do a *mitzvah* than one who does it but is not commanded (*Kiddushin* 31a).

In the Talmud, the first of these three *brachot* is worded in the positive, "Who made me a Jew." This is the version preferred by the Vilna Gaon, and is used in most Sephardic, Conservative, and Reform *siddurim*. Conservative and Reform *siddurim* also rephrase the second *brachah* ("Who has not made me a slave") to read: "Who made me free."

Instead of reading "Who has not made me a woman," the third *brachah*, women read "Who made me according to [God's] will." In the Conservative *siddur*, the *brachah* for both men and women reads: "Who made me in God's image." This *brachah* is omitted from the Reform *siddur*.

Two petitionary prayers, both beginning with the phrase "May it be Your will . . ." follow. The first asks God to protect us from the evil impulse (*yetzer hara*), which leads us to sin. The second, which was the personal prayer of Rabbi Judah the Prince, asks God to protect us from evil human beings and from evil occurrences. It is permitted to insert one's own petitions at the end of this prayer.

The next section of *Birchot HaShachar* developed in response to religious persecution under the Persian ruler Yezdejerd II. In the fifth century C.E., he forbade public worship, specifically the recitation of the *Sh'ma*, which challenged the basic dualistic teaching of the Zoroastrian religion. In response, the Jewish community developed a short liturgy to be recited at home, centered around the first line of the *Sh'ma*. The paragraph beginning "*Ribon Kol HaOlamim*" is referred to in *Yoma* (87b) as a Yom Kippur prayer.

The next section of the *Birchot HaShachar* consists of readings which relate to the sacrificial cult. Following the destruction of the *Beit HaMik-dash*, the rabbis ruled that study of texts relating to the sacrifices was as meritorious as the actual offerings (*Menachot* 110a). The readings include Numbers 28:1-8 (and verses 9-10 on Shabbat, and verses 11-15 on Rosh Chodesh), Leviticus 1:11, and chapter five of Mishnah *Zevachim*. These selections also begin the second unit of Torah study, which concludes with the introduction to the Midrash *Sifra*, which lists Rabbi Ishmael's thirteen rules by which one can interpret Torah. This entire section is omitted in some synagogues. *Kaddish d'Rabbanan* (the Rabbi's *Kaddish*), which traditionally concludes a study session, is then read, followed by Psalm 30, which is a song for the dedication of the house, and *Kaddish Yatom* (the Mourner's *Kaddish*). These prayers conclude *Birchot HaShachar*.

INSIGHTS FROM THE TRADITION

A. The second verse of the *Mah Tovu*, Psalms 5:8, (*Va'ani B'rov Chasd'cha Avo Veitecha Eshtachaveh El Heichal Kod'sh'cha B'yiratecha*) serves a special purpose in determining if there is a *minyan* present for worship. There is a Jewish aversion to counting people. This is based upon a superstition that by numbering people we invite the angel of death. The ten words in Psalms 5:8 are used to determine if there is a *minyan* present, without having to use numbers. Another approach used when counting people is to say: "Not one, not two, . . . "

B. The first of the fifteen short *brachot* literally thanks God for giving the rooster the ability to distinguish between day and night. It is taken from Job 38:36, where the word "*sechvi*" is derived from the root meaning "to see." Without the rooster's crowing, our ancestors could not have awakened at the appropriate time to start the day (with morning worship).

C. Much of the disparity between men and women in Judaism is derived from the rabbinic decision to exempt women from most positive time-bound *mitzvot*. While women were not explicitly forbidden from these *mitzvot*, in most communities throughout history the exemption was tantamount to a prohibition. Furthermore, since one who is exempt from a *mitzvah* cannot do the *mitzvah* on behalf of one who is not exempt, this ruling meant that women could not lead prayers if men were present.

D. Elie Wiesel was once asked if he found it impossible to say certain prayers. He answered: "Not any more, but it used to happen to me often. Today I know that heartbreak exists, and that prayer is tied to heartbreak. In the morning prayer, for instance, there is a phrase that says *Ashrenu ma-tov helkenu*, 'happy are we with our destiny! How pleasant is our fate! How precious is our heritage!' When I think that I recited that prayer in the camp, along with hundreds of my comrades, that we said it again and again! How could we have said such a prayer? Yet we did. So I tell myself that if we said it in the camp, what right do I have to stop saying it today?" (*Evil & Exile* by de Saint-Cheron and Elie Wiesel, p. 13. Reprinted by permission of Elie Wiesel. © 1990.)

ACTIVITIES

TEXT AND CONTEXT

1. Share with your students the pamphlet "Thanking God" from the series *Let's Discover God*. Direct students to create their own books with pictures and words which express what they are thankful for. Conclude by teaching the song *"Modeh Ani."* Resources: *The Complete Shireinu: 350 Fully Notated Jewish Songs* edited by Joel Eglash, p. 235; *Songs for Growin'* by Kol B'Seder; *Aleph Bet Boogie* by Rabbi Joe Black; *Turn It* by Mah Tovu. (K-2)

2. With the class sitting in a circle, read the series of short morning *brachot* beginning with "Who gives us the ability to distinguish between day and night." Ask each student in turn to add a *brachah* to the list. Sing the first part in Hebrew (*Baruch Atah Adonai . . .*) and the second part in English (Who has made me to be free . . .). (K-5)

3. Ask students to chart their own morning routine, being very specific (i.e., waking up, opening one's eyes, getting out of bed, washing one's face). Read through the *Birchot HaShachar* and identify the connections between the *brachot* and the students' activities. Ask each student to identify one *brachah* to learn and recite daily in conjunction with the action to which it relates. After a week, ask students to report on how it felt to do this. Did it help make them feel more connected to being Jewish? Will they continue to recite the *brachah*? Do they want to add other *brachot*? (3-8)

4. Introduce the students to *Birchot HaShachar*, providing each student with a *siddur*. Assign students to recite the *Birchot HaShachar* each morning and to keep a journal recording their thoughts and feelings about starting their day with prayer. Ask students who wish to do so to share what they wrote. Discuss how, if at all, reciting these *brachot* changed their day. (6 and up)

5. For your class, play the song "*La'asok B'divrei Torah.*" Distribute *siddurim* to your students and read this *brachah* in *Birchot HaShachar*, as well as the other *brachot* and passages for study which follow it. Discuss: Why as part of our worship service, do we actually study Torah? How does studying Torah demonstrate our praise of God? Resource: *Songs for Growin'* by Kol B'Seder. (6 and up)

6. Share the following cartoon with your students: (Reprinted with permission of Universal Press Service. © 1992.)

Read with the class the paragraph following the short *brachot* which begins "*Vihi Ratzon*" (May it be Your will). Ask students to identify the connection between the cartoon and the prayer (" . . . keep us far from an evil person . . . "). Direct students to draw their own cartoons, illustrating a similar situation from their own lives or a pretend situation. (6 and up)

7. Read with your students the blessing *Elohai N'shamah*. Listen to a recording of this *brachah*. Discuss: What does it mean to say that God created us with a pure soul? How does this idea compare with the Christian concept of original sin? Resource: *And You Shall be a Blessing* by Debbie Friedman. (9 and up)

8. Three of the *Birchot HaShachar* have generated a lot of controversy: Who has not made me a heathen . . . Who has not made me a slave . . . Who has not made me a woman. Hold a meeting of the synagogue ritual committee to discuss whether these *brachot* should be included as they were written, should be changed (see Overview), or should be eliminated. Bring in a variety of *siddurim* so students can see how the issue has been handled in various editions. You may wish to assign roles to support and oppose each position. (9 and up)

For Better or For Worse®   by Lynn Johnston

ARTS

9. Teach students to sing *Mah Tovu*, with which the morning service in the synagogue traditionally begins. Resources: *Gates of Song: Music for Shabbat* (numbers 15-18); *Snapshots: The Best of Kol B'Seder Vol. 1* by Kol B'Seder; *Only This* by Mah Tovu. (K-5)

10. Extend Activity #9 by having each student draw pictures of his/her home, synagogue, and school. Create a bulletin board with the drawings and the first phrase of *Mah Tovu*: "How goodly are your tents, O Jacob, your dwelling places, O Israel." (K-5)

11. Teach the students the phrase *Birchot HaShachar* ("The Morning Blessings"). Incorporate that phrase into a watercolor painting of the sunrise. Students might want to include images of a rooster, which is referred to in one of the *brachot*. (3 and up)

12. Listen to various recordings of "*Adon Olam.*" Discuss: How does music affect mood? Which melodies seemed most appropriate? Choose one melody for the students to learn and present at a service. Resources: *The Complete NFTY Recordings: 1972-1989*; *And You Shall Teach Your Children* by Shir Hadash; *New Traditions* by Jon Simon. (6 and up)

13. Extend Activity #12 by challenging the students to choose a familiar melody to which the words of the song "*Adon Olam*" can be sung, or to create a melody of their own. Select one of the melodies and sing it for another class. (6 and up)

14. Divide the class into small groups. Assign each group a *brachah* from *Birchot HaShachar* to dramatize. For example, the *brachah* referring to clothing the naked could be presented as a person collecting clothes for the poor. Encourage the students to be creative. For the presentation, first read the *brachah*, then present the skit. Videotape if possible. (9 and up)

15. Design and make a mosaic plaque for the entrance to your synagogue with the first line of *Mah Tovu* in Hebrew and/or English. Use small colored tiles and grout on a plywood backing. (9 and up)

BEYOND THE TEXT

16. Tell students to put their heads down and pretend to go to sleep for a short time. Talk them through waking up ("You are lying on your bed at home. You hear the birds chirping. Your room is getting lighter," etc.). Tell students to open their eyes and ask them what they are thankful for, what they look forward to doing that day. List their responses on the board or on a sheet of paper. If you recite *Modeh Ani* daily in your class, read their responses immediately before or after. (K-2)

17. Bring to class pictures of a variety of synagogues. Show these pictures to the students. Ask them to share the special things they see as they "walk into" to the synagogue. (K-2)

18. Read to your students *Peah* 1:1 and *Shabbat* 127a, which are part of the Torah study portion of *Birchot HaShachar*. Ask each student to select one of the *mitzvot* mentioned and write a short story about people who do the *mitzvah*. (3-8)

19. The study passages from *Peah* 1:1 and *Shabbat* 127a can provide the basis for a social action project. Divide the students into small groups. Direct each group to select one of the *mitzvot* from these lists and design a *mitzvah* project based on it. Have each group report to the class and choose one of the ideas to implement. (6 and up)

20. Among the authors of various passages from *Birchot HaShachar* are Rabbi Judah the Prince, Rabbi Ishmael, Daniel ben Judah, and Solomon ibn Gabirol. In groups research the life of one of these people. On a map plot out where each was from, their time period, and whether or not it would have been possible for them to know each other. Point out to the students that the *siddur* (as well as many other Jewish books) is comprised of material from disparate periods of times and different places. (9 and up)

21. *Birchot HaShachar* includes Rabbi Ishmael's thirteen rules by which one can interpret Torah. Invite the Rabbi or another knowledgeable teacher to share examples that illustrate some or all of these rules. Present passages from Jewish tradition, asking students to identify which rule was used. Resource: *Daily Prayer Book: Ha-Siddur Ha-Shalem* translated by Birnbaum, pp. 41-46. (9 and up)

22. *Birchot HaShachar* contains one *brachah* which focuses on our body and one which focuses on our soul. Using the texts of these *brachot* and other sources, students in groups or individually prepare a presentation about how Judaism views the body and the soul. Resources: *Basic Judaism* by Steinberg, pp. 71-75; "Soul" by Elior in *Contemporary Jewish Religious Thought* edited by Cohen and Mendes-Flohr; *People of the Body: Jews and Judaism from an Embodied Perspective* by Eilberg-Schwartz. (9 and up)

23. Extend Activity #22 by inviting a guest to compare and contrast Judaism's views of the body and soul with those of other religions. (9 and up)

24. "*Yigdal*," which is sung during *Birchot HaShachar*, is based on the thirteen principles of faith of Maimonides. Distribute copies of these principles to the students. Read and discuss them as a class. Compare this list with the verses of "*Yigdal*" and try to determine how each principle is represented in the song. Discuss whether the students agree with all of the principles. As a class compose contemporary principles of faith. Resources: *The Authorised Daily Prayer Book* by Hertz, pp. 248-255; *A Maimonides Reader*, Twersky, ed., pp. 417-423. (9 and up)

25. *Birchot HaShachar* contains a *brachah* beginning "*Vihi Ratzon Milfanecha*," which asks God not to give power to the *yetzer hara* (the evil inclination). Read this *brachah* with your students and ask if they have heard the terms *yetzer hara* and *yetzer hatov* (good inclination). Distribute to small groups of students one or more teachings with these terms. Each group presents a short skit reflecting the teaching. Discuss the presentations

to get a clear idea of the terms. Resources: *A Rabbinic Anthology*, Montefiore and Loewe, eds., pp. 295-314; *Aspects of Rabbinic Theology* by Schechter.

HEBREW

26. Teach the phrase "Talmud Torah" to your students. Be sure to point out that it refers not only to studying the Torah (the Five Books of Moses), but also to Torah in its broadest meaning — all of Jewish knowledge. Teach the song "*Eilu D'varim*" to the class. Resources: *The Complete Shireinu: 350 Fully Notated Jewish Songs,* edited by Joel Eglash, p. 242; *Beged Kefet: The First Album!* by Beged Kefet. (3 and up)

27. Read Numbers 24:5 in Hebrew. Now locate *Mah Tovu* in a *Sefer Torah*. Read it without vowels. Identify familiar words. Discuss why this phrase is such a blessing. (6 and up)

FAMILY

28. Hold a family workshop entitled, "Strengthening the Jewish Body and Soul." Among the topics you might include are: meditation, Israeli dancing, *halachah* and care for your body, attitude toward drug and alcohol consumption, etc. Resource: *Teaching Hot Topics* by Freeman.

29. Introduce the major *brachot* of *Birchot HaShachar* to the families using appropriate activities suggested above. Ask each family to design its own morning ritual utilizing parts of *Birchot HaShachar*, creative writings, and other material.

RESOURCES

BOOKS

Eglash, Joel , ed. *The Complete Shireinu: 350 Fully Notated Jewish Songs*. New York: Transcontinental Music Publications, 2001.

Birnbaum, Philip, ed. *Daily Prayer Book: Ha-Siddur Ha-Shalem*. New York: Hebrew Publishing Company, 2002.

Cohen, Arthur A., and Paul Mendes-Flohr, eds. *Contemporary Jewish Religious Thought.* New York: Free Press, 1988.

de Saint-Cheron, Philippe-Michael, and Elie Wiesel. *Evil & Exile.* South Bend, IN: University of Notre Dame Press, 1990.

Eilberg-Schwartz, Howard. *People of the Body: Jews and Judaism from an Embodied Perspective.* Albany, NY: State University of New York Press, 1992.

Freeman, Susan. *Teaching Hot Topics: Jewish Resources, Values, and Activities.* Denver, CO: A.R.E. Publishing, Inc., 2003.

Gates of Song: Music for Shabbat. New York: Transcontinental Music Publications, 1987.

Hertz, Joseph H. *The Authorised Daily Prayer Book.* New York: Bloch Publishing Company, 1975.

Montefiore, C.G., and H. Loewe. *A Rabbinic Anthology.* New York: Schocken Books, 1987.

Schechter, Solomon. *Aspects of Rabbinic Theology: With a New Introduction by Neil Gilman, Including the Original Preface of 1909 and the Introduction by Louis Finkelstein..* Woodstock, VT: Jewish Lights Publishing, 1999.

Steinberg, Milton. *Basic Judaism.* New York: Harcourt Brace Jovanovich, 1975.

Thompson, Marlena C. and Susan Van Dusen. *Let's Discover God.* Springfield, NJ: Behrman House, Inc., 1988.

Twersky, Isadore, ed. *A Maimonides Reader.* New York: Behrman House, Inc., 1989.

AUDIOVISUAL

Beged Kefet. *Beged Kefet: The First Album!* Livingston, NJ: Beged Kefet, 1987. Compact disc. Available from Sounds Write Productions, Inc.

Black, Rabbi Joe. *Aleph Bet Boogie.* Albuquerque, NM: Lanitunes Music, 1991. Compact disc. Available from A.R.E. Publishing, Inc.

Friedman, Debbie. *And You Shall Be a Blessing.* San Diego: Sounds Write Productions, Inc., 1989. Compact disc. Available from A.R.E. Publishing, Inc.

Kol B'Seder. *Songs for Growin'.* New York: Transcontinental Music Publications, 2001. Compact disc and songbook. Available from A.R.E. Publishing, Inc.

———. *Snapshots: The Best of Kol B'Seder Vol. 1.* West Roxbury, MA: Kol B'Seder, 2004. Compact disc. Available from A.R.E. Publishing, Inc.

Mah Tovu. *Only This.* Denver, CO: Mah Tovu, 1996. Compact disc. Available from A.R.E. Publishing, Inc.

———. *Turn It.* Denver, CO: Mah Tovu, 2001. Available from A.R.E. Publishing, Inc.

The Complete NFTY Recordings: 1972-1989. New York: Transcontinental Music Publications, 2003. Five compact disc set. Available from Transcontinental Music Publications.

Shir Hadash. *And You Shall Teach Your Children.* Vancouver, BC: Shir Hadash, 1990. Compact disc and audiocassette. Available from Sounds Write Productions, Inc.

Simon, Jon. *New Traditions.* Bethesda, MD: Silver Lining Records, 1988. Compact disc. Available from Sounds Write Productions, Inc.

CHAPTER FIVE:
P'SUKEI D'ZIMRAH

OVERVIEW

The Talmud teaches that "One should first recount the praises of God, and then pray" (*Brachot* 32a). In fulfillment of this dictum, a tradition developed of reciting psalms before Shacharit. Eventually, these selections grew until they comprised a formal section of the worship experience known as *P'sukei d'Zimrah* (Passages of Song). Whereas *Birchot HaShachar* are primarily private devotions which, originally at least, were said at home, *P'sukei d'Zimrah* are psalms and other passages designed to be sung at a public worship service.

There is a tradition that the most pious Jews would recite the entire book of Psalms daily. *P'sukei d'Zimrah* goes a way toward fulfilling that goal by including seven complete psalms on weekday mornings (Psalms 100 and 145-150) and sixteen psalms on Shabbat and festivals (plus verses from many others). Rabbi Meir of Rothenberg is credited with making this section part of the daily Shacharit service in the thirteenth century.

P'sukei d'Zimrah begins with a hymn of praise known by its first two words, *Baruch She'amar*. The word "*baruch*" occurs thirteen times in this selection, as the worshiper praises God as both creator and redeemer of the universe. *Baruch She'amar* serves as the opening *brachah* of this part of the service. It is first found in the ninth century *siddur* of Rav Amram.

Following *Baruch She'amar* is I Chronicles 16:8-36, a song which celebrates David's bringing the Ark of the Covenant to Jerusalem. The first half of this passage is almost identical to the first fifteen verses of Psalm 105, and the last half is

P'SUKEI D'ZIMRAH
(Passages of Song)

Baruch She'amar (Opening *brachah* of P'sukei d'Zimrah)

I Chronicles 16:8-36

Romemu (Verses from Psalms)

Psalm 100

On Shabbat, Festivals, and Hoshanah Rabbah: Psalms 19, 34, 90, 91, 135, 136, 33, 92, 93

Y'hi Ch'vod (May God's glory)

Ashrei (Psalm 145)

Psalms 146-150

Psalms 89:53, 135:21, 72:18-19

I Chronicles 29:10-13

Nehemiah 9:6-14

Exodus 14:30-15:18

Psalm 22:29

Obadiah 1:21

Zechariah 14:9

Nishmat Kol Chai (Shabbat and Festivals)

Yishtabach Shimcha (Concluding *brachah* of P'sukei d'Zimrah)

Chatzi Kaddish (Reader's Kaddish)

similar to Psalm 96, which probably explains its inclusion in this part of the liturgy.

Next follows a selection of verses from different psalms (beginning with the word "*Romemu*" — exalt). These verses do not appear to have any internal logic or coherence. Rabbi B. S. Jacobson suggests that "the recital of a set of such verses taken from all five books [of psalms] is held to form a substitute, as it were, for the entire Book of Psalms." (*The Weekday Siddur: An Exposition and Analysis of its Structure, Contents, Language and Ideas*, p. 83. Reprinted by permission of the publisher, Sinai Publishing Co., Tel Aviv, Israel. © 1978.)

Psalm 100, a psalm of thanksgiving, follows. It was sung while the thanksgiving offering was being sacrificed in the *Beit HaMikdash*. Since there was no thanksgiving offering on Shabbat, festivals, *erev* Pesach, the intermediate days of Pesach, and *erev* Yom Kippur, this psalm is omitted on those days.

On Shabbat, festivals, and Hoshana Rabbah, nine additional psalms are recited in the following order: Psalms 19, 34, 90, 91, 135, 136, 33, 92, and 93. These precede Psalm 145. Since there is no concern about the length of the service on these days, it is natural to add various psalms, thus distinguishing these days from the regular weekdays. In the Sephardic tradition, fourteen psalms and a mystical poem called *HaAderet V'HaEmunah* (The Power and the Faith), are added and placed before *Baruch She'amar*.

P'sukei d'Zimrah continues with another set of verses from a variety of psalms (with one verse each from Proverbs and I Chronicles interspersed), beginning *Y'hi Ch'vod Adonai L'Olam* (May God's glory endure forever). In this passage, each subsequent verse contains a word or concept which is in the prior verse. God's name is mentioned twenty-one times, perhaps to correspond to the twenty-one verses of Psalm 145, which follows.

Psalm 145 is known as *Ashrei*, the first word of the two verses (Psalms 84:5 and 144:15) which precede and introduce it. This psalm and the five that follow, Psalms 146-150, comprised the original *P'sukei d'Zimrah*. They are sometimes called the daily *Hallel*, and conclude the Book of Psalms. Even in the time of Maimonides, these psalms were optional. He wrote: "The sages regarded as praiseworthy anyone who daily reads the psalms from *Tehilah l'David* (Psalm 145) through the end of the book" (*Mishneh Torah, Tefilah* 7:12).

These psalms are followed by Psalms 89:53,

135:21, and 72:18-19, each of which is the conclusion of its psalm.

Three other biblical passages follow, each of which is a significant song or prayer. I Chronicles 29:10-13 is David's prayer at the inauguration of the building of the *Beit HaMikdash*. Nehemiah 9:6-14 is a brief survey of history through the crossing of the Sea of Reeds. This passage introduces Exodus 14:30-15:18, the Song of the Sea, which was sung by the Levites as part of the ritual accompanying the Minchah offering in the *Beit HaMikdash*, and later incorporated into *P'sukei d'Zimrah* as a way of preserving a remnant of the worship in the *Beit HaMikdash*.

The Song of the Sea is followed by three verses which proclaim God's sovereignty over all the world: Psalm 22:29, Obadiah 1:21, and Zechariah 14:9.

On Shabbat and festivals, the concluding *brachah* of *P'sukei d'Zimrah* begins with *Nishmat Kol Chai* (The breath of every living being shall bless Your name). Part of this hymn of praise is contained in the Talmud, where it is a prayer of thanksgiving for the rainfall that follows a drought (*Ta'anit* 6b, *Brachot* 59b).

On weekdays, the concluding *brachah* begins, "*Yishtabach Shimcha La'ad Malkeinu*" (May Your name be praised forever, our Ruler). This *brachah* leads into the *Chatzi Kaddish* which serves as a transition between *P'sukei d'Zimrah* and the *Bar'chu*, which leads into *Sh'ma Uvirchotehah*.

As a whole, *P'sukei d'Zimrah* is a series of psalms, other biblical passages, and rabbinic hymns and prayers which offer praise to God. Its presence at the beginning of Shacharit demonstrates the attitude that one must first praise God before offering other prayers of petition and thanksgiving.

INSIGHTS FROM THE TRADITION

A. *Tehilah L'David* (Psalm 145) has a special place in Jewish tradition. Rabbi Elazar said, "All who say *Tehilah L'David* three times every day are assured of their place in the world to come" (*Brachot* 4b). Besides being recited as a part of

P'sukei d'Zimrah, it is also chanted toward the end of Shacharit and at the beginning of Minchah.

B. The name of the Book of Psalms in Hebrew, *Tehilim*, is taken from Psalm 145, which begins with the words *Tehilah L'David*. *Tehilim* is the plural of *Tehilah*. No other psalm is introduced in this manner.

C. Psalm 145 is an alphabetical acrostic. Each verse begins with a subsequent letter of the alphabet. However, the letter *nun* is missing. According to tradition, the *nun* was omitted because the word *naflah* (fallen) begins with the letter *nun*, and one might be reminded of Amos 5:2 which speaks of Israel's fall.

D. When Saadia compiled his *siddur* in the tenth century, he included *P'sukei d'Zimrah* as an appendix. He pointed out that this section was not in the Talmud, but that the people had voluntarily taken it upon themselves to read psalms with introductory and concluding *brachot*. *Baruch She'amar* is the introductory *brachah*. On weekdays, the concluding *brachah* begins, "*Yishtabach Shimcha La'ad Malkeinu.*" On Shabbat and festivals, the concluding *brachah* begins "*Nishmat Kol Chai.*"

E. Rabbi Isaac Aboab (fifteenth century) offered a *midrash* to explain the word "*mizmor*" (song), identifying it with a word of the same root with the meaning "to prune." He wrote, "I have found it written that these hymns are called *mizmorim* in the sense of (Lev. 25:4): 'You shall not prune (*tizmor*) your vineyard.' *Zemiroth*, then, are to be understood in the sense of *zemoroth* (pruned branches). Just as the gardener prunes his vine, leaving the healthy branches and improving their fruit-bearing capacity, so does our recital of the Psalms detach and remove all obstructions and iniquities, so that when our *Tefilah* is submitted, it should obtain a hearing and be acceptable to God." (*The Weekday Siddur: An Exposition and Analysis of its Structure, Contents, Lauguage and Ideas*, p. 75. Reprinted by permission of the publisher, Sinai Publishing Co., Tel Aviv, Israel. © 1978.)

F. The origin of *Nishmat Kol Chai* has some interesting legends associated with it. One tradition credits it to Rabbi Simeon ben Shetach of the Maccabean dynasty. A legend from medieval France and Germany claims that the Apostle Peter, also known as Simon Cephas, authored it as the completion of his renunciation of the messianic claims of Jesus. This legend, however, is refuted by Rashi.

ACTIVITIES

TEXT AND CONTEXT

1. Ask your students: "How do you make cookies?" Write the responses on the board and then number the steps in the order you would do them. Introduce the words "prepare" and "preparation" as they relate to making cookies. Ask students how they prepare to do certain other things, such as going on a trip, getting ready for school in the morning, celebrating a holiday, or taking a test. Ask the students how they might get ready for prayer. Introduce *P'sukei d'Zimrah* as the way the *siddur* helps us get ready for prayer in the morning. (K-5)

2. Prior to the class session, make a large banner with the words "*P'sukei d'Zimrah*" in English and/or Hebrew. Cut up the banner like a puzzle, providing for as many pieces as there are students. Mail one piece to each student instructing him/her to bring it to the next session. (If this is not feasible, distribute the pieces as the students enter the room.) Direct the students to assemble the puzzle and read what it says. Ask if any of the students are familiar with this phrase. Translate and explain the term as the name of a section in the morning service that helps get a person in the mood to pray. (2-5)

3. Ask the students how they feel when they are praised. What words are used when they are praised? Provide students with *siddurim* and direct them to look through *P'sukei d'Zimrah* to find those words or other words of praise that are used. (3-5)

4. Discuss with the students how words stimulate and create a mood. Read through *P'sukei d'Zimrah* as a class, identifying words which fit into the following categories: beautiful, comforting, joyful, frightening. You may include other categories if you wish. Conclude by discussing what kind of mood *P'sukei d'Zimrah* expresses. (6-8)

5. According to the Mishnah (*Brachot* 5:1), the pious ones of old would wait an hour before praying in order that they might concentrate their thoughts upon the Holy One. *P'sukei d'Zimrah* was also a way to help a person prepare for the main part of the worship service. Share this information with your students and discuss: Have you thought about this period of preparation? How does it compare to preparing for a speech, test, or presentation? How does preparation affect presentation? How does this relate to prayer and to *P'sukei d'Zimrah*? (9 and up)

6. Compare *P'sukei d'Zimrah* in two or more *siddurim*, at least one of which is traditional and one of which is liberal. What are the similarities and differences? What has been omitted? Which would be more conducive for preparing a congregation for the main part of the service? (9 and up)

ARTS

7. Psalm 33, which is included in *P'sukei d'Zimrah* on Shabbat, instructs that one should "give thanks to God with the harp." Read the beginning of this psalm to your students. Invite a harpist to your class or use a recording of harp music. After listening to the harp music, ask the students what kind of mood it sets. The teacher may want to read Psalm 33 in Hebrew or English while the harpist plays some music. Resource: *City of Gold* by Sunita Stanislow. (K and up)

8. Teach the students the song "*Ivdu Et HaShem B'simcha*," the words of which are from Psalm 100. Resources: *The Complete Shireinu: 350 Fully Notated Jewish Songs* edited by Joel Eglash, p. 109; *Beged Kefet: The First Album* by Beget Kefet. (K and up)

9. Psalm 149 calls upon Israel to praise God's name with dance and to sing praises to God with the timbrel and harp. With musical instruments and song, create a dance that praises God. Resource: *Torah in Motion: Creating Dance Midrash* by Tucker and Freeman. (3 and up)

10. Have the students read through *P'sukei d'Zimrah*, choosing words of praise. Write each word on pieces of card stock of varying colors, sizes, and shapes. Put these together as a mobile. (3 and up)

11. Look at Psalm 145, and ask students to identify any unusual feature of the Hebrew text (see Insight C). It is written as an acrostic, with each verse starting with a subsequent letter of the alphabet (omitting the letter *nun*). Direct the students to write a poem of praise as an acrostic, using the letters of the alphabet as the initial letter of each line, or choosing a word or phrase whose letters will begin each verse. (6 and up)

12. Psalm 19, which is included in *P'sukei d'Zimrah* on Shabbat, states, "The heavens recount the glory of the Almighty, and the sky proclaims God's handiwork." Using florescent paints on butcher paper, create with the students scenes of the evening sky and the daytime sky. Attach to the ceiling. (6 and up)

13. *P'sukei d'Zimrah* contains three biblical passages that highlight several significant events in the evolution of the Jewish people. The passages are: I Chronicles 29:10-13; Nehemiah 9:6-14; Exodus 14:30-15:18. Read through these verses with your students and illustrate them on banners with fabric applique, in painting, or with pencil sketches. (9 and up)

14. A verse from Psalm 33 reads, "the earth is full of God's faithful care." Discuss this passage. If God has shown faithful care to the earth, have we? What are some of the good and bad things that we have done to the earth? Create a three-panel collage utilizing magazine and newspaper articles and pictures, found objects, photographs, etc. Entitle each of the panels as follows: "God's

Care for the Earth," "Humankind's Damage to the Earth," "Humankind's Healing the Earth." The collage may be embellished with stitchery, paint, crayon, or other art materials. (3 and up)

BEYOND THE TEXT

15. Extend Activity #14 by choosing an appropriate activity from *50 Simple Things You Can Do to Save the Earth* by Earthworks Group. (3 and up)

16. According to tradition, King David is the author of many of the psalms. Introduce your students to King David by reading or telling one of the following stories: "David and Goliath" from *Let's Discover the Bible* Set 2 by Shirley Rose; "David in the Days of Saul" or "David and Bathsheba" from *A Child's Bible Book 2: Lessons from the Prophets and Writings* by Seymour Rossel; "King David and the Giant" from *Elijah's Violin & Other Jewish Fairy Tales* by Howard Schwartz, pp. 44-46; one of the stories from *The Book of Legends: Sefer Ha-Aggadah* by Bialik and Ravnitzky, eds., pp. 117-122. (K-2)

17. Nissan Mindel writes, "Our Shabbat prayers have an extraordinary significance and God welcomes them with particular pleasure. It is only right that we should give God some more pleasure on Shabbat by reciting additional prayers" (*My Prayer*, p. 96). Discuss: What gives you extra pleasure, particularly on Shabbat? (3 and up)

18. In Psalm 30, David thanks God for having been saved from a deadly illness. In *To Pray as a Jew* (p. 177), Rabbi Hayim Halevy Donin writes, "In recalling the plea he made to God during his illness, David expresses a thought that is central to the Book of Psalms and to all of Judaism: the affirmation of the supreme value of life. There is no merit in death, for 'the dead do not praise the Lord' (Psalms 115:17)." Explore with your students Judaism's attitude toward martyrdom. See "*Kiddush Ha-Shem*" and "*Hillul Ha-Shem*" in *Encyclopaedia Judaica*, vol. 10, cols. 977-986. After examining this material, define with your students those situations in which Judaism permits martyrdom. (9 and up)

19. Psalm 136, which is included on Shabbat, is sometimes referred to as the "Great *Hallel*." According to Rabbi Yochanan, it is called "Great" because it refers to God as the one who gives food to all creatures (*Pesachim* 118a). The Rabbis considered the providing of food for human beings to be as difficult as dividing the Sea of Reeds. Discuss this idea with your students. Why is it so hard for us to provide food for everyone? What are some of the ways in which the students can help with this problem? Choose one project to do with your class, such as collecting non-perishable food or volunteering at a soup kitchen. Material can be obtained from MAZON: A Jewish Response to Hunger, 1990 S. Bundy Dr, Ste. 260, Los Angeles, CA 90025, P: (310) 442-0020, www.mazon.org. (9 and up)

20. Psalm 145 states, "All your works shall give thanks to you, *Adonai*; And Your loving ones shall bless You." Rabbi Joseph Hertz interprets this to mean that as Jews we must bless God not only for all the good which happens to us, but also for all the bad (*The Authorised Daily Prayer Book*, p. 87). Discuss: Why should we bless God for bad things that happen? Resource: *When Bad Things Happen to Good People* by Kushner. (9 and up)

HEBREW

21. Psalms 34 and 145, both of which are part of *P'sukei d'Zimrah*, are acrostics. Use one or both of these psalms to teach or reinforce the Hebrew alphabet. (Note: Psalm 145 omits the letter *nun*.) Two songs that teach the alphabet are: "Alef Bet Song" by Debbie Friedman and "Aleph Bet Boogie" by Rabbi Joe Black. Resources: *Debbie Friedman Live at the Del* by Debbie Friedman, *Aleph Bet Boogie* by Rabbi Joe Black. (3-5)

22. Discuss the use of acrostics in Psalms 34 and 145 and other places in the liturgy (*L'cha Dodi, Ashamnu, Al Cheit*). Have each student write a poem using each letter of his/her Hebrew name as the first letter of each line. (6 and up)

23. Divide the class into groups. Provide each group with a *siddur*. Direct the students to read through *P'sukei d'Zimrah* and make a list of words or phrases that praise God. Identify the roots that are most commonly used to praise God. (6 and up)

24. Psalm 136 contains the refrain *"Ki L'olam Chasdo"* (For [God's] righteousness is forever). Teach this phrase and its meaning to your students. Read through a few verses from this psalm, with the students repeating this phrase. To expand this activity, ask the students to give examples of God's *chesed.* (6 and up)

FAMILY

25. The psalms have played an important role in Jewish liturgy, but are often not sufficiently appreciated today. Hold a "Psalm Appreciation Day" in which selected psalms are presented to participants using a variety of formats. You may wish to choose only psalms that are from *P'sukei d'Zimrah*. A psalm could be read and interpreted in a chalk picture, painting, or clay sculpture. The melodies of some psalms could be taught. Other psalms could be experienced through interpretive dance. You might invite the rabbi, cantor, educator, or a knowledgeable layperson to lead a study session on one or more psalms.

26. *P'sukei d'Zimrah* provides a transition to prayer. Gather families together, and have each discuss and write down what their most recent "getting ready for synagogue" experience was like. Bring families together and discuss their responses. Ask what they would like to change about the way in which they get ready for services. In addition to the physical preparations, it is necessary to prepare mentally and emotionally. To assist in this preparation, suggest topics for discussion on the way to services. For example: a *tzedakah* project the family would like to do; if they went to Israel, what is the first thing they would do there? if they could be any famous Jew, who would they be?

RESOURCES

BOOKS

Bialik, Hayim Nahman, and Yehoshua Hana Ravnitzky, eds. *The Book of Legends: Sefer Ha-Aggadah.* New York: Schocken Books, 1992.

Donin, Hayim Halevy. *To Pray as a Jew: A Guide to the Prayer Book and the Synagogue Service.* New York: Basic Books, Inc., 1980.

Earthworks Group. *50 Simple Things You Can Do To Save the Earth.* Second edition. Berkeley, CA: Bathroom Reader Press, 1995.

Eglash, Joel, ed. *The Complete Shireinu: 350 Fully Notated Jewish Songs.* New York: Transcontinental Music Publications, 2001.

Encyclopaedia Judaica. Jerusalem: Keter Publishing House Jerusalem Ltd., 1972.

Hertz, Joseph H. *The Authorised Daily Prayer Book.* New York: Bloch Publishing Company, 1975.

Jacobson, B.S. *The Weekday Siddur: An Exposition and Analysis of Its Structure, Contents, Language and Ideas.* Tel Aviv: Sinai Publishing, 1978.

Kushner, Harold S. *When Bad Things Happen to Good People.* New York: Avon, 2001.

Mindel, Nissan. *My Prayer.* Newark, NJ: Merkos Linyonei Chinuch, 1998.

Rose, Shirley. *Let's Discover the Bible,* Set 2. Springfield, NJ: Behrman House Inc., 1997.

Rossel, Seymour. *A Child's Bible Book 2: Lessons from the Prophets and Writings.* Springfield, NJ: Behrman House Inc., 1989.

Schwartz, Howard. *Elijah's Violin and Other Jewish Fairy Tales.* San Francisco: Harper & Row, 1983.

Tucker, JoAnne and Susan Freeman. *Torah in Motion: Creating Dance Midrash.* New York: E-Reads, Ltd. Available only as an electronic download from www.amazon.com.

AUDIOVISUAL

Beged Kefet. *Beged Kefet: The First Album.* Livingston, NJ: Beged Kefet, 1987. Compact disc. Available from Sounds Write Productions, Inc.

Black, Rabbi Joe. *Aleph Bet Boogie.* Albuquerque, NM: Lanitunes Music, 1991. Compact disc. Available from A.R.E. Publishing, Inc.

Friedman, Debbie. *Debbie Friedman Live at the Del.*
San Diego, CA: Sounds Write Productions,
Inc., 1990. Compact disc. Available from
A.R.E. Publishing, Inc.

Stanislow, Sunita. *City of Gold.* Minneapolis, MN:
Maxemilian Productions, 1997. Compact disc.
Available from http://www.musicmax.com.

CHAPTER SIX:
SH'MA UVIRCHOTEHA

OVERVIEW

No phrase is more cherished by a Jew than the words "*Sh'ma Yisrael Adonai Eloheinu Adonai Echad*" (Hear O Israel, *Adonai* is our God, *Adonai* is One). This is often the first prayer a child learns, and these are traditionally the last words uttered before dying. Rabbi Hayim Halevy Donin has written, "The *Sh'ma* is said when our lives are full of hope; it is said when all hope is gone and the end is near. Whether in moments of joy or despair, in thankfulness or in resignation, it is the expression of Jewish conviction, the historic proclamation of Judaism's central creed." (*To Pray as a Jew*, p. 144)

In addition to its use at the beginning and end of life, the *Sh'ma* is part of *Birchot HaShachar*, *Kriat HaTorah* (the Torah Service ritual), the *Kedushah* of the Musaf *Amidah*, the last *hakafah* on Hoshana Rabbah, and the end of *Ne'ilah* on Yom Kippur.

This six word phrase is only the beginning of

SH'MA UVIRCHOTEHA
(Shema and its Blessings)

MA'ARIV (EVENING SERVICE)	SHACHARIT (MORNING SERVICE)
Bar'chu (Call to Worship)	*Bar'chu* (Call to Worship)
Ma'ariv Aravim (Creation)	*Yotzer Or* (Creation)
Ahavat Olam (Revelation)	*Ahavah Rabbah* (Revelation)
Sh'ma (Deuteronomy 6:4)	*Sh'ma* (Deuteronomy 6:4)
Baruch Shem (God's Rule)	*Baruch Shem* (God's Rule)
V'ahavta (Deuteronomy 6:5-9)	*V'ahavta* (Deuteronomy 6:5-9)
V'hayah (Deuteronomy 11:13-21)	*V'hayah* (Deuteronomy 11:13-21)
Vayomer (Numbers 15:37-41)	*Vayomer* (Numbers 15:37-41)
Ge'ulah (Redemption)	*Ge'ulah* (Redemption)
Emet V'emunah (True and faithful)	*Emet V'yatziv* (True and firm)
Mi Chamocha (Exodus 15:11, 18)	*Ezrat Avoteinu* (Help of our ancestors)
Hashkiveinu (Lie down in peace)	*Mi Chamocha* (Exodus 15:11-18)
Baruch Adonai L'olam (Blessed is *Adonai* forever; weekdays only)	*Tsur Yisrael* (Arise, O Rock of Israel)
V'shamru (Exodus 31:16-17; Shabbat only)	
Chatzi Kaddish (Reader's Kaddish)	

the *Sh'ma*, which in whole consists of three passages from the Torah: Deuteronomy 6:4-9, Deuteronomy 11:13-22, and Numbers 15:37-41. These paragraphs comprise the central part of the first section of Shacharit and Ma'ariv services, which is called *Sh'ma Uvirchoteha* (*Sh'ma* and its blessings).

Following the first sentence of the *Sh'ma* is a phrase which is not in the Torah: "*Baruch Shem K'vod Malchuto L'olam Va'ed*" (Blessed is God, whose glorious sovereignty is forever and ever). This phrase was first used in the *Beit HaMikdash* on Yom Kippur in response to the High Priest's pronouncement of the name of God. It was inserted after the *Sh'ma* by the rabbis as a commentary on the first line to emphasize that the Jews accepted the ultimate sovereignty of God alone, and not of an earthly ruler, such as a Roman emperor. This line is traditionally read silently, except on Yom Kippur, when it is read aloud. Many liberal congregations, however, always recite it or sing it aloud.

Because *kavanah* is especially important when reciting the *Sh'ma*, many people cover or close their eyes when reciting the six words. It is also traditional to gather the four *tzitzit* (fringes) of the *tallit* together and to kiss them when they are mentioned during the recitation of the third paragraph.

The first paragraph, Deuteronomy 6:4-9, contains a list of *mitzvot*:

> to love God with all one's heart, soul, and might;
> to teach the words and the intent of the *Sh'ma* to one's children;
> to bind these words on one's arm and to place them between one's eyes, traditionally interpreted as wearing *tefillin;*
> to write the words on one's doorpost and gate, which is the basis for affixing *mezuzot*.

The obligation to recite the *Sh'ma* twice daily is based upon the phrase "when you lie down and when you rise up." Therefore, the *Sh'ma* is included in both the Shacharit and Ma'ariv services.

The second paragraph of the *Sh'ma*, Deuteronomy 11:13-22, proclaims the reward Israel will receive for observing the *mitzvot* and the punishment which will result from turning aside to serve other gods. Many of the *mitzvot* contained in the first paragraph are repeated here.

The third paragraph of the *Sh'ma*, Numbers 15:37-41, begins with the *mitzvah* to wear *tzitzit* (fringes) on the corners of one's garments as a reminder to observe the *mitzvot*. It concludes with an admonition to be holy, and an affirmation of God who brought the Jews out of Egypt.

In *Gates of Prayer*, the Reform *siddur*, the entire second paragraph and the first part (Numbers 15:37-39) of the third paragraph are omitted because of repetition, theological difficulties with reward and punishment, and an effort to deemphasize the *mitzvah* of tzitzit. *Kol Haneshamah*, the Reconstructionist *siddur* for *erev* Shabbat, includes the three traditional paragraphs, but also offers a "contemporary biblical selection," Deuteronomy 28:1-6 and 30:15-19, as an alternative reading for the middle paragraph (p. 77).

While it is not clear why these particular passages were chosen to be part of the *Sh'ma*, they were originally used in the ritual of the *Beit HaMikdash* and were firmly fixed in synagogue worship by the first century C.E. That these paragraphs are Scripture and not prayers in the technical sense, demonstrates Judaism's penchant for blending Torah with worship.

The rabbis prescribed that certain blessings be recited before and after the *Sh'ma* (*Brachot* 1:4). Prior to the blessings introducing the *Sh'ma* is the *Bar'chu*, which, since ancient days, has been a call to worship. The congregation rises, the *shaliach tzibur* chants the first line, the congregation responds with the second line, and then, traditionally, the *shaliach tzibur* repeats the second line.

While the *Sh'ma* may be recited either sitting or standing, traditionally one stands for the *Bar'chu* and is then seated for the remainder of this part of the service. In most Reform services, the congregation rises before the *Bar'chu* and remains standing through the first two lines of the *Sh'ma*.

Following the *Bar'chu*, the first blessing before the *Sh'ma* focuses on the theme of creation, praising God as Creator and affirming that creation is a continuous process. The text of the prayer used in the morning differs from the text used in the evening in order to emphasize the phenomena of nature most prominent during that particular time of day.

The evening prayer, *Ma'ariv Aravim*, praises God for bringing on the evening, for controlling the flow of light and darkness, for the seasons, and for ordering the stars in heaven. The corresponding morning prayer, *Yotzer Or*, focuses on God's role as the Creator of light within the context of God's responsibility for creating all things. The traditional version of this prayer includes an alphabetical acrostic (beginning *"Eil Baruch"* on weekdays and *"Eil Adon"* on Shabbat), and a passage praising God for creating the angels, who are also depicted as praising God. The addition of these passages to the *Yotzer Or* is ascribed to mystics of the eighth century. Reform Judaism has eliminated these passages from the liturgy because of theological difficulties with angelology.

The second prayer before the *Sh'ma* is *Ahavah Rabbah* in the morning and *Ahavat Olam* in the evening, both of which are found in the Talmud. These prayers focus on God's love for the people Israel as represented by the gift of the Torah and its *mitzvot*. They therefore serve as a natural introduction to the *Sh'ma*.

Following the *Sh'ma* during Shacharit is the *Ge'ulah*, which begins the prayer *Emet V'yatziv*. This *brachah* affirms the truthfulness of God's word and the support God gave to our ancestors. It also acclaims God's redemption of Israel: the Exodus from Egypt. Two verses from the Song of the Sea (Exodus 15:11, 18), known as the *Mi Chamocha*, are included in this prayer.

During Ma'ariv, the *Ge'ulah* begins *Emet V'emunah*, and reflects the same themes as its morning counterpart, *Emet V'yatziv*, culminating in the *Mi Chamocha*. In the evening, *Hashkiveinu* is also recited, in which one asks God to watch over us as we lie down and rise up.

Examining the *Sh'ma Uvirchoteha* as a whole, one may observe a significant pattern, beginning with the theme of creation in the first *brachah* prior to the *Sh'ma*, proceeding to revelation in the next *brachah* and the *Sh'ma* itself, and concluding with redemption in the *brachah* after the *Sh'ma*. These three concepts are often cited as the cornerstones of Jewish thought (see, for example, *The Star of Redemption* by Franz Rosenzweig).

INSIGHTS FROM THE TRADITION

A. The first paragraph of the *Sh'ma* is written in the second person singular, while the second paragraph is written in the second person plural. Commentators explain that while the first paragraph is directed to the individual, the second is addressed to the people as a whole.

B. According to the Talmud, when recited in the *Beit HaMikdash*, the *Sh'ma* was preceded by the Ten Commandments. However, the Ten Commandments were eliminated from the liturgy in response to sectarians who claimed that only these commandments were revealed by God (*Brachot* 12a). The rabbis also considered including the story of Balaam (Numbers 22-24) in the *Sh'ma*, but did not because its length would have been a burden on the community (*Brachot* 12b).

C. When saying the *Sh'ma* alone, one begins with the phrase *"Eil Melech Ne'eman"* (God is a faithful Ruler). When praying with a community, this phrase is omitted, and instead the *shaliach tzibur* concludes the *Sh'ma* with the phrase *"Adonai Eloheichem Emet"* — the last two words of the *Sh'ma* plus the first word of the next prayer. In either case, the addition of three words brings the total number of words in the *Sh'ma* to 248, which according to Jewish tradition corresponds to the number of positive *mitzvot* as well as to the number of parts of the body (bones, vital organs, etc.).

D. The Talmud (*Brachot* 11b) indicates that there was a debate among the rabbis concerning whether *Ahavah Rabbah* or *Ahavat Olam* should be recited prior to the *Sh'ma*. In Ashkenazic communities, the tradition emerged to recite the former in the morning and the latter in the evening, whereas the Sephardic tradition is to recite *Ahavat Olam* both times.

E. The beginning of the *Yotzer Or* contains a quotation from Isaiah, with one significant change. Speaking in God's name, Isaiah says, "I form light and create darkness, make peace and create evil" (Isaiah 45:7). When this phrase was adopted as part of this prayer, the word "*ra*" (evil) was changed to "*HaKol*" (everything). The author of this prayer preferred to proclaim God as the Creator of all, rather than specifically to mention evil.

F. In the *Sefer Torah*, the last letter of the word *Sh'ma* (*Ayin*) and the last letter of the word *Echad* (*dalet*) are written in large letters. Abudraham, a fourteenth century Spanish Rabbi, explained that these letters form the word "*ayd*," meaning witness. By reciting the *Sh'ma*, we bear witness to God's oneness. Another explanation is that the letters are written larger so that the reader would not mistake them for other letters, which would drastically change the verse's meaning. If one mistook the *ayin* of *Sh'ma* for an *alef* and the *dalet* of *echad* for a *resh*, the phrase would mean, "Perhaps, Israel, . . . our God is another god."

G. The rabbis offer a variety of homiletical explanations for the addition in the liturgy of the phrase "*Baruch Shem K'vod . . .*" to the *Sh'ma*. According to a *midrash*, when Jacob was dying he asked his children to promise to continue following the One God. His children responded by saying, "*Sh'ma Yisrael Adonai Eloheinu Adonai Echad.*" meaning "Listen, Israel [Israel being Jacob's name], *Adonai* is our God, *Adonai* is One." Jacob, excited to hear their affirmation of God, replied, "*Baruch Shem K'vod Malchuto L'olam Va'ed*" (Blessed is God whose glorious sovereignty is forever and ever.) Just as Jacob, who was elderly, could only whisper the phrase, so too is it traditional to whisper the phrase (except on Yom Kippur when it is spoken aloud by the congregation). Another *midrash* states that Moses first heard the angels praising God with the phrase, "*Baruch Shem K'vod . . . .*" Since Moses took this phrase from the angels, it is said softly, lest the angels find out and feel insulted or angry. But on Yom Kippur, when Jews are said to be as pure as angels, we say it aloud.

According to the Mishnah (*Yoma* 6:2), when the Jews who stood in the *Beit HaMikdash* heard the High Priest say God's name aloud, which only occurred on Yom Kippur, they would kneel, prostrate themselves, and say "*Baruch Shem K'vod . . . .*"

In the Talmud the phrase "*Baruch Shem K'vod . . . .*" is said to have originated at the time of Nehemiah (fifth century B.C.E.), when the Torah was first read publicly. This view is based upon Nehemiah 9:5, the wording of which is similar. Whenever a blessing was recited in the *Beit HaMikdash*, those who heard it responded, "*Baruch Shem K'vod . . . ,*" rather than the traditional "Amen" (*Ta'anit* 16b).

H. Our sages struggled with the question of whether it is possible to command the love of God, as the first paragraph of the *Sh'ma* appears to do. According to Rashi, this phrase means that we should perform the *mitzvot* out of love of God. He explains that "with all your heart" means with all of one's feelings, "with all your soul" means even if one must give up one's life, and "with all your might" means one should use everything one has (power, strength, money, influence) to perform the *mitzvot*.

ACTIVITIES

TEXT AND CONTEXT

1. The *Bar'chu* reminds worshipers that they need to be ready to begin the worship service (or an important part of the worship service: the *Sh'ma Uvirchoteha* or the Torah reading). Ask the students if they really feel ready to praise and thank God when they get to the *Bar'chu*. What does it mean to feel ready to pray? What kind of a mood do they want to be in? What might help them get in that mood? (K-2)

2. Create a class book with each child finishing the following phrase and drawing an accompanying picture: _____(name of child) loves God and loves to _____. (K-2)

3. The *Hashkiveinu*, which follows the *Sh'ma* in the evening service, asks God to help us lie down in peace and to awaken us to life in the morning. It is recited in part to allay fears of night and darkness. Young children are often afraid of the dark. Begin the lesson by reading one of the following books on this theme: *Can't You Sleep Little Bear?* by Waddell, *Bedtime for Frances* by Hoban, *Harry and the Terrible Whatzit* by Gackenbach, *There's a Nightmare in My Closet* by Mayer. Discuss: How did the main character deal with fear of the dark? How did others help him or her? Have you ever been afraid of the dark? Who or what helped you? Explain to the students that the rabbis knew that many people were afraid of the dark and of the night. One prayer that is only recited in the evening asks God to protect us as we sleep and allow us to awaken again. Read the *Hashkiveinu* to the students and ask them if they think it might help reassure them. (K-2)

4. Teach the students how to sign the *Sh'ma*. Consider making this a regular part of the worship experience. Resource: *Signs in Judaism: A Resource Book for the Jewish Deaf Community* by Shuart. (K and up)

5. The *Ma'ariv Aravim* (of the evening service) and the *Yotzer Or* (of the morning service) present the theme of creation. Read the *Ma'ariv Aravim* or the *Yotzer Or* to the students and ask them to identify those elements of creation that it contains. Discuss why the theme of creation would be mentioned in the *siddur*. Why is it so important? What does it say about God's role in creation? You may wish to conclude this lesson by reading the story of creation in Genesis 1 and comparing it to one of these prayers. (3-5)

6. The blessing after the *Sh'ma*, the *Ge'ulah*, has the theme of redemption. It culminates with the singing of *Mi Chamocha*, which is part of the song the Jews sang during the Exodus after crossing the Sea of Reeds. Read Exodus 14 to the students as background. Sing the *Mi Chamocha* and read Exodus 15:19-21. Ask students to imagine that they were among the Israelites who crossed the sea. Direct them to write a diary entry describing what they saw and felt. Students can read their entries, put them into a booklet, or use them to create a bulletin board display. (3-8)

7. Read the first line of the *Sh'ma* with the class. Distribute an index card to each student and ask for a written response to the question: What does it mean to say that God is One? Pass around a paper bag into which each student deposits his or her index card. Then each student in turn picks one card from the bag and reads it aloud. You may wish to discuss some or all of the responses. (6 and up)

8. Write the words "Creation," "Revelation," and "Redemption" on the board. Explain that these are the themes of the prayers which accompany the *Sh'ma*. Ask students to define these words. Point out the logic of progressing from creation to revelation and then to redemption. Divide the class into three groups (or with a large class, six groups). Assign each group to explore one of the above themes using the *siddur* and other resources. Each group should create a presentation based on the theme that might include readings, poems, a song, a painting, or a sculpture. (9 and up)

9. As mentioned in Insight B, the Ten Commandments were recited as a part of the *Sh'ma* in the *Beit HaMikdash*, but were later removed from the service. Explain this to the class and discuss why they were originally included and why they were probably taken out. Ask the students if they think that they should once again be included in the liturgy. Why or why not? (9 and up)

10. The *V'ahavta* begins with the phrase "You shall love Adonai, your God . . . ." Many Jews have questioned whether it is possible to command love. Certainly one can command an action, but can one command a feeling? Rashi, for example, explained that the *V'ahavta* does not command us to love God, but to perform the *mitzvot* out of love. Discuss this issue with the students, introducing material from traditional and contemporary commentators. Resources: *Studies in Devarim: Deuteronomy* by Leibowitz, pp.

64-70; *The Commandments* by Maimonides, vol. 1, pp. 1-15. (9 and up)

ARTS

11. Teach the students to sing the *Bar'chu* and the *Sh'ma.* You may wish to use the traditional melodies, or one of the many contemporary versions. Resources: *In The Beginning* by Debbie Friedman; *The Complete Shireinu: 350 Fully Notated Jewish Songs* edited by Joel Eglash. (K-2)

12. The *Ma'ariv Aravim* speaks of the coming of evening and the *Yotzer Or* of the coming of morning light. To reflect these themes, have the students use chalk or oil pastels to make pictures of a sunrise or sunset and label them *Ma'ariv Aravim* or *Yotzer Or.* (K-5)

13. Read either *Ma'ariv Aravim* or *Yotzer Or* with the students, identifying the phrases that relate to the theme of creation. Utilizing magazine pictures or student photographs, create a montage of images which are captioned with phrases from one of these prayers. (3 and up)

14. The *V'ahavta* refers to *mezuzah* and *tefillin,* two important Jewish symbols. With the students, generate a list of Jewish symbols we wear, have in our homes, or have in the synagogue. Assign each student or group of students to research one or more symbols, writing about their findings. Generate a common list of questions to answer during the research. Collect examples of each symbol and arrange to display them, creating a museum-like setting. Students can serve as docents, narrating tours for parents and other classes. (6 and up)

15. The *V'ahavta* is the source for the *mitzvah* of putting a *mezuzah* on the doorpost of a house. Have students make their own *mezuzah* cases. Many different materials can be used to make the case. These include: Fimo (a modeling material available in craft and toy stores), clay, small wooden boxes, and test tubes. Directions for making them can be found in the following books: *The First Jewish Catalog* by Siegel, Strass-

feld, and Strassfeld, p. 14; *An Artist You Don't Have To Be!* by Magnus, p. 13; *Fast, Clean and Cheap* by Kops, p. 36, *100+ Jewish Art Projects for Children* by Sher and Feldman, p. 81-82. (6 and up)

16. The second line of the *Sh'ma* (*Baruch Shem K'vod . . .*) is not found in the Torah and is traditionally recited in a whisper. One explanation for this practice is found in the *midrash* (cited in Insight G) concerning Jacob blessing his children. Read this *midrash* to your students. Assign roles and allow the class to reenact this episode. (6 and up)

17. Teach students to sing the Debbie Friedman version of "*Ahavat Olam,*" (Resource: *In The Beginning*) or the version by Craig Taubman (Resource: *Friday Night Live*). (6 and up)

BEYOND THE TEXT

18. Gather the students into a circle for sharing responses to the following phrase: "When I look at the sunset/sunrise, I feel . . . " Tie the students' responses into the *Ma'ariv Aravim* and *Yotzer Or.* (K-2)

19. Direct each student to write (younger students to dictate) a story of how love is shown in his/her family. Allow students to read their stories to the class. Point out that families show love for each other in many different ways. Ask: What did God give the Jews to show that God loves us? How do we show that we love God? (K-5)

20. In the *Sh'ma*, God commands the people of Israel to listen. Ask the students if and when they are commanded to listen. Why is it important to listen? How does listening help protect us? What was God commanding the people of Israel to listen to? Is it possible to hear without really listening (i.e., is it possible to hear the words, without understanding what they mean)? What might happen as a result of hearing without listening? (3-5)

21. Crossing the Sea of Reeds was a major challenge for the Israelites. To personalize this event, ask each student to recall and write about a major challenge in his/her life. Among the issues to consider: What were the circumstances that created the challenge? How did the student handle it? What would the student do differently if faced with the challenge again? How does the challenge and reaction of the student relate to the experience of the Israelites crossing the Sea of Reeds? (6 and up)

22. The *Sh'ma* speaks of specific *mitzvot*, as well as the results of observing or failing to observe the *mitzvot*. Assemble a panel of speakers who represent the various movements in Judaism. Prior to the panel, brainstorm with the students questions such as: What is the policy of each branch of Judaism regarding the *mitzvot*? Can a person be authentically Jewish and not follow all of the *mitzvot*? What are the most important *mitzvot*? What are the consequences of observing or not observing the *mitzvot*? As a follow up to the panel, hold a discussion about the students' personal observance of the *mitzvot*. Did they discover that they were observing some *mitzvot* and were not aware of doing so? (6 and up)

23. The *V'ahavta* commands us to teach the *mitzvot* to our children. Ask students to pretend that they have been approached by a person who knows nothing about Judaism. What would they teach him/her? On a large sheet of butcher paper, write the phrase "What I would teach about Judaism" in the center. Each student draws a line from this phrase and writes a topic such as Shabbat, Hebrew, Moses, etc. and two or three subtopics that they would teach. (6 and up)

24. With your class, listen to one or both of the following songs about Miriam: "Miriam's Song" by Debbie Friedman and "Miriam's Slow Snake Dance" by Linda Hirschhorn. Discuss: What does each song say about Miriam? What else do the students know about Miriam? Divide the students into three groups. Assign each group to read one of the biblical passages about Miriam and present it to the other groups as a skit. The passages are Exodus 2:1-10, Exodus 15:19-20, and Numbers 12:1-16. Conclude by having each student write about ways in which Miriam is a role model for the contemporary Jewish woman. Resources: *Gather Round: Songs of Celebration and Renewal* by Linda Hirschhorn; *And You Shall Be a Blessing* by Debbie Friedman. (9 and up)

HEBREW

25. Take your class to the sanctuary or bring a *Sefer Torah* to class and unroll it to the *Sh'ma*, Deuteronomy 6:4. Read the *Sh'ma* from the text and ask the students to identify anything special about how the text is written. Explain (see Insight F) that the *ayin* is written large so that it is not mistaken for an *alef*, and the *dalet* is written large so that it is not mistaken for a *resh*, which would change the text to read: "Perhaps, Israel, . . . our God is another god." Point out that the letters *ayin* and *dalet* together form the Hebrew word "*eid,*" meaning witness. Discuss: How are we like a witness when we recite the *Sh'ma*? (3 and up)

26. In a *Sefer Torah*, show the students *Shirat HaYam*, the Song of the Sea (Exodus 15). Explain that it is written to look like a brick wall to remind us of the Jews' experience as slaves. Point out that this passage is a poem, so the lines divide naturally. Identify the passage about Miriam dancing. Have students write their own poem about the Exodus in the form of a brick wall. Resource: *This Is the Torah* by Kolatch, pp. 111-113. (3 and up)

27. Teach the song "*Emet*" to the class. Explain that the word "*emet*" means truth. Point out that the word is composed of the first letter, the middle letter, and the last letter of the Hebrew alphabet, symbolizing the idea that truth is all-encompassing. In a *siddur*, open to the *brachah* after the *Sh'ma* in the morning (*Emet V'yatziv*) or the evening (*Emet V'emunah*). Both identify God with truth. Discuss what truth means and why it is important to tell the truth. How does truth relate to God? Resource: *The Complete Shireinu: 350 Fully Notated Jewish Songs* edited by Joel Eglash, p. 63. (3 and up)

28. Distribute a *siddur* to each student or group of students. Choosing either the morning or evening *Sh'ma*, each group of 3-4 students should answer the following questions: What short phrases introduce this section? How many blessings are there between the *Bar'chu* and the *Sh'ma*? What are the names and themes of these blessings? How many paragraphs does the *Sh'ma* contain? How many blessings follow the *Sh'ma*? What are their names and themes? Each group should create a chart to present its findings. (6 and up)

29. On the board, write the following phrases in Hebrew and English: *Ahavat Olam/Ahavah Rabbah* — Everlasting Love/Great Love; *V'ahavta Eit Adonai Elohecha* — You shall love *Adonai* your God; *V'ahavta L'rei'acha Kamocha* — You shall love your neighbor as yourself. Ask students to identify the source of each phrase (the first group are the blessings before the *Sh'ma* in the evening and morning respectively; the second is from the first paragraph of the *Sh'ma*; the third is from the Torah, Leviticus 19:18). Explain that the *Ahavat Olam* and *Ahavah Rabbah* are about God's love for the people Israel; the *V'ahavta* is about Israel's love for God; the third phrase is about love for other human beings. Ask students to give examples of each type of love and write them under the appropriate heading. (6 and up)

30. Distribute *siddurim* to the students and direct them to open to the *Yotzer*. Read together the first line, through the word "*HaKol.*" Then share with the students the text of Isaiah 45:7, which is the source for this line of the prayer. There is, however, one important difference between these verses. Ask the students to identify that difference. Discuss: Why might the Rabbis have changed this phrase when adopting it for the *siddur*? Point out that in Judaism both good and evil are created by God, but the rabbis may not have wanted to emphasize God's creation of evil in the daily liturgy. (6 and up)

FAMILY

31. The *V'ahavta* presents the important idea of teaching one's children. Set up a variety of stations, each of which presents a different model for incorporating Jewish learning into their lives. At each station, participants should engage in this model of learning. These stations might include: reading and discussing the weekly *parashah*; choosing and implementing a *mitzvah* of the week; enhancing holiday and Shabbat celebrations; reading a Jewish story and doing an activity based on the story; watching and discussing Jewish videos. Leave time at the end to allow each family to decide which approach or approaches it wants to begin implementing. Resources: *Teaching Torah: A Treasury of Insights and Activities* by Loeb and Kadden; *Teaching Mitzvot: Concepts, Values, and Activities* by Kadden and Kadden; *Teaching Jewish Holidays: History, Values, and Activities* by Goodman; *Judaism Through Children's Books: A Resource for Teachers and Parents* by Musikant and Grass.

32. The source of the *mitzvah* of affixing a *mezuzah* on one's doorpost is the *V'ahavta*. The *mezuzah* is put up at a *Chanukat HaBayit* (house dedication ceremony). Present examples of such a ceremony to families and discuss its content. Direct each family to design a personal *Chanukat HaBayit* ceremony, which might include creative writing, favorite songs as well as traditional material. Each family should then have such a ceremony, putting up a *mezuzah* on one of the doors of its house. Families which already have a *mezuzah* up could take it down to inspect the scroll, as should be done every seven years, and then rededicate their home. Resources: *On the Doorposts of Your House: Prayers and Ceremonies for the Jewish Home* edited by Stern, pp. 138-142; *The First Jewish Catalog* by Siegel, Strassfeld, and Strassfeld, p. 15; *The Jewish Home* by Syme, p. 1; *The Siddur: The Prayerbook* by Bokser, p. 370.

RESOURCES

BOOKS

Bokser, Ben Zion. *The Siddur: The Prayerbook.* Springfield, NJ: Behrman House Inc., 1983.
Donin, Hayim Halevy. *To Pray as a Jew: A Guide to*

the Prayer Book and the Synagogue Service. New York: Basic Books, 1980.

Eglash, Joel, ed. *The Complete Shireinu: 350 Fully Notated Jewish Songs*. New York: Transcontinental Music Publications, 2001.

Gackenbach, Dick. *Harry and the Terrible Whatzit*. Boston: Houghton Mifflin Company, 1984.

Gates of the House: The New Union Prayerbook. New York: Central Conference of American Rabbis, 1977.

Goodman, Robert. *Teaching Jewish Holidays: History, Values, and Activities*. Denver, CO: A.R.E. Publishing, Inc., 1997.

Hoban, Russell. *Bedtime for Frances*. New York: Harper Trophy, 1995.

Kadden, Barbara Binder and Bruce Kadden. *Teaching Mitzvot: Concepts, Values, and Activities*. Revised Edition. Denver, CO: A.R.E. Publishing, Inc., 2003.

Kolatch, Alfred J. *This Is the Torah*. Middle Village, New York: Jonathan David Publishers, Inc., 1994.

Kops, Simon. *Fast, Clean and Cheap or EVERYTHING the Jewish teacher (or parent) needs to know about ART*. Los Angeles, CA: Torah Aura Productions, 1989.

Leibowitz, Nehama. *Studies in Devarim: Deuteronomy*. Jerusalem: The World Zionist Organization, 1980.

Loeb, Sorel Goldberg and Barbara Binder Kadden. *Teaching Torah: A Treasury of Insights and Activities*. Denver, CO: A.R.E. Publishing, Inc., 1997.

Magnus, Joann. *An Artist You Don't Have To Be!: A Jewish Arts and Crafts Book*. New York: UAHC Press, 1990.

Maimonides, Moses. *The Commandments*, vol. 1. New York: Soncino Press, 1967.

Mayer, Mercer. *There's a Nightmare in My Closet*. New York: Dial Publishing, 1968.

Musikant, Ellen and Sue Grass. *Judaism Through Children's Books: A Resource for Teachers and Parents*. Denver, CO: A.R.E. Publishing, Inc., 2001.

Rosenzweig, Franz. *The Star of Redemption*. Boston, MA: Beacon Press, 1972.

Sher, Nina Streisand and Margaret Feldman. *100+ Jewish Art Projects for Children*. Denver, CO: A.R.E. Publishing, Inc., 1996.

Shuart, Adele. *Signs in Judaism: A Resource Book for the Jewish Deaf Community*. New York: Bloch Publishing Company, 1986.

Siegel, Richard; Michael Strassfeld; and Sharon Strassfeld, eds. *The First Jewish Catalog*. Philadelphia, PA: The Jewish Publication Society of America, 1973.

Stern, Chaim, ed. *On the Doorposts of Your House: Prayers and Ceremonies for the Jewish Home*. New York: CCAR Press, 1994.

Syme, Daniel B. *The Jewish Home: A Guide for Jewish Living*. New York: UAHC Press, 1988.

Waddell, Martin. *Can't You Sleep Little Bear?* Cambridge, MA: Candlewick Press, 1992.

AUDIOVISUAL

Friedman, Debbie. *And You Shall Be a Blessing*. San Diego, CA: Sounds Write Productions, Inc., 1989. Compact disc. Available from A.R.E. Publishing, Inc.

———. *In The Beginning*. San Diego, CA: Sounds Write Productions, Inc., 1994. Three compact disc set. Available from A.R.E. Publishing, Inc.

Hirschhorn, Linda. *Gather Round: Songs of Celebration and Renewal*. Berkeley, CA: Oyster Albums, 1989. Compact disc, audiocassette, and songbook. Available from Sounds Write Productions, Inc.

Taubman, Craig. *Friday Night Live*. Sherman Oaks, CA: Sweet Louise Productions, 1999. Compact disc and songbook. Available from A.R.E. Publishing, Inc.

CHAPTER SEVEN:
AMIDAH

OVERVIEW

The core of the three daily worship services, Shacharit, Minchah, and Ma'ariv, is a set of *brachot* collectively known by three names: *Amidah* (standing), because it is said while standing; *Sh'moneh Esrei* (eighteen), because in its original form there were eighteen *brachot* in the weekday version; and *tefilah* (prayer).

The origins and early development of the *Amidah* are unclear. According to the Talmud, "one hundred twenty elders, among whom were many prophets, drew up eighteen blessings" (*Megillah* 17b). While the themes and some of the phrasing of the *brachot* developed during the period of the First Temple, it was not until its destruction that the order of the *brachot* and the concluding phrase of each *brachah* was set. Simeon HaPakuli and Shmuel HaKatan are said to have established the order of the *brachot* at Yavneh (*Brachot* 28b). While the theme of each *brachah* was therefore determined, the exact wording remained fluid for many centuries and was only firmly established with the creation of the earliest *siddurim*.

The *Amidah* is actually recited twice during both Shacharit and Minchah, once silently by the congregation, and then repeated aloud by the *shaliach tzibur*. At Ma'ariv it is recited once, silently, because originally it was not obligatory to recite it during this service. The first three and the last three *brachot* are of praise; the thirteen intermediary *brachot* are petitionary in nature.

Today, the traditional daily *Amidah* contains nineteen *brachot*. On Shabbat and holidays, the first three and last three *brachot* are recited, but the intermediate thirteen petitionary *brachot* are replaced by one *brachah* pertaining to that specific day. It is considered improper to petition God to fulfill a request on Shabbat and holidays.

The first three *brachot* focus on praising God based upon the passage, "A person should always utter the praises of God before offering one's petitions" (*Brachot* 32a). The first *brachah* is called *Avot* (forefathers), because it begins by identifying God as the God of our ancestors Abraham, Isaac, and Jacob. Some modern versions also include the Matriarchs: Sarah, Rebekah, Rachel, and Leah.

The second *brachah* is called *G'vurot*, which means strength. In it God is praised for healing the sick, freeing the captives, and keeping faith with the deceased. In the traditional version of this *brachah*, God's strength will be further manifested through the resurrection of the dead at the end of days when the Messiah comes. Reform Judaism, rejecting this belief in a personal messiah, replaced the words "*M'chayei HaMeitim*" (resurrects the dead) with *M'chayei HaKol* (gives life to all). In *Kol Haneshamah*, the Reconstructionist *siddur* for *erev* Shabbat, the phrase *M'chayei HaMeitim* is replaced by *M'chayei Kol Chai* (gives life to all the living).

The third *brachah*, called *Kedushat HaShem* (Sanctification of the Name), focuses on God's holiness. During Ma'ariv and when the *Amidah* is recited silently during Shacharit and Minchah, this short *brachah* begins "*Atah Kadosh*" (You are holy). However, when the *Amidah* is repeated aloud, this *brachah* is replaced by the *K'dushah*, a dramatic, responsive litany recalling how the angels on high praised God (Isaiah 6:3; Ezekiel 6:12).

AMIDAH/TEFILAH/ SH'MONEH ESREI
(The Prayer)

Adonai S'fatai (*Adonai*, open my lips, Introductory Verse)

Three *Brachot* of Praise:

Avot (Ancestors)

G'vurot (God's Strength)

K'dushat HaShem (God's holiness)/ *K'dushah* (Sanctification — when recited aloud)

K'dushat HaYom (Sanctification of the day — Shabbat and Festivals)

Thirteen Intermediate *Brachot* — Weekdays only

Da'at (Knowledge)

T'shuvah (Repentance)

S'lichah (Forgiveness)

Ge'ulah (Redemption)

R'fu'ah (Healing)

Birkat HaShanim (Blessing of the Years/Sustenance)

Kibbutz Galuyot (Ingathering of Exiles)

Din (Restoration of Judges)

Birkat HaMinim (Against Heretics)

Tzadikim (Righteous Ones)

Y'rushalayim (Jerusalem)

Y'shu'a (Deliverance)

Sh'ma Koleinu (Acceptance of Prayer)

Three *Brachot* of Thanksgiving

Avodah/R'tzei (Worship)

Hoda'ah/Modim (Thanksgiving)

Shalom Rav (Peace — Ma'ariv and Minchah only); *Sim Shalom* (Peace — Shacharit)

Elohai Netzor (Guard My Tongue from Evil)

On all days but Shabbat and holidays, thirteen petitionary *brachot* follow. In these *brachot* the worshiper asks God for knowledge and understanding; the acceptance of repentance; forgiveness; redemption from troubles; healing the sick; abundance; ingathering of the exiles; restoration of judges and counselors; punishment of slanderers; reward of the righteous, converts, and all Israel; rebuilding of Jerusalem; the arrival of the Messianic King; and the acceptance of the prayers being recited.

These petitions form a natural progression, beginning with petitions for individual well-being, and proceeding to petitions which deal with Jewish national aspirations.

Originally, there were only twelve *brachot* in this section, with the *brachot* asking for the rebuilding of Jerusalem and the coming of the Messiah as one. However, in the period of the Geonim, these became two distinct *brachot*, increasing the total number of *brachot* in the *Amidah* from eighteen to nineteen. Nevertheless, it is still called *Sh'moneh Esrei* — eighteen.

Certainly the most controversial of the thirteen petitionary *brachot* is the one directed against slanderers. At the onset, this *brachah* was directed against the early Christians. (The Hebrew word *minim* — sectarians — was used.) Abraham Millgram writes, "By adding to the *Tefillah* a benediction which contains a malediction against the Judeo-Christians, the sectarians were effectively eliminated from the synagogue" (*Jewish Worship*, p. 105). In later centuries, this *brachah* was changed to refer to *malshinim* (slanderers), primarily Jews who had become Christian and served as informers to the Roman authorities.

Gates of Prayer, the Reform *siddur*, omits this *brachah* entirely and changes many others which conflict with Reform ideology. For example, the *brachah* for gathering the exiles focuses therein on freedom in general. The *brachah* for restoring judges focuses on justice. A prayer for the peace of Jerusalem replaces the traditional *brachah* asking God to rebuild Jerusalem, and a general request for deliverance replaces the petition for the Messiah.

For Shabbat, in the traditional *siddur*, the petitionary section of the liturgy is replaced with one *brachah* which sanctifies the day. This *brachah* includes the first biblical reference to Shabbat (Genesis 2:1-3) in the evening and *V'shamru* (Exodus 31:16-17) in the morning. On holidays the content of the *brachah* includes references to the particular holiday.

On Shabbat, holidays, and weekdays, the *Amidah* concludes with the same three *brachot*. First there is a blessing for worship called *Avodah*. References to sacrifices which are contained in the traditional version have been eliminated from Reform, Reconstructionist, and Conservative *siddurim*. Instead, the *brachah* refers to the efficacy of prayer.

This *brachah* is followed by *Modim*, a prayer of thanksgiving and praise to God. On Chanukah and Purim, this *brachah* is supplemented by a special reading which begins, "*Al HaNisim*" (on account of the miracles). The Israeli progressive *siddur, Avodah Sh'BeLev,* also contains a reading for Yom HaAtzma'ut.

The *Amidah* concludes with *Birkat HaShalom*, a *brachah* for peace. During Ma'ariv and at Minchah (except on fast days), this prayer is known as *Shalom Rav*. During Shacharit, Musaf, and on fast days at Minchah, it is known as *Sim Shalom*. In the *Beit HaMikdash*, the *Kohanim* would recite the priestly benediction, *Birkat HaKohanim* (Numbers 6:24-26), as part of their prayer for peace. In modern times in traditional congregations, *Kohanim* bless the Congregation (*duchen*) during the Musaf service on Shabbat and on holidays. In some congregations, it is the reader who recites *Birkat HaKohanim* as a lead-in to *Birkat HaShalom*.

Following the last *brachah* of the *Amidah* is the private meditation of the fourth century Rabbi Mar bar Rav Rabina. It concludes the silent *Amidah* in traditional congregations and is often read as a silent prayer in other congregations. Its focus is on using one's words carefully. It includes Psalms 60:7 and 19:15, as well as a concluding line, which begins with the words, "*Oseh Shalom*."

Many of the rabbis added their own personal prayer at this point in the liturgy, a practice encouraged today among *all* worshipers as a means of increasing one's *kavanah* when reciting the established liturgy.

While the complete *Amidah* is normally recited at all services, tradition provides for a shortened form, called *Havineinu*, that could be recited if one is ill or if one did not have time for the complete version. The first three and last three *brachot* are recited in full, but the thirteen intermediate *brachot* are replaced by the paragraph *Havineinu*, which summarizes the content of the thirteen *brachot*.

The silent *Amidah* is traditionally recited standing, but when it is repeated by the *shaliach tzibur*, one stands only through the *K'dushah*. In most liberal synagogues, worshipers stand for the first three *brachot* only.

A variety of other body movements distinguish the *Amidah*. At the beginning of the *Avot*, one takes three small steps forward and bows when saying, "*Baruch Atah Adonai*." At the end, one takes three small steps backward. This reflects the etiquette of appearing before a king. Normally, one would bow every time one says "*Baruch Atah Adonai*." However, because of a concern about excessive humility (see *Brachot* 34a), one does not bow again until *Modim*. When one concludes the silent *Amidah* with *Oseh Shalom*, one takes three small steps backward, as if taking leave of a king. When the *K'dushah* is recited during the repetition of the *Amidah*, worshipers rise on their tiptoes each of the three times the word "*Kadosh*" is recited in order to elevate themselves as if toward the divine.

The first three *brachot* and the last three *brachot* were included in the Second Temple ritual, and were brought into the synagogue service after the *Beit HaMikdash* was destroyed. The intermediate *brachot* developed over a long period of time. In its earliest development, only the ending was standard, and worshipers or the *shaliach tzibur* determined the body of the prayer. Eventually these *brachot* became standardized, yet continue to undergo transformation.

INSIGHTS FROM THE TRADITION

A. Since rabbinic times, it has been customary to introduce the silent *Amidah* with the phrase: "*Adonai S'fatai Tiftach* . . . " — *Adonai*, open my lips that my mouth shall declare your praise (Psalm 51:17).

B. Beginning the *Amidah* by mentioning Abraham, Isaac, and Jacob is a reflection of the rabbinic concept *Zechut Avot* (the merit of the Fathers). Because of the great deeds of our Patriarchs, God looks kindly upon us. Moses asked God to remember Abraham, Isaac, and Jacob when Moses pleaded with God not to destroy Israel on account of the sin of the golden calf (Exodus 32:13). Therefore, we begin this series of prayers by invoking the memory of our earliest ancestors.

C. The Eighteen Benedictions open with "God of Abraham, God of Isaac, and God of Jacob" — not God of Abraham, Isaac, and Jacob — because each Patriarch sought and served God in his own way, and did not accept blindly the God of his ancestors (Baal Shem Tov).

D. The Hasidim were puzzled by the phrase "our God and God of our Fathers," which is in the *Avot*. Since these terms must be referring to the same God, why the different terminology? They concluded that the difference reflects two types of people who believe in God. The first has adopted the belief of his/her father, while the other has arrived at his/her beliefs on his/her own. The first has strong faith which cannot be shaken, but has accepted it blindly, so it is not really his/her own. The second has struggled to achieve his/her own faith, but is therefore susceptible to challenges from others. The *Avot* contains both the phrases "our God" and "God of our Fathers" because both ways of arriving at a belief in God are important for each of us.

E. In the rabbinic period, because of their dependence on agriculture, the Jews were very concerned about annual rainfall. Phrases were included in the liturgy to reflect this concern. In the *G'vurot*, the phrase "*Meishiv HaRuach U'morid HaGashem*" (Who causes the wind to blow and the rain to fall), is added from the day after Simchat Torah until *erev* Pesach. This *brachah* was chosen to acknowledge God's power over nature. The ninth *brachah*, on the theme of abundance, contains the phrase "*V'tein Brachah Al P'nei HaAdamah*," (and give a blessing on the earth). From early December until the first day of

Pesach, however, the phrase "*V'tein Tal U'matar Livrachah Al P'nei HaAdamah*," (and give dew and rain for blessing on the earth) is substituted. The reason that these words are not recited year round is because the rabbis believed that one should ask for rain only during the rainy season.

F. During the Ten Days of Repentance from Rosh HaShanah through Yom Kippur, additions and slight modifications are made to the following *brachot*: *Avot*, *G'vurot*, *K'dushat HaShem/K'dushah*, *Hashivah Shofteinu*, *Modim*, and *Shalom Rav/Sim Shalom*. These additions emphasize that God is our Sovereign and Judge, and ask God to inscribe us in the Book of life.

G. The Talmud offers the following guidelines for bowing during the *Amidah*: "Our rabbis taught: These are the *brachot* during which a person may bow: at the beginning and end of the *Avot* and at the beginning and end of the thanksgiving [*Modim*]. If one wants to bow at the end and the beginning of each *brachah*, we instruct that one does not bow." (*Brachot* 34a) The rabbis were apparently concerned about excessive humility if one were to bow during each *brachah*.

ACTIVITIES

TEXT AND CONTEXT

1. The second *brachah* of the *Amidah*, the *G'vurot*, speaks of God's might. Discuss with the students what it means to say that God is mighty. List these ideas on the board or on newsprint. What things does God do to demonstrate that might? Read the examples of God's might contained in the *brachah* and compare with the students' list. (K-2)

2. In the *K'dushah*, God is described as holy, i.e., unique, special, one-of-a-kind. *K'dushah* is a difficult word to translate. Discuss with the students what unique, special, or one-of-a-kind means to them. Ask them to give examples from their lives. Ask how God is special, unique, and one-of-a-kind. Connect these responses to the words "holy" and *"K'dushah."* (K-2)

3. The tenth *brachah* of the traditional daily *Amidah* requests an ingathering of the exiles. On a plain bulletin board, pin a giant shofar with the word "Freedom" printed in large letters. Read the *brachah* to your class. Ask the students: Where are we all to be gathered together? When? Under what circumstances? Now add a map of Israel and an Israeli flag to the bulletin board. Ask the students if they can identify groups of Jews who have sought freedom in Israel. Write these on cards and place them on the bulletin board. Add appropriate pictures from magazines and newspapers. (K-5)

4. Rabbi Avrohom Chaim Feuer explains that the eighteenth *brachah* of the traditional *Amidah*, the *Modim*, thanks God for miracles, wonders, and favors in every season. These miracles and wonders include nature. To help your students appreciate both this *brachah* and nature, take them on an outdoor field trip. Divide the class into pairs, giving each pair a sketch pad and one of the following: charcoals, oil pastels, crayons, or pencils. Each pair of students chooses a spot and sits down back to back. One students has the art materials and draws what the other student describes. After 10-15 minutes have the students switch tasks. Afterward, share the completed pictures and discuss. (3-5)

5. At the end of the *Amidah*, we recite, "My God, guard my tongue from evil and my lips from speaking deceitfully." Ask your students what these lines mean. With your students generate some general *mitzvot* of speech that would encourage them to use speech (their tongues) for good and not for bad. (3 and up)

6. On Chanukah and Purim, there are special additions to the *Amidah*. Read through these with your students. Discuss the content of each and then discuss what was miraculous about each event. Ask: What do you think a miracle is? When is something a miracle, a stroke of luck, or a chance event? How do our beliefs affect how we interpret events? (6 and up)

7. Help your students more effectively learn the contents of the *Amidah* with this "Becoming an Expert" activity. Assign each student a different *brachah* to study. Provide a file folder for each student. On the inside left side of the folder insert a copy of the *brachah* in both Hebrew and English. On the opposite side, place a sheet of paper with the following words, leaving space for students' responses: Topic, Main Idea, Details, Summary. In addition to reading their assigned *brachah* of the *Amidah*, the students may need to do supplementary research. (6 and up)

8. The eighth blessing of the traditional daily *Amidah* deals with health and healing. Invite a rabbi and a physician or nurse to discuss this *brachah* with your class. Question to consider: What role does religion, faith, and spirituality play in a person's health and recovery from illness? Resources: *Jewish Paths toward Healing and Wholeness* by Olitzky and *The Mitzvah of Healing* by Person. (9 and up)

9. Compare with your students some of the versions of the *Amidah* from different denominations. Divide students into groups and have each group examine one or more of the following (outlining the structure, names of blessings, themes, etc.): weekday Shacharit *Amidah*; weekday Ma'ariv *Amidah*; Shabbat Shacharit *Amidah*; Shabbat Ma'ariv *Amidah*; Shabbat Musaf *Amidah*; Shacharit and/or Ma'ariv Festival *Amidah*. Create a chart, and, as each group reports, fill in the chart. Discuss: Which *brachot* are always included in the *Amidah*? Which have different forms during Shacharit and Ma'ariv? Which are said only on weekdays? Explain why the intermediate *brachot* are omitted on Shabbat and holidays. (9 and up)

10. As a follow-up to Activity #9, examine with your students the text of the *Amidah* in *siddurim* from different denominations and determine whether or not the Matriarchs are included in the text of the prayer. (9 and up)

11. Explain to the students that the *Amidah* ends with a prayer for peace: *Sim Shalom* during Shacharit and *Shalom Rav* during Ma'ariv. With the students, listen to or sing a version of each. Then divide a large bulletin board in half. Label one side *Sim Shalom* and the other *Shalom Rav*. Have students draw pictures of morning and evening. For a soft look, use chalk pastels. Extend the lesson and teach the children *"boker tov"* (good morning) and *"erev tov"* (good evening). You might include these phrases on the bulletin board. Resources: *In The Beginning* by Debbie Friedman ("Sim Shalom"); *Or Shalom* by Shir Hadash ("*Sim Shalom*"); *Snapshots: The Best of Kol B'Seder Vol. 1* by Kol B'Seder ("*Shalom Rav*"); *From Strength to Strength* by Julie Silver ("*Sim Shalom*"); *Turn It* by Mah Tovu (*"Sim Shalom"*). (K-2)

12. The *Modim* blessing thanks God for all the wonderful things we have in our world. Spread a piece of butcher paper on the floor, dividing the length with lines 18" to 24" apart. Each student has a section in which to draw or paint a picture of things he/she is thankful for. (K-2)

13. Ask your students to close their eyes as you pose the following questions: What does peace look like to you? Does it have a shape? a color? a texture? Is it realistic or abstract? Hand out 9" square sheets of white paper to the students. Supply crayons, markers, and paints. Each student creates his/her image of peace. Punch holes all the way around each complete picture. With yarn, sew the pictures together to form a paper quilt. Display in the classroom or other part of the synagogue or school. (K and up)

14. Assign each student a *brachah* of the *Amidah*. Each student is to create a collage which expresses the ideas in the particular *brachah*. Pass out sheets of card stock or tagboard cut into 8" squares. Provide fabric, buttons, decorative trims, paints, markers, old magazines, scissors, and glue. Students can leave the card whole or cut it into a shape. Part of the *brachah* can be written on the card or, if it is displayed without a label, other students can try to decipher which *brachah* the collage represents. Give the students an opportunity to share and discuss the symbolism they have chosen. (3 and up)

15. There are many musical versions of the song "*Oseh Shalom*," the concluding line to the *Amidah*. Learn several with your students and discuss the mood or feeling of each version. How does the music affect the person praying? Are certain melodies better in particular situations? Ask for examples. Resources: *In The Beginning* by Debbie Friedman; *Or Shalom* by Shir Hadash; *A Day in the Life* by Sam Glaser; *Shabbat Shalom* by Cindy Paley; *Snapshots: The Best of Kol B'Seder Vol. 1* by Kol B'Seder. (3 and up)

16. Read through the *Amidah* with your students, asking them to identify pairs of words that give two sides to a subject or describe contrasting ideas such as heaven and earth, repentance and transgression, freedom and exile, slanderers and the righteous. Direct the students to write two-line poems that illustrate these contrasting ideas. (6 and up)

17. Commenting on the *brachah* of peace, the Vilna Gaon states that it refers to the perfection of one's character. Rabbi Avrohom Chaim Feuer adds, "Quality of character is truly the 'container' that seals in all other blessings because negative traits will spoil all a person's blessings, while good character traits will enhance them." (*Shemoneh Esrai: The Amidah/The Eighteen Blessings,* page 262. The ArtScroll Mesorah Series, 1990. Reprinted by permission of the publisher, Mesorah Publications.) Rabbi Yehuda stated: "Do not look at the flask, but at what it contains" (*Pirke Avot* 4:27). Discuss: How can the perfection of one's character lead to peace? Have students give examples from their own lives and from those who work toward peace in their community and in the world. Some library research may be necessary. Conclude by creating a display with photos, biographies, posters, etc., of those who have worked for peace. Conclude by singing "*Amar Rabi Yehuda*." Resource: *The Complete Shireinu: 350 Fully Notated Jewish Songs* edited by Joel Eglash, p. 16. (9 and up)

BEYOND THE TEXT

18. Read to your students the *Modim* blessing. Ask what it means to say "thank you." With the students seated in a circle, have each in turn complete the phrase, "I am thankful for . . . " You may want to record their responses on a wall chart. (K-2)

19. Read the *Avot/Imahot* to your class to introduce your students to Abraham, Isaac, Jacob, Sarah, Rebekah, Rachel, and Leah. Create paper dolls, and have each student write his/her name on a paper doll. On other dolls write the names of famous Jews, especially biblical characters, including the Patriarchs and Matriarchs. Create a chain of history to help students see the connection between Abraham's time and today. (K-2)

20. The *Amidah* concludes with three *brachot* of thanks, the first of which is called *Avodah* (or *Retzei*). Part of this *brachah* is a request that our worship be acceptable to God. Utilize the following in discussion with your students: Of all the things we pray, what do students want God to hear the most? What do students want God to accept? Ask the students how we know our prayers are successful. If we pray for a new toy or bike, but don't get it, does it mean that God wasn't listening? Are there good prayers and bad prayers? You may want to include a rabbi in this discussion. (3-5)

21. The idea of *Zechut Avot*, the merit of the ancestors, was discussed in the Overview. We remind God of the deeds of our ancestors, so God will look with favor upon us, their descendants. We also want to connect ourselves to this Jewish chain of tradition. To help our students make this generational connection, have them conduct interviews with older family members: parents, aunts, uncles, grandparents, possibly even great-grandparents. Prior to the interviews, have students generate questions about their Jewish heritage and family traditions. They may also want to include questions about customs unique to their families. In class, students can share the interview results. This process may be done by tape recorder or be handwritten. This activity may also require phone calls and/or letter writing on the part of the students and their families. (3 and up)

22. Use the *Avot/Imahot* to stimulate your students to learn about the Patriarchs and Matriarchs. Provide the students with source material, including the book of Genesis. Students should divide into groups and prepare short reports about each person. Then ask the students to complete the following: "The Patriarch/Matriarch with whom I most identify is _____ because _____." Students should write a short paragraph to explain their choices and then share with the class. (6-8)

23. With your students, conduct a thorough reading of the *Amidah*. As you are reading through, make a list on the board describing the role of God and the role of human beings that each *brachah* implies. Discuss with your class the Jewish value of human beings working as partners with God. (6 and up)

24. As a central part of the prayer experience, the *Amidah* demands a relationship between the worshiper and God. Ask students to recall how they thought about God when they were younger, and how their beliefs have changed. Then ask students to write about their personal concept of God, what their relationship to God is, and how they feel about it. Discuss with the class what it means to be on a faith journey. This activity might be a part of an ongoing journal or just a one-time period of reflection and writing. (6 and up)

25. One of the *brachot* of the traditional *Amidah* asks God to "speedily rebuild Jerusalem in our days . . . " Ask the students to describe a physically rebuilt Jerusalem, noting their responses on the board. The class would probably describe a modern city with all the usual benefits and drawbacks of contemporary living. Next discuss what the rebuilt Jerusalem referred to in this *brachah* would look like (the spiritual ideal, perfect, divine city). Again, list the responses on the board. Compare the lists to each other, noting similarities and differences. Divide the class into small groups and assign each group one of the differences. The group is to determine what steps need to be taken for the Jerusalem of today to become the "rebuilt Jerusalem." (9 and up)

HEBREW

26. The eighteenth *brachah* of the traditional daily *Amidah* is the *Modim*, recited in the evening, morning, and afternoon to thank God for the wonders and miracles of each season. Teach your students the Hebrew words for each season and the times of day. Discuss with them the wonders and miracles of each season. You might also include the holidays and the phenomena of nature: rain, wind, snow, etc. Expand this lesson by teaching a unit on weather, utilizing Hebrew vocabulary and reviewing the Hebrew names of the holidays. (3 and up)

27. Play "Vocabulary Bingo" with the words from Activity #26. Start by writing a sheet of all the vocabulary words and give each student a copy. Supply each student with a bingo grid with space for sixteen words. Students choose fifteen words off the list and fill in their bingo cards, leaving one free space. Have bingo markers ready. Have all the vocabulary written up individually on small cards. Drop these into a sack and pick out one at a time. Read the word in Hebrew, or for a further challenge, give its English translation and have the students find it in Hebrew. (3 and up)

28. Learn the names of each rubric of the *Amidah* in Hebrew (*Avot/Imahot, G'vurot*, etc.). Write each of the names on index cards. Challenge teams to put the cards in the proper order. Select categories such as weekday Ma'ariv, Shabbat Shacharit, etc., and have students gather the proper cards. (6 and up)

FAMILY

29. Use the first *brachah* of the *Amidah* as a theme for a family education program emphasizing the importance of passing Judaism on from generation to generation. Encourage families to bring important material such as genealogies, family picture albums, etc. Begin with a presentation on the Patriarchs and Matriarchs, highlighting the challenges of passing on the tradition from one generation to the next (barenness of Sarah, Rebekah, Rachel; binding of Isaac; Jacob stealing the blessing meant for Esau). In family groups have the oldest generation share stories about their parents or grandparents. Locate on maps where the family came from and trace its journey to the current city of residence. Choose one important family story and put together a skit. Perform for each of the other families, while giving a brief outline of the family's history. Provide information on genealogy for those families interested in doing further research.

30. Hold a "Shalom Fair." Include workshops about *Sh'lom Bayit* (peace in the home), *shalom* in the community, and *shalom* on a national and international level. For example, workshops on *Sh'lom Bayit* might include communications skills, celebrating Shabbat as a family, and parenting skills. *Shalom* in the community should include information on local groups that work to promote peace and justice. *Shalom* on a national and international level could focus on the Arab-Israeli conflict or other areas of global tension. Conclude by coming together for readings and songs of peace, including *Shalom Rav, Sim Shalom*, and *Oseh Shalom*, which are part of the *Amidah*.

RESOURCES

BOOKS

Avodah Sh'BeLev. Jerusalem: Movement for Progressive Judaism in Israel, 1982.

Eglash, Joel, ed. *The Complete Shireinu: 350 Fully Notated Jewish Songs*. New York: Transcontinental Music Publications, 2001.

Feuer, Rabbi Avrohom Chaim. *Shemoneh Esrei: The Amidah/The Eighteen Blessings*. Brooklyn, NY: Mesorah Publications, Ltd., 1990.

Grishaver, Joel Lurie. *19 Out of 18: The All New Shema Is for Real Curriculum*. Los Angeles:

Torah Aura Productions, 1991.

Millgram, Abraham. *Jewish Worship*. Philadelphia, PA: The Jewish Publication Society of America, 1971.

Moskowitz, Nachama Skolnik. *A Bridge to Prayer: The Jewish Worship Workbook Volume Two: The Amidah, Torah Service, and Concluding Prayers*. New York: UAHC Press, 1989.

Olitzky, Kerry M. *Jewish Paths Toward Healing and Wholeness*. Woodstock, VT: Jewish Lights Publishing, 2000.

Person, Hara. *The Mitzvah of Healing: An Anthology of Essays, Jewish Texts, Personal Stories, Meditations and Rituals*. New York: UAHC Press, 2003.

Rowe, Debi M. *Introduction to the Siddur: Vol. 3: The Amidah, The Torah Service & the Concluding Prayers*. Los Angeles: Torah Aura Productions, 1992.

The Shabbat Morning Service Book 2: The Shabbat Amidah. New York: Behrman House, Inc., 1986.

AUDIOVISUAL

Friedman, Debbie. *In The Beginning*. San Diego, CA: Sounds Write Productions, Inc., 1994. Three compact disc set. Available from A.R.E. Publishing, Inc.

Glaser, Sam. *A Day in the Life*. Los Angeles, CA: Glaser Musicworks, 1994. Compact disc. Available from A.R.E. Publishing, Inc.

Kol B'Seder. *Snapshots: The Best of Kol B'Seder Vol. 1*. West Roxbury, MA: Kol B'Seder, 2004. Compact disc. Available from A.R.E. Publishing, Inc.

Mah Tovu. *Turn It*. Denver, CO: Mah Tovu, 2001. Compact disc. Available from A.R.E. Publishing, Inc.

Paley, Cindy. *Shabbat Shalom*. Sherman Oaks, CA: Cindy Paley Aboody, 1989. Compact disc and audiocassette/songbook set. Available from Sounds Write Productions, Inc.

Shir Hadash. *Or Shalom*. Vancouver, BC: Shir Hadash, 1987. Compact disc and audiocassette. Available from Sounds Write Productions, Inc.

Silver, Julie. *From Strength to Strength*. Newton Highlands, MA: A Silver Girl Production, 1993. Compact disc. Available from A.R.E. Publishing, Inc.

CHAPTER EIGHT:
KRIAT HATORAH

OVERVIEW

In regard to *Kriat HaTorah*, reading the Torah during a worship service, Abraham Millgram has written, "To make the teaching of the tradition a cardinal principal of faith, which today is accepted quite casually as normal and natural, was in ancient times one of the most revolutionary innovations imaginable" (*Jewish Worship*, p. 108).

The custom of reading the Torah in public appears to derive from Nehemiah 8:5-8: "And Ezra opened the book in the sight of all the people . . . And when he opened it, all the people stood up. And Ezra blessed the Lord, the great God. And all the people answered, 'Amen, Amen . . . ' And [Ezra and his associates] read in the book, in the Law of God, distinctly; and they gave the sense, and caused them to understand the reading."

When we read the Torah in our synagogues today, we follow many of these same practices: the congregation rises, a blessing is said before reading from the Torah (as well as after), the text is usually translated (corresponding to "gave the sense"), and there is often an interpretation ("cause them to understand the reading").

The most elaborate ceremony for the reading of the Torah occurs on Shabbat and festivals. The ritual begins with selections from Psalms (86:8, 145:13, and 29:11) which proclaim God's uniqueness and sovereignty. A short Rabbinic passage *Av HaRachamim*) asks God to build the walls of Jerusalem. The *Aron HaKodesh* is then opened as the congregation sings *Va'y'hi Binso'a* (Numbers 10:35-36). This recalls how the the Ark of the Covenant was carried before the people in the Sinai desert.

Ki Mitzion (Isaiah 2:3) follows, proclaiming that God's word comes from Jerusalem. The *Sefer Torah* is removed from the *Aron HaKodesh* as worshipers recite *Baruch Shenatan*, which praises God for having given Israel the Torah.

On festivals and the High Holy Days, Exodus 34:6-7, which enumerates the thirteen attributes of God, is recited three times. An additional supplication is silently read on the festivals, followed by *Yih'yu L'ratzon* (Psalm 19:15) and *Va'ani Tefilati* (Psalm 69:14).

In some congregations a selection from the *Zohar* beginning "*Brich Sh'mei*" follows. This extols God as Ruler and pleads for redemption and well-being for God's people.

The reader and congregation then recite the *Sh'ma*, followed by a Rabbinic response (*Echad Eloheinu*). The reader then bows toward the *Aron HaKodesh* while reciting *Gad'lu l'Adonai* (Psalm 34:4). The congregation responds with *L'cha Adonai* (I Chronicles 29:11) as the *Sefer Torah* is carried in a *hakafah*, a circuit around the synagogue. (On Simchat Torah, all *Sifrei Torah* are removed from the *Aron HaKodesh* and are carried for seven *hakafot*.) Other songs pertaining to the Torah such as *Romemu* (Psalm 99:5,9) and *Al Sh'loshah D'varim* (Pirke Avot 1:2) are often sung until the procession is complete and the Torah has made its way to the *bimah*.

It is traditional never to turn one's back on the Torah. During the *hakafah*, worshipers turn to follow the Torah around the room. As the Torah passes by, many worshipers will touch its covering with the *tzitzit*, the *siddur*, or fingertips, and then kiss the object that has just touched it. It is also traditional to kiss the Torah (before and

KRIAT HATORAH
(Reading of the Torah)
(Shabbat and Festivals)

Ein Kamocha (There is none like You)

Adonai Melech (*Adonai* is King)

Av HaRachamim (Merciful Father)

Va'y'hi Binso'a (When the Ark was carried)

Ki Mitzion (Torah will go forth from Zion)

Baruch Shenatan (Blessed is the One Who gave Torah)

Adonai, Adonai (Exodus 34:6-7 — Festivals only)

Sh'ma (Deuteronomy 6:4)

Echad Eloheinu (Our God is One)

Gadlu l'Adonai (Psalms 34:4)

L'cha Adonai (To You, *Adonai,* is the greatness)

Birchot HaTorah (Torah blessings)

Kriat HaTorah (Torah reading)

Birkat HaGomeil (Blessing for one who has survived a dangerous experience)

Mi Shebeirach (On behalf of each person called to the Torah)

Chatzi Kaddish (Reader's *Kaddish*)

V'zot HaTorah (Deuteronomy 4:44, Numbers 9:23)

Birchot Haftarah (Haftarah blessings)

Kriat Haftarah (Haftarah reading)

Y'kum Purkan (May salvation come — Shabbat only)

Prayer for the Government

Birkat HaChodesh (Blessing of the new month, on the Shabbat before Rosh Chodesh)

Ashrei (Psalm 145)

Y'hal'lu (Let them praise)

Hodo Al Eretz (Psalm 148:13-14)

Psalm 29 (On Shabbat)

Psalm 24 (On Festivals)

Uv'nucho Yomar (When the ark rested Moses said)

Chatzi Kaddish (Reader's *Kaddish*)

after) an *aliyah*, by touching the *tzitzit* to the first word (and the last) word of the reading and then kissing the *tzitzit*.

When the Torah arrives at the *bimah*, its cover and adornments are removed, and it is set down on the reading desk. A medieval doxology (a paean of praise to God) is sometimes read silently. In some congregations, the reader then recites a short *piyyut* (poem) from the school of Rashi (*Av HaRachamim*) and another paragraph praising God (*V'ya'azor V'yagein*).

The first person to be honored with an *aliyah* is then called to the Torah. Traditionally, only men were called to recite the Torah *brachot* or to read from the Torah, but now women are also called for *aliyot* in Reform, Reconstructionist, and most Conservative congregations. As each *aliyah* approaches the *bimah*, the reader recites a short paragraph: "*Baruch Shenatan Torah L'amo Yisrael Bik'dushato*" (Blessed be the One Who in holiness gave the Torah to Israel), and the congregation responds "*V'atem Had'veikim Eloheinu Chayim Kulchem HaYom*" (And you who cling unto the Eternal your God are alive every one of you this day).

Before reading from the Torah, the *aliyah* then recites the *brachah*, which begins "*Barchu Et Adonai HaM'vorach.*" This assures that the congregation is ready for this most important part of the service. This *brachah* affirms that God chose Israel from all peoples and gave Israel the Torah. A selection from the Torah is then read, followed by the *brachah* after the Torah reading, which again mentions the giving of the Torah, as well as an assurance that God "planted in us eternal life." This procedure of blessings and readings is repeated until the entire *sedra* has been read.

The Torah is divided into fifty-four portions, each of which is called a *parashah* (plural, *parashiyot*) or *sedra* (plural, *sidrot*). A *parashah* is read each week beginning with the Shabbat following Simchat Torah, when the first *parashah*, *B'reishit*, is read. During a non-leap year, when there are fewer than fifty-four weeks, certain *sidrot* are combined and read on the same Shabbat.

While the entire *parashah* is read in Orthodox synagogues, a section of the *parashah* is read in most Reform, Reconstructionist, and Conservative congregations. Some read a third of the portion, based upon the ancient Palestinian tradition of a triennial cycle, as opposed to the Babylonian annual cycle. A different third is then read each year.

In addition, there are special readings for the *Yamim Nora'im* (High Holy Days) and the festivals, which reflect on the themes appropriate for the day.

After the Torah has been read (and often translated), two individuals are called to the *bimah* to lift (*hagbahah*) and to roll and dress (*g'lilah*) the Torah. The person lifts the Torah from the reading desk, turns to face away from the congregation, and holds the scroll aloft so that part of at least three columns can be seen. Meanwhile, the congregation recites *V'zot HaTorah* (Deuteronomy 4:14), which affirms that Moses placed the Torah before Israel at God's behest.

The Haftarah, a reading from *Nevi'im* or *Ketuvim* (Prophets or Writings sections of the Tanach) follow. Haftarah means conclusion (because it is read at the conclusion of the Torah service). The word "Haftarah" is not linguistically related to the word "Torah."

There are various theories explaining the origin of the Haftarah. One claims that it was instituted in response to the Samaritans who did not recognize these books as sacred. According to Abudraham, the reading of the Haftarah developed in response to a prohibition of the reading of the Torah by Jews in the days of Antiochus Epiphanes of the Chanukah story. Other scholars believe that the Haftarah reading was instituted by Rabbi Akiba in response to the prohibition by Hadrian, the Emperor of Rome, against reading the Torah.

Whatever the reason, we now read a passage from the Prophets or Writings which is in some way related to the Torah portion. The reading is preceded by one *brachah* and followed by four *brachot* that are read as one. The *brachah* before the reading affirms that God chose prophets of truth and righteousness. The themes of the blessings following the reading are God's truthfulness and faithfulness; the return to Zion (Jerusalem); the coming of the Messiah; and thanksgiving for Torah, worship, the prophets, and Shabbat (or the particular holiday). Many of the *brachot* following the Haftarah reading have been eliminated in Reform ritual.

A number of special prayers often follow the Haftarah. These include:

> Y'kum Purkan, a prayer for the Rabbinical academies, Rabbis, and students
> a prayer for the congregation and its leaders
> a prayer for the government
> a prayer for the state of Israel
> a blessing for the coming month, recited on the Shabbat before Rosh Chodesh
> a prayer remembering martyrs, recited on certain Shabbatot only

The ritual for returning the Torah to the *Aron HaKodesh* begins with *Ashrei*, Psalm 145, (see Chapter 5). As the Torah is placed in the *Aron HaKodesh*, the reader says "*Y'hal'lu Et Sheim Adonai Ki Nisgav Sh'mo L'vado*" (Let them praise God's name, for God's name alone is worthy of exaltation) from Psalm 148:13-14. The congregation responds with "*Hodo Al Eretz . . . Hallelujah,*" praising God. On Shabbat, *Mizmor L'David* (Psalm 29) is recited, whereas on festivals which fall on weekdays, Psalm 24 is recited.

Then verses referring to the Ark of the Covenant are recited (Numbers 10:36, Psalms 8-10), followed by Proverbs 4:2 (*Ki Lekach Tov*) and Proverbs 3:18, 17 (*Eitz Chayim*) and Lamentations 5:21 (*Hashiveinu*). The *Chatzi Kaddish* is then chanted to mark the end of the Torah service and to serve as a transition to the next part of the service.

Besides being read at Shacharit service on Shabbat and festivals, Torah is also read at Shacharit on Mondays and Thursdays and at Minchah on Shabbat and Yom Kippur. Mondays and Thursdays were so chosen because they were market days in ancient times. This also assured that three days could not pass without the Torah being read. A small selection of the forthcoming *parashah* is read on these days. At Minchah on Shabbat, a small section of the upcoming week's *parashah* is read. The ritual accompanying the Torah reading is greatly abbreviated on these occasions. Neither is there a Haftarah reading, except at Minchah on Yom Kippur, when the entire book of Jonah is read.

INSIGHTS FROM THE TRADITION

A. The number of *aliyot* varies between three and seven. According to tradition, on Mondays, Thursdays, and Shabbat afternoons, there are three. On the intermediate days of the festivals of Pesach and Sukkot, there are four. On the first and last days of the festivals of Pesach, Shavuot, Rosh HaShanah, and Sukkot, five *aliyot* are called to the Torah. On Yom Kippur, there are six, and on Shabbat there are seven *aliyot*.

The first *aliyah* is traditionally given to a *Kohen* (someone descended from the High Priest of Israel). The second *aliyah* is traditionally given to a *Levi* (someone descended from the second level of priests). Thus our priestly heritage is remembered. The third and following *aliyot* are given to a *Yisrael* (someone from a non-priestly family).

B. While it is now customary for the *hazzan*, the rabbi, or a *ba'al koray* (Torah reader) to read the Torah, it was not always so. Originally, each person called to the Torah would read a section of the text. The first reader would chant the *brachah* before the Torah and then read from the text. Each successive reader would read only from the text. The last reader would conclude with the *brachah* after the Torah.

As Jews became less familiar with the biblical text, it became common to have a designated reader for those unable to read from the Torah. Eventually, in order not to embarrass anyone, this reader read the entire portion, while each person recited the *brachot*.

C. The origins of the *D'var Torah* or *drashah* (words of commentary) can be traced to the Talmudic period, when various rabbis customarily expounded on the text after it was read (*Brachot* 30a). In some congregations the *D'var Torah* has been replaced by a sermon delivered by the rabbi.

D. It is customary to honor a person who has recovered from a serious illness or returned from a long trip with an *aliyah*. Following the *aliyah*, this person recites "*Birkat HaGomeil*," to express gratitude to God for having been delivered from danger. The congregation responds by saying, "May the One who has shown you kindness deal kindly with you in the future." Rabbi Hertz reports that after an enemy bombing of a city in England resulted in 587 deaths during World War II, an entire congregation recited this *brachah* together (*The Authorised Daily Prayer Book*, pp. 487-488).

E. After each person reads or chants the *aliyah*, it is traditional for a *Mi Shebeirach* to be recited. This *brachah* asks God who blessed our ancestors to bless the person called to the Torah and his or her family. There are a variety of formulas for the *Mi Shebeirach* depending on the reason for the *aliyah* (naming of a daughter, Bar Mitzvah, upcoming marriage, etc.). It is a custom to make a donation to the congregation after receiving an *aliyah*.

F. The historian George Foot Moore commented upon the uniqueness of the public reading and teaching of the Torah in the ancient Middle East. "The religion of the household in Egypt or Greece or Rome was a matter of domestic tradition, perpetuated by example rather than by instruction . . . ; the religion of the city or the state was a tradition of the priesthoods in whose charge the public cultus was . . . . If the usage of the sanctuary was reduced to writing it was done privately or for the convenience of the priests themselves. The possession of a body of sacred Scriptures, including the principles of their religion as well as its ritual and the observances of the household and the individual, of itself put the Jews in a different case." (In Millgram, *Jewish Worship*, pp. 69-70)

G. The Reconstructionist movement, which does not accept the concept of Jews as a chosen people, substitutes in the blessing before the Torah reading "Who has brought us close to God's service" in place of "Who has chosen us from all peoples."

H. On the last day of Pesach, Shavuot, and Sukkot, and on Yom Kippur, a brief memorial service called *Hazkarat Nishamot* — but better known as *Yizkor* — (the name of one of its prayers) is recited as part of the Torah service. This service begins with an introductory reading composed of verses from Psalms and Ecclesiastes. Individuals then silently recite the *Yizkor* prayer for a parent, sibling, spouse, or child who has passed away. The service usually ends with *Eil Malei Rachamim*.

ACTIVITIES

TEXT AND CONTEXT

1. Bring a *Sefer Torah* to the classroom. With the students, practice undressing and then dressing the Torah. As this is done, identify each of the ritual objects by its name (see Chapter 13). When the students are proficient with the naming, ask the Rabbi to include them in this role during a service. Listen to the song "The Torah" by Kol B'Seder. (For other activities pertaining to the Torah ornaments, see Chapter 13.) Resource: *Songs for Growin'* by Kol B'Seder. (K-2)

2. As part of an ongoing classroom activity, create a large Jewish calendar. At each class session, go over the Hebrew date and name of the week's *parashah*. Include Jewish holidays as they occur. You may also want to include the dates according to the secular calendar so that students understand that as Jews we live by both calendars. (K-2)

3. To teach the students when the Torah and Haftarah are read, create a chart on a large sheet of tagboard with three columns: one column with a *Sefer Torah* at the top; one column with a *Sefer Torah* and a book representing the Haftarah at the top; and one blank at the top. Distribute cards which have the days of the week in English or Hebrew and names of the following holidays: Shabbat, Rosh HaShanah, Yom Kippur, Sukkot, Pesach, and Shavuot. One student at a time reads his/her card and places it in the correct column. Teacher or other students correct when necessary. Continue until all cards have been put into the appropriate columns. Discuss the results so that students understand that the Torah is traditionally read on Mondays and Thursdays, in addition to Shabbat and holidays, and that there is a Haftarah on Shabbat and holidays. (3-8)

4. Individually, or as a class, attend a Torah service, pretending to be reporters and closely observing what happens. Ask the students to recall everything that occurred, listing each step on the board. Answer any questions that the students have, and ask your own questions to make sure the students understand everything that happened. (3-8)

5. Follow up Activity #4 by going to the sanctuary and role playing a Torah service. Assign students to be the rabbi; cantor; *gabbai* (*shamash*, beadle, sexton); *aliyot* (persons called to the Torah to recite the *brachot* before and after the reading); *magbiah* (person who lifts the Torah after it is read); *goleil* (person who rolls and dresses the Torah); etc. Go through the Torah service with each person taking a part. Afterward, discuss the experience. (3-8)

6. It has been said that the Torah service reenacts the giving of the Torah to the people at Mount Sinai. Read Exodus 19-20 with the students and discuss how the experience of the ancient Hebrews compares with what happens during the Torah service today. What are the similarities and differences? How could the Torah service be changed to make it more similar to the giving of the Torah? (6 and up)

7. Compare the Torah *brachot* in the Reconstructionist *siddur* with the traditional Torah *brachot*. What is different? Explain how this difference stems from differing beliefs regarding the Jews as the chosen people. Discuss the meaning of this concept. Do the students feel chosen? If so, in what ways? Why were the Jews chosen? Is there an obligation that goes with chosenness? (9 and up)

ARTS

8. Teach the students the song "*Al Sh'loshah D'varim*," which is often sung as part of a Torah service, or other songs which are sung as part of

Kriat HaTorah at your synagogue. Resources: *The Complete Shireinu: 350 Fully Notated Jewish Songs* edited by Joel Eglash, p. 311; *Shabbat Alive* by Rick Recht, *The Bridge* by Sam Glaser. (K-2)

9. Extend Activity #8 by creating a large banner based on the saying "*Al Sh'loshah D'varim*." Divide the banner into three parts labeled: *Al HaTorah*/On Torah, *Al HaAvodah*/On Worship, and *Al G'milut Chasadim*/On Acts of Kindness. Provide crayons or markers for students to decorate each section appropriately. (K-5)

10. Teach the song "*Romemu*," which is often sung during the *hakafah*. Extend this activity by looking up the source for this song, Psalm 99:5. Resource: *Friday Night Live* by Craig Taubman. (3-8)

11. Create a symbolic tree of life. Fill a coffee can with plaster of paris. Place a tree branch in the can. Allow the plaster of paris to harden. As children enter the room, give each child a piece of paper cut in a leaf shape. Share with the students the concept that the Torah is a tree of life. Discuss what this means. Direct each student to write on the paper leaf one way that the Torah is a tree of life. Punch a hole in the corner of each leaf, thread with yarn, and attach to the branch. Conclude the lesson by singing one version of "*Eitz Chayim Hee*" (Tree of Life). Resources: *In The Beginning* by Debbie Friedman; *Or Shalom* by Shir Hadash, *Only This* by Mah Tovu, *Presence* by Sam Glaser. (3-8)

12. On the Shabbat prior to the beginning of a new month, a *brachah* is recited during the Torah service announcing Rosh Chodesh, the beginning of a new month. Encourage students to observe the moon over the period of a month, drawing its shape each night or every few nights. Students bring their drawings of the phases of the moon to class at the end of the month and create mobiles with them. The shapes of the moon can be decorated with glitter, markers, or other material. Using wooden dowels and string, make the mobiles and hang them from the classroom ceiling. (3-8)

13. Create a Torah service cantata (working with the cantor or music specialist, if possible). Select from among the many contemporary and classical versions of the prayers that are part of the Torah service. Present the cantata as part of a worship service. (6 and up)

14. During the Torah service, a *Mi Shebeirach* is often recited for one who is ill or facing surgery. Debbie Friedman has composed a melody for an egalitarian version of this *brachah*. Learn this song and present it at an appropriate time at a service. You may also wish to sing it as a class when one of the students or a member of a student's family is ill. Resource: *And You Shall Be A Blessing* by Debbie Friedman. (6 and up)

15. Ask the students if they have ever heard the Torah or Haftarah chanted. Using a Chumash or Tanach, point out the musical notations which are called trope marks. Invite the cantor or a member of the congregation (or students) to demonstrate one or more of the melodies, or listen to taped versions. Resources: *Parashah: Chanting Your Torah and Haftarah Portion* (each *parashah* is a separate cassette) from Transcontinental Music Publications; *Preparing for Your Bar Mitzvah/Bat Mitzvah* from MitzvahVision; *Trop Trainer* from Kinnor Software. (6 and up)

16. Distribute a *siddur* to each student and read together the "Prayer for the Country" or the "Prayer for the State of Israel." Discuss why these prayers are important, and why they have become part of the liturgy. Ask students to write their own version of one of these prayers. Collect them into a booklet that can be used during worship services. (9 and up)

BEYOND THE TEXT

17. Bring a Torah to the classroom. Take a photograph of each student holding the Torah. Have each student write or dictate a caption for the picture which states, "Torah is important to me because . . . " (K-2)

18. Read to the students the following book that describes the making of a Torah: *Sofer: The Story of a Torah Scroll* by Ray. Discuss the differences between the making of a Torah and the making of a regular book. (K-5)

19. View and discuss the video *For Out of Zion*, which is about the making of a Torah. Review the video by discussing these questions with the students: What is the individual called who copies the Torah? How is a Torah made? With what materials is a Torah made? How long does it take to complete a Torah? Do you think this is a difficult job? Would you like to do this? How can someone who is not trained as a scribe fulfill the *mitzvah* of writing a Torah scroll? (3-8)

20. As a follow-up to Activity #18 or #19, invite a *Sofer* (scribe) to the classroom to explain and, if possible, demonstrate that profession. The *Sofer* should bring examples of the types of documents that he writes, including a *mezuzah*, *ketubah*, *get*, and *tefillin*, explaining the significance of each. (3 and up)

21. Ask the students if they have ever seen anyone kiss ritual objects in the synagogue. When? What objects? List the students' responses on the board. (Besides the Torah, it is traditional to kiss the *tallit* before putting it on, to kiss the *tefillin* before putting them on and after taking them off, to kiss the fingers after touching the *tefillin* during the *V'ahavta*, to kiss the *tzitzit* at the end of *Baruch She'amar* and when it is mentioned during the *Sh'ma*, to kiss a *mezuzah* when entering a house, and to kiss a *siddur* or Chumash if it is dropped, or after using it.) Discuss: Why would this be a part of Jewish worship? How do students feel when they kiss someone? How do they feel when they are being kissed? How is this similar to the feelings one has when kissing a ritual object? (3-8)

22. Using a Jewish calendar, teach students how to find the weekly *parashah* and Haftarah readings. Provide each student with a Chumash to practice finding the *parashah* and Haftarah. Bring a perpetual calendar to class so students can look up their Bar/Bat Mitzvah *parashah* and those of their parents. Resource: *The Standard Guide to the Jewish and Civil Calendars* by Reiss. (5-8)

23. To help students become familiar with the section of the Tanach from which the Haftarot are taken, assign students to do a prophet report. The reports should include basic biographical material, important sayings, and a summary of the prophet's contributions to Judaism. Create a time line to show the place of each in Jewish history. The reports should be presented to the class or at another appropriate occasion. Resources: *An Introduction to Kings, Later Prophets and Writings* by Newman; *Think Prophets* by Grishaver and Bolton; *The Gift of Wisdom: The Books of Prophets and Writings* by Steinbock. (5 and up)

24. Ask the students if they have ever noticed the relationship between the Torah and Haftarah readings. Encourage them to recall their Bar/Bat Mitzvah portions. Distribute a Chumash to each student or pair of students and direct them to examine different Torah and Haftarah portions and attempt to determine the relationship. Each in turn should briefly summarize the portions and identify the connection for the other students. Summarize the theories as to the origin of the Haftarah readings as contained in the Overview. (9 and up)

25. When the Torah is lifted, it is traditional to sing *"V'zot HaTorah"* (This is the Torah which Moses placed before Israel, according to the word of God through the hand of Moses). Since the nineteenth century, liberal Jewish thought has reflected the conclusions of some biblical scholars that the Torah is composed of a number of traditions which were handed down orally for many generations before being written down and eventually brought together, and that the majority of the text does not go back to the time of Moses. Present and discuss this view with your students. (An excellent summary can be found in *The Torah: A Modern Commentary*, edited by Plaut, pp. xxi-xxiv.) What are the implications of accepting this view as opposed to the traditional view of Jewish belief and practice? Should one who accepts this view still say *V'zot HaTorah* . . . ? (9 and up)

HEBREW

26. Teach the students how to call someone to the Torah. You will need to know the person's Hebrew name, including whether that person is a *Kohen* or *Levi*. Have the students practice calling each other up to the Torah. Resources: *The Second How-To Handbook for Jewish Living* by Olitzky and Isaacs; *This Is the Torah* by Kolatch, p. 151. (3-8)

27. Teach the students the Hebrew terminology relating to the Torah service. Among the words to include are: *aliyah, Kohen, Levi, Yisrael, Mi Shebeirach, hagbahah, g'lilah, Maftir,* and Haftarah. Create a pantomime for each of the words to help reinforce its meaning. (3-8)

28. Bring a *Sefer Torah* to class and unroll it. Point out to the students the crowns on certain letters. Which letters have crowns and which do not? Discuss the reason why some letters have crowns. Resource: *This Is the Torah* by Kolatch, pp. 100-103. (3-8)

29. Look at a Torah portion in a *Tikkun*, which has the pointed and unpointed Torah text in adjacent columns. Compare the pointed with the unpointed version. Discuss how Torah readers use the *Tikkun* to prepare. Invite a Torah reader to talk about the process. Students who have become a Bar/Bat Mitzvah can also share their experiences about their preparation. (6-8)

FAMILY

30. Introduce the custom of a family *aliyah* in your synagogue or Junior Congregation. Rather than calling a single person for an *aliyah*, call an entire family to the *bimah* to recite the *brachot* together. Those wearing a *tallit* can wrap it around all the family members as they recite the *brachot*.

31. It is a *mitzvah* for each person to write a *Sefer Torah*. While this is usually not practical today, each family can create its own "Torah," which tells the story of the family. Tell families to bring pictures, documents, and other material for this project. Provide each family with a long roll of white paper. Each family creates its own "Torah" which includes family history and genealogy, stories and pictures about the family, recipes and family traditions, pictures and drawings, and anything else which might be appropriate. Attach each end of the paper to pre-cut dowels. Encourage families to continue to add to their "Torah" and to use it as part of important family occasions.

RESOURCES

BOOKS

Eglash, Joel, ed. *The Complete Shireinu: 350 Fully Notated Jewish Songs*. New York: Transcontinental Music Publications, 2001.

Grishaver, Joel Lurie and Scott Bolton. *Think Prophets*. Los Angeles, CA: Torah Aura Productions, 2000. Fourteen Instant Lessons on various prophets available.

Hertz, Joseph H. *The Authorised Daily Prayer Book, Revised Edition*. New York: Bloch Publishing Company, 1975.

Kolatch, Alfred J. *This Is the Torah*. Middle Village, NY: Jonathan David Publishers, Inc., 1994.

Millgram, Abraham. *Jewish Worship*. Philadelphia, PA: The Jewish Publication Society of America, 1971.

Newman, Shirley. *An Introduction to Kings, Later Prophets and Writings*. West Orange, NJ: Behrman House, Inc., 1981.

Olitzky, Kerry and Ronald H. Isaacs. *The Second How-To Handbook of Jewish Living*. Jersy City, NJ: KTAV Publishing House Inc., 1996.

Plaut, W. Gunther, ed. *The Torah: A Modern Commentary*. New York: UAHC Press, 1981.

Ray, Eric. *Sofer: The Story of a Torah Scroll*. Los Angeles, CA: Torah Aura Productions, 1986.

Reiss, Fred. *The Standard Guide to the Jewish and Civil Calendars*. West Orange, NJ: Behrman House, Inc., 1986.

Steinbock, Steven E. *The Gift of Wisdom: The Books of Prophets and Writings*. New York: UAHC Press, 2001.

Teutsch, David A., ed. *Kol Haneshamah: Shabbat Vehagim*. Elkins Park, PA: The Reconstructionist Press, 2002.

AUDIOVISUAL

For Out of Zion. Teaneck, NJ: Ergo Media Inc., 1973. Videocassette, 15 minutes, not rated.

Friedman, Debbie. *And You Shall Be A Blessing*. San Diego, CA: Sounds Write Productions, Inc., 1989. Compact disc. Available from A.R.E. Publishing, Inc.

———. *In The Beginning*. San Diego, CA: Sounds Write Productions, Inc, 1994. Three compact disc set. Available from A.R.E. Publishing, Inc.

Glaser, Sam. *The Bridge*. Los Angeles, CA: Glaser Musicworks, 2002. Compact disc. Available from A.R.E. Publishing, Inc.

———. *Presence*. Los Angeles, CA: Glaser Musicworks, 2003. Compact disc. Available from A.R.E. Publishing, Inc.

Kol B'Seder. *Songs for Growin'*. New York: Transcontinental Music Publications, 2001. Compact disc and songbook. Available from A.R.E. Publishing, Inc.

Mah Tovu. *Only This*. Denver, CO: Mah Tovu, 1996. Compact disc. Available from A.R.E. Publishing, Inc.

Parashah: Chanting Your Torah and Haftarah Portion. New York: Transcontinental Music Publications. Audiocassettes.

Preparing for Your Bar Mitzvah/Bat Mitzvah. Seattle, WA: MitzvahVision. Instructional videotapes.

Recht, Rick. *Shabbat Alive*. St. Louis, MO: Vibe Room Records/Banana Head Publishing, 2001. Available from A.R.E. Publishing, Inc.

Shir Hadash. *Or Shalom*. Vancouver, BC: Shir Hadash, 1987. Compact disc and audiocassette. Available from Sounds Write Productions, Inc.

Taubman, Craig. *Friday Night Live*. Sherman Oaks, CA: Sweet Louise Productions, 1999. Compact disc and songbook. Available from A.R.E. Publishing, Inc.

Trop Trainer. Key West, FL: Kinnor Software. Available from www.kinnor.com.

CHAPTER NINE:
ALEINU

OVERVIEW

The central prayer of the concluding part of the service is the *Aleinu*. The *Aleinu* combines the themes of particularism (praising God for giving the Jews a unique destiny) and universalism (looking forward to the day when all peoples will accept God's sovereignty).

The first paragraph of the *Aleinu* concludes with Deuteronomy 4:39, which affirms that our God is the only God in heaven and earth. The second paragraph, which expresses the desire to witness the perfection of the world and the turning to God of all people, concludes with two biblical quotations. The first, Exodus 15:18, affirms God's eternal rule; the second, Zechariah 14:9, looks forward to the universal recognition of God's sovereignty.

The *Aleinu* originated as an introduction to the *Malchuyot* portion of the Rosh HaShanah Musaf *Amidah*. The third century Babylonian sage Rav is credited with editing this *Amidah*, including the *Aleinu*. However, because it mentions neither the rebuilding of the *Beit HaMikdash*, nor the restoration of the Jewish state, both of which would have been appropriate additions to a prayer which looks toward the end of time, many scholars conclude that it was at least partially written prior to the destruction of the *Beit HaMikdash* (70 C.E.). According to one tradition, it was written by the rabbis of the Great Assembly during the Second Temple period. Another tradition claims Joshua instituted its recital after conquering Jericho.

While the *Aleinu* was used in Palestine quite early as an introductory morning prayer, it only became a concluding prayer of the daily services in the twelfth or thirteenth centuries. The *Machzor Vitri* is the first to include the *Aleinu* in all services. The *Aleinu* assumed its more prominent position, at least in part, because it was often recited by Jewish martyrs in medieval times as an affirmation of their faith in God as they went to their deaths.

The *Aleinu* has been one of the most controversial Jewish prayers, and was often censored, both by government censors and by Jewish leaders attempting to eliminate the controversy. The problem concerned the beginning of the prayer which originally read: "It is incumbent upon us to praise the God of all, to attribute greatness to the Creator, Who did not make us like the nations of the lands, nor placed us like the families of the earth; Who has not given our portion like theirs, nor our lot like all of their multitude. For they worship and bow before vanity and emptiness and pray to that which is of no avail, but we bend our knees and bow down and thank the King of the king of kings, the Holy One Who is blessed."

The phrase "For they worship and bow before vanity and emptiness and pray to that which is of no avail" is no longer included in Ashkenazic *siddurim*, but is contained in Sephardic liturgy. Censors from the Catholic church claimed that the words "vanity" and "emptiness" referred to the Christian divinity because the numerical value (gematria) of the letters in the Hebrew word *"vareik"* (and emptiness) is the same as the value of the Hebrew for Jesus. In response to this claim, Jews pointed out that both the biblical sources for these terms, Isaiah 30:7 and 45:20, and the prayer itself predate Christianity, and that even if the controversial verse could be attributed to Rav, he had no contact with Christianity.

Many non-Orthodox prayerbooks go beyond eliminating this controversial phrase by omitting or replacing all particularistic references in the entire prayer or by offering alternative versions from which to choose. (See, for example, *Gates of Prayer*, pp. 615-621 and *Kol Haneshamah: Shabbat Eve*, pp. 130-136.)

The *Aleinu* is traditionally read or sung standing, facing the *Aron HaKodesh* (which is closed) as if one is testifying as a witness. In most Reform synagogues, the *Aron HaKodesh* is opened at the beginning and closed after the phrase "the Holy One Who is blessed," at which point the congregation is seated.

It is traditional to bend one's knees and to bow at the waist when reciting the words describing these actions. Originally, worshipers would kneel and fully prostrate themselves. This practice is still followed by some during the repetition of the Musaf *Amidah* of Rosh HaShanah and Yom Kippur by the *shaliach tzibur*.

INSIGHTS FROM THE TRADITION

A. In the fourth century B.C.E. the rulers of Persia were called the "king of kings." To affirm God's supremacy, the Jews of Persia referred to God as "the King of the king of kings," a phrase found in the first paragraph of the *Aleinu*.

B. Manasseh ben Israel devoted a chapter in his 1656 book *Vindiciae Judaeorum* to defending the *Aleinu*. He reports that when Sultan Selim read a Turkish translation of the *siddur* he said of the *Aleinu*: "Truly this prayer is sufficient for all purposes; there is no need of any other."

C. Joseph HaCohen has written in *Vale of Tears*, "During the persecution of the Jews of Blois (France) in 1171, where many masters of the Torah died at the stake, an eye-witness wrote that the death of the saints was accompanied by a solemn song resounding through the stillness of the night, causing the Churchmen who heard it from afar to wonder at the melodious strains, the like of which they had never heard before. Afterwards, it was determined that the martyred saints had used the *Aleinu* as their dying song." (Hertz, *The Authorised Daily Prayer Book*, p. 209)

D. The Hebrew word "*reik*," meaning "emptiness," can also mean "spittle." It was a custom among some worshipers to spit when reciting this word, a practice discouraged by the rabbis. The Yiddish phrase, "*er kummt tsum oysshpayen*," meaning "he arrives at the spitting" and referring to a person who enters the service late, is derived from this practice.

E. In expressing his opposition to the particularism of the first part of this prayer, Abraham Geiger wrote, "The separation between Israel and the other peoples, which existed at one time, has no right to be expressed in prayer. Rather ought there to be an expression of the joy that such barriers are increasingly falling." (In Petuchowski, *Prayerbook Reform in Europe: The Liturgy of European Liberal and Reform Judaism*, p. 299. Reprinted by permission of the publisher, The World Union for Progressive Judaism, Ltd. © 1968.)

ACTIVITIES

TEXT AND CONTEXT

1. Ask the students what happens when someone goes before a king or queen. Provide a crown and let the children take turns being the ruler and the person coming before the ruler, who bows and rises. Explain that we talk about God as being the Ruler of the universe. The *Aleinu* tells us to bow before God. (K-2)

2. The *Aleinu* begins by saying that "It is our responsibility to praise God." Ask the students the following questions: What is praise? What are words of praise? With what words can we praise each other? With what words can we praise God? How does it feel when someone praises you? (K-5)

3. Teach the traditional choreography associated with the *Aleinu*. One bends the knees at "*Va'anachnu Korim,*" bows at "*Umishtachavim,*" and then stands up straight at "*Umodim.*" Explain that at one time, worshipers actually prostrated themselves (which is what the word *mishtachavim* means literally). Even today in some synagogues the *shaliach tzibur* does so during Musaf on Rosh HaShanah and Yom Kippur. (3-5)

4. To help the students understand the concept of the chosen people that is reflected in this prayer, do the following activity. Tell the class that you have something very special for a few of the students to do, and that you need to choose the students who will do this task. After a few moments, choose two or three of the students and tell them that they will be doing their special thing later. Ask the students how they felt being chosen and not being chosen. Then ask the students to suggest on what basis you chose the students, writing their suggestions on the board. Add to the list so that all of the following are included: random choice, best students, oldest students, students who could best do the task, students who could benefit most from the task, students whom the teacher likes the best. Explain that it is often not possible to know why a person or a group of people has been chosen. Ask the students if they have heard the Jews referred to as the chosen people. What does this mean? Review the first part of the *Aleinu* and discuss how it reflects the idea that the Jews are the chosen people. (6 and up)

5. Write on the board the statement attributed to Sultan Selim by Manasseh ben Israel: "Truly this prayer is sufficient for all purposes; there is no need of any other" (see Insight B). Divide the class into groups of three or four students. Ask each group to find three statements in the *Aleinu* which support this claim. Conclude this activity by asking each group to share and explain its choices. (6 and up)

6. Hold a mock synagogue meeting called to discuss what version of the *Aleinu* should be used. Among the roles to assign: rabbi, cantor/soloist, members of this synagogue, and Jews from other synagogues who report on how they do *Aleinu*. Students should use both the text of the *Aleinu* and the Overview to prepare their arguments. Conclude the meeting with a vote. (6 and up)

7. Because the traditional text of the *Aleinu* is controversial, some liberal *siddurim* offer alternate versions. Provide each student with the traditional text and at least one other version. Direct students to compare the texts and determine what has been changed and why it might have been changed. Ask students to choose which version they prefer and explain their choice. In this context, you might point out that even the traditional version in the Ashkenazic tradition has been edited to exclude a phrase (see Overview) that is still used in the Sephardic tradition. Resources: *Gates of Prayer*, pp. 615-621; *Kol Haneshamah: Shabbat Eve*, pp. 130-137. (6 and up)

8. Divide the class into two groups to debate the following topic: "All references to the Jews as the chosen people shall be eliminated from the *siddur*." (Note: Other prayers that would be affected are the Shabbat *Kiddush* and the blessing before reading from the Torah.) Divide the class into two groups and assign one the "pro" position and the other the "con" position. Resource: *The Book of Jewish Belief* by Jacobs, Chapter 5. (9 and up)

9. Distribute a Machzor to each student and direct the class to turn to the *Aleinu* in the *Malchuyot* portion of the Rosh HaShanah Musaf *Amidah*. (Note: In *Gates of Repentance* it is in the Shofar Service that is incorporated in Shacharit, pp. 139-143.) Briefly discuss the theme of this section of the service (God's sovereignty) and ask the students to find phrases in the *Aleinu* that reflect this theme. Explain that the *Aleinu* was initially a part of this service, and only later became a concluding prayer for the daily services. (9 and up)

ARTS

10. Write the last line of the *Aleinu* on the board: "God shall be ruler over all the earth. On that day God shall be One and God's Name shall be One."

Discuss what this means. What will the world be like when this happens? Have each student create a drawing of such a world. An example to share with the class is on page 17 of *Gates of Wonder*. (K-5)

11. Create a fabric applique wall hanging illustrating the phrase in the *Aleinu* which describes God as "stretching out the heaven and establishing the earth." Materials needed: 1 large piece of background fabric hemmed to the desired dimensions; a variety of fabric scraps, trims, lace, beads, etc. Create a design on paper. Cut the design apart using the pieces as patterns for cutting out the fabric. With stitches, applique the pieces onto the background fabric. Embellish with lace, trim, beads, etc. (3 and up)

12. Use the context of the *Aleinu* to introduce the importance of choreography to Jewish prayer. As a class, create a list of body movements associated with Jewish prayer. These include: standing, shuckling, bowing, kissing, rising on one's tiptoes, bending the knees, taking small steps, turning to face the Torah during a *hakafah*, and turning to face the door. Discuss what such choreography adds to prayer and how such movement relates to *kavanah*. Teach the body movements associated with the *Aleinu* (and other selected prayers if you wish). Hold a service in which you encourage students to experiment with traditional and creative body movements. Discuss how it felt and how the students might incorporate some of these movements into their own practice. Resource: "Movement of Prayer" by Saltzman in *The Second Jewish Catalog*, pp. 292-295. (6 and up)

13. Listen to a few different melodies for the *Aleinu*. With the students choose one of the melodies and create an interpretive dance. You may wish to incorporate some of the traditional body movements associated with the *Aleinu* into the dance. Resources: *In The Beginning* by Debbie Friedman; *The Jazz Service* by Bruce Benson. (6 and up)

14. Using the themes found in the *Aleinu*, direct students to write their own versions. Discuss the themes and provide a variety of translations and interpretations. Students may use poetry or prose. (9 and up)

BEYOND THE TEXT

15. The *Aleinu* speaks of God as stretching forth the heavens and establishing the earth. To help students understand God's role in our world, read *God's Paintbrush* by Sasso. Choose a few of the questions that are found throughout the text for discussion. (K-5)

16. The *Aleinu* tells us that the Jews are a unique people. To encourage students to see themselves as being special, do a proud whip with your class. Gather students into a circle. Each student in turn completes the phrase: "I am proud to be a Jew when . . . " or "I am proud to be Jewish because . . . " (K-5)

17. Another way to personalize the concept that the Jews are unique is to have each student make an "I am unique" poster. Provide the students with fabric, glue, and trims. Give each student one large piece of felt or fabric, about 2' x 3'. Direct students to cut out appliques that show significant Jewish occasions in their lives, holiday celebrations and special Jewish memories. Glue these onto the large fabric. Display on an appropriate occasion. (3-8)

18. The prominence of the *Aleinu* is due in part to its use by martyrs during the Middle Ages. As a class, create a memorial book for destroyed Jewish communities. You might or might not want to limit it to those communities destroyed during the Crusades. Students, working in pairs, select and research a community and write a one-page description. Compile these into a memorial book. Be sure to explain the tradition of the memorial book to students. Resources: *Encyclopaedia Judaica*, vol. 5, cols. 1135-1145; *The Encyclopedia of Jewish Life Before and During the Holocaust* edited by Spector. (6 and up)

19. Share with the class the information about censorship contained in the Overview. Invite a guest speaker from the library commission, the ACLU, People for the American Way, or another organization to speak about censorship today. (6 and up)

20. Someone once remarked that if what has happened to the Jews in history is a result of being the chosen people, maybe God could choose someone else next time. Conduct a poll on the question of whether being Jewish is a blessing or a burden. Students should interview parents, other relatives, friends, Jewish professionals, and lay leaders in the community, etc. Students should record comments, share them with the class and put together a summary of their findings for publication in the synagogue's bulletin or another forum. (6 and up)

21. Although the *Aleinu* would have us look forward to the day when all people will serve one God, it does not mean that everyone will become Jewish. But it does mean that all people will abide by a basic moral code. In groups, students should create a set of basic laws and guidelines for such a society. Students should limit their lists to ten or fewer rules. Share the rules with each other and draw up a composite list. Introduce the students to the idea of the Noachide laws, which are the basic laws that everyone is expected to follow in order to merit entering the world to come. Compare the Noachide laws to the students' lists. Resource: "Noachide Laws" in *Encyclopaedia Judaica*, vol. 12, cols. 1189-1191. (6 and up)

22. The *Aleinu* contains the seemingly contradictory themes of particularism and universalism. With the class, define these terms and ask students to identify which phrases in the *Aleinu* reflect each theme. Divide the class into two groups and assign each group to explore one of these themes. They should give examples of Jewish teachings and prayers that reflect the themes and analyze their importance to Judaism. After each group presents its findings, discuss whether they are contradictory or whether they are compatible. Are they both necessary for Judaism to survive and flourish? (9 and up)

HEBREW

23. Ask students to identify the Hebrew word for king, *melech*. Explain the concept of "root" in Hebrew as three consonants that appear in the same order in most forms of the word. Direct students to read through the *Aleinu* and identify all words with the root *mem, lamed, kaf*. (It occurs eleven times.) Discuss the significance of this root occurring so many times vis-a-vis the theme of the prayer. (3 and up)

24. The *Aleinu* contains many names and terms for God including: *Adon HaKol*/Lord of all, *Yotzeir B'reishit*/Creator, *Melech, Malchei HaMelachim*/King of the king of kings, *HaKadosh Baruch Hu*/The Holy One Who is blessed, *Eloheinu*/our God, *Malkeinu*/our King, *Adonai*/Lord, *Shaddai*/God almighty. Have students find these names in the prayer and learn to read them. Discuss why there are so many different names and phrases referring to God. What are some of the other terms for God? What does each add to our understanding of God? (6 and up)

25. With the students, identify and translate the biblical passages contained in the *Aleinu* — Deuteronomy 4:39, Exodus 15:18, Zechariah 14:9. (6 and up)

FAMILY

26. The conclusion of the *Aleinu* looks forward to the day when all people will recognize the God of the Jews as their God. This time is called the Messianic Age. What will this age be like? Encourage families to imagine what it would be like to live during that time. Ask each family to choose a problem that exists in the world and come up with a solution to that problem. Each family should share its solution with the other families. The group as a whole should then choose one or two of the problems and begin to implement the suggested solutions.

27. One of the themes of the *Aleinu* is Jewish uniqueness. Have families make albums in which they record significant Jewish events in their lives with creative writing, photos, and mementos. Provide each family with a blank book. On the cover, each family may create a coat of arms using its last name or other important characteristics. Begin this session by having families recall noteworthy experiences, about which they can write. Encourage families to use a variety of forms of creative expression in their books.

RESOURCES

BOOKS AND PERIODICALS

Encyclopaedia Judaica. Jerusalem: Keter Publishing House Jerusalem Ltd., 1972.

Gates of Prayer: The New Union Prayerbook. New York: Central Conference of American Rabbis, 1975.

Gates of Wonder: A Prayerbook for Very Young Children. New York: Central Conference of American Rabbis, 1989.

Hertz, Joseph H. *The Authorised Daily Prayer Book*, Revised Edition. New York: Bloch Publishing Co., 1975.

Jacobs, Louis. *The Book of Jewish Belief*. New York: Behrman House, Inc., 1984.

Kol Haneshamah: Shabbat Eve. Wyncote, PA: The Reconstructionist Press, 1989.

Petuchowski, Jakob J. *Prayerbook Reform in Europe: The Liturgy of European Liberal and Reform Judaism*. New York: The World Union for Progressive Judaism, Ltd., 1968.

Saltzman, Shulamit. "Movement of Prayer." In *The Second Jewish Catalog*, compiled and edited by Sharon Strassfeld and Michael Strassfeld. Philadelphia, PA: The Jewish Publication Society of America, 1976.

Sasso, Sandy Eisenberg. *God's Paintbrush*. Woodstock, VT: Jewish Lights Publishing, 1992.

Spector, Shmuel, ed. *The Encyclopedia of Jewish Life Before and During the Holocaust*. Washington Square, NY: New York University Press, 2001.

AUDIOVISUAL

Benson, Bruce. *The Jazz Service*. Oakland, CA: Bensongs, 1986. Compact disc. Available from Sounds Write Productions, Inc.

Friedman, Debbie. *In The Beginning*. San Diego, CA: Sounds Write Productions, Inc., 1994. Three compact disc set. Available from A.R.E. Publishing, Inc.

CHAPTER TEN:
KADDISH

OVERVIEW

The *Kaddish* is one of the most familiar Jewish prayers, but it is also one of the most unusual and misunderstood. Rabbi Hayim Halevy Donin writes, "No prayer in all of Jewish liturgy arouses greater emotion than *Kaddish*. No prayer instills greater reverence. No prayer projects more mystery." (*To Pray as a Jew*, p. 216)

When most Jews hear the word *Kaddish* they think of the Mourner's *Kaddish* (*Kaddish Yatom*, literally Orphan's *Kaddish*), but in fact there are actually four other forms of the *Kaddish*:

Chatzi Kaddish, literally half-*Kaddish*, but more commonly called Reader's *Kaddish*

Kaddish d'Rabbanan, Rabbis' *Kaddish*

Kaddish Shalem, Complete *Kaddish*

Kaddish L'itchadata, *Kaddish* of Renewal, also called Burial *Kaddish*

Part of the mystery surrounding the *Kaddish* in general is its origin. "Just how and when the *Kaddish* originated is not altogether clear, but it is certain that not all of it was composed at the same time. Each sentence, sometimes each phrase, comes down to us through devious routes, from different times and as parts of prayer for different occasions." (Garfiel, *Service of the Heart: A Guide to the Jewish Prayer Book*, p. 75. Reprinted by permission of the publisher, Wilshire Book Co., North Hollywood, CA. © 1975.)

The oldest part of the *Kaddish* is a phrase cited in the Talmud and other rabbinic literature. According to *Brachot* 3a, when God hears the people say, "*Y'hei Sh'mei Rabba M'varach, L'olam Ul'almei Almaya*" (May God's great name be blessed forever and ever), God grieves over the destruction of Jerusalem.

Reciting this phrase with all one's strength can cause the gates of paradise to open and can annul a decree of lifelong suffering (*Shabbat* 119a). In addition, saying this prayer after studying *Aggadah* helps assure the continued existence of the world (*Sotah* 49a).

This key phrase is the major congregational response to the recital of the *Kaddish*. It closely reflects two biblical passages which may have influenced its origin: Psalms 113:2: "Let the name of the Lord be blessed now and forever," and Daniel 2:20: "Let the name of God be blessed forever and ever." The passage from Daniel is written in Aramaic, the common language of the Jews in Palestine and Babylonia during the rabbinic and post-rabbinic years, and the predominant language of the *Kaddish*. As early as the second century, the *Kaddish* was used at the end of a study session, which would have been conducted in Aramaic. It therefore made sense to conclude with a prayer in Aramaic. However, the last line of all forms of the *Kaddish* except the *Chatzi Kaddish*, the line which begins "*Oseh Shalom Bimromav*" (May the One Who makes peace in heaven), is in Hebrew. This short prayer for peace actually paraphrases the Aramaic prayer for peace which immediately precedes it.

The phrase beginning "*Oseh Shalom*" is also found at the conclusion of the *Amidah* and the *Birkat HaMazon*, reflecting the importance of praying for peace in Jewish tradition.

The beginning words of the *Kaddish*, "*Yitgadal V'yitkadash*" (May God's Name be magnified and sanctified) may be reflective of Ezekiel's messianic vision, which uses these identical Hebrew roots in different forms (Ezekiel 38:23).

Another distinguishing characteristic of the *Kaddish* is that it is written entirely in the third person. Whereas most prayers composed by the rabbis of the Talmud contain the phrase *"Baruch Atah Adonai"* (Blessed are You, *Adonai*), using the second person to address God directly, the *Kaddish* does not contain this phrase. Furthermore, the most common liturgical terms for God, *Adonai* and *Eloheinu,* are also absent; instead, the phrases *"Sh'mei Rabba"* (God's great Name) and *"D'Kud'sha B'rich Hu"* (the Holy One Who is blessed) are used.

KADDISH YATOM

In the eighth century, two sentences were added to the *Kaddish,* beginning *"Y'hei Sh'lama"* and *"Oseh Shalom."* This longer version was recited at the end of a study session, including the study session which followed *shiva* (the week-long mourning period) for a scholar. Since Judaism teaches that all are equal in death, the *Kaddish* was eventually recited at the end of every *shiva* period, and thus became associated with death.

While this version of the *Kaddish* may have been part of the regular liturgy as early as the eighth century, it was not until the thirteenth century that it became a mourner's prayer, recited at the end of the service. This custom emerged in Germany at the time of the Crusades in response to intense persecution. It thus became known as *Kaddish Yatom.*

Kaddish Yatom is not only recited at the end of the service, after the *Aleinu,* it is also recited as part of the preliminary prayers during Shacharit and after Psalm 93 at Kabbalat Shabbat. Traditionally, one recites *Kaddish Yatom* daily during the eleven months following the death of a parent (beginning after the burial), and in some communities for thirty days following the death of a sibling, spouse, or child. *Kaddish Yatom* is also said for *Yahrzeit* (the anniversary of the death) of one's relatives. The obligation of saying *Kaddish Yatom* is traditionally placed upon males. In liberal Judaism, the obligation falls equally upon females.

In Orthodox and Conservative synagogues, only mourners and those observing *Yahrzeit* recite the *Kaddish Yatom.* However, the entire congregation responds with *"Amen"* (each time it appears), and recites the phrases *"Y'hei Sh'mei Rabba . . ."* and *"B'rich Hu."*

In most Reform synagogues, the entire congregation rises to recite the *Kaddish Yatom.* This change was made so as not to embarrass a mourner who may not know the words, and also to emphasize the community joining together to share moments of sadness, and to say *Kaddish Yatom* for the many Jews who died in the Holocaust leaving no one to say *Kaddish* for them.

CHATZI KADDISH

This short form of the *Kaddish* is also the earliest version. Although *Chatzi Kaddish* literally means half-*Kaddish,* it is commonly called Reader's *Kaddish* because it is recited by the *shaliach tzibur* to mark the conclusion of a section of the worship service. During Shacharit it occurs after *P'sukei d'Zimra,* after the *Amidah,* and after the Torah reading. During Minchah, Ma'ariv, and Musaf, it is recited after the *Sh'ma Uvirchoteha.*

KADDISH D'RABBANAN

The *Kaddish d'Rabbanan,* or Rabbis' *Kaddish,* consists of the entire text of *Kaddish Yatom,* plus an additional paragraph asking blessing upon teachers, their students, and all those who study Torah. The *Kaddish d'Rabbanan* is recited at the end of a study session which includes *midrash,* and after studying portions of the liturgy such as those contained in *Birchot HaShachar* and *Kabbalat Shabbat.*

While anyone may recite *Kaddish d'Rabbanan,* it is now the custom for mourners only to recite *Kaddish d'Rabbanan* in addition to *Kaddish Yatom.*

KADDISH SHALEM

Kaddish Shalem, the full *Kaddish,* is also called *Kaddish Titkabal* (or *Kaddish Titkabeil*) because it contains an additional paragraph beginning with the word *"titkabal"* (*titkabeil* in some versions). This extra phrase asks God to accept the prayers and supplications of Israel. It is recited by the *shaliach tzibur* prior to the *Aleinu*. However, on days when Musaf is said, the *Chatzi Kaddish* is said instead, followed by the Musaf *Amidah*.

KADDISH L'ITCHADATA

A special form of the *Kaddish*, called *Kaddish L'itchadata*, the *Kaddish* of Renewal, or the Burial *Kaddish*, is traditionally recited by mourners at the cemetery immediately following burial. The first paragraph of this *Kaddish* mentions "reviving the dead and raising them to eternal life," as well as the rebuilding of Jerusalem. This *Kaddish* is also recited when concluding the study of a tractate of Talmud.

INSIGHTS FROM THE TRADITION

A. During the *Yamim Nora'im*, the ten days of repentance from Rosh HaShanah through Yom Kippur, the words "*L'eila Min Kol Birchata*" are replaced by the words "*L'eila U'l'eila Mekol Birchata.*" The addition of the word "*U'l'eila*" (meaning "well beyond") is based upon the Aramaic translation of a phrase from Deuteronomy 28:43, and is used to emphasize that God is way beyond our praises. In the Italian and Yemenite traditions, this repetition occurs at all times.

B. The tradition of mourners reciting *Kaddish* may in part be based upon a story told about Rabbi Akiba. In a cemetery, an old man appeared carrying a heavy load of wood. Rabbi Akiba asked this man why he was doing such hard work, and offered to redeem him if he was a slave or help support him if he was poor. The man explained that he had been condemned to burn in hell and that he had to carry the wood for his own suffering. Akiba asked if there was any way for him to be relieved of his suffering. He replied that he would be free of the judgment if his young son were to say the first part of the *Kaddish* and the people were to respond, "*Y'hei Sh'mei Rabba . . . ,*" or if he were to say the first line of the *Barchu*, with the people answering with the second. Rabbi Akiba searched for the man's son, found him, and

taught him what he needed to know. The son recited the *Kaddish*, and his father's soul was saved from punishment (*Netiv Binah I,* pp. 367-368).

Based upon this legend, the belief that the recitation of the *Kaddish* could influence the soul of one's deceased parent became widespread in the Jewish community through much of the Middle Ages. Many leading rabbis, however, condemned this belief as a baseless superstition.

C. The practice of reciting *Kaddish* for eleven months rather than a full year is based upon the legend of the previous insight. It was believed that reciting *Kaddish* could influence the fate of a deceased parent's soul up to one year following death. However, if one said *Kaddish* for a full year, it implied that it was *necessary* to recite *Kaddish* for a full year to redeem his/her soul. Therefore, it became a custom to recite *Kaddish* for only eleven months following death. This eleven month tradition is observed even during a Jewish leap year, when there would be thirteen months between death and the first *Yahrzeit*.

D. During the recitation of *Kaddish Yatom*, the congregation says "*Amen*" at four different places in the *Kaddish*. This Hebrew word has entered many languages as an affirmation of what has been stated, as if to say, "so be it." As early as the time of King David, the people responded to a blessing with "*Amen*" (I Chronicles 16:35). According to the Talmud, the three Hebrew letters that comprise the word *Amen* stand for the Hebrew words "*Eil Melech Ne'eman,*" meaning "God is a faithful King" (*Shabbat* 119b). Responding "*Amen*" to a prayer recited by the *shaliach tzibur* fulfills one's obligation to recite the prayer oneself. One fulfills the obligation of reciting a *brachah* by saying "*Amen*" upon hearing another person recite the *brachah*.

E. Rabbi Levi Yitzhak of Berditchev, one of the leading Hasidic masters of the third generation, authored a famous private prayer challenging God called "Lawsuit with God," but better known as the *Kaddish* of Rabbi Levi Yitzhak. It reads:

Good morning to You, Master of the

Universe.

I, Levi Yitzhak, son of Sarah of Berditchev,
I come to You with a Din Torah [lawsuit] from
    Your people Israel.
What do You want of Your people Israel?
For everywhere I look it says, "Say to the
    Children of Israel,"
And every other verse says, "Speak to the
    Children of Israel,"
And over and over, "Command the Children
    of Israel,"
Father, sweet Father in Heaven,
How many nations are there in the world?
    Persians, Babylonians, Edomites.

The Russians, what do they say?
    That their Czar is the only ruler.
The Prussians, what do they say?
    That their Kaiser is supreme.
And the English, what do they say?
    That their King is the sovereign.
But I, Levi Yitzhak, son of Sarah of
    Berditchev, say,
"Yisgadal v'yiskadash shmei raboh —
Magnified and sanctified is Thy Name."

And I, Levi Yitzhak, son of Sarah of
    Berditchev, say,
"From my stand I will not waver,
And from my place I shall not move
Until there be an end to this Exile.
Yisgadal v'yiskadash shmei raboh —
Magnified and sanctified is only Thy Name."

(From *Arguing with God: A Jewish Tradition* by
Anson Laytner. Reprinted by permission of
the publisher, Jason Aronson, Inc., Northvale,
NJ. © 1990.)

F. A version of the *Kaddish* in memory of the
Holocaust can be found in *The Six Days of
Destruction: Meditations toward Hope* by Wiesel and
Friedlander, pp. 86-87. Names of ghettos, concentration camps, and other places in which Jews
died in the Holocaust are interspersed with the
words of the *Kaddish*.

G. The *Kaddish* has been a very influential prayer
for Judaism, and has also had a significant influence on Christianity. Many scholars believe that
the Lord's Prayer, which is found in different
versions in Matthew 6 and Luke 11, was influenced by the *Kaddish*. Both versions contain the
phrases "may your name be hallowed" and "may
your sovereignty come," which are very similar to
phrases contained in the *Kaddish*.

ACTIVITIES

Note: In teaching the *Kaddish*, it is important to
point out that the *Kaddish* is not just a mourner's
prayer, but is said in a variety of circumstances.
Also, the *Kaddish* does not mention death, but
praises God. Mention these points wherever appropriate in conjunction with the following activities.

TEXT AND CONTEXT

1. To help the students understand the word
"magnified," the initial word of the *Kaddish* in
most translations, use a magnifying glass or cube
to view a variety of objects. Discuss what the
word magnified means. Ask the students to
suggest other words that mean the same thing,
such as "great," "big," "expanded," "enlarged,"
"emphasized," etc. (K-5)

2. Learn to sing one or more of the versions of
"*Oseh Shalom*," which is the last line of the *Kaddish*.
Resources: *And the Youth Shall See Visions* by Debbie
Friedman; *Snapshots* by Kol B'Seder. (K-5)

3. Ask the students what they do to observe or
celebrate the end of an activity, school year, etc.
For example, pizza party at the end of a sports
season, bridging ceremony from one level of
scouts to another, graduation ceremony. Introduce the *Kaddish* as a prayer that is used to mark
completions: the *Chatzi Kaddish* to mark the completion of a section of the service, the *Kaddish
Yatom* to mark the completion of someone's life,
the *Kaddish d'Rabbanan* to mark the end of a
study session. For the end of a unit of study, plan
a celebration which includes a festive meal called

Se'udat Mitzvah and a recitation of *Kaddish d'Rabbanan.* (3-8)

4. Allow students to experience the difference between the traditional manner of reciting *Kaddish Yatom* in which only the mourners rise to say it and the liberal practice in which the entire congregation rises and says it. First, gather the students together, distribute the *siddurim*, and recite the *Kaddish Yatom* in unison. Then ask for volunteers, either individually, or a few at a time, to recite the *Kaddish*. The rest of the class should join in for the congregational responses. Ask the students what the differences were. How did it feel to read alone? with a few other students? all together? If they were a mourner, how would they prefer to do it? (6 and up)

5. Invite to class someone who has observed the traditional eleven month mourning period by reciting *Kaddish* daily. Compile a list of questions ahead of time such as: For whom were you reciting *Kaddish*? Where did you recite it? Did you ever miss a day? Why did you choose to do it? How did it affect your life? Afterward, discuss with the class members what observing this ritual might mean to them. (6 and up)

6. Distribute *siddurim* to the class and direct the students to compare the various versions of the *Kaddish*. What are the similarities and differences? How is each version used? How is each version appropriate to its situation? This activity can be done using either the Aramaic text or English translation. (9 and up)

7. Hold a mock congregational meeting to discuss and debate whether the *Kaddish Yatom* should be recited with all worshipers standing, only mourners standing, or whether each worshiper should be allowed to decide who will rise to recite the *Kaddish*. Assign roles such as the rabbi, cantor, synagogue president, a person who has just completed reciting *Kaddish* daily, etc. (9 and up)

ARTS

8. The concluding line of the *Kaddish Yatom*

speaks about peace. Prepare a dove-shaped template as large as you like. Each child needs to cut out two of these shapes, staple or glue the edges together (leaving an adequate opening to stuff later), decorate each side, stuff with crumpled newspaper, and close the opening. Each student composes his or her own short message of peace, which is written on a strip of paper. These strips are attached to the dove's beak. Hang the completed doves from the ceiling. (K-5)

9. Read to the class *The Tenth Good Thing about Barney* by Viorst. Ask students to suggest a different tenth good thing about Barney. (K-5)

10. The *Kaddish* includes many words of praise for God. Create a mobile using synonyms for the word "praise." Read through the *Kaddish* to create a list, and also use a thesaurus. (3-5)

11. What if your *siddur* could talk? What would it say about the *Kaddish* prayer? It might speak about the content or about a particular mourner or congregant. The students assume the role of the *siddur* and write a short story. (6 and up)

12. Help set the mood for the *Kaddish* prayer. Examine a variety of *siddurim*, paying particular attention to the introductory readings to the *Kaddish Yatom*. The students should then create their own poems, prayers, or readings. (6 and up)

13. Distribute a large sheet of white paper and charcoal to each student. Play parts of a recording of *Kaddish* by Leonard Bernstein. Direct younger students to create an abstract drawing reflecting the mood, tone, and feeling of the music. For older students, discuss how the composer conveyed the mood of the *Kaddish*. Resource: *Symphony No. 3 Kaddish* by Leonard Bernstein. (7 and up)

14. With your class read *Kaddish d'Rabbanan*. Discuss how it differs from the *Kaddish Yatom*. Listen to "*Kadish d'Rabanan*" by Debbie Friedman. Resource: *And You Shall Be a Blessing* by Debbie Friedman. (9 and up)

15. Read to your students *Grandma's Soup* by Karkovsky or *A Candle for Grandpa* by Techner and Hirt-Manheimer. These stories are about relationships between a young child and a grandparent. Ask the students to recall special people in their lives and the memories they have created together. Point out that it is these memories that keep people with us at all times, even after they have died. (K-2)

16. Create an *Oseh Shalom* chart for the classroom on which you list actions and activities that the students have done that promote peace between individuals or groups of people. Examples: sharing toys, helping at home, saying you are sorry, etc. Set aside a time during each class period to allow students to share what they have done. (K-5)

17. Use the film *The Corridor: Death* to spark a discussion about students' experiences with the death of a family member, friend, or pet. What rituals were observed? Was the *Kaddish* recited? Who said it and for how long? (6-8)

18. Invite the rabbi or another knowledgeable guest to speak about Jewish customs and beliefs pertaining to death, burial, and life after death. Brainstorm questions with the students ahead of time. Tell the speaker to focus particularly on the role of *Kaddish* in the mourning process. (6 and up).

19. Plan a study session to be used at a house of mourning. Discuss the tradition of holding a study session after the death of a scholar. The session might focus on the weekly Torah portion, a particular area of Jewish law or practice, or another Jewish topic. Introduce the *Kaddish d'Rabbanan* as the form of the *Kaddish* recited at the end of a study session. Pay particular attention to the extra paragraph that differentiates this form of the *Kaddish* from the *Kaddish Yatom*. (6 and up)

20. The *Kaddish* of Rabbi Levi Yitzhak of Berditchev (see Insight E) is an example of how one rabbi has used the *Kaddish* as part of a prayer of protest directed at God. Distribute a copy of this *Kaddish* to each student and read it aloud. Discuss its theme and why the *Kaddish* is used as part of this reading. Expand the discussion to the theme of protesting against God. Is this appropriate? If so, under what circumstances? Use the book *Arguing with God* by Laytner as a resource for other examples of this practice in the Jewish tradition. Create a worship service on the theme of protesting against God, utilizing texts from the book and the students' own writings. This service would be particularly appropriate for Shabbat *Va'yera*, which includes Abraham protesting God's decision to destroy Sodom and Gemorrah or Shabbat *Ki Tisa*, which includes Moses challenging God who wanted to destroy the people because of the golden calf. (9 and up)

21. Discuss with your class the tradition of reciting *Kaddish Yatom* for a deceased relative. Ask: For whom is it recited? Who recites it according to Jewish tradition? What happens if there is no male child to recite it? Read to your class the letter which Henrietta Szold wrote to Haym Peretz. How did her family solve this dilemma? Be sure to point out that this letter was written in 1916. How has liberal Jewish tradition evolved over time to reflect the attitude expressed in this letter? Resource: *Four Centuries of Jewish Women's Spirituality: A Sourcebook*, edited by Umansky and Ashton, pp. 164-165. (9 and up)

HEBREW

22. The root *kuf, dalet, shin*, occurs in many important Hebrew words related to the liturgy such as *Kaddish, Kiddush, K'dushah, K'dushat HaShem*, and *K'dushat HaYom*. To show the students how important this root is in Jewish tradition, hold a "Holy Scavenger Hunt" with your class. (6 and up)

Holy Scavenger Hunt
1. There are many Hebrew words and terms with the root *kuf, dalet, shin*, which means holy. How many can you identify?
   a. Prayer over the wine_____
   b. Prayer said in memory of the dead and at

other times in the worship service_____

    c. Word in candle blessing_____

    d. Part of the *Amidah* in the morning service_____

    e. Name for the Temple in Jerusalem_____

2. Read Leviticus 19:1-19 and list as many ways to be holy as you can find in that chapter.

3. Go into the synagogue and list those objects that you consider holy.

4. Find three people and ask them what being holy means to them.

5. What does "holy" mean to you?

This activity is reprinted with permission from *Teaching Torah: A Treasury of Insights and Activities* by Sorel Goldberg Loeb and Barbara Binder Kadden. Denver, CO: A.R.E. Publishing, Inc. 1997.

23. The *Kaddish* is one of the few prayers written not in Hebrew, but in Aramaic, a related Semitic language. Ask the students to examine the text of the *Kaddish* for words that appear familiar, but may be slightly different from the Hebrew words they know. Point out other liturgical passages that are in Aramaic, such as *Kol Nidrei* for Yom Kippur and *Ha Lachma Anya* of the Pesach Haggadah. Explain that prayers which are in Aramaic tended to be popular with the general worshipers who were more familiar with Aramaic, the language they spoke daily, than with Hebrew. (6 and up)

FAMILY

24. Gather together families that have lost loved ones and wish to participate in a bereavement group. Suggested activities: Within family groups, each member writes a letter about his/her loved one who has passed away. They then take turns reading their letters to each other. Create quilted fabric squares that include words and pictures illustrating the life of their loved one. These squares are sewn together and become part of a memory quilt. You may wish to conclude the program with the group reciting *Kaddish* together. (Some traditional Jews may not want to recite *Kaddish* when it is not called for by tradition.) Resources: *When a Grandparent Dies: A Kid's Own*

Remembering Workbook for Dealing With Shiva and the Year Beyond by Liss-Levinson; *A Time to Mourn, A Time to Comfort: A Guide to Jewish Bereavement and Comfort* by Wolfson.

RESOURCES

BOOKS AND PERIODICALS

Donin, Hayim Halevy. *To Pray as a Jew: A Guide to the Prayer Book and the Synagogue Service.* New York: Basic Books, Inc., 1980.

Garfiel, Evelyn. *Service of the Heart: A Guide to the Jewish Prayer Book.* Northvale, NJ: Jason Aronson Inc., 1999.

Karkowsky, Nancy. *Grandma's Soup.* Rockville, MD: Kar-Ben Copies, Inc., 1989.

Laytner, Anson. *Arguing with God: A Jewish Tradition.* Northvale, NJ: Jason Aronson Inc., 1998.

Liss-Levinson, Nechama. *When a Grandparent Dies: A Kid's Own Remembering Workbook for Dealing With Shiva and the Year Beyond.* Woodstock, VT: Jewish Lights Publishing, 1995.

Loeb, Sorel Goldberg and Barbara Binder Kadden. *Teaching Torah: A Treasury of Insights and Activities.* Denver, CO: A.R.E. Publishing, Inc., 1997.

Techner, David and Judith Hirt-Manheimer. *A Candle for Grandpa.* New York: UAHC Press, 1993.

Umansky, Ellen M. and Dianne Ashton, eds. *Four Centuries of Jewish Women's Spirituality: A Sourcebook.* Boston, MA: Beacon Press, 1992.

Viorst, Judith. *The Tenth Good Thing about Barney.* New York: Atheneum Books, 1971.

Wiesel, Elie and Albert H. Friedlander. *The Six Days of Destruction: Meditations toward Hope.* New York: Paulist Press, 1988.

Wolfson, Ron. *A Time to Mourn, A Time to Comfort: A Guide to Jewish Bereavement and Comfort.* Woodstock, VT: Jewish Lights Publishing, 1996.

AUDIOVISUAL

The Corridor: Death. Teaneck, NJ: Ergo Media Inc., 1989. Videocassette, 25 minutes, not rated.

Friedman, Debbie. *And You Shall Be a Blessing.* San Diego, CA: Sounds Write Productions Inc.,

1989. Compact disc. Available from A.R.E. Publishing, Inc.

———. *In The Beginning*. San Diego, CA: Sounds Write Productions Inc., 1994. Three compact disc set. Available from A.R.E. Publishing, Inc.

Kol B'Seder. *Snapshots: The Best of Kol B'Seder Vol. 1*. West Roxbury, MA: Kol B'Seder, 2004. Compact disc. Available from A.R.E. Publishing, Inc.

Symphony No. 3 *Kaddish* by Leonard Bernstein. Israel Philharmonic Orchestra. Deutsche Grammophon. Compact Disc #423582-2-GH.

CHAPTER ELEVEN: KABBALAT SHABBAT

OVERVIEW

On the eve of Shabbat, the service begins with a group of psalms and the liturgical poem *L'cha Dodi*, collectively called Kabbalat Shabbat (receiving the Sabbath). As early as the ninth century, it was a custom in Babylonia to recite six psalms prior to Shabbat to symbolize the six shofar blasts which in the days of the Temple signaled the approach of Shabbat (*Shabbat* 35b). In the sixteenth century, the Jewish mystics of Safed, a city in northern Israel, would go to the open fields and sing psalms and songs to welcome Shabbat. The custom of welcoming Shabbat in synagogues with psalms and songs quickly spread to other Jewish communities.

Kabbalat Shabbat begins with Psalms 95-99 and 29, each representing one of the weekdays. Rabbi Moses Cordovero, a member of the Safed community, selected these particular psalms. They contain the themes of worshiping God with song, proclaiming God's glory to all the world, and affirming God's sovereignty and righteous judgment.

These psalms introduce *L'cha Dodi*, a poem written by another member of the Safed community, Rabbi Shlomo Halevi Alkabetz. He drew on a number of biblical phrases and themes, many from Isaiah. For the refrain, he utilized the Talmudic image of the Shabbat as *kallah* (bride) and *malkah* (queen). The passage in the Talmud, *Shabbat* 119a, reports that Rabbi Chanina, dressed in fine garments, stood at sunset on *erev* Shabbat and exclaimed, "Come let us go forth to welcome the Shabbat queen!" Rabbi Yannai would also dress in fine clothes and call out, "Come, O bride! Come, O bride!"

KABBALAT SHABBAT
(Welcoming Shabbat)

L'chu N'ran'na (Psalm 95)

Shiru l'Adonai (Psalm 96)

Adonai Malach, Tageil Ha'aretz (Psalm 97)

Mizmor Shiru l'Adonai Shir Chadash (Psalm 98)

Adonai Malach, Yirg'zu Amim (Psalm 99)

Mizmor L'David (Psalm 29)

Ana B'choach (With Strength)

L'cha Dodi (Welcoming the Sabbath Bride)

Mizmor Shir L'yom HaShabbat (Psalm 92)

Adonai Malach, Gei'ut Laveish (Psalm 93)

Kaddish Yatom (Mourner's *Kaddish*)

Bameh Madlikin (*Mishnah Shabbat*, Chapter 2)

Kaddish d'Rabbanan (Rabbinical *Kaddish*)

While the first two stanzas of *L'cha Dodi* refer to Shabbat, stanzas three through eight contain the themes of rebuilding Jerusalem, the coming of the messiah, and the redemption of Israel. The final stanza returns to the theme of the Shabbat bride. Traditionally, worshipers stand, face the door of the synagogue, and bow when singing "*Bo'i Kallah*" (Come, O bride), as if one were welcoming a bride. *L'cha Dodi* is a popular text for writers of liturgical music, with over 2000 melodies.

Kabbalat Shabbat concludes with Psalm 92, a song for Shabbat, and Psalm 93, which affirms God's sovereignty. Psalm 92 was sung by the

Levi'im in the Temple on Shabbat, and Psalm 93 was recited on Fridays (*Tamid* 7:4). Although neither psalm appears in the earliest *siddurim*, Maimonides claims that their recitation on *erev* Shabbat is an ancient custom.

When Shabbat coincides with a festival or with one of the intermediate days of a festival, or if a festival is to begin on *Motza'ay Shabbat* (Saturday evening) as Shabbat ends, it is traditional to omit the first six psalms and *L'cha Dodi*, and to begin the service with Psalm 92. This change, which only occurs in the Ashkenazic tradition, reflects an attempt to refrain from overshadowing the festival. In the Sephardic tradition, the service begins with Psalm 29 and only the first two and last two stanzas of *L'cha Dodi* are sung.

While mourners remain at home during *shiva*, mourning is suspended on Shabbat, and mourners are encouraged to attend the synagogue. Since Shabbat is considered to begin officially with the completion of *L'cha Dodi*, it is a custom in some congregations for the mourners to enter the synagogue at this point of the service. As they enter, the leader, on behalf of the congregation, greets them with the words: "May God comfort you among the other mourners of Zion and Jerusalem." The *Beit HaMikdash* contained a special gate for mourners.

INSIGHTS FROM THE TRADITION

A. Medieval Jewish poets often used acrostics in their poetry. Rabbi Shlomo Halevi Alkabetz wrote *L'cha Dodi* so that the first letter of each verse (except the last) spells out his name (Shlomo Halevi). Another approach was to write each word, phrase, or verse so that they begin with the letters of the alphabet in order. Examples from the liturgy are *Ashrei, El Baruch*, which is part of the traditional *Yotzer*, and *Ashamnu* and *Al Cheit* from the Yom Kippur *Amidah*. The Tanach also contains acrostics, for example, Psalms 111, 112, and 119; Proverbs 31:10-31; Lamentations 1.

B. The first verse of *L'cha Dodi* reads, "*Shamor V'zachor B'dibur Echad*," reflecting the rabbinic

understanding that God said "*Shamor*," keep Shabbat (Deuteronomy 5:12) and "*Zachor*," remember Shabbat (Exodus 20:8) at the same time. This teaching attempts to explain why the *mitzvah* pertaining to Shabbat differs in the two versions of the Ten Commandments.

C. The theme of Shabbat as *kallah* is related to a *midrash* which states that each of the six weekdays has a partner: the first day has the second, the third has the fourth, and the fifth has the sixth. When Shabbat complained that it didn't have a partner, God responded, "The community of Israel is your partner" (*B'reishit Rabbah* 11:8). It was once a custom to chant Song of Songs prior to Shabbat, as if one were wooing the Sabbath bride with these ancient songs of love.

D. The Talmud cites Psalm 29 as the source of the tradition that the weekday *Amidah* contained eighteen *brachot* and the Shabbat *Amidah* seven *brachot*. These numbers correspond to the number of times God's name occurs in this psalm and to the number of times the phrase "voice of God" occurs, respectively (*Brachot* 28b-29a). This connection explains its place in Kabbalat Shabbat as a transition from the weekday to Shabbat, as well as the custom of standing when reciting it.

E. Jewish mystics added the prayer *Ana B'choach* following Psalm 29. Ascribed to the Talmudic sage Nechunya ben Hakanah, it contains forty-two words, the initial letters of which form the secret forty-two letter name of God, which was once used in place of YHVH (*Kiddushin* 71a). In addition, the initials of each verse form seven divine names corresponding to the seven voices of God in Psalm 29.

F. In some congregations it is customary during Kabbalat Shabbat to read all or part of the second chapter of *Mishnah Shabbat*, known by its opening words "*Bameh Madlikin*" (With what may we light?). First introduced into the service in ninth century Babylonia, it is usually read between Psalm 93 and the *Bar'chu*. However, it was originally read at the conclusion of the service, probably to lengthen it so that latecomers would be able to complete their prayers. This particular passage was likely chosen because of its primary theme of lighting candles to welcome the Shabbat. This practice was condemned by the Karaites, who interpreted literally the biblical command forbidding the kindling of a fire on Shabbat. Reciting this passage thus served to exclude the Karaites from worshiping with the rest of the Jewish community.

G. In some congregations Kabbalat Shabbat is led from the *bimah* where the Torah is read (rather than from the podium where prayers are usually conducted) to indicate that this part of the liturgy is not required. The prayer leader may not put on a *tallit* until after Kabbalat Shabbat for the same reason.

ACTIVITIES

TEXT AND CONTEXT

1. *L'cha Dodi* symbolizes Shabbat as bride and queen. Have each girl in turn dress up as a bride or queen. While dressed up, each student says how it feels to be a bride or queen. Boys can dress up as they would to greet a bride or queen, then welcome the bride or queen. Discuss (girls): How would it feel to be special — to be a bride or a queen? How does it feel to be welcomed in? Discuss (boys): How would it feel to be in the presence of royalty? How would they act in such a situation? Discuss (girls and boys): Why do we want feelings such as these to be part of Shabbat? (K-2)

2. Brainstorm a list of things that a person might do to prepare for Shabbat. Point out the contrast between the weekdays (noisy, active, busy) and Shabbat (peaceful, quiet, relaxed) and discuss how Kabbalat Shabbat helps make the transition. (K-8)

3. To help the students understand that Kabbalat Shabbat serves as an introduction to the evening Shabbat service, do the following activity. Bring a ball to class, gather the students, and announce, "Let's start the game." Throw the ball into the air and voice words of encouragement that the game should get started, without explaining what game to play. After a couple of minutes, stop playing and discuss: What happened? What was missing from the activity? How did it feel? Explain the need for preparation, direction, and structure before a group can play a game. Make the connection between preparation for a game and preparation for Shabbat. (3 and up)

4. Investigate how your congregation observes Kabbalat Shabbat. Begin by brainstorming questions as a class. Then divide into groups to examine the *siddur* and interview the rabbi and/or cantor. Pay attention to the issues raised in the Overview. Conclude the activity with each group reporting its findings to the class. (6 and up)

5. Teach your students the term *Shomer Shabbat*, which refers to someone who observes the traditional Shabbat *mitzvot*. Introduce the thirty-nine activities that are prohibited on Shabbat. These can be found in *Mishnah Shabbat* 7:2 or in *The First Jewish Catalog* by Siegel, Strassfeld, and Strassfeld, p. 105. Discuss the origin of these prohibited acts and how they have been expanded to include technological developments, such as electricity, the automobile, etc. If your students are *Shomrei Shabbat*, discuss how this observance affects their lives. If you teach in a liberal Jewish setting, consider inviting a guest speaker who is *Shomer Shabbat*. Expand this activity by asking the students to spend a Sabbath being *Shomer Shabbat*. Plan ahead with family involvement. Afterward, have students write a paper expressing their views about their experience. Students should share these with the class. (6 and up)

6. The second chapter of *Mishnah Shabbat* is traditionally read at Kabbalat Shabbat. Divide your students into seven groups and assign each group one of the sections to teach to the others by means of a short skit, song, or other creative expression. (Note: *Mishnah* 6 of this chapter, which says that women die in childbirth for transgressing certain *mitzvot*, needs to be handled particularly sensitively.) (9 and up)

7. Teach the students the traditional phrase with which worshipers greet mourners during Kabbalat Shabbat (see Overview). Explain the custom of suspending mourning during Shabbat. Resources: *The Jewish Way in Death and Mourning* by Lamm; *A Jewish Mourner's Handbook* by Isaacs and Olitzky. (9 and up)

ARTS

8. Create a large banner for Kabbalat Shabbat. Write Kabbalat Shabbat in Hebrew and English in large outline letters in the center of the banner. Using crayons or markers, students should decorate the banner with symbols of Shabbat, flowers, or other Jewish symbols. Display at a Shabbat dinner or worship service. (K-2)

9. Invite the Cantor or music specialist to teach the class a variety of melodies for *L'cha Dodi* and/or other songs whose words are from the Kabbalat Shabbat psalms: *"Adonai Oz," "Mizmor Shir L'Yom HaShabbat," "Yismechu HaShamayim," "Tzaddik Katamar,"* and *"Or Zaru'a."* Perform them at a Shabbat service. Resources: *The Complete Shireinu: 350 Fully Notated Jewish Songs* edited by Joel Eglash, pp. 4, 163, 226, 371, 379; *Sing Unto God* by Debbie Friedman (*"Yismechu"*); *Israel Folkdances* by Israel Yakovee (*"Tzaddik Katamar"*); *Shabbat Shalom* by Cindy Paley (*"Mizmor Shir"*); *Snapshots: The Best of Kol B'Seder Vol. 1* by Kol B'Seder (*"Or Zarua"*); *The First Album* by Beged Kefet (*"Yis-m'chu"*). (All grades)

10. Teach the class the dance *Tzaddik Katamar*. Be sure to point out that the text comes from Psalm 92. Discuss with the students the meaning of the phrase, *"Tzaddik Katamar Yifrach"* (The righteous one shall flourish like a palm tree). Resource: *Israeli Folkdances* by Israel Yakovee. A simplified version of this dance for grades K-2 can be found on *20 Israeli Folk Dances for Young Children, Part A*. (3 and up)

11. Select four *L'cha Dodi* melodies reflecting different cultures. Distribute a large white sheet of paper and crayons or chalk pastels to each student. Instruct the students to divide the paper into four parts, and as each melody is played, to create an abstract illustration reflecting the mood of that melody. After finishing the drawings, discuss the differences, and how each melody reflects the culture from which it originated. Resources: *Shaarei Shira: Gates of Song; In The Beginning* by Debbie Friedman; *Ki Sarita* by Bruce Benson; *Celebrate With Us: Shabbat, Chanukah, Passover* by Jewish Family Productions; *New Traditions 2* by Jon Simon; *Shabbat Shalom* by Cindy Paley. (6 and up)

BEYOND THE TEXT

12. Introduce the term "Kabbalat Shabbat" to the students. Read any of the following books to the class: *Mrs. Moskowitz and the Shabbat Candlesticks* by Schwartz, *Shabbat Can Be* by Zwerin and Marcus, or *Hurry, Friday's a Short Day* by Gold. Ask the students what they can do to prepare for Shabbat. (K-2)

13. Create a Shabbat corner in your classroom. This corner should include a small table, chairs, place settings, candle holders, candles, *challah* cover, broom, mop, dust cloth, etc. Individually or in groups, students can prepare for and celebrate Shabbat in this experiential play area. When the Shabbat corner is initially set up, discuss how the elaborate preparations for Shabbat help us to get in the mood for celebrating Shabbat. (K-2)

14. Teach the students the word "psalm." Ask: What word does it sound like? Explain that psalms were a type of ancient song often sung at the *Beit HaMikdash*. Turn to the Book of Psalms in a Tanach. Explain that psalms are not in the Torah, but are in another part of our Tanach. Read to the students Psalm 92:1-6. Discuss: Why is this psalm appropriate for Shabbat? What words or phrases would you use in a psalm for Shabbat? As a class or in small groups, have students compose a psalm for Shabbat. (3-5)

15. *"L'cha Dodi"* uses the metaphor of Shabbat as *kallah*. Sit in a circle and invite each student in turn to contribute a sentence that explains the metaphor. For example, the teacher might begin, "Just as a *kallah* is radiant, so too are the Shabbat candles. Just as a *kallah* wears white, so too does our Shabbat table wear a white cloth." You may wish to repeat the activity using the metaphor of Shabbat as *malkah*. (3-8)

16. In order for the students to understand the significance of Safed for the creation of Kabbalat Shabbat, view the video *Shalom of Safed*. Supplement the video with postcards or pictures of Safed. Discuss how the physical features of Safed might have influenced the creation of Kabbalat Shabbat. (3 and up)

17. Psalms comprise the bulk of Kabbalat Shabbat and are also used on a variety of other occasions. Prepare a presentation for a service or an open house about the role of psalms in Judaism. Assign each student one of the psalms. The student should briefly summarize its contents and explain when it is used in the Jewish tradition. Then each student should read the psalm. Begin the program with an introduction about the significance of psalms in Judaism, and include songs which are taken from the psalms. Resources: *Bringing the Psalms to Life: How to Understand and Use the Book of Psalms* by Polish; *Keeping Faith with the Psalms: Deepen Your Relationship with God Using the Book of Psalms* by Polish; *Encyclopaedia Judaica*, vol. 13, "Psalms, Book of," especially cols. 1323-1325, "In the Liturgy." (9 and up)

18. Mysticism is a difficult subject to teach, but is an important subject as it relates to Kabbalat Shabbat. To introduce mysticism, read the dialogue, "God Talk" by Joel Lurie Grishaver in Appendix A, pages 187-188. Discuss: According to the characters, what is mysticism? How does it differ from magic? What role does God play in mysticism? Have the students ever had a mystical experience? Other resources: *The Invisible Chariot: An Introduction to Kabbalah and Jewish Spirituality* by Kerdeman and Kushner; "Kabbalah" in *Encyclopaedia Judaica*, vol. 10, cols. 489-653. (9 and up)

HEBREW

19. Teach the students the word "*kallah*" (bride), which is in *L'cha Dodi*, and the word "*chatan*" (groom). Teach the song "*Od Yishama*," which contains these words. Resource: *The Complete Shireinu: 350 Fully Notated Jewish Songs*, edited by Joel Eglash. (K and up)

20. Ask the students who was the author of *L'cha Dodi*. Tell them the author hid his name in the text. If the students are still stumped, ask them to call out the first letter of each verse. Write them on the board. Explain the various traditions of using acrostics (see Insight A). Have the students create their own acrostics on the theme of Shabbat, using either their names, the alphabet, or a special word or phrase relating to Shabbat. (6 and up)

21. Compare the two versions of the Fourth Commandment (Exodus 20:8-11 and Deuteronomy 5:12-15) in the original Hebrew. Discuss the difference between keeping (*shamor*) Shabbat and remembering (*zachor*) Shabbat. How do the activities we do on Shabbat (lighting candles, saying *Kiddush*, going to synagogue, making Havdalah, etc.) reflect these two terms? (6 and up)

FAMILY

22. Help families plan their Kabbalat Shabbat observance at home. Set up learning stations that might include teaching the *brachot*, teaching Shabbat songs, baking *challah*, and discussing general preparations for Shabbat. After attending all the stations, each family sits together and plans its own Shabbat celebration.

23. Create a mural for *L'cha Dodi*. Assign each family one or two verses of *L'cha Dodi*. Direct each family to create a drawing that reflects the contents of the verse, which should be written in Hebrew and/or English under the drawing.

RESOURCES

BOOKS AND PERIODICALS

Eglash, Joel, ed. *The Complete Shireinu: 350 Fully Notated Jewish Songs*. New York: Transcontinental Music Publications, 2001.

Encyclopaedia Judaica. Jerusalem: Keter Publishing House Jerusalem Ltd., 1972.

Gold, Yeshara. *Hurry, Friday's a Short Day: One Boy's Erev Shabbat in Jerusalem's Old City*. Brooklyn, NY: Mesorah Publications, Ltd., 1986.

Isaacs, Ron H., and Kerry M. Olitzky. *A Jewish Mourner's Handbook*. Hoboken, NJ: Ktav Publishing House, Inc., 1991.

Kerdeman, Deborah, and Lawrence Kushner. *The Invisible Chariot: An Introduction to Kabbalah and Jewish Spirituality*. Denver: A.R.E. Publishing, Inc, 1986.

Lamm, Maurice. *The Jewish Way in Death and Mourning*. Revised and Expanded Edition. New York: Jonathan David Publishers, 2000.

Polish, Daniel F. *Bringing the Psalms to Life: How to Understand and Use the Book of Psalms*. Woodstock, VT: Jewish Lights Publishing, 2000.

_____. *Keeping Faith with the Psalms: Deepen Your Relationship with God Using the Book of Psalms*. Woodstock, VT: Jewish Lights Publishing, 2003.

Schwartz, Amy. *Mrs. Moskowitz and the Shabbat Candlesticks*. Philadelphia, PA: The Jewish Publication Society of America, 1983.

Shaarei Shira: Gates of Song. New York: Transcontinental Music Publications, 1987.

Siegel, Richard; Michael Strassfeld; and Sharon Strassfeld, eds. *The First Jewish Catalog*. Philadelphia, PA: The Jewish Publication Society of America, 1973

Zwerin, Raymond A. and Audrey Friedman Marcus. *Shabbat Can Be*. New York: UAHC Press, 1979.

AUDIOVISUAL

20 Israeli Folk Dances for Young Children, Part A. Adi Sulkin-Vardit Publications. Audiocassette.

Beged Kefet. *The First Album*. Livingston, NJ: Beged Kefet, 1987. Compact disc or audiocassete. Available from Sounds Write Productions, Inc.

Benson, Bruce. *Ki Sarita*. Oakland, CA: Bensongs. Compact disc or audiocassete. Available from Sounds Write Productions, Inc.

Celebrate With Us: Shabbat, Chanukah, Passover. San Diego, CA: Jewish Family Productions, 2003. Two compact disc set. Available from A.R.E. Publishing, Inc.

Friedman, Debbie. *In The Beginning*. San Diego, CA: Sounds Write Productions, Inc., 1994. Three compact disc set. Available from A.R.E. Publishing, Inc.

Israeli Folkdances. Israel Yakovee. Audiocassette.

Kol B'Seder. *Snapshots: The Best of Kol B'Seder Vol. 1*. West Roxbury, MA: Kol B'Seder, 2004. Compact disc. Available from A.R.E. Publishing, Inc.

Paley, Cindy. *Shabbat Shalom*. Sherman Oaks, CA: Cindy Paley Aboody, 1989. Compact disc or audiocassette/songbook set. Available from Sounds Write Productions, Inc.

Shalom of Safed. Teaneck, NJ: Ergo Media Inc., 1969. Videocassette, 30 minutes, unrated.

Simon, Jon. *New Traditions 2*. Bethesda, MD: Silver Lining Records. Compact disc. Available from Sounds Write Productions, Inc.

CHAPTER TWELVE:
TACHANUN, HALLEL, AND HOLIDAY LITURGY

OVERVIEW

TACHANUN

Tachanun is a group of penitential prayers which, as part of the weekday liturgy, follow the *Amidah* during Shacharit and Minchah. While these originated as personal prayers, and remained unstructured and optional for many centuries, they have now taken on a standard form and are included in Orthodox and Conservative *siddurim*. *Tachanun* is omitted from Reform and Reconstructionist *siddurim* in an effort to shorten the liturgy, although individual petitions can be made during silent prayer.

There are two versions of *Tachanun*, a long version recited Mondays and Thursdays, and a short version recited on the other weekdays. In the rabbinic period, Mondays and Thursdays were market days, when many people would gather in the city square. The Torah was read on these days, and therefore the service was of greater importance. People did not have to rush back to work, so the service could be longer. On Mondays and Thursdays, *Tachanun* commences with seven prayers of supplication, the first of which begins "*V'hu Rachum.*" While most of these prayers are of post-biblical origin, verses from Psalms and other biblical books are interspersed throughout them. This section ends with the *Sh'ma* (Deuteronomy 6:4).

The next part of *Tachanun* is a brief confessional which begins with II Samuel 24:14, in which King David speaks to the prophet Gad. After this verse is recited silently, the *shaliach tzibur* recites the following confessional: "Merciful and gracious One, I have sinned before you; *Adonai,* full of mercy, have mercy on me and receive my supplications." This section concludes with Psalms 6:2-11 (Psalm 25 in the Sephardic ritual), a series of short verses from a medieval penitential prayer, and a prayer for protection, *Shomeir Yisrael* (Guardian of Israel).

On Tuesday, Wednesday, Friday, and Sunday, *Tachanun* begins with II Samuel 24:14, continues with the brief confessional quoted above and Psalm 6, and concludes with *Shomeir Yisrael*.

Tachanun is not recited on days of a festive nature because its serious and at times sorrowful theme might interfere with the mood of the day. Among the days *Tachanun* is omitted are Shabbat, Pesach, Shavuot, Sukkot, Rosh HaShanah, Yom Kippur, Rosh Chodesh, Chanukah, Tu B'shvat, Purim, the entire month of Nisan, Yom HaAtzma'ut, Lag B'omer, and Yom Yerushalayim. It is also omitted if a bridegroom is present, or if either the father, *Sandek*, or *Mohel* who are to participate in a *Brit Milah* are present. (See Donin, *To Pray as a Jew*, pp. 207ff. for a complete list and explanation of when *Tachanun* is omitted.)

The traditional posture for reciting *Tachanun* is seated, bent over, with one's face resting on the left forearm (or the right forearm if *tefillin* are worn on the left arm).

HALLEL

The *Hallel*, sometimes referred to as the Egyptian *Hallel* because of its references to the Exodus from Egypt, consists of Psalms 113-118. It is said after the *Amidah* during the Shacharit service on Pesach, Shavuot, Sukkot, Chanukah,

Rosh Chodesh, and as part of the Pesach *Seder*. It is not, however, recited on Purim because the miracle occurred outside of the land of Israel and because the Jews did not achieve complete independence. In recent years, it has been recited on Yom HaAtzma'ut and Yom Yerushalayim as well.- *Hallel* is said standing, preceded by a short *brachah* indicating one is performing a *mitzvah* by reciting *Hallel*. The psalms which comprise *Hallel* praise God for all the wonderful things that God has done, particularly delivering the people from Egyptian bondage. *Hallel* concludes with a *brachah* on the theme of praising God.

COUNTING OF THE OMER

In the days of the *Beit HaMikdash*, a forty-nine day period during the grain harvest was observed by the waving of an *omer,* a measure of barley, by the officiating priest. This ceremony began the second day of Pesach and culminated with Shavuot, the Feast of Weeks, which occurs seven weeks after the second day of Pesach. (The word Shavuot means weeks.) Shavuot celebrates among other things the wheat harvest. Since the destruction of the *Beit HaMikdash,* the waving of the grain has ceased, but the counting of the days from Pesach to Shavuot has remained a part of the liturgy.

Counting the *omer* is usually done at the conclusion of Ma'ariv. It begins with a brief statement of intention, which includes Leviticus 23:15-16. The *brachah* for performing the *mitzvah* is recited followed by the counting of the day by the *shaliach tzibur* ("Today is the first day of the *omer,*" etc.). The ceremony concludes with a prayer for the restoration of the *Beit HaMikdash* and Psalm 67.

This ritual is observed in Orthodox and most Conservative congregations and in some Reform and Reconstructionist congregations.

PIYYUTIM

Beginning in the seventh century, the worship service was often embellished by adding religious poems known as *piyyutim*. These poems vary significantly in both style and content depending on when, where, and for what purpose they were written. While many *piyyutim*

are no longer a part of our liturgy, some are still included, especially on the High Holy Days. Many well-known songs were originally written as *piyyutim,* among them *"Adon Olam," "Yigdal," "Ein Keiloheinu,"* and *"L'cha Dodi."*

A sub-category of *piyyutim* are *Selichot,* penitential prayers. While many synagogues have a *Selichot* service on the Saturday evening preceding Rosh HaShanah (or two Saturdays before if Rosh HaShanah begins on Sunday evening), *Selichot* are traditionally said on fast days and at every service beginning the week before Rosh HaShanah and concluding with Yom Kippur.

Another collection of *piyyutim* are the *Hoshanot* prayers said during Sukkot as one circles the *bimah* with the *lulav* and *etrog,* a ritual which dates from the days of the *Beit HaMikdash.*

HIGH HOLY DAYS

On the High Holy Days, the basic daily prayer service is followed. There are, however, a number of important additions to the liturgy.

Avinu Malkeinu is a special supplication recited on Rosh HaShanah, Yom Kippur, the weekdays between, and, in an abbreviated form, on certain fast days. It is traditionally omitted on Shabbat because of its association with fast days and also because of its theme of supplication. However, many Reform congregations recite *Avinu Malkeinu* when Rosh HaShanah or Yom Kippur falls on Shabbat because of its strong identification with the holiday. Like *Tachanun,* it is recited after the *Amidah.* It is said standing before the open *Aron HaKodesh.*

Avinu Malkeinu consists of forty-four lines, each beginning with the words *Avinu Malkeinu* (Our Father our King). Some of the phrases are attributed to Rabbi Akiba (*Ta'anit* 25b), but the prayer was not composed by one person or at one specific time. In the *siddur* of Rav Amram (ninth century) *Avinu Malkeinu* contains twenty-five verses, but because of persecution, other verses were added over the centuries. Liberal *Machzorim* contain an edited version, including verses that pertain to the themes of the High Holy Days, but omitting verses which do not reflect modern sensibilities. For example, phrases which ask God to "annul the plans of our enemies" and "frustrate the counsel of our foes" are omitted.

While most of the phrases are petitions, asking God to do something for the people, the first two lines confess that we have sinned and proclaim that we have no ruler but God. Like many of the prayers of the High Holy Day liturgy, *Avinu Malkeinu* is written in the first person plural, recognizing our shared destiny as one community.

CONFESSIONALS

Since the days of the *Beit HaMikdash*, confession has characterized the Yom Kippur ritual. The short confessional begins with a prayer by the rabbinic sage Mar Samuel, followed by *Ashamnu*, an alphabetical list of sins. The long confessional follows, beginning with a prayer by the sage Rav, and continuing with *Al Cheit*, which is written in the form of a double acrostic. Each line begins "*Al Cheit Shechatanu Lifanecha B'* . . ." (On account of the sin we have sinned before you by . . .) and then lists a specific sin, the first two beginning with *aleph*, the next two with *bet*, etc. The sins reflect primarily ethical transgressions, many of them pertaining to speech (gossip, slander, etc.). After each group of sins, worshipers ask God to "forgive us, pardon us, grant us atonement."

The confessionals are said standing, at the end of the *Amidah*. Like *Avinu Malkeinu*, these prayers are written in the first person plural. They are said as a community, with everyone confessing to each and every sin, whether or not one may have committed any of them in the previous year.

SHOFAR SERVICE

The Rosh HaShanah Musaf *Amidah* includes the sounding of the shofar, introduced by significant liturgical material. Three substantial *brachot*, on the themes of *Malchuyot* (God's Sovereignty), *Zichronot* (Remembrances), and *Shofarot* (Shofar blasts heralding redemption), are included. Each begins with one or more prayers, continues with ten brief biblical verses: three from the Torah, three from the Prophets, three from the Writings, and one more from the Torah, and concludes with a final supplication. The opening prayer of the *Malchuyot* is the

Aleinu, which originated as part of this ritual, and only later became part of the daily liturgy (see Chapter 9). The shofar is also sounded during the Shacharit service, after *Kriat HaTorah*.

AVODAH

On Yom Kippur, the *Amidah* of the Musaf service contains a special section called the *Avodah*, which is a detailed description of the ritual at the *Beit HaMikdash* on the Day of Atonement. Although the prescribed ritual cannot be performed because of the destruction of the *Beit HaMikdash*, reading about the ritual was considered to be an effective substitute.

KOL NIDREI

Although technically *Kol Nidrei* is not a prayer, it is an important part of the Yom Kippur ritual. *Kol Nidrei* is a legal declaration proclaiming that all vows and obligations that can not be kept in the year ahead shall be null and void. It was inserted into the Yom Kippur liturgy in the Middle Ages when Jews were often forced to make vows against their will which they could not keep.

Kol Nidrei traditionally begins before sundown, as such a declaration cannot be made on the holiday itself. The *Sifrei Torah* are removed from the *Aron HaKodesh* and held before the congregation as everyone rises. The setting is reminiscent of a *Beit Din*, (a Jewish Court which consists of three rabbis), with the *Sifrei Torah* representing the rabbis. *Kol Nidrei* is traditionally chanted three times because such a declaration would be made three times before a *Beit Din*.

Kol Nidrei is recited in Aramaic. Although there was originally a Hebrew version, too, the common people preferred the Aramaic because it was the language they spoke in daily life. Its popularity also assured its continued place in the liturgy despite controversies. Some Christians have claimed that because of *Kol Nidrei*, one cannot trust the word of a Jew. In response to such a charge, it was at times removed from the *Machzor*. However, because of the people's strong attachment to its words and melody, it has always found its way back into the service.

BIRKAT KOHANIM

Another ritual of the *Beit HaMikdash* which has made its way into the liturgy is the *Birkat Kohanim*, the Priestly Benediction (Numbers 6:24-26). In the days of the *Beit HaMikdash*, the *Kohanim* would raise their hands during the morning and evening offerings and recite these verses from a platform, called a *duchen*. The term *duchenin* is still used to refer to this ritual.

Prior to *Birkat Kohanim*, the *Kohanim* go to another room, where the *Levi'im* pour water on their hands, symbolizing the ritual purification. The *Kohanim* then come before the *Aron HaKodesh*, face the congregation, and pull their *tallitot* over their heads. Their hands are outstretched, with spaces between the thumb and first finger and between the third and fourth fingers. The *Kohanim* repeat each word of the *brachah* after the reader.

This ritual is observed only during the Musaf *Amidah* on festivals in the Ashkenazic community outside of Israel. It is observed in Israel and in all Sephardic congregations daily during Shacharit, and on Shabbat and festivals during Musaf. Even if the ritual is not performed, the *brachah* is read by the *shaliach tzibur* during the repetition of the *Amidah*.

Because the Reform and Reconstructionist movements do not espouse the rebuilding of the *Beit HaMikdash* and do not recognize the special status of *Kohanim* and *Levi'im*, this ritual is not performed in these synagogues. It is also omitted in some Conservative congregations. However, the verses from Numbers are sometimes incorporated into the Shacharit service on holidays and are read by the *shaliach tzibur* at the appropriate place in the service.

INSIGHTS FROM THE TRADITION

A. Abraham Millgram describes the prayers which make up *Tachanun* thusly: "They speak repeatedly of Israel's unending suffering, which, they say, are a just retribution for Israel's unfaithfulness to the covenant. Nonetheless, they plead for God's forgiveness. Underlying all these pleas is the abiding faith that the 'living and everlasting God' will not forsake His people." (*Jewish Worship*, p. 462)

B. Rabbi Hayim Halevy Donin offers this comment about the omission of *Tachanun* on certain occasions relating to the life cycle of a member of the community. "Nowhere else in religious worship do we find such a striking example of how the entire congregation is made to share the joy or sorrow of the individual. The rules that govern the omission of *Tachanun* from the services are an expression of the Jewish community's concern with and responsibility for the individual. No Jew is ever alone. He is always part of an extended family that shares his sorrow and his joy." (*To Pray as a Jew*, pp. 208-209)

C. A number of lines of *Avinu Malkeinu* were instituted in response to the massacres of Jews and the destruction of Jewish communities which occurred in fourteenth century Europe. This was a reaction to the Black Death for which the Jews were blamed. One line asks God to have compassion upon us for the sake of those who died *Al Kiddush HaShem* — as martyrs.

D. Commenting on the *Ashamnu*, Macy Nulman has written, "The alphabetical form impresses upon us that our sins have their source in our neglect of the entire Torah that was formed with the twenty-two sacred letters" (*The Encyclopedia of Jewish Prayer*, p. 38).

E. Rabbi Samson Raphael Hirsch says about *Hallel*: "Hallel is the Jewish song of jubilation that has accompanied our wanderings of thousands of years, keeping awake within us the consciousness of our world-historical mission, strengthening us in times of sorrow and suffering, and filling our mouths with song of rejoicing in days of deliverance and triumph. To this day, it revives on each Festival season the memory of Divine redemption, and our confidence in future greatness." (Hertz, *The Authorised Daily Prayer Book*, p. 756)

F. Reciting *Hallel* is an example of a *mitzvah* not explicitly found in the Torah. Nevertheless, we precede it with a blessing which says that God commands us to do it. Other examples of such *mitzvot* are washing of hands and lighting Chanukah candles. These *mitzvot* are based on Deuteronomy 17:11 which states: "according to the law which they shall teach you, you shall do." "They" is understood to be the rabbinic authorities.

G. Judaism's sensitivity to the suffering of Israel's enemies is demonstrated by the shortening of *Hallel* on the last six days of Pesach and on Rosh Chodesh. The "Half *Hallel*" as it is sometimes called, omits the first eleven verses of both Psalm 115 and Psalm 116. "Because Egyptians suffered in the process of our deliverance, the sages decreed that *Hallel* be shortened to symbolize the lessening of the festival joy" (*Yalkut Shimoni* 247). (See *To Pray as a Jew* by Donin, p. 266).

H. Maimonides explains the significance of the counting of the *omer* thusly: "Just as one who awaits a most intimate friend on a certain day, counts in ardent expectation the days and even the hours till his coming, so we count the days from the anniversary of our departure from Egypt till the Festival of the Giving of the Torah. For the latter was the aim and object of the exodus from Egypt." (Hertz, *The Authorised Daily Prayer Book*, p. 938)

I. According to *Targum Onkelos*, the *Birkat Kohanim* offers a person a blessing in three distinct areas of life. "May God bless you and protect you" is a blessing for success in work and protection from danger. "May God's countenance shine upon you and be gracious to you" refers to learning through Torah study. "May God's countenance be lifted upon you and may God grant you peace" asks that God listen to our prayers.

ACTIVITIES

TEXT AND CONTEXT

1. Ask the students when they have had to say "I'm sorry." Was it difficult or easy? Why is it important to say "I'm sorry?" How do they feel when someone says "I'm sorry" to them? How do they feel after saying "I'm sorry" to someone else?

Explain that there are prayers which help us say "I'm sorry." These include: *Al Cheit*, *Tachanun*, and *Avinu Malkeinu*. Give examples from one of these prayers to show how it helps us say "I'm sorry." (K-2)

2. Read through the *Al Cheit* prayer from a High Holy Day Machzor and ask each student to identify one thing that is particularly meaningful. Students may share why it is meaningful. A children's version of the *Al Cheit* can be found in *Gates of Repentance for Young People* edited by Abrams and Citrin, p. 43. (3-5)

3. The teacher chooses a posture that expresses an emotion. After assuming this posture, ask students to identify the emotion. Have students volunteer to express emotions through posture, with other students guessing what emotion is represented. Introduce *Tachanun*, explaining what it is. Then read through it with the students and show them the posture one traditionally assumes while reciting it. (For a picture of this posture, see *To Pray as a Jew* by Donin, p. 204.) Ask students how posture reflects the words of prayer. (3-5)

4. The shofar blasts are often compared to a wake-up call, a call to action, or a nudge to change our behavior. With your students read through, examine, and discuss the three significant *brachot* (*Malchuyot*, *Zichronot*, and *Shofarot*) of the Rosh HaShanah Musaf *Amidah*. Each student should have a *Machzor* to facilitate the conversation. Focus the discussion on the ten biblical verses included with each of these *brachot*. What do these verses call us to do? How do the shofar blasts punctuate the conclusion (with a question mark or an exclamation point)? How can the reading of these verses affect our behaviors, attitudes, and approaches to Judaism? (6 and up)

5. Divide students into small groups and assign each group to one of the prayers from this chapter. Students are to create a Fact File about their prayer. The students use primary and secondary sources to gather information about the prayer. Students compile the information into a one-page fact sheet. These might be displayed on a bulletin board or put together to form a booklet. (6-8)

6. Arrange for students to attend a service at which *Birkat HaKohanim* is included or invite someone to class to describe the ritual. Discuss whether this ritual has a place in contemporary Judaism. Resources: "In Praise of Birkhat Kohanim" by Gillman in *"Sh'ma: A Journal of Jewish Responsibility,"* 22/436 September 4, 1992; *To Pray as a Jew* by Donin, pp. 132-137; *The Encyclopedia of Jewish Prayer* by Nulman, pp. 109-112.

7. Provide students with a copy of the *Al Cheit* prayer. Read through it, explaining that it is recited as a communal confession of sins. Discuss: How do Jews confess? What does it mean to share in the guilt? Why should we confess to sins we did not commit? Why, if we are innocent, should we confess with the guilty? Why share responsibility? (9 and up)

ARTS

8. Make an *omer* calendar. The calendar needs to contain forty-nine spaces, numbered sequentially. Students should decorate the spaces, with special designs for Shabbat, Lag B'omer, and other important occasions during this time period. (K-5)

9. Make a crayon and water resist painting that illustrates one of the occasions on which *Hallel* is recited (see Overview). Each student or group of students draws a different occasion. To make a crayon and water resist painting, first create a crayon drawing on watercolor paper. Then, making sure spaces have been left without crayoning, paint watercolors over the entire painting. Try different colors painted on in bands horizontally or vertically. Remind the students not to blend the watercolors as they will make the picture muddy.

10. Design a CD cover for an album featuring a *Hallel* concert. Read through and discuss the themes, ideas, and mood of *Hallel*. Using the medium of their choice (e.g., paint, oil, pastels, or colored markers), students create their own interpretation. Purchase empty CD cases for the

students to display their completed designs. (3-5)

11. To extend Activity #9 or #10, create a display gallery and invite parents, or display for the congregation the next time *Hallel* is a part of the service. (K-5)

12. Learn to sing one or more of the psalms from *Hallel*, utilizing the cantor or music specialist if you have one. Resources: *A Passover Haggadah: The New Union Haggadah*, p. 107-109; "B'tzeit Yisrael" and "Hodu" on *In The Beginning* by Debbie Friedman; "Hallelu" on *Or Shalom* by Shir Hadash; "Halleluyah" and "B'tzeyt Yisrael" on *A Singing Seder* by Cindy Paley. (3-8)

13. Extend Activity #10 by taking the melody of a popular song and create a song of praise with new lyrics which could be part of a modern *Hallel*. You may wish to look at some of the psalms of *Hallel* before creating your song. (3-8)

14. Utilizing the interpretation of *Birkat HaKohanim* offered in *Targum Onkelos* (see Insight I), design a triptych. A triptych is a set of three panels, either hinged or folded, with pictures or designs arranged so that the two side panels may be folded over the central one. Each panel should reflect one of the phrases from *Birkat HaKohanim*. (6-8)

15. Compare the lyrics of "Sabbath Prayer" with the content of *Birkat HaKohanim*. Discuss: What are the meaning and message found in "Sabbath Prayer" and *Birkat HaKohanim*? Resource: *Fiddler on the Roof* soundtrack. (6 and up)

16. Explain to your students the significance of the *Hoshanot* prayers. With the students, create a modern dance interpretation of the *Hoshanot*. (9 and up)

17. Many of the songs we sing on Shabbat were originally *piyyutim*. Learn to sing at least one version of the following: "Adon Olam," "Yigdal," "Ein Keiloheinu," "L'cha Dodi." Present a musical Shabbat with students singing these songs as part of the service. Resources: *In The Beginning* by Debbie Friedman; *And You Shall Teach Your*

Children by Shir Hadash; *Gates of Song: Music for Shabbat.* (9 and up)

BEYOND THE TEXT

18. Ask the students if they can think of any songs that are sung for special occasions, such as "Happy Birthday," or "The Star Spangled Banner" at the beginning of a baseball game. Explain to the students that we have special songs for special occasions in Judaism. An example is *Hallel*, which is sung on holidays. Summarize for the students the significance of *Hallel* using the material in the Overview. (K-2)

19. Bring a variety of musical instruments to class, including a shofar. Compare their shapes and the sounds they make. Allow students to try to get sounds from them. Discuss how the sounds make the students feel. Resources: "The Announcing Tool," a story in *Does God Have a Big Toe?* by Gellman, pp. 85-88. (K-5)

20. Explain to the students that there are special poems called *piyyutim* that are sometimes read during a service. Choose a holiday and, as a class, create a poem about it. First, discuss the holiday and brainstorm ideas for the poem, and then write it together. Recite it as a class as part of a worship service or at an assembly. (K-5)

21. Prepare brief descriptions of skits that involve misunderstandings or the committing of a wrongdoing taken from the *Al Cheit* prayer. Divide students into groups and give one description to each group. Present each skit to the whole class. After each skit, the class discusses how the situation might be resolved. (6-8)

22. Read with the students some of the High Holy Day prayers, such as *Avinu Malkeinu* or *Al Cheit*. Discuss with the students the themes reflected in the liturgy, particularly the concept of committing sins and asking forgiveness for what we have done wrong. An important part of this process is taking a personal inventory, which begins with reflection on one's own behavior. Direct students to write a letter to themselves,

noting what they have done during the past year that they want to change or not repeat during the year ahead. Each student puts the letter in an envelope, seals it, and writes his/her address on it. Teacher collects these and mails them later in the year as a reminder. (6 and up)

23. According to the Overview, some of the phrases of *Avinu Malkeinu* are attributed to Rabbi Akiba. Direct students to research this famous rabbi to find information about his life and important quotations and teachings. Among the resources to use: *Pirke Avot* (which is found in many *siddurim*); *Pass the Torah, Please* by Silver; *Encyclopaedia Judaica*; *The Book of Legends: Sefer Ha-Aggadah* by Bialik and Ravnitzky; *The Legends of the Jews* by Ginzburg; and books of Jewish quotations. Students should share the material they find. Then discuss what might have influenced Rabbi Akiba to write some of the phrases of *Avinu Malkeinu*. (7 and up)

24. In recent years, *Hallel* has been recited on Yom HaAtzma'ut and Yom Yerushalayim. With your students create an appropriate celebration for one of these occasions. Select songs about Israel or Jerusalem, readings from the Tanach, Talmud, and other Jewish literature, and selections from *Hallel*. You may wish to encourage the students to write poetry or prose for the service. Present the service to the school or congregation. (7 and up)

HEBREW

25. Counting the *omer* provides an excellent opportunity to teach or reinforce Hebrew numbers. Teach the students the numbers one through fifty, with emphasis on reciting them aloud and reading them with understanding. Use one or more of the following number games to help learn them: Students count in turn, but every multiple of five (or another number) say "*Omer*" instead of the number; count by twos or threes; *Bingo*. (3-8)

26. Many of the prayers of the High Holy Day liturgy are written in the first person plural, such as *Avinu Malkeinu* or *Al Cheit*. Use these prayers to teach or review the suffix *"nu"* which means our, we, or us. Distribute a *Machzor* to each student and direct each to turn to *Avinu Malkeinu* (or another prayer). Ask the class to identify all of the words that have this ending. Try to translate each of the words with this ending. Conclude by discussing why many of the prayers are written in the first person plural. (6-8)

27. Compare the vocabulary of *Kol Nidrei* with *Kaddish Yatom.* Compile a list of commonly used Aramaic terms and create a glossary. (6 and up)

FAMILY

28. Hold a workshop for families to develop *Selichot* rituals to be held in the home before Rosh HaShanah. Begin by discussing the tradition of *Selichot* and the need for preparation for the High Holy Days. Among the other activities to include are teaching simple songs from the liturgy; sharing prayers and appropriate readings or stories; taking an opportunity to apologize to each other for behavior during the past year; setting goals as a family for the coming year. If someone in the family can blow the shofar, suggest that this practice might also be included. Resource: *Selichot: A Family Service* by Abrams.

RESOURCES

BOOKS AND PERIODICALS

Abrams, Judith Z. *Selichot: A Family Service.* Rockville, MD: Kar-Ben Copies, Inc., 1990.

Abrams, Judith Z. and Paul J. Citrin, eds. *Gates of Repentance for Young People.* New York: Central Conference of American Rabbis, 2002.

Bialik, Hayim Nahman, and Yehoshua Hana Ravnitzky, eds. *The Book of Legends: Sefer Ha-Aggadah.* New York: Schocken Books, 1992.

Bronstein, Herbert, ed. *A Passover Haggadah: The New Union Haggadah.* New York: Central Conference of American Rabbis, 1974.

Donin, Rabbi Hayim Halevy. *To Pray as a Jew: A Guide to the Prayer Book and the Synagogue Service.* New York: Basic Books, Inc., 1991.

Encyclopaedia Judaica. Jerusalem: Keter Publishing House Jerusalem Ltd., 1972.

Gates of Song: Music for Shabbat. New York: Transcontinental Music Publications, 1987.

Gellman, Marc. *Does God Have a Big Toe? Stories About Stories in the Bible.* New York: Harper-Collins, 1993.

Ginzburg, Louis, ed. *The Legends of the Jews.* Philadelphia, PA: Jewish Publication Society of America, 2002.

Hertz, Joseph H. *The Authorised Daily Prayer Book,* Revised Edition. New York: Bloch Publishing Company, 1975.

Hoffman, Lawrence A., ed. *Gates of Understanding 2: Appreciating the Days of Awe.* New York: Central Conference of American Rabbis, 1984.

———, ed. *Tachanun and Concluding Prayers.* Woodstock, VT: Jewish Lights Publishing, 2002.

Millgram, Abraham. *Jewish Worship.* Philadelphia, PA: The Jewish Publication Society of America, 1971.

Nulman, Macy. *The Encyclopedia of Jewish Prayer: Ashkenazic and Sephardic Rites.* Northvale, NJ: Jason Aronson Inc., 1995.

Sh'ma: A Journal of Jewish Responsibility. 22/436 September 4, 1992.

Silver, Cherie Ellowitz. *Pass the Torah, Please: Jewish Leaders from Mattathias to Saadia.* Denver, CO: A.R.E. Publishing, Inc., 1990.

AUDIOVISUAL

Fiddler on the Roof. RCA Cassette #OK-1005; CD #RCDI-7060.

Friedman, Debbie. *In The Beginning.* San Diego, CA: Sounds Write Productions, Inc., 1994. Three compact disc set. Available from A.R.E. Publishing, Inc.

Paley, Cindy. *A Singing Seder.* Sherman Oaks, CA: Cindy Paley Aboody. Compact disc. Available from Sounds Write Productions, Inc.

Shir Hadash. *And You Shall Teach Your Children.* Vancouver, BC: Shir Hadash, 1990. Compact disc and audiocassette. Available from Sounds Write Productions, Inc.

———. *Or Shalom.* Vancouver, BC: Shir Hadash, 1987. Compact disc and audiocassette. Available from Sounds Write Productions, Inc.

CHAPTER THIRTEEN:
SYNAGOGUE

OVERVIEW

HISTORY

The origins of the synagogue (*Beit Knesset*) are uncertain. According to Abraham Millgram, "the synagogue had its origins in spontaneous informal gatherings among the Jewish exiles in Babylonia" (*Jewish Worship*, p. 64). Virtually all historians agree that the institution emerged during the Babylonian exile; some consider the references to the assembly of the elders before Ezekiel (Ezekiel 8:6, 14:1, 20:1) or to the "small sanctuary" (Ezekiel 11:16) as reflections of its beginnings. There are a few historians who maintain that the synagogue came into existence during the days of the Maccabees in the second century B.C.E.

The first explicit evidence of the existence of a synagogue comes from an inscription on a marble slab discovered near Alexandria, Egypt which states that the Jews dedicated a synagogue to Ptolemy III Euergetes, who reigned from 246-221 B.C.E., and to his queen Bernice.

By the first century C.E., a variety of literary sources indicate that the synagogue was a well established, important religious institution in the land of Israel, as well as in the Diaspora. Archeological discoveries have confirmed the existence of synagogues in first century Palestine. Ironically, the earliest literary source attesting to a great number of synagogues in the Diaspora is Acts of the Apostles from the Christian scriptures.

According to the Babylonian Talmud, 394 synagogues existed before the destruction of the Temple in 70 C.E. (*Ketubot* 105a). The Jerusalem Talmud gives the number as 480 (*Megillah* 3:1). Although these figures may be exaggerations, the synagogue was clearly an important institution while the *Beit HaMikdash* still functioned.

After the destruction of the *Beit HaMikdash*, the synagogue became the focus of Jewish religious life, adapting certain of its rituals and terminology, while eschewing others that were considered only appropriate for the *Beit HaMikdash*. For most of subsequent Jewish history, the synagogue was not only a place of worship, but also of study and communal activities.

During the Middle Ages, virtually every area of a Jew's daily life was reflected in the life of the synagogue. In modern times, the synagogue continues to be the most important religious institution of Judaism.

ARCHITECTURE

While the synagogue has been a fixture in virtually every Jewish community since the first century, no distinct, universal style of architecture developed. In fact, synagogues often reflect the architectural characteristics of their host culture. For example, medieval German synagogues reflected contemporaneous church architecture. Many Sephardic synagogues borrowed from Spanish Moorish architectural styles.

The Talmud contains a few guidelines for the synagogue. It should be the tallest building; a city with roofs higher than the synagogue will be destroyed (*Shabbat* 11a). However, Jews could not always fulfill this teaching due to hostility toward them from the non-Jewish community and its leaders.

The Talmud also stipulates that a synagogue

have windows. This tradition is based upon the story of Daniel, "in whose upper chamber he had windows made facing Jerusalem, and three times a day he knelt down, prayed, and made confession to his God" (Daniel 6:11). Later Jewish law states a synagogue should have twelve windows.

This passage also may be the source of the tradition of facing Jerusalem when one prays. Synagogues are designed so that worshipers, when they are facing the *Aron HaKodesh*, are facing Jerusalem. In North America and Europe, synagogues therefore face east. In Israel they face Jerusalem and in Jerusalem they face the Temple Mount.

There are two basic layouts of synagogues. In Sephardic and most Orthodox congregations, the *bimah*, the raised platform from which the Torah is read, is in the center of the room, with seating around it. The Torah is read on the *bimah* facing the *Aron HaKodesh*. The central place of the *bimah* in the synagogue emphasized the centrality of the Torah in Judaism. The reader faces the *Aron HaKodesh*, i.e., toward Jerusalem.

In most Reform, Conservative, and Reconstructionist synagogues, the term *bimah* refers to the entire raised area at the front of the room; pews or chairs face the front. The Torah is read from a reading desk on the *bimah*, facing the congregation. This layout reflects church architecture. The prayer leader now faces the congregation, which changes this role from being one of the community to being a separate religious functionary.

Another architectural feature of most Orthodox synagogues is the women's gallery. In the back or in a balcony, this area is usually separated from the rest of the synagogue by a divider (a screen, a wall, a curtain) called a *mechitzah*. The primary purpose of the separation of the sexes during worship is to eliminate inappropriate contact between men and women and reduce distractions. In some Orthodox synagogues, men and women sit separately without a *mechitzah*. Reform, Conservative, Reconstructionist, and some Traditional synagogues allow mixed seating.

RITUAL OBJECTS

At the front of every synagogue is the *Aron HaKodesh*. Just as the tablets of the Ten Com-

mandments were placed in the Ark of the Covenant in the wilderness, our *Sifrei Torah* (Torah scrolls) are kept in the *Aron HaKodesh*. In some Sephardic synagogues, one can actually walk into the Ark, which is called the *Heichal*. The Torah scrolls are kept in niches in the wall.

These scrolls are handwritten on parchment and contain the first five books of the Bible. The parchment is attached at each end to a wooden roller called an *Eitz Chayim*, a tree of life (plural, *Atzei Chayim*). The Torah itself is often called an *Eitz Chayim*, based on Proverbs 3:18, a passage often sung when returning the *Sefer Torah* to the *Aron HaKodesh*.

An *Aron HaKodesh* will often have a curtain, called a *parochet*, which originally referred to the curtain which screened off the Ark of the Covenant in the Tabernacle (Exodus 40:21).

In some Sephardic traditions, the *Sifrei Torah* are enclosed in round wooden cases, often elaborately decorated. In the Ashkenazic tradition, the scroll is dressed with a variety of items, reminiscent of the garments worn by the priests of the Tabernacle (Exodus 28).

The scroll is bound by a belt (*avneit*) or a long piece of cloth called a wimple. A mantle (*m'eel*) is placed over the scroll. A breastplate (*choshen*) hangs from the *Atzei Chayim*. Its original purpose was to indicate which scroll was to be used for a specific reading on occasions when more than one selection is read. Breastplates are often elaborately decorated with Jewish symbols including lions of Judah, crowns, Ten Commandments, and trees. The breastplate is also a reminder of another aspect of priestly garb. Hanging from one *Eitz Chayim* is a *yad* (pointer), used to keep one's place while reading from the Torah and to protect the writing from being smudged with use.

The *Atzei Chayim* themselves are covered by a *keter* (crown) or by two finials called *rimonim* (pomegranates), so named because they resemble that fruit. The *keter* or *rimonim* are reminiscent of the head covering worn by the high priest in the Tabernacle and in the *Beit HaMikdash*.

The *keter* or *rimonim* and often the breastplate contain bells, which serve to announce that the Torah is approaching, so that worshipers can pay due respect. It is traditional to touch the Torah with a corner of one's *tallit* or *siddur*, and then to kiss the *tallit* or *siddur*, reflecting one's love for Torah. Furthermore, one should never turn one's back on the Torah. During a *hakafah*, when the Torah is paraded through the congregation, worshipers turn to follow its movement around the room.

Torah ornaments are traditionally silver rather than gold, so as not to bring to mind the sin of the golden calf.

Besides the *Aron HaKodesh* containing the Torah scrolls, the other universal fixture in the synagogue is the *Ner Tamid* (the Eternal Light). Usually a lamp hanging in front of the *Aron HaKodesh*, the *Ner Tamid* symbolizes the branch of the Temple *menorah* which was always left burning as a reminder of God's eternal presence. Despite the prohibition against making an exact replica of the *menorah* which stood in the Temple (*Avodah Zara* 43b), many synagogues have in their sanctuary a seven branched *menorah* made in any of a variety of sizes, shapes, and materials. Often the light of the middle branch is replaced by a *Magen David* (Star of David) to emphasize its difference from the *menorah* of biblical times. Some synagogues also contain other hanging Shabbat lamps.

Most synagogues will have the Ten Commandments prominently displayed, either above the *Aron HaKodesh* or on one of the walls.

Some liberal synagogues contain two candlesticks for kindling the Shabbat and festival candles. While this ritual is traditionally associated with the home, it is sometimes incorporated at the beginning of the evening service so that everyone can experience it.

Yahrzeit plaques containing the names and dates of death of those who have passed away are on the walls of some synagogues, sometimes inside the sanctuary, sometimes outside. In some instances, there are lights by the names which are lit on the anniversary (*yahrzeit*) of the death and on Yizkor (a special memorial service held on Pesach, Shavuot, Yom Kippur, and Shemini Atzeret).

INSIGHTS FROM THE TRADITION

A. While the English words "temple" and "synagogue" are sometimes used interchangeably, there is an important distinction in their origin. The Temple refers to the First Temple and/or the Second Temple which stood in Jerusalem. Throughout most of Jewish history, the word synagogue (or its equivalent) referred to institutions where Jews gathered to pray and often also to study.

In modern times, most Reform congregations have incorporated the word Temple into their names, reflecting the view that the Temple in Jerusalem will not be rebuilt and that the current houses of worship have fully taken its place.

B. The sanctity of the ritual objects of the synagogue is reflected not only in how they are treated when they are usable, but also how they are treated when they can no longer be used. The general principle is to ascend in matters of sanctity. A *Sefer Torah*, considered the holiest object, cannot be sold to purchase a synagogue or other ritual objects, but may be sold to ransom captives and therefore fulfill the important *mitzvah* of saving a life. An *Aron HaKodesh*, because it contains the *Sifrei Torah*, is next in sanctity. It may be sold to purchase a Torah, but not to buy a synagogue or other item. (*Megillah* 26a)

When a *Sefer Torah*, a *siddur*, or other ritual object can no longer be used, it is not simply discarded, but is placed in a special storeroom called a *genizah*. Ultimately, such objects are buried in a Jewish cemetery.

C. According to Rav Avraham Kook, the requirement for a synagogue to have windows comes to teach us that when we pray, we must be aware of the world around us.

D. The absence of any representation of a human figure, and a general reluctance to decorate the synagogue with other figures, is a result of a strict interpretation of the second commandment: "You shall not make for yourself a sculpted image, or any likeness of what is in heaven above, or on the earth below, or in the waters of the earth" (Exodus 20:4). This concern is often in tension with the concept of *Chidur Mitzvah*, the beautification of objects used in performing a *mitzvah*. In recent years, many Jewish artists have created elaborate ritual objects for the synagogue. It is forbidden to decorate the *Sefer Torah* itself (although scrolls of Esther are often elaborately illustrated because that book does not contain God's name).

E. In some communities it was traditional to make a wimple from the fabric which swaddled an infant at the *Brit Milah* (circumcision). The wimple often contained the infant's name, date of birth, and the prayer " . . . that as he entered the covenant, so may he be brought to the study of Torah, to be married under the *chupah* (wedding canopy), and do good deeds." The wimple would be wound around the Torah for important occasions during the child's life, such as his becoming a Bar Mitzvah and the *aufruf* prior to his wedding.

F. The origin of separate seating for men and women during prayer may derive from a story in the Talmud about a celebration at the *Beit HaMikdash* of *Beit HaShoeivah* (water drawing). While the men were kept out of the Court of the Women where this ceremony took place, the four gates were opened so that the men could see the festive ceremony. One year, the men entered the women's section, leading to some improper behavior. To prevent a recurrence, the authorities decreed that a balcony be built for the women, while the men were allowed to occupy the main area. (*Sukkot* 51b)

G. In her book *Women Leaders in the Ancient Synagogue: Inscriptional Evidence and Background Issues*, Bernadette Brooten has written about nineteen Greek and Latin inscriptions from the first century B.C.E. through the sixth century C.E. "that refer to women as 'president of the synagogue,' 'leader,' 'elder,' 'mother of the synagogue,' and 'priestess'" (Plaskow, *Standing Again at Sinai*, p. 44). She concludes that these were more than honorary titles, and that they indicate that at least some women held leadership roles in the early years of the synagogue.

ACTIVITIES

TEXT AND CONTEXT

1. Introduce the students to the synagogue utilizing one or more of the folders *Let's Discover the Synagogue* by Adam Siegel and Ruby G. Strauss. Take the class to the synagogue and identify the objects that they learned about in the folders. (K-2)

2. With the class present, undress a *Sefer Torah*, identifying each item as it is removed from the Torah. Place the items on a table. Cover the items with a cloth and ask the students to close their eyes. Remove one object from the table. Have the students open their eyes and guess which item is missing. Repeat until the students are able to identify all the objects. (K-2)

3. Make up a lotto game that has picture images of the ritual objects found in a synagogue. Each student receives a lotto card with the same objects, but in different locations on the card. Play proceeds like Bingo, but the teacher calls the names of objects, rather than numbers. First student to complete a row wins, and must name each object. (K-2)

4. View the video *For Out of Zion: The Torah*. This film introduces the students to Torah and its importance in Judaism, with emphasis placed on the making of a Torah. (3 and up)

5. Choose one student at a time to assume the role of a ritual object. The other students ask questions that can be answered "yes" or "no," and then try to guess which object the student represents. (3-8)

6. Train your students to be docents for a tour of the synagogue. First take your class to the synagogue and identify and list each ritual object that will need to be explained. Each student is responsible for researching and writing a few paragraphs about one or more of the items. First, give a tour to each other. Then invite parents, church groups, younger classes, or others for a tour of the synagogue. (6 and up)

7. Create a crossword puzzle or word search using ritual objects of the synagogue. For older students, have the students make up their own crossword puzzle or word search. (6 and up)

ARTS

8. Listen and learn the songs *"Bimah"* by Jeff Klepper and Susan Nanus (*Especially Jewish Symbols)* and/or "To Be a Torah" by Rabbi Joe Black (*Aleph Bet Boogie*). (K-2)

9. Ask your students to imagine what it would be like to be a Torah. Discuss some of the things the Torah might say about what it is wearing, how it is carried, lifted, and read. Each student then dictates to an older student a story about what it is like to be a Torah. Students may wish to illustrate their stories. (K-2)

10. Take your class to the synagogue and have the students sit in the seats. Turn off or dim the lights and ask the students to imagine that it is the middle of the night and suddenly the ritual objects come alive. Begin telling a story such as: "One evening the *Sefer Torah* jumped out of the *Aron HaKodesh* and began shouting: 'I'm lost, I'm lost!' The *Ner Tamid* was frightened. 'Where are you going?' the *Ner Tamid* asked the Torah." Point to one of the students who continues the story and then points to another student. Continue until each student has had a chance to add to the story. Encourage students to include all of the ritual objects of the synagogue. (3-8)

11. Create with your students a dollhouse-sized synagogue. Brainstorm all the elements needed to make an accurate synagogue. Refresh everyone's memory by taking a walking tour of your synagogue. Begin by making the exterior of the little synagogue, using a large cardboard carton or lightweight wood box. Make the synagogue furnishings from inexpensive supplies, such as small boxes, fabric, foil, modeling clay, polymer clay, paint, pre-made doll house furnishings, etc. Use your imagination! (3-8)

12. Make models of the *Ner Tamid* with your students. You will need the following supplies: a large tin can for each student, nails, hammers, small votive candles. Clean and fill the cans about three quarters full with water. Freeze until solid. Students make a design on the cans using permanent markers. With the hammers and nails, students hammer holes along the design lines. After the ice melts, dry the inside of the can and place a candle at the bottom. Be careful of sharp edges. (6-8)

13. In some synagogues, the *Aron HaKodesh* includes a special curtain called a *parochet*. As a class, create a *parochet* for the *Aron HaKodesh* in your synagogue. Take the measurements and purchase appropriate fabric. Create a design using applique, embroidery, or fabric paint, or a combination of these media. For design ideas, consult a Judaica artist or one of the following sources: *Jewish Folk Art from Biblical Days to Modern Times* by Ungerleider-Mayerson; *Jewish Ceremonial Art and Religious Observance* by Kanof; *Jewish Art and Civilization* edited by Wigoder. (9 and up)

14. In small groups, direct the students to design their own synagogue sanctuary. Consider inviting an architect or interior designer to explain some of the issues that need to be considered when designing such a space. Students should also look at pictures of synagogues for ideas. Designs can either be two-dimensional or three-dimensional. Display the results at an appropriate occasion. Resources: *The Synagogue* by de Breffny; *The Story of the Synagogue: A Diaspora Museum Book* by Wigoder; *And I Shall Dwell Among Them: Historic Synagogues of the World* by Folberg and Assis; *Synagogues: Architecture and Jewish Identity* by Jarrassé. (9 and up)

15. One of the most famous synagogue floors is the mosaic discovered at Bet Alpha in Israel. Bring to class a picture of this floor and discuss its features, particularly the use of the zodiac theme. Students can do their own mosaic as a group or individually using tiles or small colored squares of paper. Source: *Encyclopaedia Judaica*, vol. 8, cols. 651; *The Story of the Synagogue: A Diaspora Museum Book* by Wigoder, p. 21. (9 and up)

BEYOND THE TEXT

16. For this activity you will need a large felt board and felt cut-outs of the Torah and all of its ritual objects. Place the "Torah" in the center of the board. Divide students into two teams. A member of each team in turn takes one of the ritual objects and places it in the appropriate place on the Torah. Leave the game in a free-play area so that students can practice on their own. (K-2)

17. Bring to the classroom a variety of ritual objects found in the synagogue. With students seated in a circle, pass the objects one at a time, allowing the students to describe each object using as many of their senses as possible. (K-5)

18. Invite a *sofer* (or a Hebrew calligrapher) to the class to speak to the students. Prepare a list of questions ahead of time. (3 and up)

19. Create a bulletin board that illustrates how a synagogue is used as more than a place of worship. Divide the class into groups and allow each group to choose a particular type of activity, such as education, youth work, social action, etc. Students should use the newsletter as a resource and should also interview members and staff who are involved in these areas. The finished product might include photographs, drawings, interviews, and short reports. (6-8)

20. Learn the history of your synagogue. Consult records and archives, members, and staff as resources. Choose a format to present the results of your research, such as a play, video, power-point presentation, or brochure. (6 and up)

21. With your class, attend a service at a synagogue with a *mechitzah*. Afterward, discuss the similarities and differences between that synagogue and the students' synagogue, as well as the worship experiences. What impact did the *mechitzah* have? What kind of environment was created with the *mechitzah*? Invite a person who regularly prays in a setting with a *mechitzah* to come to class and describe the experience from his/her point of view. (6 and up)

22. To find out how one goes about founding a synagogue, contact the national body to which your synagogue belongs (Union for Reform Judaism, United Synagogue of America, Federation of Reconstructionist Congregations, Union of Orthodox Jewish Congregations of America, etc.). You may wish to invite a guest speaker representing this group, or someone who has been involved in founding a synagogue. Have the students brainstorm the steps necessary in the founding of a new synagogue, and some of the decisions that have to be made regarding philosophy, leadership, ritual practice, architecture, etc. (9 and up)

HEBREW

23. Have each student create a rebus story about the synagogue. A rebus uses pictures in place of some words. With your students go over the Hebrew words for various parts of the synagogue and its ritual objects (Torah, *bimah*, *Ner Tamid*, *Aron HaKodesh*, *parochet*, etc.). Whenever one of these words is used in the story, students draw a picture instead. The students should read their finished stories aloud. (3-8)

24. Investigate the (Hebrew) name of your synagogue and other synagogues in your community. What is its source? What does it mean? Why was it chosen? (6 and up)

25. Create a glossary of Hebrew synagogue terms. Advanced students should write the definitions in Hebrew. (6 and up)

FAMILY

26. Hold a "Synagogue Scavenger Hunt." Prepare a list of questions the answers to which can be found by walking around the synagogue. For example: How many *Sifrei Torah* are in the *Aron HaKodesh*? How many steps lead up to the *bimah*? Is there an inscription over or near the *Aron HaKodesh*? What does it mean? Gather the families together and divide into teams, giving each team a list of the questions. Teams should divide up and search for the answers. After the time limit is reached, gather teams and go over the answers, giving an appropriate award to the winning team and recognition to all participants.

27. There is an old Jewish tradition of creating a wimple (Torah binder) from a baby's swaddling cloth. Expand this tradition by having each family design and make a wimple honoring itself. There are a variety of ways to create a wimple. Typically, it is a long sash (7" to 8" wide and 9' to 12' long) of cotton, linen, or silk fabric decorated with fabric paint or embroidery. The families may wish to include their Hebrew names, a biblical quote, abstract or realistic designs of ritual objects, holidays or life cycle events, etc. Resource: *The Second Jewish Catalog* by Strassfeld and Strassfeld, pp. 40-43.

RESOURCES

BOOKS AND PERIODICALS

Berman, Melanie. *Parts of the Synagogue: A Primary Instant Lesson.* Los Angeles, CA: Torah Aura Productions, 1988.

Brooten, Bernadette J. *Women Leaders in the Ancient Synagogue: Inscriptional Evidence and Background Issues.* Brown Judaica Studies 36. Chico, CA: Scholars Press, 1982.

Building Jewish Life: Synagogue (Activity Book). Los Angeles, CA: Torah Aura Productions, 1991.

de Breffny, Brian. *The Synagogue.* New York: Macmillan Publishing Co., Inc., 1978.

Encyclopaedia Judaica. Jerusalem: Keter Publishing House Jerusalem Ltd., 1972.

Folberg, Neil and Yom Tov Assis. *And I Shall Dwell Among Them: Historic Synagogues of the World.* New York: Aperture, 2001.

Jarrassé, Dominque. *Synagogues: Architecture and Jewish Identity.* Paris: Vilo International, 2001.

Kanof, Abram. *Jewish Ceremonial Art and Religious Observance.* New York: Harry N. Abrams, Inc., n.d.

Millgram, Abraham. *Jewish Worship.* Philadelphia, PA: The Jewish Publication Society of America, 1971.

Plaskow, Judith. *Standing Again at Sinai: Judaism from a Feminist Perspective.* San Francisco, CA: HarperCollins Publishers, 1990.

Rosenblum, Richard. *The Old Synagogue.* Philadelphia, PA: The Jewish Publication Society of America, 1989.

Rowe, Alan. *The Well Dressed Torah: A Primary Instant Lesson.* Los Angeles, CA: Torah Aura Productions, 1986.

Siegel, Adam and Ruby G. Strauss. *Let's Discover the Synagogue.* Springfield, NJ: Behrman House, Inc., 1997.

Strassfeld, Sharon, and Michael Strassfeld, eds. *The Second Jewish Catalog.* Philadelphia, PA: The Jewish Publication Society of America, 1976.

Ungerleider-Mayerson, Joy. *Jewish Folk Art from Biblical Days to Modern Times.* New York: Summit Books, 1986.

Wigoder, Geoffrey, ed. *Jewish Art and Civilization.* Fribourg, Switzerland: Chartwell Books, Inc., 1972.

Wigoder, Geoffrey. *The Story of the Synagogue: A Diaspora Museum Book.* San Francisco, CA: Harper & Row, 1986.

AUDIOVISUAL

Black, Rabbi Joe. *Aleph Bet Boogie.* Albuquerque, NM: LaniTunes Music, 1991. Compact disc. Available from A.R.E. Publishing, Inc.

For Out of Zion: The Torah. Teaneck, NJ: Ergo Media Inc., 1973. Videocassette, 15 minutes, not rated.

Klepper, Jeffrey and Susan Nanus. *Especially Jewish Symbols.* Denver, CO: A.R.E. Publishing, Inc., 1977. Audiocassette/songbook set.

CHAPTER FOURTEEN:
TALLIT, TEFILLIN, AND KIPAH

OVERVIEW

TALLIT

In the Torah God tells Moses to speak to the Israelites "and instruct them to make for themselves a *tzitzit* (fringe) on the corners of their garments." Each fringe was to contain a blue thread. The Israelites were told to look at the fringe in order to "recall all the *mitzvot* of God and do them, and not turn away after your hearts and your eyes and lust after them." (Numbers 15:37-40)

Originally, these fringes were attached to the four corners of the cloak worn by Jews in ancient times. This cloak was called a *tallit* (plural, *tallitot*) in Hebrew. When Jews stopped wearing these garments as they adopted the dress habits of their neighbors, they continued to wear *tzitzit* on a special prayer shawl which was called a *tallit*.

According to tradition, males wear a *tallit* during Shacharit and Musaf services. In some communities males begin wearing the *tallit* when they become Bar Mitzvah, in others upon marriage. The only time the *tallit* is worn in the evening is on Yom Kippur. Males traditional in their observance wear a *tallit katan*, a small *tallit*, under their clothes at all times.

Though the *tallit* is traditionally worn draped over one's shoulders, some worshipers place the *tallit* over their heads at certain points in the service to promote *kavanah* and to reduce distractions.

Though women are not required to wear a *tallit* (because it is a positive time-bound *mitzvah* from which women are exempt), neither are they prohibited from wearing one. Some women wear a *tallit* whenever tradition prescribes that men wear one; others wear one when called to the Torah.

Before putting on a *tallit*, one recites the following blessing: *Baruch Atah Adonai Eloheinu Melech HaOlam Asher Kidshanu B'mitzvotav V'tzivanu L'hitateif Ba'tzitzit* (Blessed are You, O Eternal our God, Sovereign of the universe, Who has made us holy with *mitzvot* and commanded us to wrap ourselves with fringes).

It is also customary to read Psalms 104:1-2, which describes God as "robed in glory and majesty" and "wrapped in light as in a garment."

It is traditional to kiss the *tzitzit* at the end of *Baruch She'amar* and during the recitation of the *Sh'ma* when the *tzitzit* are mentioned. It is also customary to kiss the *tallit* at the ends of the *atarah* (neckband) after reciting the blessing and just before putting it on.

A *tallit* may be made of linen, wool, or silk, but may not contain both linen and wool because of the prohibition of mixing fabrics (*shatnez*) in the same garment (Leviticus 19:18). The *tzitzit* must be of the same material as the *tallit*.

A traditional *tallit* is white with black or blue horizontal stripes. However, these stripes may be of any color or combination of colors. The strand of blue that was part of the *tzitzit* in ancient times is no longer included because the exact shade of blue is no longer known, although some groups in Jerusalem are incorporating the blue thread.

Since the *tallit* is used for morning prayer, the question of when it is morning is answered by holding up the *tallit* to the natural light. When one can clearly distinguish between the colored horizontal stripes and the white, it is morning.

TEFILLIN

The tradition of wearing *tefillin*, or phylacteries, during prayer is based upon four biblical verses which refer to "a sign upon your hand and a symbol between your eyes" — Exodus 13:9, Exodus 16; Deuteronomy 6:8, Deuteronomy 11:18. *Tefillin* consist of two small leather boxes called *bahtim* (houses) which contain the four paragraphs from the Torah. One box is placed on one's left upper arm (left-handers place it on the right arm), and the other box is placed on one's forehead. They are held in place with leather straps, thus literally fulfilling the requirement "to bind them" (Deuteronomy 6:8 and 11:18).

Tefillin are traditionally worn during the weekday Shacharit service by males who have reached Bar Mitzvah age. They are not worn on Shabbat or festivals because of the prohibition against carrying an object on those days. Furthermore, because Shabbat is a sign of the covenant between God and Israel, it is not necessary on that day to wear *tefillin*, which are also referred to as a sign. Women may wear *tefillin*, but are not required to do so.

When one wears both *tallit* and *tefillin*, one puts on the *tallit* first. Next, the *tefillin* is placed on one's arm, and the following blessing is recited: *Baruch Atah Adonai Eloheinu Melech HaOlam Asher Kidshanu B'mitzvotav V'tzivanu L'Haniach Tefillin* (Blessed are You, O Eternal our God, Sovereign of the universe, Who has made us holy with *mitzvot*, and commanded us to put on *tefillin*). The strap is then wound seven times around the forearm and around the palm of one's hand.

The other *tefillin* is then placed on one's forehead and the following blessing is said: *Baruch Atah Adonai Eloheinu Melech HaOlam Asher Kidshanu B'mitzvotav V'tzivanu Al Mitzvah Tefillin* (Blessed are You, O Eternal our God, Sovereign of the universe, Who has made us holy with *mitzvot* and has commanded us concerning the *mitzvah* of *tefillin*). This is followed by *Baruch Shem K'vod Malchuto L'olam Va'ed* (Blessed is God, whose glorious majesty is forever and ever).
It is also customary to recite Hosea 2:21-22: "I will betroth you to myself forever; I will betroth you to myself in righteousness and in justice, in kindness and in mercy. I will betroth you to myself in faithfulness; and you shall know the Eternal." The *tefillin* symbolically binds the Jew to God as a groom is bound to his bride.

KIPAH

Whereas wearing *tallit* and *tefillin* are *mitzvot*, wearing a *kipah* (plural, *kipot*), a head covering, is a custom. However, this custom has taken on an obligatory nature among traditional Jews. The head covering is called a *kipah* in Hebrew, but is more commonly known by the Yiddish word *yarmulke.*

The origin and development of the custom of wearing a *kipah* is unknown. The Tanach describes the priest's head covering (Exodus 28:4, 40) which was worn along with other garments for honor and glory. Covering one's head was considered a sign of mourning in biblical times (2 Samuel 15:30, 19:5; Jeremiah 14:3-4; Esther 6:12) and in the rabbinic period.

The Talmud exhorts the people to cover their heads "so that reverence for God be upon you" (*Shabbat* 156b). Rav Huna would not walk four cubits bareheaded (*Kiddushin* 31a). When a certain man passed before a distinguished Rabbi without covering his head, one of his colleagues said, "How impudent is that man" (*Kiddushin* 33a). From these few references, it is clear that while covering one's head may have been customary in rabbinic times, it was not obligatory (*Nedarim* 30b).

The option of wearing a head covering appears to have continued through the Middle Ages. Maimonides states that the sages kept their heads covered, but there are references to men being called to the Torah bareheaded in thirteenth century France and Germany.

In the late Middle Ages, the practice of covering one's head became obligatory in many European communities, in part as a reaction to the practice by Christian males of uncovering heads during prayer.

In modern times, traditional Jewish men keep their heads covered at all times, not just during worship. All men are required to wear a *kipah* in Orthodox and Conservative synagogues. Some men wear a *kipah* when studying Torah and eating (because of the practice of reciting the *Birkat HaMazon* after eating).

In the late nineteenth century, Reform Judaism abandoned the practice of covering the head during prayer. Some Reform synagogues prohibited the wearing of *kipot*. However, as Reform Judaism rediscovered the significance of religious ritual in the 1900s, the practice of covering one's head became more common, and today is optional and usual in Reform synagogues.

Kipot may be made of any material and may be any color or shape. Certain Jewish communities developed distinctive types of head coverings. The Jews of Bukhara wear the colorful, distinctive box-like *kipah*. Modern Orthodox Jews often wear tightly crocheted *kipot* which fit closely to the head. Hasidic communities developed the *streimel*, a felt hat with fur trim around the brim, which is worn in addition to a *kipah*.

INSIGHTS FROM THE TRADITION

A. The *tallit* is not worn in the evening because the passage which requires it to be worn (Numbers 15:37-40) says that we should "look at it." This phrase was interpreted to mean that we should look at the fringes by natural daylight, and therefore only wear it for daytime services. Since the *erev* Yom Kippur service begins before sunset with *Kol Nidre*, the *tallit* is worn for that service.

B. The *tzitzit* are tied in such a way as to remind us of our responsibility to observe the 613 *mitzvot*. The letters in the Hebrew word *tzitzit* have numerical values which add up to 600. To that number one adds the eight strands and five knots of each fringe to arrive at 613. Also, each fringe is tied as follows: double knot, seven coils, double knot, eight coils, double knot, eleven coils, double knot, thirteen coils. There are a total of thirty-nine coils which equals the value of "*Adonai Echad*" (God is One). The *tzitzit* thus reminds us of this central Jewish belief.

C. The reason that women are traditionally exempt from wearing *tallit* and *tefillin* is that wearing either of these is a positive time-bound commandment. The Rabbis exempted women from almost all positive time-bound commandments because of the expectation that they would be busy with the responsibilities of being a wife and mother, i.e., bearing and caring for children and running a Jewish home. For most of Jewish history, this exemption has been tantamount to a prohibition. However, in modern times, many women have begun to wear these ritual objects.

D. In recent years, some women have considered the wearing of a *kipah* as a way of demonstrating equality. There is no explicit prohibition of this practice, except by those who consider it to fall under the commandment not to wear men's clothing (Deuteronomy 22:5). Some women wear *kipot* similar to those worn by men, while others have created unique styles.

E. The practice of women covering their heads is not directly related to the custom of wearing a *kipah*, but rather was considered to be a sign of modesty. This concept has its origin in the Tanach. A woman did not have to cover her head until marriage, from which time on she was required to wear a head covering in public. Her husband could divorce her without returning her dowry if she violated this precept (*Ketubot* 7:6). Toward the end of the eighteenth century, some women began to wear a wig, called a *sheitl* in Yiddish, to cover their natural hair. Some women who do not normally cover their hair will wear a scarf or other head covering in a synagogue.

F. For much of history, some Jewish communities required worshipers to remove their shoes before entering the synagogue. This practice dates to biblical times. Moses, on beholding the burning bush, was told: "Remove your sandals from your feet, for the place on which you stand is holy ground" (Exodus 3:5). The priests of the *Beit HaMikdash* performed their duties barefooted.

"During the Talmudic and Geonic periods the removal of one's shoes before entering a synagogue was a well established custom in Eastern Jewish communities. At prayer, the Jews would sit on the floor, cross-legged and barefooted. This practice is still common among the Moslems and in some oriental Jewish communities" (*Jewish Worship* by Millgram, p. 350). The practice of wearing tennis shoes on Yom Kippur, rather than one's regular leather shoes, may also derive from this custom.

G. The following *midrash* explains the significance of the *tzitzit*: A person is thrown from a boat into the water. The captain stretches out a rope and tells the person to take firm hold of it, for the person's life depends on it. The rope is like the *tzitzit*, the drowning person is like Israel, and the captain is like God. The *tzitzit*, which provides a lifeline for adherence to the commandments, is life itself. (*Numbers Rabbah* 17:6)

ACTIVITIES

TEXT AND CONTEXT

1. Invite to the class an adult or older student who traditionally wears a *kipah*, *tallit*, and *tefillin*. Ask students to identify each object and to share when they have seen people wearing it. Have students volunteer to put on one or more of these items. Ask: How do you feel wearing it? Does it make you feel different? Would you be more comfortable if everyone else in the room were wearing it? You may also wish to take pictures of each student wearing the different ritual items and have the student write or dictate an appropriate caption for the pictures. (K-2)

2. Bring to class pictures of people dressed in uniforms. Show the pictures to the class and ask the students to identify what the person does. Discuss why some people wear uniforms. Point out that uniforms help us identify someone. For example, if we need a police officer, we can recognize one by what she or he is wearing. Ask the students if Jews sometimes wear a special "uniform." Show the students, and pass around for them to feel, examples of *kipot*, *tallitot*, and *tefillin*. Discuss when each is worn, and demonstrate how they are worn. (K-2)

3. Bring to class several *tallitot*. Ask students to examine them carefully and to describe their characteristics. List these on the board. What are the similarities and differences? Ask: What makes a *tallit* a *tallit*? (the *tzitzit* at each corner) Show the students how the *tallit* is put on and allow each to put one on. Teach the students the *brachah* for putting on the *tallit* (see Overview). Resource: *Gates of Prayer*, p. 282; *Siddur Sim Shalom*, edited by Cahan, p. 4; *The First Jewish Catalog* by Siegel, Strassfeld, and Strassfeld, pp. 51-57. (3-5)

4. View the video *Wrapped: The How and Why of Tallit and Tefillin*, available in traditional or egalitarian versions. Discuss how wearing these ritual items might affect their ability to pray and to connect to God. (3-8)

5. Teach the students the proper way to put on *tefillin*. Directions can be found in *The First Jewish Catalog*, pp. 59-61. It is helpful to invite someone to class who lays *tefillin* regularly to help show the students how to do it. Obtain as many sets as possible so that students can do it all at the same time. Also teach the students the appropriate blessings. Resource: *Siddur Sim Shalom*, edited by Cahan, p. 4. (6-8)

6. Provide students with the traditional text of the *Sh'ma*. Ask them to read through it and identify the phrases that refer to the *tallit*, *tefillin*, and *kipah*. (They will not be able to find anything referring to the *kipah*.) Point out that the wearing of a *kipah* is a custom, not a *mitzvah* (commandment). Discuss: Could the phrases that are interpreted to mean that one wears the *tallit* and *tefillin* have been interpreted differently? Encourage the students to imagine what other sorts of ritual objects might have developed from these phrases. (6 and up)

7. Divide students into three or more groups and assign each group to do a report on one of the ritual items. The reports should include history, usage, and examples reflecting different traditions relating to the chosen item. Each group should prepare an oral presentation for the other groups, parents, or other classes. (6 and up)

8. Investigate your synagogue's policies of wearing *tallit*, *tefillin*, and *kipah*. Are they required? Are they optional? Are they required when one is on the *bimah*, but optional when one is in the congregation? Are these policies the same for males and females? Compare your policies with the policies of other synagogues and religious institutions in your community. (9 and up)

ARTS

9. Listen to the song *"Kipah"* on the album *Especially Jewish Symbols* by Jeff Klepper and Susan Nanus. What does it say about the *kipah*? Bring a variety of *kipot* to class and pass them around for the students to try on. (K-2)

10. Create *kipot* for the students using muslin fabric. Prepare the *kipot* ahead of time by cutting the fabric into rounded triangles, approximately 6" on each side. Using quarter inch seams, sew the triangles together in pairs. Then sew two pairs together, along the long edges to make one *kipah*. Students decorate with fabric paint. Encourage them to use Jewish symbols or their Hebrew names. An alternative would be to order plain white or black *kipot* (available from Ktav) and decorate them. Resources: *Hats and Caps of the Jews* by Davis and Davis; "Head, covering of the," in *Encyclopaedia Judaica*, vol. 8, cols. 1-2. (K-5)

11. Many Judaic artists weave fabric that is used in making *tallitot* and other Jewish ritual objects. Take your class on a field trip to a weaver (preferably an artist who does Judaica art). The weaver should explain the loom, the materials used, and how they are brought together to produce fabric. Another option is to visit an artist who creates silk *tallitot* with painted designs. (3-8)

12. To extend Activity #11, students can create their own *tallitot*. Each child needs fabric (approximately 22" x 72") to make the body of the *tallit*. To make the *atarah*, students need a piece of decorative fabric (approximately 3" x 24") or plain fabric that they can decorate with fabric markers, paint, or embroidery. Sew the *atarah* onto the *tallit*, centered on one of the long edges of the

tallit. On each corner of the *tallit*, sew a 3" x 3" square of plain or decorative fabric. In the center of each square make a buttonhole using a sewing machine. Obtain *tzitzit* from a local Judaica store or online. Directions for tying *tzitzit* can be found in *The First Jewish Catalog* by Siegel, Strassfeld, and Strassfeld, p. 52-53. (3-8)

13. Bring to class a set of *tefillin* with boxes that may be opened. Examine the scrolls that are inside. Note that the *tefillin shel yad* (hand) contains one scroll with all four passages, while the *shel rosh* (head) contains four separate scrolls. Students can practice calligraphy using chisel point markers. Resources: *Hebrew Calligraphy: A Step-by-Step Guide* by Greenspan; *A Guide to Hebrew Lettering* by Prusan. (6 and up)

14. Create a video or power-point presentation with pictures and images of people wearing *tallit*, *tefillin*, and *kipot*. Incorporate music, original poetry, and prose. Utilize this show as part of a worship service, retreat, or assembly. (9 and up)

BEYOND THE TEXT

15. Bring to class a variety of head coverings (or pictures) that are worn by people in Israel and elsewhere in the Middle East. Allow the students to try them on and look at themselves in a mirror. Discuss the importance of covering one's head in the Middle East to protect oneself from the intensity of the sun. Point out that Judaism has adopted this practice as a religious custom. (K-5)

16. Bring to class a life preserver with an attached rope. Ask the students what it is and when and how it is used. Tell the students the *midrash* which explains the significance of the *tzitzit* (see Insight G). With the students sitting in a circle, each in turn completes the following statement: "When I see the *tzitzit* on a *tallit*, I think of . . . " (K-5)

17. Create a bulletin board based upon the *midrash* which explains the significance of the *tzitzit* (see Insight G). Bring a life preserver and rope to class. Cut the rope into short lengths so there is one for each student. Attach the life preserver and ropes to the bulletin board. Tell the students the *midrash* and ask them what ties them to Judaism and to the Jewish people. Have each student write a response to this question neatly on a sheet of paper and pin it to the bulletin board at the end of a rope. (6 and up)

18. Prepare with the students a list of questions to ask people who wear *tallit, kipot,* and *tefillin.* Invite a few people to the classroom who do, and allow the students to interview them in groups. Afterward, discuss the answers. Does everyone wear the item in the same situation and for the same reasons? (6 and up)

19. Use the *tzitzit* to introduce the students to *gematria,* Jewish numerology. Create a chart of each letter of the alphabet and its numerical value. Ask the students to calculate the value of some words, including the word *tzitzit.* Ask students to count the number of double knots and strands on the *tzitzit.* Together with the numerical value of *tzitzit,* these total 613, which corresponds to the number of *mitzvot.* Resource: *B'chol L'vavcha* by Harvey J. Fields, p. 5. (9 and up)

21. The first *mishnah* of tractate *Bava Metzia* begins with the phrase, "Two people are holding on to a *tallit.*" The *mishnah* discusses what happens when two people appear before a court, both claiming possession of the same garment. Study and discuss this *mishnah.* Resources: *The Talmud: The Steinsaltz Edition, Vol. 1: Tractate Bava Metzia, Part 1; The Jewish Law Review Vol. II: The Mishnah's Laws of Lost and Found* by Gamoran. (9 and up)

HEBREW

22. Create with the students an illustrated dictionary of the ritual objects and their component parts. Words to include: *kipah/kipot, tallit/tallitot, atarah, tzitzit, tefillin, bahyit shel rosh, bahyit shel yad, klaf* (parchment scroll in the *tefillin*), *retzu'ah* (leather strap of the *tefillin*). Advanced students should define the words in Hebrew. (3 and up)

23. Teach the *brachot* for putting on *tallit* and *tefillin* (see Overview). (3 and up)

24. Read in Hebrew (and translate) the passages from the Torah about the *tallit* and *tefillin*: Exodus 13:9-10, 16; Numbers 15:37-40; Deuteronomy 6:4-9, 11:18-20. (6 and up)

FAMILY

25. Hold a *tallit*-making workshop for families. Ask families to bring fabric they wish to use. For a full size *tallit,* fabric should be about 45" wide and 72" long (smaller for children). At the workshop have the following stations: cutting and hemming the fabric; making an *atarah* using a plain contrasting fabric, painting or embroidering an appropriate phrase or design; learning to tie the *tzitzit;* studying the sources for wearing a *tallit* and learning the blessing. Resource: *The First Jewish Catalog* by Siegel, Strassfeld, and Strassfeld, pp. 55-56.

26. For Consecration, Confirmation, or another special class occasion, create with the help of parents a giant *tallit.* Each family should bring a 45" square piece of fabric. Using fabric and felt cutouts, fabric paints, trims, and ribbons, each family creates a design on its fabric reflecting what Judaism means to them. When these are completed and have dried, sew them to each other. Tie large *tzitzit* to the four corners. Use this *tallit* at an appropriate time during the ceremony, such as when the rabbi blesses the students.

RESOURCES

BOOKS AND PERIODICALS

Cahan, Leonard, Ed. *Siddur Sim Shalom for Shabbat and Festivals.* Rev. ed. New York: The Rabbinical Assembly, 1998.

Davis, Eli, and Elise Davis. *Hats and Caps of the Jews.* Jerusalem: Massada Ltd. Publishers, 1983.

Encyclopaedia Judaica. Jerusalem: Keter Publishing House Jerusalem Ltd., 1972.

Fields, Harvey J. *B'chol L'vavcha*, revised edition. New York: UAHC Press, 2001.

Gamoran, Hillel. *The Jewish Law Review Vol. II: The Mishnah's Laws of Lost and Found*. Los Angeles: Torah Aura Productions, 1991.

Gates of Prayer: The New Union Prayerbook. New York: Central Conference of American Rabbis, 1975.

Greenspan, Jay Seth. *Hebrew Calligraphy: A Step-by-Step Guide*. New York: Schocken Books, 1981.

Harlow, Rabbi Jules, ed. *Siddur Sim Shalom: A Prayerbook for Shabbat, Festivals, and Weekdays*. New York: The Rabbinical Assembly/The United Synagogue of America, 1985.

Millgram, Abraham. *Jewish Worship*. Philadelphia, PA: The Jewish Publication Society of America, 1971.

Oberman, Sheldon. *The Always Prayer Shawl*. Honesdale, PA: Boyds Mills Press, 1994.

Pinkwater, Daniel. *Bare-Knuckled Rituals: A Look at How Jewish Ceremonies Speak to Us*. (Instant Lesson) Los Angeles: Torah Aura Productions, 1989.

Prusan, Peretz. *A Guide to Hebrew Lettering*. New York: UAHC Press, 1981.

Siegel, Richard; Michael Strassfeld; and Sharon Strassfeld, eds. *The First Jewish Catalog*. Philadelphia: The Jewish Publication Society of America, 1973.

Tallit: An Instant Lesson. Los Angeles: Torah Aura Productions, 1986.

The Talmud: The Steinsaltz Edition, Vol. 1: Tractate Bava Metzia, Part 1. New York: Random House, 1989.

AUDIOVISUAL

Klepper, Jeff, and Susan Nanus. *Especially Jewish Symbols*. Denver, CO: A.R.E. Publishing, Inc., 1977. Audiocassette and Songbook.

Wrapped: The How and Why of Tallit and Tefillin. Teaneck, NJ: Ergo Media Inc., 2001. Videocassette, 31 minutes, not rated. Available in traditional and egalitarian versions.

PLAIN KIPOT

Available from Ktav Publishing House, Inc., P. O. Box 6249, Hoboken, NJ 07030-7205.

CHAPTER FIFTEEN: SHALIACH TZIBUR, HAZZAN, RABBI, AND GABBAI

OVERVIEW

While rabbis and/or cantors usually lead the worship service, it is only in recent times that these religious functionaries have filled such a role on a regular basis. Actually, a Jewish worship service can be led by any knowledgeable Jew (adult male in Orthodox synagogues).

For much of Jewish history, the majority of Jews was very familiar with the prayers and could therefore lead the service. A member of the congregation would be accorded this honor when observing *Yahrzeit* or mourning a recent death.

However, in recent centuries, there has been, especially in non-Orthodox congregations, a trend away from laypersons leading the service toward professionally trained rabbis and cantors. There are a number of reasons for this trend. Few laypersons are familiar enough with the liturgy or comfortable enough with the Hebrew to lead the worship service. Many laypersons have come to expect the service to be led by professionals who were trained for that purpose. As the role of the rabbi has evolved to reflect the role of Christian clergy in their congregations, the rabbi has become more involved in leading worship. Nevertheless, in many congregations, laypersons lead services or parts of services, at least on some occasions.

SHALIACH TZIBUR

The "generic" term for a person who leads the worship service is *shaliach tzibur*, literally "messenger of the congregation." The *shaliach tzibur* is not an intermediary between members of the congregation and God. Rather, the *shaliach tzibur* recites prayers on behalf of the congregation, particularly those worshipers who are not able to do so; they need only to respond *"Amen"* to fulfill their obligation of reciting the prayer. In some congregations the major function of the *shaliach tzibur* is to set the pace for the worship service by chanting aloud the concluding section of each *brachah*. In some congregations it is customary to choose a mourner as the *shaliach tzibur*.

Other terms used for the worship leader include *shatz* (acronym for *shaliach tzibur*), *ba'al tefilah* (Master of Prayer), and *hazzan* (cantor).

HAZZAN

In the rabbinic period, the *hazzan* was a communal official. The Talmud describes his responsibilities as bringing out the *Sifray Torah* when they were to be read and sounding a horn to announce the beginning of Shabbat and festivals. He would also lead the service when requested to do so.

By the Middle Ages, the *hazzan* was the major worship leader of the congregation. "When the musical rendition of the service began to play a central role in the worship during the Middle Ages, the title *hazzan* became associated exclusively with the person who distinguished himself in the musical rendition of the prayers" (Millgram, *Jewish Worship*, p. 519). However, during this period, *hazzanut* (the art of chanting) was mostly an avocation rather than a profession.

A *hazzan* would often serve as teacher, *sofer* (scribe), or *shochet* (ritual slaughterer) to supplement the income he received from his duties as *hazzan*.

Beginning in the late Middle Ages, some congregations hired *hazzanim* as full-time professionals responsible for leading the worship. This tradition became widespread in the nineteenth century, with the *hazzan* sometimes having voice training. The position of *hazzan* was an honored one in the community. The *hazzan* was elected by the congregation, and the position was frequently passed down from one generation to the next.

In most liberal congregations, "cantor" has replaced "*hazzan*" as the term used for the professional who leads the musical part of the service. The cantor usually shares the leading of the worship with the rabbi. In Reform, Reconstructionist, and Conservative synagogues, women may serve as cantor or *hazzan*.

There are two types of training to become a *hazzan*. One can enroll in a seminary, such as Hebrew Union College, The Jewish Theological Seminary, or Yeshiva University, and take the required courses. In order to enroll, one must have a good voice, some musical background, knowledge of Hebrew, and a strong commitment to Judaism. The course of study includes musical training, cantillation, *nusach* (musical motif) of the liturgy, as well as courses in Jewish history and liturgy. An alternative approach is to become a student of a particular *hazzan*. As an apprentice one studies all the necessary material and one would have opportunities to lead parts of the service.

The *hazzan* with whom one is studying makes the ultimate determination as to whether one has adequately learned the material. Individuals who study with a *hazzan*, but are not formally invested by a seminary, are sometimes given the title of Cantorial Soloist.

Either course of study requires mastering the different forms of *nusach* for weekdays, Shabbat, festivals, and High Holy Days. These different musical motifs help set the appropriate mood for the day, and serve to identify them as different from one another. The *hazzan* also usually chants the Torah and/or Haftarah selections, using the musical notations called trope. These marks not only indicate how each word is to be sung, but also serve as punctuation marks and accents. While it is traditional for a *hazzan* to sing *a cappella*, many liberal congregations include

instrumental music in the worship service. A variety of instruments, including the shofar, trumpet, harp, and lute, were part of the ritual at the *Beit HaMikdash*. However, following its destruction, instrumental music (apart from the shofar) was banned from worship in the synagogue (*Shulchan Aruch Orach Chayim* 560:3). In the nineteenth century, Reform congregations introduced organ music to the synagogue. Today, it is common for a guitar or other instrument to be used in the worship service of a Reform or Reconstructionist congregation.

RABBI

The word "rabbi" is derived from the word "*rav*," meaning master. It was first used as a title for scholars and sages in the generation after Hillel in the first century C.E. During the period of the Talmud, the rabbis were primarily responsible for interpreting the Tanach and rendering legal decisions. Their teachings comprise the bulk of the Talmud and classical *midrash*. Some works of *midrash* are collections of rabbinic sermons called *drashot*. During this period, most rabbis earned their livelihood by another occupation.

The role of the rabbi developed during the Middle Ages and often included the responsibilities of teaching and service as spiritual leader of the congregation and community. Sermons were normally given only twice a year — on the Shabbat before Pesach to remind the congregation of the legal aspects of the holiday, and on *Shabbat Shuvah*, the Sabbath between Rosh HaShanah and Yom Kippur, to rouse the people to repentance. Even the greatest rabbis of this period, too, earned their living in other occupations. Rambam (Maimonides), for example was a physician; Rashi was a vintner.

While many well-known rabbis served from time to time as *shaliach tzibur*, especially on the holidays, it did not become a regular duty until the modern period.

Reform Judaism in the nineteenth century redefined the role of the rabbi as a full-time professional with responsibilities of leading worship (often with a cantor), officiating at weddings and funerals, and regular preaching. The modern rabbi's responsibilities often include teaching, pastoral visits, and counseling as well. In the Reform, Reconstructionist, and Conservative movements, women may also be ordained as rabbis.

Training to become a rabbi, as with becoming a *hazzan*, can be done through a seminary or in private study with a rabbi or group of rabbis. The primary seminaries are The Jewish Theological Seminary (Conservative), Reconstructionist Rabbinical College, Yeshiva University (Orthodox), Hebrew Theological College (Orthodox), and Hebrew Union College (Reform). While the course of study at each seminary varies, in each students study the full range of Judaic subjects (e.g., Hebrew, Aramaic, Talmud, Midrash, Codes of Jewish Law, history, philosophy), as well as receiving training in practical rabbinics.

GABBAI

While the *gabbaim* (plural form of *gabbai*) were originally responsible for collecting and distributing the *tzedakah* of the synagogue, in the eighteenth century, they took over the logistical responsibilities of the service. This included selecting the *shaliach tzibur*, assigning and calling up *aliyot*, reciting the *Mi Shebeirach* (a prayer asking God's blessing on an individual or community usually recited after an *aliyah*), and correcting the pronunciation or the trope of the *ba'al korei* (Torah reader). In most synagogues there were two *gabbaim* who stood on either side of the Torah as it was read.

The *gabbai* took over many of the duties of an earlier functionary called a *shamash, shamas,* sexton, or beadle. The *shamash* had a variety of duties including: cleaning and heating the synagogue, setting the *Sifrei Torah*, and rounding up people for a *minyan*.

INSIGHTS FROM THE TRADITION

A. The *Shulchan Aruch,* recognized as the official law code by Orthodox Jews, states that a *hazzan* should have the following qualifications: "He should be a man free of transgressions and with a good reputation that has not been soiled even in his youth. He should be of humble and pleasing personality. He should possess a sweet voice, and should be fluent in the reading of the Torah, the Prophets, and the Writings. If such a person is not available, the best man in terms of scholarship and piety is to be chosen." (*Shulchan Aruch, Orach Chayim* 53:4-5)

B. The issue of whether a rabbi should be a salaried professional has been quite controversial. According to Solomon Schechter, Rabbi Judah ben Asher, of fourteenth century Toledo, Spain, "still retained his antiquated German prejudices, and could never reconcile himself to the idea of accepting a remuneration for his services to the community as rabbi and teacher. As the community insisted on his accepting the salary, he saved up all the money which he received from his congregants and converted it in his will into a bequest for various educational and charitable purposes." (Millgram, *Jewish Worship,* p. 537)

C. The term often used to denote rabbinic ordination is *s'michah,* literally "to lean on," but referring to the laying on of hands. When Moses appointed Joshua to succeed him, he laid his hands upon him (Numbers 27:18-23). The rabbis of the Talmud revived this tradition of *s'michah* and taught that there was an unbroken chain going back to Moses. Following the Bar Kochba revolt, the Romans made *s'michah* a capital offense, but it continued until the early fifth century when it was abandoned apparently because it had been adopted by Christianity. In modern times, the tradition has been revived once again by all denominations.

D. Rabbi Hayim Halevy Donin explains the reason for the *gabbai*. "That one does not stand alone on the *bimah* when reading from the Torah is based on a Talmudic teaching which emphasizes the point that God gave the Torah to Israel through an intermediary (Moses). In that same spirit, we arrange to always have at least three persons standing on the *bimah*. The Torah reader is then, so to speak, the intermediary between the synagogue official who summons people to the Torah (as God summoned

Israel) and the one called to the Torah who represents the people receiving the Torah." (*To Pray as a Jew*, pp. 247-248)

ACTIVITIES

(Note: In these activities we have used the term cantor. If your congregation or community uses the term *hazzan*, use this term with the students.)

TEXT AND CONTEXT

1. Ask your students the following questions. Record the answers on the board. What is our rabbi's name? What is our cantor's name? What is our *gabbai's* (Administrator's) name? What are some of the things each does at the synagogue? How can you recognize them? What do they do on the *bimah*? How do they help the congregation? the community? all Jews? What do you think is the best/worst thing about being a rabbi or cantor? (K-2)

2. Invite the rabbi or cantor to your classroom to tell a story, teach a song, and talk about aspects of their jobs. (K-2)

3. Ask your students what the rabbi or cantor does. Use their answers as part of a webbing activity. Write the word "rabbi" or "cantor" on the board (or on a large piece of paper if you want to save it). Circle the word and extend lines from the circle, writing various tasks of the rabbi or cantor as the students offer them. If any tasks are clearly related, have them diverge off the same main branch. (3-5)

4. To extend the previous activity, invite the rabbi or cantor to your classroom to discuss the web. The students should interview the rabbi or cantor and make additions and/or corrections to the web. You may wish to publish this web in the congregation's bulletin. (3-5)

5. What is a day like in the life of a rabbi or cantor? Ask one of them to reproduce a week or month of their calendars, removing names or other confidential and personal references. Students examine this calendar and then write a personal diary account of one day in their life as if they were either a cantor or rabbi. (6-9)

6. Have your students write essays entitled, "When I grow up I would/would not like to be a rabbi or cantor because . . . " (6-9)

7. Arrange with your rabbi and/or cantor for students individually or in small groups to "shadow" them for a day or part of a day. The students should keep a journal of what they do during the day and prepare a brief presentation for the rest of the class. (6 and up)

8. How does one become a Jewish professional? Have the students write letters to the seminaries and schools that train rabbis, cantors, educators, social workers, and Jewish communal workers. Their task is to find out about professions in the field, the educational requirements, and also to ask for brochures, class catalogues, and other material. Compile all the resources and create a display for the religious school and the synagogue. Addresses: The Jewish Theological Seminary of America, 3080 Broadway, New York, NY 10027; Yeshiva University, 500 West 185th St., New York, NY 10033; Hebrew Theological College, 7135 Carpenter Rd., Skokie, IL 60077; Hebrew Union College-Jewish Institute of Religion, 3101 Clifton Ave., Cincinnati, OH 45220; Reconstructionist Rabbinical College, Church Road at Greenwood, Wyncote, PA 19095; Touro College, 30 West 44th St., New York, NY 10036; Wurzweiler School of Social Work, 2495 Amsterdam Ave., New York, NY 10033; Spertus College of Judaica, 618 S. Michigan Ave., Chicago, IL 60605; Baltimore Hebrew University, 5800 Park Heights Ave., Baltimore, MD 21215; Brandeis University, Waltham, MA 02254. (9 and up)

ARTS

9. Listen to the song *"Bimah."* Take turns allowing one or two students to sit on the *bimah* during services, leading the Torah procession.

Take oral dictation as students describe how they felt on the *bimah*. Resource: *Especially Jewish Symbols* by Jeff Klepper and Susan Nanus. (K-2)

10. Give the students large sheets of paper and have them draw pictures of the rabbi and/or cantor. These can be sent as gifts to them. (K-2)

11. Have the students draw a cartoon or comic strip about something funny that could happen to a rabbi or cantor. (3-5)

12. With your class, write a song entitled, "These Are the People in My Synagogue" using the melody of the *Sesame Street* song "These Are the People in My Neighborhood."(K-3)

13. Take snapshots of your students' heads and do one or more of the following:
a. Using the snapshots as the head, students draw the rest of their body as if they were a cantor or rabbi.
b. Find Jewish newspapers and magazines that include photographs of rabbis/cantors. Replace the faces with the student snapshots and rewrite the headlines and/or accompanying story. (3-5)

14. Assign your students to write a haiku about their rabbi/cantor, which might reflect what a rabbi or cantor does, the responsibility of working with the Jewish community, or other related topics. A haiku is a non-rhyming poem made up of three lines. The first line has five syllables, the second line has seven syllables, and the last line has five syllables. (4 and up)

15. Either individually or in groups, use a popular song and replace the words with a song about your rabbi or cantor. Sing this as part of a school assembly or other gathering. (6 and up)

16. Invite to class the cantor or a guest artist who knows the *nusach* for chanting the Torah, Haftarah, and various *Megillot*. The person should demonstrate some of these melodies and then discuss with the students how particular melodies are used to set certain moods. (6 and up)

17. Read the story *Ima on the Bimah* by Portnoy to your class. Discuss: What does the rabbi do? Are all rabbis women, or are all rabbis men? How is a rabbi's family similar to and how is it different from your family? (K-2)

18. Tour the synagogue. Meet the people who do all the different jobs needed to run the synagogue. Take photos of the students with these people. Create an "Our Synagogue" book with the students writing the captions for pictures. (K-2)

19. There are many storybooks and folk tales that include a rabbi as a main character. Collect a variety of these, and have students do book reports or thumbnail sketches of the rabbi from the story they read. Each student can make a decorated representation of the rabbi from the story (puppet, stick figure paper doll, or fabric covered stick figure, drawing or painting). Do a bulletin board display of their work. Also, discuss with the students if they thought the story was a realistic portrayal of a rabbi, if the story influenced how they thought and felt about rabbis, how rabbis should look and what they should do. Suggested books: *Partners* by Syme; *A Children's Treasury of Chassidic Tales* adapted from Zevin's *A Treasury of Chassidic Tales* by Adler; *The Rabbi and the Twenty-nine Witches* by Hirsh. (3-5)

20. Today, running a synagogue oftentimes requires more than just the rabbi, cantor, and volunteers. Have the students investigate what it takes to run the synagogue. They can conduct interviews, read old/new synagogue bulletins, and examine the local Jewish newspaper (where available). Things for the student investigators to consider: Who works in your synagogue (professional, support, lay/volunteer)? The students can interview these individuals. They should determine why these people are needed. They might consider what additional staff might do or suggest what might change if any of these jobs went unfilled. (6 and up)

21. Ask the students to list some of those who

have served the congregation as rabbi, cantor, *gabbai, shaliach tzibur*. Are there photos of these individuals available? Can you or the students locate information through old synagogue records about these people? With your students create a "Hall of Fame" or "Hall of Synagogue Memories." Use photos or drawings, excerpts of sermons, descriptions of projects the rabbi(s) or other synagogue professionals accomplished, etc. (6 and up)

22. Arrange for your students to be able to hear liturgical music played by a variety of instruments: piano, organ, harp, guitar, flute, or others. You may also listen to recordings of some of these instruments. Discuss with the students how music might enhance or detract from the worship experience, and how particular instruments influence the mood of a prayer. Which instruments are the students used to hearing as part of a service? (6 and up)

23. Introduce the topic "Rabbis who have made a difference." Each student researches a different rabbi. Utilize the *Encyclopaedia Judaica, Who's Who in the Talmud* by Kolatch, and other appropriate sources. (9 and up)

24. View a movie that has a rabbi (or rabbinical student) or cantor as a major character, such as *The Chosen, The Jazz Singer, Crimes and Misdemeanors, Frisco Kid, Yentl,* or *Keeping the Faith.* Discuss how the rabbi/cantor is portrayed. Was that a typical rabbi/cantor for that time period? How does this description compare to a rabbi/cantor of today? (9 and up)

25. Role play a rabbinic/cantorial search committee. The committee should do each of the following: Create a job description and a classified advertisement, collect resumes (which can be created by class members), make a list of questions, conduct interviews. (9 and up)

HEBREW

26. Teach the students the Hebrew terms for the synagogue personnel: *rav* (rabbi); *hazzan* (cantor); *gabbai* (sexton); *shaliach tzibur* (prayer leader). (3-9)

27. Have students take turns being rabbi, cantor, *shaliach tzibur, ba'al koray* (Torah Reader) and *gabbai.* Give each student an appropriate task to do based on his/her Hebrew ability, such as leading a prayer, reading a *Mi Shebeirach*, calling up an *aliyah*, etc. The rest of the class should play the role of the congregation. (6-9)

FAMILY

28. Conduct a Family Education Day with activities led by professional and lay leaders of your synagogue. Choose a theme for the program, such as "Creating Peace" or "Making Shabbat." Each of the leaders prepares a presentation or activity based on the theme appropriate to his or her discipline. For example, the cantor might teach songs or help create a song. The rabbi might teach Jewish texts that relate to the theme.

29. Hold an appreciation day for leaders of your synagogue. Ask families to bring with them pictures and other material for a scrapbook, as well as favorite stories. Families put together a book for each person honored and make other gifts for them. Conclude with a ceremony presenting each with the gifts. Presenters should share with the group stories about the person.

RESOURCES

BOOKS

Adler, David A. *A Children's Treasury of Chassidic Tales*, adapted from S.Y. Zevin's *A Treasury of Chassidic Tales*. Brooklyn, NY: Mesorah Publications, Ltd., 1983.

Donin, Hayim Halevy. *To Pray as a Jew: A Guide to the Prayer Book and the Synagogue Service*. New York: Basic Books, Inc., 1980.

Encyclopaedia Judaica. Jerusalem: *Keter* Publishing House Jerusalem Ltd., 1971.

Hirsh, Marilyn. *The Rabbi and the Twenty-nine Witches*. New York: Scholastic Book Services, 1976.

Kolatch, Alfred J. *Who's Who in the Talmud*. Middle Village, NY: Jonathan David Publishers, Inc., 1964.

Millgram, Abraham. *Jewish Worship*. Philadelphia, PA: The Jewish Publication Society of America, 1971.

Portnoy, Mindy Avra. *Ima on the Bimah: My Mommy Is a Rabbi*. Rockville, MD: Kar-Ben Copies, Inc., 1986.

Syme, Deborah Shayne. *Partners*. New York: UAHC Press, 1990.

AUDIOVISUAL

The Chosen. 1981, 108 minutes, rated PG. Available in video stores.

Crimes and Misdemeanors. 1989, 107 minutes, rated PG-13. Available in video stores.

The Frisco Kid. 1979, 122 minutes, rated PG. Available in video stores.

The Jazz Singer. 1980, 115 minutes, rated PG. Available in video stores.

Keeping the Faith. 2000, 128 minutes, rated PG-13. Available in video stores.

Klepper, Jeff, and Susan Nanus. *Especially Jewish Symbols*. Denver, CO: A.R.E. Publishing, Inc., 1977. Audiocassette/songbook set.

Yentl. 1983, 132 minutes, rated PG. Available in video stores.

SEEKING SPIRITUALITY:
NEW TRENDS IN JEWISH WORSHIP
INTRODUCTION

Rabbi Raymond A. Zwerin

The buzzword of this generation in religious circles is "spirituality." In Hebrew, it is most commonly rendered as *"ruchaniut"* from the word for wind or breath or spirit. Spirituality has been the subject of countless recent sermons and scholarly papers. Days, weekends, even entire weeks have been devoted to the study of the topic at academic colloquia and symposia and at congregational gatherings. Though there has been no lack of effort to fathom the meaning of the term, still our definition remains vague; though there has been no lack of effort to achieve it and transmit it, still our means of teaching it is sketchy, and techniques for incorporating it into our lives are tenuous at best. Discussion about how to "do" spirituality invariably leads to certain "exercises" that incorporate meditation, dance, song, mantras, *niggunim*, and the like in a variety of settings that are so constructed as to evoke the senses or to suspend them. Like the wind, the concept of spirituality is ephemeral.

I dare say that spirituality has been neither a religious nor a cultural focus of Judaism. We tend to associate the concept primarily with eastern religions — Buddhism and Hinduism. Spirituality is more the aspiration of the Ashram than it is of the *shul* or the *Beit Midrash*. Neither Torah nor Talmud commands us to seek the "spiritual path." Rambam in his *Mishneh Torah* deals with all sorts of life situations, but has no laws or customs for achieving or acknowledging a "spiritual" condition. There are no spiritual *mitzvot* to perform, no blessings to recite, and there is no personal "vision-quest" to endure as a part of our Jewish life cycle.

One could argue that the mystics of Spain and Safat had a spiritual bent — that their teachings concerning *ma'aseh b'reishit* and *ma'aseh merkavah* were about achieving a spiritual nexus. Indeed, Gershom Scholem in his great work on the subject informs us that the earliest mystics who were responsible for the *hechalot* literature prescribed extensive meditations, fasts, and bodily preparations for the purpose of reaching a mental state receptive to mystical illumination. Aryeh Kaplan's books on Jewish meditations using biblical and Talmudic sources also open to us the possibility of achieving a transcendent mental state out of a Jewish frame of reference. But in the scope of normative Jewish living, these are really sidebars for many and diversions for most.

If authoritative Jewish sources such as Torah and Talmud and Maimonides do not promote our aspiring to spirituality, what then is the primary goal that they set for us? What is the ideal state of being for a Jew to achieve? The answer, in a word, is *kedushah* — holiness. "You shall be holy for I Adonai am holy," Leviticus 19 instructs us. The holiness of the divine is recounted and rehearsed in prayer after prayer in our liturgy — "Holy, holy, holy is *Adonai Tz'va'ot*, whose *kavod* fills the whole earth"; *"Yitgadal v'yitkadash Sh'mei rabbah . . .* — Great and holy is the divine Name . . ." From the *Kiddush* over wine to the *Kiddushin* of marriage to *Kaddish* at the passing of a dear one, holiness is intrinsic to the nature of the divine and our task as Jews is to develop ourselves in emulation of that attribute.

And how are we to achieve holiness in our lives? Through the study of Torah, the recitation of blessings, the performance of rituals, the observance of *mitzvot*, the incorporation of Jewish values and virtues in our thoughts and deeds, and through *tefilah* — personal and communal worship.

In brief, spirituality is internal. It is a personal quest; it is about the struggle to become emotionally and/or religiously centered. Holiness on the other hand is external. It is about relationships; it is about the struggle to find the divine in our interpersonal dealings with relatives, friends, and strangers. Within a Jewish construct, spirituality is a by-product of our striving toward holiness. The Jew who bypasses the path toward holiness is likely to end up disconnected — from community, from family, from heritage, and ironically from the very source of all that spirituality implies — from God.

That is why it is critical to teach our children the formulae of Jewish observance, to guide them as they seek both spirituality and holiness. In this special new section of *Teaching Tefilah*, six experts in their respective fields present ways of reaching our students in various settings, and from the standpoint of different disciplines, and by employing different techniques. The focus of this section is on the overall theme of "seeking," because that is exactly what our children are encouraged to do. Oftentimes, for children as well as for adults, it is in the seeking that a path is found, a question answered, a commitment formed, a dilemma resolved.

In "Seeking Relationship: Worship Experiences for Very Young Children," Maxine Segal Handelman talks about how the main goal in worship for children is developing a relationship with God. She explores the many ways in which such relationship evolves, and explains how children grow and thrive from prayer experiences that are rich in both *keva*, the fixed routine of worship, and *kavanah*, the spontaneous, heartfelt intention of prayer.

Cantor Wally Schachet-Briskin in "Seeking Community: Worship in the Jewish Camp Setting" explains why the development of community is a key ingredient in the success of worship at camp. He suggests that the intense, round-the-clock Jewish environment that children experience at camp promotes a special community bond and provides unique opportunities for young Jews to experience "living Judaism." Cantor Wally identifies the various elements that

make camp worship successful and offers suggestions for further enhancing the worship experience in both camp and school settings.

In "Seeking Connection: Prayer in the Jewish Renewal Movement," Rabbi Daniel Siegel defines Renewal prayer as joyous, as profound, and as misunderstood. He outlines the basic principles of Jewish Renewal and explains the key concepts, expressions, and techniques of prayer in that Movement.

Music and prayer are inextricably linked in Jewish tradition. Merri Lovinger Arian, who has much experience in teaching Jewish music and leading congregations and groups in song and worship, explores this relationship in her chapter "Seeking Harmony: Music, Prayer, and Sacred Community." She discusses music as a means of building sacred community, and focuses specifically on how music can be used to empower and engage participants in meaningful worship experiences. Craig Taubman, co-creator of "Friday Night Live" and "One Shabbat Morning," adds some practical guidelines for creating a musical worship experience that is emotional, powerful, and engaging.

Nan Gefen is a writer of note on the subject of meditation. Her chapter "Seeking the Silence Within: Jewish Meditation" explores the techniques and the benefits of the discipline. She assesses the historical roots of Jewish meditation, explains the connection between meditation, mysticism, and Kabbalah, and discusses the various forms of Jewish meditation in use today. Rabbi David Cooper, who has been called "one of today's leading teachers of Jewish meditation," adds a description of one particular meditative technique.

Reaching out to others with our visits, our prayers, and through worship is the subject of "Seeking Wholeness: The Jewish Way of Healing" by Rabbi Nancy Flam. Jewish tradition has long recognized that there is both a physical and spiritual dimension to the experience of illness. Rabbi Flam, a pioneer in the field, reminds us that there is a difference between *curing* and *healing*. Jewish healing does not seek to replace conventional medicine, but rather to complement and supplement medical practice by establishing — or perhaps re-establishing — a relationship between the community and those in need of healing. Additional contributions by Rabbi Rachel Cowan, Debbie Frideman, and Rabbi Shefa Gold offer insights into traditional Jewish healing practices such as the recitation of psalms, the *Mi Shebeirach* prayer, and chanting.

All of these chapters point out the essential thrust of the Jewish endeavor, namely, that holiness is achieved in our relationships *bein adam l'atzmo, bein adam l'chaveiro, u'vein adam l'Makom* — between us and ourselves, us and others, us and God. As we seek to strengthen these relationships through study, value-based actions, religious observances, personal prayer, and positive communal worship, we aspire toward *kedushah*, holiness — emulating the divine. That process in turn is also our path toward spirituality.

———————————————

Rabbi Raymond A. Zwerin is co-founder and formerly president of A.R.E. Publishing, Inc. A pioneer in the field of Jewish education, Rabbi Zwerin has written and edited countless books, articles, and sermons. Ordained as a Rabbi from the Hebrew Union College-Jewish Institute of Religion in 1964, Rabbi Zwerin is the founding rabbi at Temple Sinai in Denver, Colorado. He received a Doctor of Divinity degree from HUC-JIR in 1989.

CHAPTER SIXTEEN:
SEEKING RELATIONSHIP
WORSHIP EXPERIENCES FOR VERY YOUNG CHILDREN

Maxine Segal Handelman

Young children approach the world with a sense of awe and wonder. God and prayer are subjects young children handle with ease, given the opportunity. "Tot Shabbat" services are designed to draw both children and parents in to the joy of ritual, prayer, Torah, and community. *T'fillot* can be meaningfully integrated into a morning circle in the preschool classroom, and the *Sh'ma* can ease daycare children into nap every day. When we strive to nurture the spiritual side of children, we enable them to build a meaningful and life long relationship with God.

God is central to Jewish life. Judaism has long had a tradition of ethical monotheism. The covenantal relationship between God and the Jewish people as expressed through Torah laid the foundation for a both a people and a God that were expected to act ethically, justly, and compassionately. Prayer is a way of acknowledging the importance of this relationship to God in our lives.

RELATING TO GOD

Jewish tradition upholds a belief in one God. But monotheism does not mean that there is only one way to think about God or relate to God. Our ancestors, Abraham and Sarah, Isaac and Rebekah, Moses, King David, Elijah, and Maimonides each had differing views of God. On one end of the spectrum, Abraham communicated often with God. They challenged one another. Abraham even argued with God. On the other end of the spectrum, Maimonides believed that one could say with certainty what God is not, but could not conceive of what God is. Although a fervently

committed and scholarly Jew, God's presence was much more complicated and remote for Maimonides than it was for Abraham.

Doubting and questioning are normal in understanding and relating to God. Abraham questioned God's sense of justice in wanting to destroy the righteous along with the wicked in Sodom and Gomorrah. Throughout the wilderness experience the Israelites expressed doubt again and again that God's promises would be fulfilled. Rabbi Daniel Gordis reminds us that Jews are *B'nai Yisrael*, the Children of Israel (1999). *Yisrael* means "to wrestle with God," as our biblical forefather, Jacob, wrestled with an angel. Subsequently, Jacob's name was changed to Israel; we are named for him. Jews are "God-wrestlers;" we continually wrestle with our ideas of God. As Jewish adults, we have many doubts about what God is, and how we personally relate to God. These doubts and uncertainties are part of Judaism.

God commands. The *mitzvah* system is based on two kinds of commandments: those between God and human beings, and those between one person and another. In a Hassidic tale, one person asks: "Which is more important: to love God or to love your neighbor?" The teacher answers, "To love your neighbor. By loving your neighbor, you show your love for God. The opposite is not always true." How we treat others points to our view of God.

Moral behavior is mixed with this sense of human beings being commanded. Therefore, moral behavior implies an underlying spirituality. Much of "God-talk" revolves around concerns such as a sense of being *Kadosh* (holy), imitating God (*B'tzelem Elohim*), doing the right thing

(*Derech Eretz*), and caring for others (*G'milut Chasadim*).

PRAYER

Prayer takes on many different forms. Prayer can arise spontaneously from the heart or occur at set times in fixed forms. Praying is our conscious reminder and expression of our connection to God. When we recite prayers, we bless, praise, thank, petition, or exalt God. The Jewish prayer service has a fixed order and set of prayers that for all the variations in language, melody, and philosophy are remarkably similar for Jews around the world. Prayer can be one person's utterance, or an experience recited in unison by a *minyan* (prayer community). Prayer can be uttered in one's home, or in the synagogue, or walking on the way. Prayers are often spoken whenever and wherever Jews assemble for a wedding, a funeral, during *tashlich* near running water, a conference in a meeting center, or a family gathering in a restaurant.

Aside from the daily, Shabbat, and holiday prayer services, many occasions throughout the days, weeks, months, and lifetime of a Jew are cause for a prayer. The basic function of eating is an opportunity to recite blessings before and after a meal or snack. *Birchot Ha'Nehenin* (blessings for enjoyment) contain blessings for all sorts of events that occur in nature and society such as hearing a clap of thunder, smelling a fragrant spice, or seeing a scholar. Life cycle events, the holidays, and new experiences give rise to many *shehecheyanu* moments that reveal our days as being filled with blessing and joy. There are also special prayers that are meant to comfort us when we experience sorrow and pain.

PRAYING WITH KAVANAH

Kavanah is the concept of praying with intention and fervor. It means paying attention to what we are doing and saying. Its opposite is *keva*, which refers to prayer as a routine or set part of our lives. In fact, both are needed to make prayer a spiritual experience. Spirituality in a Jewish context balances that which is fixed and routine, *keva*, with that which is spontaneous and heartfelt, *kavanah*. These are a constant struggle in terms of prayer. While the tradition often emulates and upholds the importance of the fixed and obligatory aspects of Jewish ritual and prayer, another tendency is strongly felt for making the experiences meaningful and passionate.

Music, dance, and movement are ways of reaching a level of *kavanah*, especially with young children. Music is an important part of praying. Traditional liturgy, Torah and Haftarah chanting, and many *brachot* have *nusachim* (melodies) associated with them. Psalm 150 is a reminder of the various instruments — cymbals, harp, timbrel, horn, and lute — that were used to praise God in the Temple in Jerusalem. Today, melodies of all styles are written as interpretations of the prayers. Music is used to enhance or heighten the prayer experience and to inspire the prayer participant. This prayer music is not only sung in the synagogue but is played on cassettes and CD players in cars, homes, and classrooms as well.

Young children are familiar with music as a learning tool and a way of expressing their emotions. Music is a wonderful way to capture their attention, hearts, and minds. Early childhood classrooms are filled with songs that teach children about values and relationships, remind them of rules and behaviors, and challenge their minds and imaginations. The challenge is for the early childhood educator to use music and instruments to enrich the experience of *kavanah*, of learning to pay attention to prayers and praying.

Children are constantly in motion. Coordination of all sorts is a challenge to them. They learn about the parameters of what their bodies can and cannot do through the normal course of daily activity. Many of their successes and accomplishments relate to acquiring skills, from walking to somersaulting, eating with utensils to writing letters, painting with their fingers to cutting with scissors. Dance and movement can be used to capture the energy of using the body and motion, increasing the ability of the young child to connect to prayers and praying. Many of the prayers come with their own "choreography." When we recite the phrase in the *K'dusha*, "Holy,

Holy, Holy," we rise up on our toes toward the heavens. Our bodies naturally move along with the *lulav* as we shake it in all directions, up, down, forward, backward, to the right, and to the left. It is not uncommon to find dancing in the aisles at services to set a mood, to accompany the Torah when it is taken out of the ark, or to celebrate a special *simchah* (joyful occasion), such as a wedding blessing.

The daily, Shabbat, and holiday prayer services are models of the way Jews view the world. Many of the prayers reflect the central narratives in Jewish tradition: creation, revelation, and redemption. Other prayers give us a sense of how Jews have survived over the ages. Prayers mirror the relationship between the Jewish people and God. Prayer is an expression of our highest ideals and expectations. It is the expression of a longing for a better world. The language of prayer is one of addressing and speaking to You, God: Baruch *Atah* — We praise *You*.

The Torah service is a special part of many prayer services. It is a reenactment of the giving and receiving of the Torah at Mt. Sinai. Tradition says that we all stood at Sinai, and the Torah service recreates that experience. We stand when we take the Torah, God's words, out of the *Aron Kodesh* (Ark). In many synagogues, one takes the Torah down from the *bimah* (pulpit) and brings it to the people standing, much as Moses took the tablets from the mountaintop down to the Israelites. We read the words from the Torah that God spoke to Moses. At the end, we raise the Torah up, show off the words, and declare that they were the words that Moses received from God.

YOUNG CHILDREN, GOD AND PRAYER

With the right guidance, young children can come to stand at Sinai. Children are born with a sense of wonder about the world. Unless they are actively stifled, children take extreme pleasure in exploring, in asking questions, in discovering the "whys" of their world. Robert Coles, professor of psychiatry at Harvard Medical School, and author of the book, *The Spiritual Life of Children*, writes,

"boys and girls are attuned to the heart of spirituality and have a natural ability to look inward in search of meaning and purpose . . . Children pursue their questions while drawing pictures, stories and poems, while indulging in the exploration of this wondrously enchanting planet" (Coles, 1996, p. 118). Coles further notes that all children need a spiritual life which is validated by their parents and other significant adults, including teachers. Even preschool children are aware of the gift of life, and are busy trying to understand it and figure out what they should do with it.

To this end, children ask lots of questions. Rabbi David Wolpe, author of *Teaching Your Children About God*, points out that very young children ask questions about God's beginnings: Was God born? What does God look like? Does God have a body? As children get older, they turn their focus more toward what God *does*. Does God speak to people? Is God still creating new things? Gordis (1999) notes that when children ask about God, they are often not seeking information about God. Instead, children use God as one way to create order in their world, a way to construct a world that makes sense, a world that is loving and not cruel.

Rabbi Harold Kushner warns adults to listen carefully when children ask questions, in order to know what the real question is. Kushner reminds us of Piaget's description of the functional orientation of the child's mind. When a child asks about what something is, she is really interested in knowing what it does, and how it is relevant to her life (1995). When children ask, "Where is God?" Kushner suggests rephrasing the question. "Where is God?" implies that God is a physical being, that God has a location. Even if we tell children that God is not a person, that God is everywhere, we may miss a great opportunity. Kushner recommends replacing the "where" question with "When is God?" This question suggests that God is not an object, but rather a relationship, a feeling, something that happens when the right elements are in place (when we light Shabbat candles, when we appreciate nature, and so on). Children tend to ask the most questions about God from the ages of four to fourteen. Adults can foster children's sense of wonder, and initiate God-talk, even with younger children. With the right nurturing, as pre-literal children get older, they can translate their wonders into questions.

The young child needs something concrete in particular to help him/her learn. God presents a special challenge to the need for something tangible. While Judaism has many different beliefs about God, there is general agreement that God has no human body or form. Thus, pictures or images of God are not to be made by Jews. When God is mentioned in anthropomorphic (human like) ways, for example, God rescued the Jews from Egypt with "an outstretched arm," this reference is taken as symbolic or metaphorical — not literally.

How does one meet the concrete needs of the young child when teaching about God? The names of God are a particularly fertile source to help address this concern. A name is something to which children can relate. Children know their own names well before they can even speak. Older children may know that their names have alternative meanings (e.g., Ari is a lion or Sarah is a person from the Torah). They also often know that they were given their name to honor a relative, living or dead, thereby giving names personal associations and history.

The Torah, *siddur* (prayer book) and other Jewish texts, both classical and modern, are filled with names for God. In addition to the more traditional sources, the many names of God are also found in songs, stories, and blessings. These names for God are suggestive of how we understand and relate to God. For example, we call God *Melech* (King or Ruler), *Avinu* (our Father or Parent), and *Borei* (Creator). Although these names are meant to be understood on a metaphorical level, we can use the many names of God to help us think about God. How do we act around a king or queen? What does a parent do? How is God like a parent? What types of feelings do parents have for their children? What types of feelings do children have for their parents? How does God create things? (see *Sacred Fragments* by Neil Gillman for further reading). Young children can relate to these names for God when they are tied to their experiences or captivated by their imaginations. Stories about their lives and about others, real or fictional, can stimulate a deeper understanding of and relationship to God when connected to the various names of God.

Using different names of God can also be a meaningful way to connect young children to the experience of prayer. As children begin to explore the concept of God, they will eventually seek to find ways to talk with God. Being exposed to many different names for God allows each child, each with different experiences and backgrounds, needs and desires, to find the most meaningful concept of God to use when thinking about God and addressing God in prayer.

Young children's images of God are very much affected by their everyday experiences. Their understanding of God is influenced and shaped by their relationships to authority figures, parents and teachers alike. Children are used to being commanded, to having someone set rules and regulations. They associate reward and punishment with following rules because they love or care for the person who sets the expectations and limits.

Young children are open to the experience of prayer. They are comfortable imitating behaviors of others and eager to touch, experience, and try out new things. Preschoolers enjoy performing new rituals, exploring symbols, and developing new competencies. As they are learning to verbalize things, it is just as natural for them to learn *b'samim* as it is to learn the term "spice box." "Blessed are You, Lord Our God, Ruler of the universe" is as foreign to them as *"Baruch Atah Adonai Eloheinu Melech HaOlam."* They enjoy repeating words over and over again until they master them.

Young children grow and thrive from a prayer experience that is rich in both *keva* and *kavanah*. Even before they can read, it is worthwhile for young children to use or at least see a *siddur*, to know that a prayer service or experience has an order and consistency that can be counted on. Children learn through repetition. Basic prayers and songs, such as *Sh'ma* and *Oseh Shalom*, should be a consistent part of each prayer experience.

At the same time, it is essential that children are enabled and empowered to find themselves in their prayer, that something in the prayer service draws on personal experiences and interests.

Allowing children to relate their own stories to prayer (e.g., "I am thankful for my new baby sister. Please God, help me to be a good big brother.") and involving children in every way we know children learn (linguistically, musically, kinesthetically, even mathematically) helps children pray with intention and fervor, and helps them pay attention to what they are doing and saying.

Involving children in t'fillah from a very young age gives children the tools they need to build their own relationship with God. Prayer experiences help children grow and explore their spiritual selves, enriching how they relate to the world around them, to other people, and to themselves. Through meaningful prayer experiences, children develop a deeper understanding of moral, Jewish behavior that will sustain them and their relationship to the Jewish people for their entire lives.

A child's relationship to God and prayer will change drastically with age. Although most children do not start asking questions about God until around the age of four, there are many ways to infuse the classroom with "God concepts" from the earliest age. Developmentally appropriate concepts of God and prayer change with age. Building prayer experiences accordingly will help children continue to develop their relationship with God and explore as they grow. Following are some "God-concepts" for every age.

Infants to 24-month-olds experience wonder as a part of every day. It is appropriate for children this young to hear blessings and God-talk, and to see Jewish ritual objects every day. Many of the things that are a part of everyday life for these young children, such as rituals and routines and quality relationships with parents and caregivers, provide a foundation for experiencing prayer and forming a relationship with God. Just as Adam and Eve named the animals in the Torah, so too do children begin speaking and connecting to their world by naming things and people. Finally, the act of commanding and mitzvot (commandments) between God and the People appears in early speech patterns, as children command in order to act within their world.

Two-year-olds build on the concepts appropriate for younger children. Two-year-olds begin to understand that prayer and blessings are a way to talk to God. The concept of being kadosh (holy) begins to have meaning for two-year-olds. They can try to be kadosh like God. Older twos are beginning to become moral beings. They begin to understand that when they treat other people with love and hesed (mercy), they are being like God.

Three-year-olds can truly begin to meaningfully question their world. Wonder is encouraged and fostered with exploratory questions. As they build on the concepts appropriate to younger children, three-year-olds can now understand that each and every person is created B'tzelem Elohim (in the image of God), and deserves to be treated accordingly. As three-year-olds begin to think about what God does, they can learn that God created the world, and on Shabbat, God rests. Three-year-olds can begin to assess what in the world is created by God, and they can communicate thankfulness for God's gifts through prayer.

Four- and five-year-olds are highly capable in spoken language and are becoming more aware of and proficient in written language. These skills take them beyond the concepts applicable to younger children, to understand that it is possible to talk to God with prayers that other people wrote, or prayers that they make up in their own hearts, and that blessings are a way of saying thank you to God. It is useful to share with four- and five-year-olds that God has many names. Shabbat and holidays provide different experiences, prayer opportunities, and metaphors of God. The capacity for moral behavior grows, as four- and five-year-olds understand that every person is treated with respect and compassion because each person is created B'tzelem Elohim. Four- and five-year-olds can find evidence of God in other people, in nature, in themselves, etc. As they ask more questions, they can be directed to find answers from the Torah, the siddur, and Jewish stories. At the same time, children this age can understand that no one knows everything about God, so we each need to keep asking. Four- and five-year-olds should be encouraged to explore their understandings of and relationship with God by talking with grown-ups like parents, teachers, and rabbis.

PRAYER EXPERIENCES WITH YOUNG CHILDREN

Young children can experience God and prayer in many different contexts. In the classroom, at synagogue, and at home, Jewish life is rich with the opportunity to think about and talk to God.

Marvell Ginsburg, Director Emeritus, Department of Early Childhood, Community Foundation of Jewish Education in Chicago, advises teachers that God may come into the classroom, whether or not teachers consciously put God in the curriculum. If children are free to explore and encouraged to wonder, then children will bring God in through their discoveries and with their questions. If teachers do not support exploration and wonder with warmth and respect, then God is likely to be conspicuously absent from the classroom.

In order to let God into the classroom, teachers must be at least somewhat comfortable talking and thinking about God. This is certainly not to say that teachers must know what (or when) God is, or be completely fluent in Jewish liturgy. If that were the case, very few people would consider themselves qualified to teach about God! Wolpe (1993) assures us that when it comes to talking about God and making meaning of our lives, we can often give what we don't have. In fact, it is not the task of adults to transmit to children an exact copy of their faith and idea of God, or to teach children to pray exactly the way they pray. It is a teacher's responsibility to help children develop their own ideas of God in a way that is valuable and true both to the traditions held by the community and to what teachers know about the world.

To help children, teachers do need to have some sense of their own faith, or spirituality, or idea of God. Before teachers can really hear and deal with children's questions about God, they need to have asked their own questions about God, and have sought out some answers. Teachers don't need to have necessarily *found* the answers, but they must be looking. Remember, Jews are God-wrestlers — doubt is part of the equation. Yet Gordis (1999) warns against sharing too many doubts with young children. In every aspect of

life, it is a teacher's duty to assure children that they are living in a good, secure, safe world. The same guidelines apply to helping children think about God. Though it is never permissible to lie to children, it is not dishonest to help children grow up believing that God is loving and caring and treasures every human being, including them.

To expose children to prayer and help them learn traditional ways to talk with God (*keva*) and their own ways to immerse themselves in a conversation with God (*kavanah*), teachers need to have a basic familiarity with Jewish liturgy, know the standard Hebrew formulas for blessings, and have explored the best ways they personally connect with prayer. Teachers must be comfortable with the prayers and blessings that will make up the daily or weekly rituals that will happen with children. Music is essential in creating classroom prayer experiences and rituals. Some teachers use movement and dance as well to involve children in prayer, Torah, and in developing a relationship to God (See the chapters "Encountering God in Dance" by JoAnne Tucker and "Encountering Spirituality through Movement: Incorporating Nonverbal Expression into Jewish Education" by Kate Mann in *Teaching about God and Spirituality*, edited by Roberta Louis Goodman and Sherry H. Blumberg, 2002).

Teachers should never be afraid to tell a child, "I don't know." It's okay, in fact important, for children to know that grown-ups don't have all the answers about God (or most anything else in life). Rather than make up an answer to a child's question, which will only cause the child to mistrust or to have to unlearn later, tell a child, "I don't know. What do you think?" Then *listen* to the child's answer, and ask questions to help the child expand on her own ideas of God.

Our job as teachers is to allow children the space and safety to explore God. There are many strategies to help children think about how the world works. The most valuable world explorations come when children learn that each person is created *B'tzelem Elohim* — in the image of God. Being created in God's image means that every person has value, every person is deserving of respect and caring. When children know that they are created *B'tzelem Elohim*, their own self worth is bolstered, and it is safer, and easier, to ask questions about God and the rest of their world.

Tot Shabbat services can serve to draw in both children and parents to the joy of ritual, prayer, Torah, and community. The experience should be relatively short, less than an hour, as is appropriate for young children. The children who bring their parents to Tot Shabbat might range from a few months old to around seven years old. This range provides role models for younger children, allows children to grow into leadership roles within the service, and gives families a broad opportunity to build a community within a prayerful context. Songs, games on a felt board, and stories help round out the prayer experience, appealing to every kind of learner.

Siddurim for a tot Shabbat service should be small, brief, and full of pictures. Consistent use of age-appropriate *siddurim* allows children to feel comfortable and take ownership of the service, being able to predict or "read" what comes next. The service should involve repetition, familiar melodies, movement, and of course, food (a *Kiddush* afterward with juice and challah).

The children who attend Tot Shabbat services regularly know that the synagogue is their home, and they will sometimes choose to come to Tot Shabbat over other tempting offers. The families who come are a community — celebrating births and grieving when longtime members move away.

Tot Shabbat is a gateway into the celebration of Shabbat. It deeply affects those who join in month after month. These families — not just the young children, but their parents and sometimes grandparents and aunts and uncles as well — discover that Judaism is full of joy and that Judaism, and the synagogue, are significant, welcoming places.

Children who experience prayer at school and at synagogue will bring these experiences home. Blessings before eating, singing *Modeh Ani* upon waking and singing the *Sh'ma* before going to bed will become natural ways to talk with God throughout the day. A child's spiritual self will grow and become enriched in every realm of life when the child is consistently and comfortably encouraged to explore his or her relationship with God through questions and prayer.

RESOURCES

BOOKS FOR ADULTS

Coles, Robert. *The Spiritual Life of Children*. Boston, MA: Houghton Mifflin, 1990.
A fascinating investigation of children from several religions and cultures, and their relationships to God and their spiritual selves.

Kushner, Harold. *When Children Ask About God: A Guide for Parents Who Don't Always Have All the Answers*. New York: Schocken Books, 1995.
This book, originally published in 1971, was one of the first guides for Jewish parents on how to talk to their children about God. Kushner's advice is timeless.

Gillman, Neil. *Sacred Fragments: Recovering Theology for the Modern Jew*. Philadelphia: Jewish Publication Society, 1990.
A thoughtful, informative review of leading ideas and issues in Jewish philosophy. Recipient of a National Jewish Book Award.

Goodman, Roberta Louis and Sherry H. Blumberg, eds. *Teaching about God and Spirituality*. Denver, CO: A.R.E. Publishing, Inc., 2002.
A comprehensive anthology with chapters that present theory and practice on teaching about God and spirituality.

Gordis, Daniel. *Becoming A Jewish Parent: How To Explore Spirituality And Tradition With Your Children*. New York: Harmony Books, 1999.
A guide for parents who want to introduce Judaism into their homes so that their children can grow up loving, understanding, and cherishing their heritage.

Handelman, Maxine Segal. *Jewish Every Day: The Complete Handbook for Early Childhood Teachers*. Denver, CO: A.R.E. Publishing, Inc. 2000.
This book will enable every teacher to create a Jewish developmentally appropriate classroom, one in which Jewish values and themes permeate every learning experience every day.

Wolpe, David J. *Teaching Your Children About God: A Modern Jewish Approach*. New York: Henry Holt and Company, 1993.
A beautiful book, filled with midrashim *(stories); perfect for helping adults help children to discover God.*

BOOKS FOR CHILDREN

Brichto, Mira Pollak. *The God Around Us: A Child's Garden of Prayer.* Revised Edition. New York: UAHC Press, 1999.
Blessings for the wondrous experiences of everyday life, over mountains, blooming trees, and different kinds of people, to list a few. (Ages 2 to 5)

Edwards, Michelle. *Blessed Are You.* New York: Lothrop, Lee & Shepard Books, 1993.
Traditional everyday Hebrew prayers. (All ages)

Groner, Judye, and Madeline Wikler. *Thank You God!* Rockville, MD: KarBen Copies, 1993.
A Jewish child's book of prayers. (All ages)

Hample, Stuart and Eric Marshall, eds. *Children's Letters To God: The New Collection.* New York: Workman Publishing, 1991.
An insightful and hysterical look at the questions children ask God. (Ages 2 to adult)

Rossoff, Donald. *The Perfect Prayer.* New York: URJ Press, 2003.
The Queen is is on a quest for the sounds of the perfect prayer. As each of her advisors presents a sound, and important aspect of the Sh'ma is explained. (Ages 2 to adult)

Sasso, Sandy Eisenberg. *In God's Name.* Woodstock, VT: Jewish Lights Publishing, 1994.
Everyone and everything in the world has a name. What is God's name? (Ages 4 to 8)

———. *What is God's Name?* Woodstock, VT: Jewish Lights Publishing, 1999.
An abridged, board book version of Sasso's In God's Name. *In this book, children will see and hear the many names people have for God. (Newborn to age 4)*

MUSIC

Friedman, Debbie. *Shirim Al Galgalim: Songs on Wheels.* San Diego, CA: Sounds Write Productions, Inc., 1995. Compact disc.
Shabbat and holiday songs and blessings for young children. Available from A.R.E. Publishing, Inc.

Mah Tovu. *Days of Wonder, Nights of Peace.* Springfield, NJ: Behrman House, Inc., 2001. Compact disc and activity booklet.
Family prayers in song for morning and bedtime, with engaging activities.

Taubman, Craig. *Friday Night Live.* Sherman Oaks, CA: Sweet Louise Productions, 1999. Compact disc and songbook.
Contemporary versions of the Shabbat evening service prayers. Available from A.R.E. Publishing, Inc.

CHILDREN'S SIDDURIM

Orkand, Robert, Joyce Orkand and Howard I. Bogot. *Gates of Wonder: A Prayerbook for Very Young Children.* New York: Central Conference of American Rabbis, 1989.
A very simple book about prayer, God, and wonder. From the Reform movement. (Ages 2 to 5)

Maxine Segal Handelman is a Jewish Early Childhood Consultant. She holds a Master's Degree in Early Childhood Education from Pacific Oaks College in Pasadena, California, and a Master's Degree in Jewish Education from Hebrew Union College-Jewish Institute of Religion in Los Angeles. Max is the author of Jewish Every Day: The Complete Handbook for Early Childhood Teachers *and* What's Jewish about Butterflies? (*both from A.R.E. Publishing, Inc.*) *and* The Shabbat Angels (*UAHC Press*). *Max is also a sought-after speaker, a professional storyteller, and leader of Tot Shabbat services for young families.*

Chapter Seventeen:
Seeking Community
WORSHIP IN THE JEWISH CAMP SETTING

Cantor Wally Schachet-Briskin

THE MAGIC OF CAMP

The Jewish camp setting, specifically the sleep-away summer camp, provides a unique and wonderful experience. In this mini-society, young people, typically eight through seventeen years old, live, eat, sleep, learn, explore, and succeed in small, age-specific groups. Every moment of the camp day is planned with the health, safety, and emotional needs of the campers in mind. They are supervised by a high school or college-aged student, often only a few years older than themselves, who is perceived more as an "older sibling" than as a "parent." There are no cars, and campers travel by foot to all areas of their world. That world is insular, with no intrusion by television, newspapers, or other distractions of the "outside world," save communications from family. Meals are served family-style, and cleanup is a shared group responsibility. In fact, nearly every aspect of camp life, from cabin cleanup to sports activities to singing after meals, is communal in nature. The intensity of this collective environment fosters close relationships, strong peer support, and lasting bonds among campers. It's often said that friends made at camp are friends for life.

The Jewish camp environment is also the perfect setting for children to experience Jewish life on a level that goes beyond their usual routine. Campers put aside concerns of "normal" life for most of their two to three week camp stay, and explore their connection to Judaism in an intense, round-the-clock Jewish environment.

Positive Jewish role models — rabbis, cantors, educators, songleaders, artists, and others — are accessible and approachable. Wearing t-shirts and shorts, they climb the same hills, swim in the same pool, and eat at the same table while modeling Jewish values and virtues.

Jewish music and Hebrew language mark every point of the camp day, from the singing of *"Modeh Ani"* at morning flag raising to the blessings sung before and after each meal, from the guitar accompaniment of the daily and Shabbat worship service to the "good and welfare" songs sung around the friendship circle at bedtime.

It is within the context of a natural, perhaps rustic outdoor environment that all of these elements combine to create the perfect, magical setting for Jewish living — or to put it another way, for campers to experience a world of "living Judaism." It's no accident that the latter part of the name of the Union for Reform Judaism's Camp Swig in Saratoga, California, an hour's drive from San Francisco, is "Institute for Living Judaism." Indeed, the founder of the first Reform Jewish camp, Rabbi Herman E. Schaalman, saw the success of Jewish summer camping in developing "fond emotional responses to Judaism, (making) Judaism exciting, vibrant, beautiful — maybe even to some extent romantic...."[1]

Camp Swig, along with dozens of other Jewish camps across North America, establishes each summer a unique environment that incorporates Judaism into every aspect of daily life. Each activity that takes place in camp is punctuated by the use of Hebrew, the demonstration of Jewish

---

[1] Goldberg, Edwin Cole. "The Beginnings of Educational Camping in the Reform Movement," *Journal of Reform Judaism*, Fall 1989, p. 9.

values and virtues, and the rhythms of Jewish life. At camp, Jewish education becomes exciting and tangible — counselors are transformed into *shtetl* dwellers, the maintenance truck becomes the ship *Exodus*, and the songs campers sing after they've been turned into ancient Egyptian slaves are really telling Pharaoh, "Let my people go!" These Jewish experiences do not simply play out in front of the campers; rather, campers are firsthand participants. They take *"la'asok b'divrei Torah,"* immersing oneself in learning and history, to a whole new level.

GOD MOMENTS

All of these elements of the Jewish camp provide unique opportunities for young Jews to be open to, and to experience, "God-moments." A God-moment can be described as an awareness of the presence of God in life, and an understanding of the sacred relationships between humanity and God. Watching a sunrise from the top of a mountain peak or witnessing the vastness of a star-filled sky bring an awareness of God that is too often overlooked in everyday life. The pace of camp life provides opportunities to stop and recognize the wonder of God's creation all around, and to sanctify those moments through Jewish ritual, blessings, and prayer. Interpersonal relationships, too, take on a deeper meaning when children learn to see others as created *"B'tzelem Elohim"* — in God's image. Seemingly mundane activities like caring for horses, maintaining a wilderness trail, visiting a sick friend in the infirmary, and even recycling soda cans all become teachable moments within the camp day, moments when children can recognize the presence of God and the importance of humankind's partnership with God.

WORSHIP IN THE CONTEXT OF THE CAMP SETTING

Prayer and worship in the camp setting provide opportunities for translating religious concepts into real experience, and help to transform children into knowledgeable, practicing Jewish adults. Prayer moments are built into the daily routine at camp, and come to be "normal" and expected. At flag raising, everyone sings *"Modeh Ani,"* thanking God for restoring each person's soul after the night's rest. Before and after each meal the appropriate communal blessing is recited, thanking God for providing us with food. Daily and Shabbat worship services become part of our schedule. Before going to bed, everybody gathers in a circle to sing *"Hashkiveinu"* and *"Sh'ma"* as a community. Even within routine camp activities — hiking, swimming, sports — the values expressed and the particular lens through which these activities are viewed can be an extension of the worship experience.

Camp is also a safe environment in which to experiment with Jewish ritual. A child who has never worn a *kippah*, tried a *tallit*, or wrapped *t'fillin* can experiment in a supportive, welcoming environment. Many children experience *Havdalah* for the first time at camp, and come to love the beauty and symbolism of the ritual that bids goodbye to Shabbat. Camp worship may be very different from a child's home, synagogue, or religious school worship experience, with unique advantages for instilling the notion of "living Judaism." It can also allow children to take part in writing or leading a service for the first time, an experience that provides training for future leadership within their synagogue or the larger Jewish community.

Historically, Jewish camps have been a testing ground for "pushing the envelope" of worship practice. Undoubtedly, the first Jewish campers prayed from the *siddurim* they brought with them from their home synagogues, but soon the need for a creative and innovative style of camp worship became clear. Folk songs and poetry began to replace the typical psalms and responsive readings. Music became an important element in the camp worship service — in fact, many of the prayer melodies widely used in synagogues today, by composers such as Debbie Friedman, Jeff Klepper, and Craig Taubman, were first introduced in our Jewish camps. Today, camp worship services range from the traditional to the "way out," and may include nature walks, bibliodrama, or guided imagery mind journeys. Still, in most cases the camp worship service will adhere to the basic structure of a Jewish worship service, with all the required prayers in the proper order. This too is part of the educational process, helping campers to become familiar and comfortable with the structure and order of Jewish worship.

WHAT MAKES CAMP WORSHIP WORK?

Camp gives participants the opportunity to be outdoors, in a natural environment. This heightens the awareness of God in creation, and provides a tactile way of sanctifying holy space and holy time. Openings exist to experiment with prayer space, musical style, and creative expression. Campers often get an opportunity to lead and to provide personal offerings within the service. The repetition of daily prayers allows opportunities for experiencing many layers of meaning in a particular piece of liturgy. The communal setting allows campers to pray while, perhaps, counselors spread *tallitot* over them, allowing them to experience firsthand the feeling of a *sukkat shalom*, a shelter of peace. Or, campers disperse from the *beit t'filah* and sit quietly alone, eyes closed, and enjoy the natural soundscape. Another example of a powerful camp prayer moment might be to lie down on a hillside after a sunrise hike and listen to guided imagery, then take time for silent meditation followed by a meaningful song. For the most part, when done well, participants will leave camp with *t'filah* experiences that have been positive, educational, and engaging.

A list of the elements that make camp worship successful would include the following:
- *T'filah* is part of the life of the community, not just part of the schedule. It is an integrated and important component of the communal experience.
- *T'filah* is sacred time, taking place in sacred space. The atmosphere of worship is distinct from that of other activities.
- *T'filah* is transformative, or at least provides portals through which transformative experiences are possible.
- *T'filah* is viewed as an expression of our love of Judaism. Through Hebrew, music, and ritual one can connect oneself to the traditions of the Jewish people.

- *T'filah* is not just for the heart, but also for the head. A teaching component woven into the experience ensures that everyone takes something away with them.
- Particpants are personally engaged through stories, lessons, personal reflections, and other means that help them understand the themes of the liturgy and make them meaningful in their lives.
- Empowered *t'filah* leaders create an empowered congregation. Worship leaders are knowledgeable, dynamic, and welcoming.
- Music and singing are an important part of the worship experience.
- *Minhagim* (customs, such as standing or sitting for *"Sh'ma"*), reasons that an individual prays (giving thanks, praising, asking for things), and other prayer topics are discussed in a supportive, nurturing environment so that worshipers can fully participate.
- *T'filah* provides a safe environment for participants to experiment with Jewish ritual (to try wearing a *kipah* or *tallit* for the first time, for example).
- Alternative methods of worship — creative expression through the arts, guided imagery, nature walks, etc. — are embraced.
- *T'filah* extends beyond the synagogue setting, and includes times such as *Hamotzi, Birkat Hamazon, Siyum (Sh'ma/Hashkiveinu)*, and *Havdalah*. God-moments permeate the day, and one can take time to recognize them.

SOMETIMES IT MIGHT NOT WORK

While it would seem that most ingredients for successful worship experiences occur naturally in a camp environment, sometimes it just might not work. There can be difficulties in providing positive camp *t'filah* experiences. *Chanichim* (campers) or *madrichim* (staff) may not be engaged or may be distracted — outdoor chapels, common in camps, often have a lot of distracting elements, ranging from sticks and rocks to chirping birds and loudly babbling streams. The prayer text may not be appropriate for all ages, certainly a concern when the camp community ranges from eight-year-olds to adults. Scheduling services at less than ideal times for campers' energy levels, or when appropriate dress is an issue (for example, immediately following pool time) can lead to disruption or non-participation. At one camp high in the Colorado Rocky Mountains, evening services become difficult late in the summer because the weather turns cool by late afternoon. Other potential pitfalls include lack of adequate supplies (not enough prayer books or songsheets), unqualified or underprepared prayer leaders, out-of-tune guitars, and worship styles which become rusty, or quaint, or no longer pertinent.

Sometimes, even a model that worked well on one occasion can fail. For example, asking participants to write personal *iyyunim* (meditations) can deepen the meaning of certain prayers. This works well with older campers who have some knowledge of the meaning of the liturgy. However, younger campers who have not had time to learn and reflect upon the prayers may write *iyyunim* that are irrelevant, or worse, inappropriate. This can lower the quality of the service experience, and cause frustration among the campers as well as the adult worship leaders.

Being aware of these pitfalls can help *t'filah* leaders anticipate and avoid them. Understanding the larger issues can help create positive worship experiences for children at camp or in any other setting.

KEYS TO SUCCESS

There are several keys to ensuring the success of a camp worship program. First, it is important that there are clearly articulated standards for worship. These may come from the camp's parent institution, or may be part of the history of the camp. They should be developed in consultation with the relevant stakeholders — rabbis, cantors, temple educators, camp directors, the camp educational oversight committee, and members of the camp board. Such standards would identify which components must be present in every worship experience, which are optional, and which methods or techniques would be unacceptable. Standards can address such wide-ranging topics as liturgy, music, setting, dress, and the suitability of "alternative" techniques such as meditation,

dance, or guided imagery. At the same time, it is important to recognize that standards may change over time. For example, it wasn't that long ago that few if any Reform institutions included the *Mi Shebeirach* prayer as part of their worship. Today, thanks in large part to Debbie Friedman's well-known musical setting, *"Mi Shebeirach"* is almost universally included in Reform worship, and in most camp settings as well.

Second, it is essential to have at least one qualified worship leader to help guide the group. This should be an adult, a staff member, or an older camper; one who is familiar with the liturgy and the melodies, and is comfortable in leading the group. A capable songleader or guitarist, while not crucial, can be a great enhancement to the quality of the worship experience, and can allow the introduction of new melodies to keep the prayer experience fresh and engaging.

Third, preparation and education are vital. A camper group that will be leading a service must be adequately prepared, and preferably must have some knowledge and understanding of the worship to be led. This involves knowing the order of the service, the cues for rising and sitting, the proper tempo of congregational readings, and much more. Many camps have a rabbi, cantor, educator, para-rabbi or rabbinic student who works with groups of campers to prepare them to lead *t'filah*, and is available to step in and avert disaster if needed. This preparation not only makes the worship service itself run more smoothly, but provides a positive educational experience for the campers and prepares them for future leadership at camp or in their home congregations.

Finally, flexibility and a willingness to try different techniques can make camp worship dynamic and always new. For example, the Rocky Mountain camp mentioned above switched from evening worship to morning worship in the latter part of the summer to avoid the cool evening weather. The different liturgy of the morning service presented opportunities to introduce new songs, explore new themes, and start the camp day with a meaningful community gathering. Greeting the morning with the sun on their faces and the fresh mountain air in their lungs provided campers and staff alike with an invigorating change. Perhaps an alternative site in camp, such as a sports field or grassy hill, may lend itself to a less distracting or more beautiful worship experience than the appointed "outdoor chapel" on occasion.

TAKING IT HOME

When done well, camp worship can provide some of the most powerful and meaningful experiences that campers will have during their stay. Many campers report that they love *t'filah*, and the extended Shabbat experience that most Jewish camps embrace is always a special, cherished time. For Jewish educators, then, the question becomes: how can this positive camp worship experience be brought home? Apart from lifting what already works in the sleep-away summer camp experience and dropping it into a temple or youth group retreat weekend, what elements will translate to synagogues and religious schools so that students will feel the same about worship in those settings as they do at camp?

Recreating the magic of camp in a religious school or synagogue setting is certainly a challenge. As "Uncle" Max Frankel, a lifelong camp director and Jewish educator once said, one can't paint trees on the classroom windows and expect it to feel like camp. Above, many elements that make for successful camp worship were identified. These same elements can invigorate the prayer service wherever one is. Boiled down to their essence, they fall into the following categories:

CREATING COMMUNITY

The sense of a close, supportive community is really the "glue" that holds everything together at camp. How can one create this sense of community in a school setting, when students spend just a few hours each week together? This is an important and ongoing challenge in Jewish education, and the answers are well beyond the scope of this article. However, viewing worship as an opportunity to build community, rather than simply another activity that students "do," is key. One could try holding services "in the round" so that everyone

feels equally involved. Engage the group in a few minutes of communal singing to create a proper mood for prayer. Encourage older students to sit with younger children and help them follow along in the *siddur*. Let B'nai Mitzvah students practice their skills by leading sections of the service or chanting their Torah portion. Allow students to speak aloud the names of those in their lives in need of healing before singing *"Mi Shebeirach,"* or to recite the names of loved ones for whom they are reciting *"Kaddish."* Engage in a few minutes of paired discussion or brief *chevruta* study of the weekly *sedra* or of the theme of a selected prayer. Such activities that encourage interaction between students within the context of the worship service will help build community bonds.

PARTICIPATION AND LEADERSHIP

At camp, children have opportunities to create and lead their own worship services, engaging them directly in the process and giving them a sense of ownership. Each class or grade can have a turn at creating and leading school *t'filah* during the year, or in preparing a special Shabbat evening service for the entire congregation. Or, each class can be assigned a specific section of the service to lead each week. Rotate sections so that during the course of the year a class can learn about and have a chance to lead each prayer. Allow aspiring songleaders to join in leading the worship music. Even simple tasks — for example, asking younger students to distribute and collect *siddurim* or songsheets — provide an extra level of involvement and ownership.

Adult leadership is critical as well, as has been noted previously. Rabbis, cantors, and others who lead students in worship should pay particular attention to the presence or absence of a sense of community, and to making sure that everyone is engaged in the worship experience.

MUSIC

Music can provide perhaps the most direct connection to students' fond memories of worship at camp. Incorporate favorite camp melodies into the service, and be sure to teach them to non-campers as well. Stick with a limited repertoire at first; later, as students become comfortable with the music, the *t'filah* leader can introduce new tunes. Try to choose melodies that reflect the *kavanah* — the intent — of each prayer. Be sure to have the words available, either in the *siddur* or on a songsheet (or poster, or overhead, etc.), to promote student participation. Provide them not only with the English and transliterated Hebrew words, but with the actual Hebrew text itself so that they become more comfortable with the language of Jewish prayer.

The presence of a cantor or songleader with camp experience is of great benefit, but any music leader with energy, enthusiasm, and a good understanding of the mechanics of the worship service can greatly enhance the service. A communicative face and a positive attitude toward prayer can say much more to observing students than any words on the page.

NON-TRADITIONAL TECHNIQUES

The freedom to try something "outside the box" is invigorating. Nature walks, meditations, guided imagery, and creative liturgy aren't just for camp. These techniques have the potential for success because they fully immerse participants in the experience. Be creative, and try something different. Dance, movement, bibliodrama, creative writing — these and many other wonderful activity suggestions can be found elsewhere in this book.

SACRED TIME, SACRED SPACE

God-moments aren't exclusive to camp. They happen everywhere, all the time. Recognizing them in a school setting may just take a little more work. Special times and places for worship are set aside, yet God doesn't "dwell" in the *beit t'filah* at camp any more or less than in the synagogue sanctuary. Both are special places where one slows down, acts differently, and opens him or herself to God's presence. One might help students to recognize and celebrate the God-moments happening all around them. Teach them to discover the divine sparks in all life. Emphasize that all are created *B'tzelem Elohim*, and

that when people treat each other with love and respect, they are striving to be like God. Identify and reinforce the themes of Jewish worship — blessings, thankfulness, awe, peace — and weave them into the culture of the school. Creating an awareness of the sacred will enhance the strength of the community.

CONCLUSION

So, is it possible to re-create a successful camp-like worship experience outside of the camp environment? Absolutely. By focusing on the elements of Jewish worship that work so well in the camp environment, and understanding that a certain amount of adaptation is required, one can bring a little bit of the magic of camp home — without having to paint trees on the windows.

RESOURCES

BOOKS AND ARTICLES

Goldberg, Edwin Cole. "The Beginnings of Educational Camping in the Reform Movement." *Journal of Reform Judaism*, Fall 1989, p. 6.

Hoffman, Rabbi Lawrence. *The Art of Public Prayer: Not For Clergy Only*. Washington, DC: The Pastoral Press, 1988.

Salkin, Jeffrey K. "NFTY at Fifty: An Assessment." *Journal of Reform Judaism*, Fall 1989, p. 18.

Schachet-Briskin, Cantor Wally. "The Music of Reform Youth." Masters' thesis, Hebrew Union College-Jewish Institute of Religion School of Sacred Music, 1996.

Schwartz, Shuly Rubin. "Camp Ramah: The Early Years, 1947-1952." *Conservative Judaism*, vol. 40, no. 1 (1987), p. 14.

Will-Boxt, Cantor Rosalie. "Cantors and Campers: Bringing Youth into the Worship Service." Masters' thesis, Hebrew Union College-Jewish Institute of Religion School of Sacred Music, 2001.

MUSIC AND SONGBOOKS

Eglash, Joel N., ed. *The Complete Shireinu: 350 Fully Notated Jewish Songs*. New York: Transcontinental Music Publications, 2001.

Richards, Stephen, ed. *Manginot: 201 Songs for Jewish Schools*. New York: Transcontinental Music Publications, 1992.

Schachet-Briskin, Wally. *The Cantor Wally Songbook*. Northridge, CA: Six Point Productions, 1997. Available at www.cantorwally.com.

Taubman, Craig. *The Best of the Rest*. Los Angeles, CA: Craig 'n Company, 2003. Compact disc and songbook. Available from A.R.E. Publishing, Inc.

UAHC Camp Institutes for Living Judaism Camp Swig. *Tov Lanu Lashir: It is Good for Us to Sing*. San Francisco, CA, 1975. Compact disc. Available from Sounds Write Productions, Inc.

———. *Shir Mi-libeinu: A Song From Our Heart*. San Francisco, CA, 1984. Compact disc. Available from Sounds Write Productions, Inc.

UAHC Camp Institutes for Living Judaism Camp Newman. *Shir L'Yom Chadash: A Song for a New Day*. San Francisco, CA, 1999. Compact disc. Available from Sounds Write Productions, Inc.

Various artists. *Ruach 5761: new Jewish tunes*. New York: Transcontinental Music Publications, 2001. Compact disc and songbook.

———. *Ruach 5763: new Jewish tunes*. New York: Transcontinental Music Publications, 2003. Compact disc and songbook.

———. *The Complete NFTY Recordings 1972-1989*. New York: Transcontinental Music Publications, 2003. Five compact disc set.

WEB SITES

A.R.E. Publishing, Inc.
http://www.arepublish.com
A wide selection of contemporary Jewish music, popular in Jewish camp settings.

National Ramah Commission: Ramah Library
http://www.campramah.org/library.html
Compact discs and books from the Conservative movement's camping system.

Sounds Write Productions, Inc.
http://www.soundswrite.com
Online music store featuring many recordings of melodies from camp worship.

Transcontinental Music Publications
http://www.etranscon.com/
Sheet music and CD publishers of the Reform Movement, including NFTY.

Association of Jewish Sponsored Camps
http://www.jewishcamps.org
New York area Jewish summer camps of all affiliations.

Union for Reform Judaism (URJ) Camps
http://urjcamps.org
Information about and a directory of the camps of the Reform Movement.

Cantor Wally Schachet-Briskin, a 1996 graduate of the Hebrew Union College-Jewish Institute of Religion's School of Sacred Music (HUC-JIR SSM), serves at Leo Baeck Temple in Los Angeles, California. Wally treasures the opportunity to be a faculty member and musician-in-residence each summer for "Hagigah" at the Union for Reform Judaism (URJ) Camp Institutes for Living Judaism in Northern California. Wally has released several recordings of original Jewish music, and is active in the Los Angeles Jewish community as a songleader, performer, lecturer, event leader, and guest cantor. Visit his Web site at www.cantorwally.com.

The Southern California division of the Camp Swig/Camp Newman Education Council contributed to this article.

CHAPTER EIGHTEEN:
SEEKING CONNECTION
PRAYER IN THE JEWISH RENEWAL MOVEMENT

Rabbi Daniel Siegel

When Rabbi Noah, Rabbi Mordecai's son, assumed the succession after his father's death, his disciples noticed that there were a number of ways in which he conducted himself differently from his father, and asked him about this. "I do just as my father did," he replied. "He did not imitate, and I do not imitate."

(Martin Buber, *Tales of the Hasidim, Vol. 2: Later Masters*, p. 157)

The movement for Jewish spiritual renewal, or Jewish renewal, is an outgrowth of the work of an intergenerational collaboration. Inspired mostly by the teachings and encouragement of Rabbis Zalman Schachter-Shalomi and Shlomo Carlebach, a number of people responded to a perceived spiritual crisis by founding new synagogues and *havurot*, projects in social action, lay leadership training, innovations in liturgy, a retreat center, a rabbinic program focused on spiritual skills in pastoring and prayer, and more recently a rabbinic association and network of communities. One area of great importance has been the reinvigoration of prayer, both communal and individual, and this chapter will explore some of these developments. In particular, we will describe key concepts such as paradigm shift and the psycho-halachic process, and key practices of the Renewal movement, including the use of music, movement, and chant in prayer.

WHAT IS JEWISH RENEWAL?

Like the Hasidism of Eastern Europe, what we now call Jewish renewal (or the movement for

Jewish spiritual renewal) is a response to a set of needs rather than an ideology in search of adherents. The great up-welling of yearning for deeper meaning from the central Jewish practice of prayer, the desire for the relinking of the practice of *mitzvah* to the totality of life, and the hunger for a rekindling of the joy in serving the Holy Blessed One are what have given rise to this movement of people seeking connection with one another as they seek for connection to the Source of Meaning. Just as the Hasidism of Eastern Europe was a response to a time of relative peace and prosperity following the wars and pogroms of the recent past (see Moshe Rosman, *Founder of Hasidism*), so also the neo-Hasidism of today follows a time of forced migration and the tragedy of the destruction of European Jewry and emerges during a period of relative security and calm.

While there is no formal creed to which those who consider themselves part of Jewish renewal subscribe, some points of commonality are central to this grassroots movement. Rabbi Zalman Schachter-Shalomi, the founder and catalyst of so much of Jewish renewal and whom we know as Reb Zalman, has suggested the following parameters as culled from his teachings and writings:

• We are living in a time of Paradigm Shift, similar to that in which the founders of the Jewish rabbinic tradition lived. For them, the destruction of the Temple and the end of a place-centered spiritual practice meant the development of a theology to explain and give meaning to these seemingly catastrophic events and the shifting of the Divine presence, the *Shechinah*, to the world of *halachic* practice. For us, the catalysts include the twin realities of a Jewish state and a new manifestation of the Diaspora in societies based on individuals and their gifts rather than on the groups to which individuals belong. Given that this paradigm shift means that we live in a qualitatively different environment rather than one which has changed only incrementally from the recent past, the exploration of the implications of that change require us to rethink our most basic ideas concerning God and the place of Judaism in the world.

• God must be no less than the consciousness that fills all of the natural world. Humanity experiences the transcendence of the Divine from within that immanence. This means that our primary experience of God is in the consciousness of the planet, Gaia, on which we live and of whose systems we are a part.

• A planetary consciousness requires us to rethink traditional *kashrut* to include the ethical and environmental implications of our eating habits.

• The increasingly visible web of interconnectedness leads us to reevaluate our sense of the place of Judaism in the world. We are now aware of the existence of other spiritual paths whose practices and goals are in harmony with ours. Thus, Judaism can live in a collaborative relationship with its sister spiritualities, accepting that Jews have much to learn from others even as we have much of our own to share. Further, in the increasingly open world in which we live, people will move in and out of all spiritual traditions as they seek the place most in harmony with who they are at different stages of their lives.

For example, an expression of this more collaborative approach to the role of Judaism in the world in a liturgical context is the way in which Reb Zalman wrote the following English to go with his reworking of the exclusiveness in the original Hebrew of the *Aleinu* prayer:

We rise to praise You Source of All

עָלֵינוּ לְשַׁבֵּחַ לַאֲדוֹן הַכֹּל

Your generous work as Creator of All

לָתֵת גְּדֻלָּה לְיוֹצֵר בְּרֵאשִׁית

You made us one with all of Life

שֶׁלֹּא עָשָׂנוּ עִם גּוֹיֵי הָאֲרָצוֹת

You helped us to share with all humankind

וְלֹא שָׂמָנוּ עִם מִשְׁפְּחוֹת הָאֲדָמָה

You linked our fate with all that lives

שֶׁלֹּא שָׂם חֶלְקֵנוּ עִמָּהֶם

And made our portion with all in the world.

וְגוֹרָלֵנוּ עִם כָּל הָעוֹלָם

(see *Siddur Kol Koreh*, among other places)

• This leads to the need to introduce a new category into the *halachic* process, which Reb Zalman calls "psycho-halachah." This is the recognition that the practice of *mitzvot* is a means to a spiritual and social end and must be evaluated by whether or not given *mitzvot* actually accomplish the purposes for which they are intended.

• We affirm the chosenness of the Jewish people as a significant organ in the body of humanity and the planet. We also affirm that other peoples are chosen in ways different but no less significant from ours. Just as the Jewish people can see itself as a part of the human species, so also, in the words of Rabbi David Wolfe-Blank of blessed memory, "each self can also know its Jewish flavor, its Kabbalistic coloration, *Sefira* markers, Hassidic *niggun*, and its special Hebrew letter with all the cosmic, golden trail of Divine creativity, antiquity, and adaptability that that implies."

As a result of the common agreement on these basic principles, several practical directions emerge:

• Jewish renewal is fully egalitarian. In a sense, this statement no longer seems as radical as it was only a few years ago, which is a tribute to the rate of change in Jewish life to which Jewish renewal is a major contributor. In fact, the board of ALEPH: Alliance for Jewish Renewal, added a statement on gay marriage to the principles that have guided this organization for over ten years:

ALEPH welcomes, includes and recognizes the sanctity of every individual regardless of sexual orientation or gender identity. We recognize respectful and mutual expressions of adult human sexuality as potentially sacred expressions of love, and therefore we strive to create communities that include and welcome a variety of constellations of intimate relationships and family forms — among them gay, lesbian, and heterosexual relationships as well as single life-paths....

For us, the God of liberation Whose Name was revealed to Moses at the Burning Bush as "I Will Be Who I Will Be" calls in our generation for the strengthening of holy marriage through the inclusion of same sex couples in its joys and responsibilities, both spiritual and legal.

• Jewish renewal especially honors the mystical texts and traditions of Judaism as guides for the further development of consciousness and for their unique way of interpreting the primary texts of the Torah.

• The welcoming of individuals through the creation of safe environments and communities is a priority. Over sixty congregations and *havurot* have been formed under this guiding principle, which also governs all events and programs under the aegis of various renewal organizations.

• Jewish renewal is committed to developing a program of social action that affirms the special place of a self-governing Jewish homeland in the community of nations and affirms the right of all people seeking autonomy and self-government, including the Palestinians.

• Jewish renewal is committed to developing the resources that help people, not only on their first entry into Jewish spiritual life, but throughout their lives.

Jewish renewal is a movement in harmony with our people's tradition of creativity. Just as it is traditional to recite the prayers our ancestors wrote, it is traditional to write prayers, as our ancestors did. Where would be we be today if Rabbi Amnon had not used the pain of his own experience to compose the *U'netaneh Tokef* prayer that we all recite, chant, and sing every Rosh HaShanah and Yom Kippur? Where would we be today if Rabbi Judah the Prince, Rav Safra, and Rabbi Alexandri had not written their own personal meditations for ending their prayers? Not only would we be missing the meditation we use most often after the *Amidah*, we would also be without one of the morning blessings and the traditional Shabbat prayer welcoming the new month. Where would we be today if the Hasidim of Eastern Europe had not composed hundreds of melodies and showed us how music, even without words, can lift us higher and deeper than we ever dreamed possible? Where would we be today if

Moses de Leon had decided to read only books that were already part of everyone's library and had not compiled the *Zohar*?

Our commitment to learning and study also takes many forms. For many, study means deep contemplation of the books written into our souls, which we access through silence and then writing. For others it means allowing the Divine to emerge in color on paper, canvas, or silk. For yet others, it means listening to the music of our souls down through the ages and across worlds, emerging into chant and *niggun*. For still others, it means giving expression to the experience of meditation. And, for many, it means delving into our traditional sacred literature, uncovering new levels of meaning, spiritual richness lying dormant within waiting for us to retranslate, reframe, rediscover, and share.

The trust which the psycho-halachic process places in the individual is greater than in the past, and has special prominence in the movement for Jewish spiritual renewal. The psycho-halachic process reconnects us to the old idea that *minhag*, the custom of the people of a particular place or family, is a significant part of the larger *halachic* process. We are learning to be comfortable again with a variety of practices coexisting, creating a rich and colorful tapestry of what constitutes Judaism in our time.

It is important to note that this interaction between the individual and the communal does not license us to do whatever we want, to make Shabbat for ourselves. Rather we are called to grow, to learn, to reach a level of knowledge, insight, and compassion that merits the trust required for this flexibility. And, we trust that each person will learn how to balance his or her own individual needs with that of a functional and healthy community so that we and others can be nurtured for generations to come.

THE WORLD OF PRAYER

In Jewish renewal, prayer goes beyond the obligatory. We take literally the call to involve our bodies ("let all my bones praise God!"), to "go beyond the words of David, son of Jesse," to "praise God with the horn and the harp." Prayer is an opportunity neither to be missed nor hurried, a chance to bring our creativity to the service of the Holy One, to create harmony and experience connectedness. We sing new music as well as old, celebrate the morning blessings and verses of praise as moments of appreciation for the gifts of body and world, prolong the recitation of the *Sh'ma*, and include personal prayers in our *Amidah*.

THE WORLD OF PRAYER: CONCEPTS

FOUR WORLDS DAVVENEN

Our work is the spiritual renewal of Judaism. We place ourselves firmly within the tradition of creativity, renewal, and change that is as central to our people as is our deep loyalty to the traditions of the past. In particular, we look to the theory and practice of the great Jewish mystics for our models.

Lurianic *kabbalah* offers a dramatic description of Creation as a four stage process, through which ongoing emanations of Divinity evolve successive degrees of separateness from the Divine Infinite. Guided particularly by the teachings of *hasidut* and of Rabbi Zalman Schachter-Shalomi, we have come to appreciate these "Four Worlds of Divine Emanation" as illustrating processes by which God unfolds not only in the cosmos, but within the self as well.

The Four Worlds are called *Assiyah* (doing), *Y'tzirah* (forming), *B'riyah* (creating), and *Atzilut* (emanation, or closeness). In relationship to prayer, they can be described as follows: *Assiyah* is the reality of task-oriented work approached in a spiritual way. In prayer, *Assiyah* is when we acknowledge our bodies and their functioning, accept the reality of this world's multiplicity, and mostly through blessing, express our awareness of its connection to the Divine Source. In prayer, we might express this level by including stretching exercises which loosen the muscles and by asking people to share the blessing of which they are most aware at that moment.

Y'tzirah is the world in which affect, emotional nuance, and modes of feeling are at the center.

This is the realm of myth and archetype. In prayer, this is when we celebrate God as the creator of the natural world, every aspect of which sings God's praises through the medium of our ability to listen and to sing. Chanting, singing, and reciting psalms are the most common liturgical expressions of prayer in *Y'tzirah*. Melodies in rounds or with harmonies, and dancing — both spontaneous and choreographed — are the most common expressions of prayer on this level in Jewish renewal.

B'riyah is the world in which we engage our intellects in Divine service, allowing our minds to open to the highest wisdom. It is here we comprehend our own mission and give voice to our inspiration. In prayer, this is the moment when we link creation, revelation, and redemption and, by reciting the *Sh'ma*, accept God as both transcendent and immanent, distant and intimate. In this world, our prayer may be more traditional in its form, or it may be a time for contemplation and guided meditations.

Atzilut is hardly a "world" at all. Here we strive to erase boundaries and become permeable to each other and to God. In *Atzilut* we seek to know ourselves as vessels for the Divine energy itself. In prayer, this is the time of the *Amidah*, when, through naming our needs, we express our aspirations in the context of being vessels for the Divine. Thus, in Jewish renewal, people are often encouraged to seek out the place, either inside the room or outside, where they feel they can best express themselves in a personal way before God. Often, as in traditional services, we may begin the *Amidah* together. At times, this section of the service will only be in silence.

"NAMING" GOD

Traditional liturgy has chosen to limit the number of names by which we address God. Most often the divine name is read as *Adonai*, "Lord." *Elohim* is also familiar, and when reciting a full psalm, we might recognize the shorter form of *Yah*. In keeping with our understanding of the significant changes taking place in our worldview, we tend to look for more names, rooted in tradition, to express or reinterpret the relationship we have with God. In her *Siddur for Shabbat Morning,* Rabbi Marcia Prager, known for her inspired *davvenen,* describes the way that we give names to God:

The Hebrew letters יהוה, "*Yud-Hay-Vav-Hay,*" constitute the unpronounceable four-letter Name of God which subsumes and unites all the descriptions which Jewish tradition has evolved in its quest for the Divine. The letters are aspirate consonants: letters which, in the absence of vowels, can only be "pronounced" by breathing. This breathing of the Divine Name informs our community's frequent "translation" of יהוה as "The Breath of Life." The Name can also be understood as a causative verb: "(The One Who) Is!" It also resembles God's enigmatic words to Moshe: *Eh'yeh Asher Eh'yeh,* "I Am Who I Am" (Exodus 3:14). Thus יהוה hints at the absurdity of assigning a name to an ineffable Divinity.

Printed thus

יְ
הֹ
וֹ
ה

the arrangement of the letters hints at a human form, reminding us that we are in the Divine Image, and that the energies of the letters which manifest ultimate divinity also flow through us. Historically, it became common to substitute the God-Name *Adonai* when encountering the unpronounceable name in spoken prayer. However, its literal translation as "Lord" is problematic and results in much distress for us. In the Jewish mystical tradition, *Adonai* is understood as a reference to *Shechinah* (the feminine aspect of God) and the *S'firah* of *Malchut* (the feminine gateway into which Divinity flows and then emerges as the manifest universe). In many Jewish renewal communities, the God-Name "Yah," so popular in the psalms, is commonly used in prayer, as this Name shares the first two letters of יהוה and is also suggestive of the link between the ineffable Name and breath.

Throughout Jewish literature and prayer, there are abundant other Names and descriptions of the One Power which is our Source. While we understand God to be entirely inclusive of and also beyond all gender, Hebrew — a rich, evocative, and potent language of prayer — is also an intrinsically gendered language. As you pray, feel free to use the God-Names and gender in both Hebrew and English which reflect your experience of the Divine.

"BLESSING" GOD

The traditional formula for "blessing" God serves several purposes. At its deepest level, reciting the formula makes us conscious of being the channels through which the longing of the universe to reconnect with its source is fulfilled. Thus, that which we are appreciating, ingesting, or doing, moves from the level of physical *Assiyah* to that of spiritual *Assiyah.* Eating becomes the channeling of potential energy to the actual service of God as wheat is transformed into bread and its energy then released into prayer and good deeds. The fragrance of flowers is transformed from personal pleasure to appreciation of the Creator of all creation. In blessing each other we cultivate a connection to the Divine in the other and an appreciation of the unique gifts and purposes of each person.

The direct address used in most forms of blessing also affirms our personal relationship with the Divine. We speak directly to God, who is close to us and responds. At the same time, God is sovereign over all creation, source of all life, the object of our awe through whom we too are connected to all that is, was, and will ever be. Finally, it is our relationship with God which is the source of our belief in being commanded, or invited, to share in the ongoing process of creation and redemption simply by becoming conscious of the infinite in each part of creation and elevating it to its source.

Over the years, we have experimented with many ways of expressing these beliefs within the framework of our traditional formula. Some are ways of changing the traditional wording into the feminine, while others are more radical, redefining the way in which we express our relationship with God. Below, taken from *Siddur Kol Koreh,* are samples of various possibilities for the language of a blessing. People are encouraged to use them both when leading and when praying on their own.

Alternative Masculine:

בָּרוּךְ אַתָּה יָהּ אֱלֹהֵינוּ מְקוֹר הַחַיִּים

Blessed are You, Yah our God, Source of Life.

Alternative Feminine:

בְּרוּכָה אַתְּ שְׁכִינָה אֵם כָּל חָי

Blessed are You, *Sh'chinah*, Mother of all life.

(From *Siddur Kol Koreh*, ALEPH: Alliance for Jewish Renewal)

THE WORLD OF PRAYER: EXPRESSIONS AND TECHNIQUES

Until recently, the form and expression of prayer in most synagogues were limited to reciting the text of the prayer book, some congregational singing and reading, and a teaching or sermon delivered by a rabbi in the form of a lecture. In Jewish renewal, some of these forms are maintained, especially key parts of the traditional liturgy. These include the basic structure of the service, as well as specific prayers such as the *Sh'ma* and the *Amidah*, the *Kaddish* in its various forms, and the Torah reading. Jewish renewal has also reintroduced practices that, while traditional, had fallen out of use over the past century. These would include the freedom to move about the sanctuary during prayer, the welcoming of children, more spirited singing in the Hasidic style, and an informality around the Torah service which encourages discussion and the writing of new *midrashim*. In addition, Jewish renewal teachers and communities have adapted practices from other spiritual traditions and expanded some Jewish practices beyond their traditional limits as ways of responding to the needs of people in this time. Some examples of this creativity are:

MUSIC

The focus on song and melody as a crucial aspect in Jewish renewal prayer is difficult to describe in words. Perhaps most significantly, we combine the recent custom of congregational singing most prevalent in liberal synagogues with the intensity of the Hasidic *niggun*, or melody, whose ability to lift the soul depends both on the way the melody reaches into the heart and on repetition. For the many people for whom Jewish

renewal is their reentry point and even their first introduction to Jewish prayer, reducing the volume of words and slowing the speed at which they are recited is crucial to discovering meaning in prayer.

Early in the history of this movement, prayer leaders decided to use melody as a way to increase the time spent on those words that were retained. The decision as to which were allowed to be omitted and which had to be kept was made on traditional grounds. Thus, one would find few renewal services where central prayers such as the *Sh'ma* and *Amidah* are not said in one form or another. At the same time, the custom emerged to sing words with special significance, allowing participants to experience their meaning in a profound way. This practice also led to the composing of hundreds of melodies, not only for those parts of the service most familiar, though this is where it began, but also to individual lines of psalms and parts of prayers written for Shabbat and holidays.

Many composers have also been drawn to those parts of the service for which the least music already existed. Because of the emphasis on bringing all four levels of consciousness into play at every service, described above as the four "worlds" of Jewish prayer, Jewish renewal has paid much more attention to the early parts of the morning services, in particular the morning blessings and verses of praise, which are so often recited in a monotone and as quickly as possible in traditional prayer. There are melodies and chants for the blessings relating to the return of the soul to the body after the night's sleep, especially for *Modeh Ani* and "the soul which you have given me is pure." There are numerous melodies and chants for *Baruch She'amar*, lines of the *Ashrei* and psalms that follow, and parts of the *Nishmat* prayer.

It is not uncommon for services in Jewish renewal settings to have as much time allocated for the morning blessings and verses of praise as for the formal Shacharit, or morning service itself. During these times, there will be much singing, meditative chanting, and periods of silence. Thus, people have a chance to allow the meaning of the words to penetrate deeply enough to become influential in their lives and for them to be able to carry them into their normal environments outside the synagogue.

CHANTING

More than any other single person, Rabbi Shefa Gold has been responsible for bringing the art of sacred chant from the Sufi tradition into Jewish prayer. As you will see from what she says in *Siddur Kol Koreh*, chanting is not the same as singing:

Chanting, the repetition of a sacred phrase, is a way of transforming the words of liturgy into doorways. They become entrances into expanded states of consciousness. They become the lanterns by which our inner journeys may be illuminated. Rabbi Abraham Joshua Heschel says, "It is only after we kindle a light in the words that we are able to behold the riches they contain." We kindle a light in the words through careful and loving attention to breath, intention, meaning, sound, melody, harmony, tone, rhythm, and through the will to repeat a phrase long enough that a shift in consciousness can occur.

The art of chanting in community requires a double focus — on the ever-deepening center of one's being, and on the group energy that is emerging. With each repetition of the phrase, the chanter has an opportunity to strengthen and refine both these points of focus. By opening the heart, the chanter finds within herself more to give the group. And by becoming a servant to the group, the chanter is given access to the deeper realms of her own heart.

When the sound of a chant has ended, the most subtle, transformative and powerful part of the practice can begin. By entering into the silence after a chant, we can receive both the Divine influx and the gifts that bubble up from the soul. The silence after a chant is a completely different, yet complementary practice to the chant itself. At the end of a chant, the silence helps to focus attention on the breath moving gently in and out of the heart. One surrenders to the power that the chant has generated, letting it do its work within. In the silence, the chanter notices everything possible, knowing

that a heightened attention is necessary in order to enter in through whatever doors have been opened by the power of the chant. Awareness of a state magnifies its benefit.

In a prayer service a chant can be used to enter the liturgy from an expanded mind-state, to build soul-connection between the chanters, to release the blocks to prayer, to open the heart to new possibilities, and to build and refine energy which can then be used for further prayer and healing.

TRANSLATIONS AND PRAYING IN ENGLISH

Again, in a way reminiscent of the Hasidic movement of Eastern Europe, the meaning of the words recited in prayer is of special importance in Jewish renewal. While I know that many people in the other movements within Judaism feel that maintaining traditional forms is the higher value, the intensity of the relationship with the Divine which is at the core of Jewish renewal virtually requires that the words of the prayers have meaning for those reciting them.

In addition, the large numbers of people coming to Jewish renewal with little or no familiarity with Hebrew makes it necessary to compose English translations which can be sung in the same melodies as the Hebrew originals. Thus, many of the melodies composed for parts of the service also contain English verses that translate or supplement the Hebrew.

A case in point is the last verse of Psalm 90. This verse is enigmatic in the Hebrew, lending itself to many possible translations. In the Reconstructionist movement's Shabbat and festival prayer book *Kol Haneshamah*, this verse reads: "Let our divine protector's pleasure be upon us, and the labor of our hands, make it secure, the labor of our hands ensure!" (p. 194). In an earlier prayer book of the Conservative movement, this same verse reads: "And let Thy graciousness, O Lord our God, be upon us; Establish Thou also the work of our hands for us; Yea, the work of our hands establish Thou it" (Morris Silverman, *Sabbath and Festival Prayer Book*, p. 68). In an early Jewish renewal prayer book for Shabbat, Rabbi Burt Jacobson translated this same verse as follows:

"May the beauty of God rest on us. May God establish the works of our hands and may the works of our hands establish God."

This last translation resolves the ambiguities of that verse with a clear expression of the sense of being in partnership with the Divine in the ongoing unfolding of creation and history. It is deeply meaningful within the context of Jewish renewal's focus on the Divine feminine, the "indwelling presence of God," and the sense that humanity is the *Shechinah's* voice in the process of reunifying all of life within a consciousness of God. It makes concrete the familiar saying of the Kotzker Rebbe that God dwells wherever God is let in.

A beautiful example of the use of translation to bring new meaning to the Hebrew is the following interpretation written by Rabbi David Wolfe-Blank for the second paragraph of the *Sh'ma*, printed in *Siddur Kol Koreh*:

And it will come to pass,
that when you deeply listen to the underlying
    patterns of the commandments
with which I enjoin you here this day,
namely, to love and accept your Creator
and to dedicate yourself with heart and soul,
then your joy will manifest in your physical
    surroundings as good seasons.
You will be able to attain satisfaction of all
    your needs here in a joyful world.
When you eat you will feel satisfied.
Watch yourselves
that you do not miss the point of connection
    to your Godplace
and be left with rituals that are meaningless to
    you.
Your own anger and disappointment will then
    echo against yourselves,
causing you to lose alignment with your
    divine connection.
This misalignment will reverberate through-
    out your lives,
causing needless unhappiness and suffering.
Return again to the depth of these words with
    heart and soul,
bind yourselves into them with every physical
    act and thought,
study and teach the truth to your children,
remind yourselves frequently even as you sit

in your house,
as you travel, dream and wake.
May your days and the days of your children
    be full on the earth,
as God has always intended and so promised
    to your parents' parents,
that you may enjoy the most heavenly benev-
    olence
right here as you live on this land.

MOVEMENT AND DANCE

Prayer in Jewish renewal releases those who have always wanted the freedom to express themselves through movement. While small Orthodox congregations allow for a certain amount of movement by the men, it is still rare for a liberal synagogue to encourage people to move in their places or dance. In Jewish renewal, the custom of moving freely to the music of the service, joining others in spontaneous dance, and even learning choreographed dances as part of prayer, is common. Several Jewish renewal teachers spent time with North American Sufis and learned the movements to *Zikr*, sacred Sufi dancing, which they have then reinterpreted for a Jewish environment.

Many years ago, during a *Hallel* led by the Rosh Chodesh group of Or Shalom in Vancouver, British Columbia, a gate was made by two people as the community danced to a melody for the verse *Pitchu li sha'arei tzedek*, "open for me the gates of righteousness." People joined hands and danced as couples through that gate and this informal dance became a regular part of *Hallel* in that community for many years. In B'nai Or of Boston, it is often the case that preparations for the High Holiday services include dancing parts of the service and setting the Torah reading to movement and dramatization. An example of a choreographed dance, again using the last verse of Psalm 90, is the following developed by Rabbi Hanna Tiferet Siegel, which goes with the melody she composed for this verse:

Vi'hi Noam Partner Dance

This song acknowledges the creative energy that flows through our hands. It is the chant of the artist, and we are all artists in life. This dance makes use of the hands in many different ways.

Choose a partner. Stand next to each other.

Form a large circle, facing the center.

Vi'hi Noam	Circle right arm above head, then left arm above head.
Adonai	Hands on heart
Eloheinu	Rest arms on backs of people next to you in circle.
Aleinu	Feeling blessed as one, bend forward together slowly, then backward.

Repeat the pattern above.

uma'aseh yadeinu	Face your partner and look into his/her eyes. Allow your palms to touch at heart level and then mirror each other, circling up, out, down and back to center.
kon'nah aleinu	Place hands on partner's head, blessing him/her.
uma'aseh yadeinu	Extend right hand to shake hands with your partner and gently place your left hand on the outside of the handshake. Say goodbye with eye contact as you extend your left hand and greet your new partner (allemande right and left).
kon'neihu	Cross right hand over left in a double handshake. Lift arms up and let go. Turn to center of circle with arms extended above and begin again.

HEALING

A prominent feature of prayer services in Jewish renewal for decades has been a focus on healing. Many of the people drawn to this spiritually based approach to Judaism suffered abuse in childhood, loss of significant family members to illnesses, or the trauma of being the children of Holocaust survivors. The strong sense of community and caring which is central to most Jewish renewal communities led to the practice of making prayers for healing central and personal. In *Siddur Kol Koreh*, there are three prayers for healing in addition to the traditional one often recited during the Torah reading. It is not uncommon for healing prayers to be offered on Friday evenings as well, with people in need coming to the center of the circle and the rest of the congregation standing around them offering blessing. The practice of calling out the names of others for whom people are praying is also one of long standing.

This practice has been further developed in the emerging Jewish healing centers, and services especially devoted to healing have been added in many communities. For the most part, however, Jewish renewal communities tend to continue the earlier practice of including healing as a significant part of regular Shabbat services.

Many of the healing prayers use the prayer which Moses said on behalf of his sister Miriam (Numbers 12:13). What follows is an example of such a healing prayer written by Rabbi Aryeh Hirschfield:

From deep within the home of my soul,
Now let the healing, let the healing begin.

אָנָּא אֵל נָא רְפָא נָא לָהּ

Heal our bodies, open our hearts,
awaken our minds
E'he'ye (or) *Sh'chinah*

CONCLUSION

In the preface to the second edition of his book *Ivdu Et Hashem B'Simcha: Serve the Holy One with Joy!*, Rabbi David Zaslow expresses an attitude toward prayer which will resonate for many people in Jewish renewal. In this *siddur* he also gives voice to what we hope will become infused into the prayer life of Jews who already pray and provide a way for others to begin to pray:

A few final words about *davvenen*. It's joyous, it's profound, it's misunderstood, and it takes practice. Traditionally we were taught that praying from a *siddur* is supposed to be done in a particular way; every word is read clearly and pronounced accurately. Our attitude, we were taught, was to be formal and serious. The image we have inherited is that during the *Amidah* we are having a 'private meeting with the King of Universe.' Given the seriousness of the situation, formality and awe are in order. Yet, for many traditional *davveners* the actual experience is personal, sweet, and informal.

There seems to be a rhythm to praying whose musicality is affected by many factors: mood, weather, climate, time constraints, etc. Once I accept the reality that there is no perfect *davvenen*, then I can begin to accept the perfection of my own imperfection. At that point I can start to enjoy my prayer-life, and actually experience God's presence.

The most important impact that Reb Zalman's teachings on davvenology have had on my own prayer life, is that when I *davven* I envision myself as entering into a conversation with God. I am not trying to get through a service, read a certain number of pages, or do something right.

It is normal for a particular prayer to speak to me one day, and ignore me the next day. In this way, each prayer comes alive, and becomes an opportunity for me to speak with God through the language of my ancestor. A prayer should not be a chain that holds us back from God because we lack Hebrew or experience. Rather, a prayer can be seen as the string of a kite keeping us both grounded and soaring in the same moment. *Boruch Hashem*!"

RESOURCES

For more information about Jewish renewal and a list of resources and links, see the website of ALEPH: Alliance for Jewish Renewal and their ReSources Catalog at http://www.aleph.org.

To experience prayer in a Jewish renewal context, spend a week at Elat Chayyim, the Jewish Retreat Center in Accord, New York (http://www.elatchayyim.org), or attend the biennial ALEPH Kallah.

For a list of communities affiliated with the Network of Jewish Renewal Communities, visit the ALEPH website.

RESOURCES CITED IN THIS CHAPTER AVAILABLE FROM THE ALEPH RESOURCES CATALOG:

SIDDURIM

Prager, Marcia. *A Siddur for Shabbat Morning.* N.p., n.d. Also available is a *siddur* for Friday night.

Siegel, Daniel, ed. *Siddur Kol Koreh.* N.P., n.d.

Tiferet, Hanna. *I Am My Prayer: The Hanna Tiferet Songbook.* Boston, MA: Hanna Tiferet, n.d. Also available from http://www.hannatiferet.com.

Wolfe-Blank, David. *Meta Siddur: Recipes for Jewish Renewal.* N.P., n.d.

Zaslow, David, ed. *Ivdu Et Hashem B'Simcha: Serve the Holy One with Joy!* Ashland, OR: N.P., n.d. Also available from Rabbi David Zaslow, shalomrav@aol.com.

TEACHINGS OF RABBI ZALMAN SCHACHTER-SHALOMI

A Guide for Starting Your Next Incarnation: Reb Zalman on T'shuvah
Hashir V'hashevach (The Song and the Praise), compiled by Rabbi David Zaslow
The Kabbalah of Tikkun Olam
Spiritual Economics
The Ten S'firot and Sacred Time
Yom Kippur Kattan and the Cycles of T'shuvah

AUDIOTAPES AND CDS OF SERVICES

Davvening with Reb Zalman (cd/*siddur*)
For Your Healing (Reb Zalman)
P'nai Or Kabbalat Shabbat with Rabbi Marcia Prager and Hazzan Jack Kessler
Shir Tikvah Live (Reform/Renewal Synagogue in Troy, Michigan)
Words of Light Shabbaton

MUSIC

Recordings of Jewish renewal music are available from the composers and in many Jewish stores and catalogues. A partial list includes:

Rabbi Tirzah Firestone
Rabbi Jack Gabriel
Rabbi Shefa Gold (www.rabbishefagold.com)
Rabbi Aryeh Hirschfield
Rabbi Yitzchak Husbands-Hankin
Rabbi Geela Rayzel Raphael
Rabbi Hanna Tiferet Siegel
(www.hannatiferet.com)

OTHER RESOURCES

Buber, Martin and Olga Marx. *Tales of the Hasidim, Vol. 2: Later Masters.* New York: Random House, 1961.

Cooper, David A. *God Is a Verb: Kabbalah and the Practice of Mystical Judaism.* New York: Riverhead Books, 1997.

Prager, Marcia. *The Path of Blessing: Experiencing the Energy and Abundance of the Divine.* New York: Bell Tower, 1998.

Rosman, Moshe. *Founder of Hasidism: A Quest for the Historical Ba'al Shem Tov.* Berkeley, CA: The University of California Press, 1996.

Schachter-Shalomi, Zalman. *Paradigm Shift.* Northvale, NJ: Jason Aronson, 1993.

———. *Wrapped in a Holy Flame: Tales and Teachings of the Hasidic Masters.* San Francisco, CA: Jossey-Bass, 2003.

Weiner, Shohama Harris and Jonathan Omer-Man, eds. *Worlds of Jewish Prayer: A Festschrift in Honor of Rabbi Zalman M. Schachter-Shalomi.* Northvale, NJ: Jason Aronson, 1993.

Rabbi Daniel Siegel is the Director of Spiritual Resources for ALEPH: Alliance for Jewish Renewal, an organization of those who are dedicated to reclaiming the Jewish people's sacred purpose of partnership with the Divine in the inseparable tasks of healing the world (tikkun olam) and healing of the heart (tikkun halev). ALEPH offers teleconferencing classes for adults, sponsors numerous retreats and events, and edits and publishes the teachings of Reb Zalman Schachter-Shalomi and others. Rabbi Siegel serves the ALEPH Rabbinic Program in several capacities, including teacher, director of studies, and consultant. As well as serving as editor of Siddur Kol Koreh *and other resources for prayer, Rabbi Siegel is a trained mediator and is available to individuals and communities in conflict and transition. Along with his life partner Rabbi Hanna Tiferet Siegel, he is also the co-spiritual leader of B'nai Or of Boston.*

CHAPTER NINETEEN:
SEEKING HARMONY
MUSIC, PRAYER, AND SACRED COMMUNITY

Merri Lovinger Arian

From the very earliest of times, music and prayer have been inextricably linked in Jewish tradition. As prayer is often an attempt to express the inexpressible, to reach out to the unknowable, and to ask for the seemingly unattainable, it is not surprising that one looks to music to help in this sacred task. Referring to prayer, Rabbi Abraham Joshua Heschel writes, "The inadequacy of the means at our disposal appears so tangible, so tragic, that one feels it a grace to be able to give oneself up to music, to a tone, to a song, to a chant."[1] It is in the music of the Jewish people that one finds "the joys and triumphs, the tenderness and warmth, the agony and sorrows, the prayer and the protest . . ."[2]

THE TRADITION OF MUSIC WITHIN JEWISH WORSHIP

Sacred music is first mentioned in the Bible during the time of King David.[3] When the Ark was first transferred to Jerusalem (c. 1000 B.C.E.), the ceremony featured instrumental music and dance (II Sam. 6). Immediately thereafter, even before the First Temple was built, singers were appointed to be in charge of the singing that accompanied the daily and special offerings (I Chron. 6: 16-33). Music continued to accompany the sacrificial worship throughout the First

Temple period. During the Second Temple era, the music accompanying the service may have been even more elaborate. It featured Levitical choirs and accompanying instrumentation that included woodwinds, percussion, brass, and strings.

Toward the end of the Second Temple period, as synagogues began to develop, the worship music that emerged reflected the Halachic prohibitions against the use of musical instruments in certain settings. In respect for the destruction of the Temple, the role of music was somewhat deemphasized. Early synagogue music was dominated by different types of chant. There is evidence that the art of chanting biblical verses may date back to the time of the Second Temple. The actual codification of the scripture cantillation, as we know it today, didn't happen until the seventh to ninth centuries, culminating in the sophisticated system of notation created by the Masoretic school of Tiberias.

By the twelfth century, one finds reference to Jewish Psalm singing, often antiphonal in nature. Prayer modes, linked to specific times and seasons, developed. These traditional motifs were known as "*nusach*," pertaining to a version or manner of style in which the prayers are executed musically according to a given tradition. *Nusach* became the normative form of musical expression in worship, with different versions (Ashkenazic, Sephardic and others) developing in different geo-

---

[1] Abraham Joshua Heschel, *Man's Quest for God.* (Scribner's, 1954), p. 39, quoted in Samuel H. Dresner, ed., *I Asked For Wonder: A Spiritual Anthology* (New York: Crossroad, 2002), p. 32.

[2] Judith Kaplan Eisenstein, *Heritage of Music: The Music of the Jewish People* (Wyncote, PA: The Reconstructionist Press, 1990), p. 3.

[3] Much of the historical overview that follows is based on Eliyahu Schleifer, *"Jewish Liturgical Music from The Bible to Hasidism,"* quoted in Lawrence A. Hoffman and Janet R. Walton, eds., *Sacred Sound and Social Change* (Notre Dame, IN: University of Notre Dame Press, 1992), p. 13, and Lawrence A. Hoffman, *"Musical Traditions and Tensions in the American Synagogue ,"* quoted in David Power, Mary Collins, and Mellonee Burnim, eds., *Music and the Experience of God: Concilium 222* (Edinburgh: T. and T. Clark, 1989), p. 30.

graphic regions. In many places, specialists (*hazzanim* or cantors) were appointed to serve as *shlichei tzibbur* (prayer leaders; literally, "representatives of the public") to lead the chanting in worship. For these professionals, *nusach* was the basis for their *hazzanut* (cantorial art), a framework from which they improvised according to their individual talent and skill.

The rise of Hasidism in Eastern Europe in the early eighteenth century in many ways represented a populist rebellion against the professionalization of Jewish prayer life. The Baal Shem Tov and his followers taught that through prayer, God could be accessed by everyone. A favorite Hasidic musical form is the *niggun* — a simple, wordless tune that can be sung easily by every member of the community, not only by trained musical specialists.

In the eighteenth and nineteenth centuries, reformers in Western Europe made changes in the style of synagogue worship, by enhancing decorum and formality and by borrowing elements from the worship practices of their Christian neighbors. These changes were reflected in synagogue music, with the introduction of the organ as a staple in liberal congregations. Cantorial art changed as well, becoming increasingly formal. Composed (as opposed to improvised) music, performed by a trained cantor and choir, became the norm in many congregations.

In the late twentieth century and into the twenty-first, music continues to play a critical and sometimes controversial role in synagogue worship. Congregants increasingly come to synagogue looking for connection and community. Synagogues have responded to this by becoming more intimate in many ways. The architecture of newer synagogues emphasizes closer proximity between the clergy and the congregant, creating a more intimate space. Clergy are creating moments for congregants to share their stories within worship, seeking to promote connectedness between members of the congregation. Music, too, has followed suit. The more intimate sound of the guitar or piano is often used to replace the overwhelming power of the organ as the instrument of choice in worship. Newer synagogue compositions often invite congregational singing,

rather than (or, in addition to) cantorial performance. These trends are reflected in Orthodox congregations as well. The melodies of Shlomo Carlebach, which invite congregational participation and encourage informality, increasingly supplant more traditional *hazzanut* in many Orthodox setttings.

In each age of Jewish history, Jewish sacred music grows and develops, reflecting the particular needs of the age and the growth of the liturgy itself. In every age, worship has been enhanced by the unique power of music.

THE POWER OF MUSIC

I never cease to be amazed by the indisputable power of music. In my work as a music therapist, music educator, song leader, and prayer leader, I have seen music touch people in a way that nothing else comes close to achieving.

I remember as a music therapist, sitting with geriatric patients who could barely tell me their children's names. Yet, the moment I began to play a melody for them on the piano, the lyrics of the song would pour out of them, word for word, with astonishing accuracy. Something about the engaging quality of music managed to stay locked securely in their memories, and the instant they heard those familiar tunes the words came tumbling forth. Similarly, when these patients would sit and speak with me about their lives, invariably they would share wonderful memories they had of singing in their synagogue or church choirs. A smile would form on their lips as they shared stories of communal religious moments they experienced through participation in these choirs. These "performing" groups served a function that their choir leaders may never have imagined. These choirs forged lifelong relationships and memories that brought a sparkle to these seniors' eyes, too often dimmed by aging and loss.

For example, there was the middle-aged gentleman who, recovering from surgery performed on a malignant brain tumor, shared that what he had missed most during his convalescence were his weekly synagogue choir rehearsals. He could well do without the board meetings and countless other committee meetings that he was missing, but eagerly awaited his return to his synagogue choir community.

As an educational tool, music has been proven to be effective in the learning of new material. How did each and every one of us learn to recite the letters of the alphabet? We sang them, of course! Many a Hebrew teacher teaches body parts, colors, days of the week, and members of the family through songs composed for just that purpose. My husband learned the names of the first thirty-seven presidents of the United States of America in much the same way. Music compartmentalizes information in a way that is easier for people to store and master. Similarly, the liturgy of our worship services is most effectively taught through the various musical settings that are available to us. An example of the efficacy of music in this arena is best exemplified by Debbie Friedman's setting of the *Mi Shebeirach* prayer. For most Reform Jews, this liturgy was completely foreign prior to Debbie's composition. Now, most can recite this text almost as easily as they can the *Sh'ma* or *Bar'chu*. This musical setting breathed life into a liturgical text that for many was completely unfamiliar. Music teachers in our religious schools harness this most accessible medium as a tool unparalleled in the school setting.

The educational power of music to which I refer is grounded in current educational theory. Dr. Howard Gardner, Professor of Cognition and Education at the Harvard Graduate School of Education, developed the Theory of Multiple Intelligences.[4] In it he describes seven distinct "intelligences" — pathways through which people learn. These include:

• Logical-Mathematical Intelligence
• Linguistic Intelligence
• Spatial Intelligence
• Musical Intelligence
• Bodily-Kinesthetic Intelligence
• Personal Intelligences
• Intrapersonal Intelligence

By activating a wide assortment of intelligences, teaching can facilitate a deeper understanding of the subject material. Gardner's specific reference to music as one of these portals of learning speaks exactly to my point.

It has been said that music is the heartbeat of a people, and if one is to study the culture of a people, one can learn volumes just by hearing their music. The music of a people tells their story. Judith Kaplan Eisenstein put it beautifully when she stated, "When we live for a moment with that music, we are touching the pulse itself, and our own is quickened in turn."[5]

Music touches, teaches, transforms, and has the capacity to help individuals transcend their solitary existence to become part of something much greater.

MUSIC AS A MEANS OF BUILDING SACRED COMMUNITY

As I have already suggested, music is a medium which bonds people together, our synagogue choirs being a case in point. As a song leader in a number of Jewish camps, time and again I would be reminded of the central role that music played in building these camp communities. Whether it be the highly spirited "A-minor medley" of Israeli folksongs that brought the community to its feet dancing hand in hand, or the more mellow section of the repertoire that had people rocking back and forth, arm in arm, music was at the forefront, helping all of this to happen, carefully orchestrated in such a way as to respect and respond to the community it served.

But what about "sacred" community — *kehillah k'dosha*? Synagogue 2000, a trans-denominational synagogue transformation project that is committed to helping synagogues examine their current structure and reimagine ways to be better at what they already do, devotes the first eighteen months of its three-year curriculum to the study of sacred community. A sacred community is defined as one in which its members are welcoming, caring, and responsive. The conversations

---

[4] Gardner, Howard. *Frames of Mind: The Theory of Multiple Intelligences.* (New York: Basic Books Inc., 1983).

[5] Eisenstein, p. 3.

that happen within a sacred community are different from those you would hear elsewhere. The committees that make up a sacred community are seen as teams with common goals. Its members "check in" with one another in a formalized manner, to assure that people are caught up with what is going on in one another's lives. People study together, pray together, sing together, and share one another's life's journeys.

Where does music fit into this community? In its rituals, celebrations, programs, and, perhaps most importantly, in its modes of worship. For it is when the community comes together to pray that one can most easily see the sacred at work. Music is, once again, in the forefront. How one selects music, "performs" music, teaches music, and uses music within worship directly affects the strength of the sacred community it seeks to create. For as Rabbi Pinchas Koretz taught: "… Alone I cannot lift my voice in song — Then you come near and sing with me. Our prayers fuse, and a new voice soars. Our bond is beyond voice and voice. Our bond is one of spirit and spirit. . . ." [6]

MUSIC AS A MEANS FOR CREATING MEANINGFUL WORSHIP

For the traditional Jew, prayer is a commandment. One comes to the synagogue to pray because one is commanded to do so. Music can heighten that prayer experience and enhance the text in such ways as to bring deeper meaning to the ancient words. The *nusach* chanted during the worship service sets the tone of the service, signaling a particular time in the Jewish calendar, connecting the prayer with all the history and meaning of that particular time. The familiar melodies connect the person praying to a tradition and a long history — an understanding that the sacred act that she is involved in is a link in a long chain. Those melodies intensify the prayer experience as they bring to mind parents and grandparents who came before, uttering these

very same words and melodies, hundreds of years before. These melodies serve as touchstones — guideposts — as one proceeds through the prayer experience.

For the less traditional Jew, though, prayer services can be somewhat daunting — the language foreign and difficult to pronounce, and the customs unfamiliar and awkward. Often it is the music that can help ease these people into the prayer experience, for music is the universal language and music can help level the "praying field"!

BEGINNINGS

How we *begin* the prayer experience is important. We need to recognize where the congregants are coming from — a missed train, a late babysitter, a hassled week at work, a week of being indoors with a sick child. They need to be welcomed into the prayer experience. I was reminded recently about how important this *Kabbalat Shabbat* experience can be. As I sat in Congregation B'nai Jeshurun in New York City, I couldn't help noticing that we sang together in prayer for a solid half hour, before reaching *L'cha Dodi*. This conservative synagogue is not alone in its recognition of the importance of this beginning time. At Kol HaNeshama, a Reform congregation in Jerusalem, Rabbi Levi Weiman-Kelman also takes this warm-up time, this welcoming of the Shabbat, equally seriously. In synagogues spanning the entire range of Jewish observance, from "Rock 'n Roll Shabbat" at Temple Beth Jacob in Redwood City, California to the Religious Zionist Youth Movement's Carlebach Minyan in Syndey, Australia, we learn that taking the time is important. It needs to be inviting, and *not* intimidating.

We need to be cognizant of who it is that plans our worship services. The Jewish professionals of the congregation plan our worship — those who do this "religion thing" as a profession. Getting into prayer is something that most probably comes easily to them! But not true for

---

[6] Rabbi Pinhas of Koretz, as quoted in *Entrances to Holiness Are Everywhere* (White Plains, NY: Congregation Kol Ami, 1998), p. 10b.

the layperson. She needs to be nurtured and guided into the experience. The opening music is our first chance! The music needs to be relatively easy to access, and familiar. I do not want the congregant to be focused on an awkward rhythm, or difficult melody. I want her to be looking inward and focusing on prayer. When carefully planned, the music at the beginning of the service can help her do just that.

TRANSITIONS

How one transitions from one part of the service to another greatly affects the prayer experience. The music that one selects during these transitional times needs to support the feeling that one is creating. For example, how one moves in and out of silence is terribly important. There needs to be a sense of quieting down, a slowing of the pace. Silence is not a familiar space for many of us whose lives are usually accompanied by a din of competing calls for our attention. Yet, the silent prayer is often cited as the part of the service that people most look forward to. When we select music that precedes the silent prayer, we need to help guide people to this special place. Similarly, when we come out of this silence, we want to help people hold on to the calm that they have just experienced, and so we select music that matches that quietude, gradually increasing the dynamics and tempo as we proceed onward through the liturgy.

It was not until the death of my father that I understood the importance of the transition needed following the Mourner's *Kaddish*. In most congregations, the next moment is filled with either announcements or a closing hymn. For the first time, I understood as a mourner how jolting that closing hymn or congregational announcement could be, coming on the heels of that intense prayer. Attention needs to be given to that transition, in such a way as to provide closure for the person saying *Kaddish*. In some congregations, that transition is accomplished by the rabbi reciting something in English, acknowledging how we as a congregation take the names of all of these people into our hearts. This transition can also be handled musically, with the insertion of an *a cappella* refrain, that is appropriately contemplative in nature, possibly using the text of *Oseh Shalom*. We ask people to open their hearts, and be present in prayer, and we need to be sensitive and respectful of their needs and their vulnerability.

ENHANCING THE TEXT

The music that we use in our worship services needs to reflect the texts that it accompanies. Surely we understand that our liturgical texts are sacred and enduring, yet sometimes we say the words, not really thinking about their meaning. Music is an opportunity to "check in" on the meaning of the text. When chosen sensitively, music can enhance and sometimes even bring new or deeper meaning to these age-old prayers. Think about that time in our service when we ask God to grant peace to us, and our people. Think of all the beautiful melodies that have been written for *Sim Shalom*, *Shalom Rav*, and *Oseh Shalom*, to name just a few prayers. Those melodies that you remember are the ones that truly gave extra meaning to those moments. What about the joy of the Israelites crossing the Red Sea, as they spoke those ancient words: *Mi chamocha ba-eilim Adonai*? Again, we can almost hear the joyful, triumphant melodies that have been composed expressly for that moment. And what about all of the new melodies that have been written to support the healing moments that congregations are now creating within their regular worship settings? These melodies capture the urgency of peoples' prayers of healing for loved ones in a way that the text alone simply cannot do.

Our worship is made ever more meaningful by the inclusion of music that helps guide people into prayer, helps them make transitions within the service, and enhances and deepens the meaning of the text.

MUSIC IN WORSHIP TODAY

We are living in a time of transition. Worship renewal is in the consciousness of people across the spectrum of observance. It is no surprise, then, that we are witnessing a renewed burst of creative energy around Jewish music. Everyone may not be in agreement as to how that music should sound, or how that music should be "performed" but all agree that music is crucial to the prayer life of a congregation.

There was a time when people yearned to be spoken to and sung to! People flocked to Carnegie Hall in large numbers to hear great orators like Rabbi Stephen Wise, and great *hazzanim* like David Kousevitsky. They were uplifted and inspired by these experiences, and they walked out of these great halls having transcended their mundane, day-to-day existence. That was the same generation who went to their doctor's office, heard the doctor's diagnosis, and left the office knowing just which pill to take for what ailed them. When asked, though, why the doctor had prescribed that particular medication, or whether or not they had questioned a particular procedure that was being suggested, the answer would always be, "No. He is the professional. He knows best."

Those times are long gone. People want to be involved in a very different way. They want to discuss the doctor's diagnosis. They want to understand the doctor's prescription, and they want to be part of the conversation. Similarly, people want to be empowered in prayer. They quite literally want a voice in prayer. They want to be able to sing the sacred texts. As my dear friend and colleague, Cantor Benjie Ellen Schiller states, "Singing gives them the sacred key that allows their access to Jewish sacred tradition." [7]

---

[7] Benjie Ellen Schiller, *"The Many Faces of Jewish Sacred Music."* Quoted in Synagogue 2000 *Itinerary for Change: Prayer* (Los Angeles: Synagogue 2000, 2002), pp. 6-18.

PRINCIPLES OF ONE SHABBAT MORNING
Craig Taubman

Craig Taubman's dynamic music has been an integral part of Jewish worship for nearly twenty-five years. In 1998, Craig, along with Rabbi David Wolpe, created "Friday Night Live," a unique musical worship service at Temple Sinai in Westwood, California. Held one Shabbat each month, Friday Night Live continues to attract some 2,000 worshippers who sing and sway, dance and pray to Craig's powerful and inspirational music. Though not the first service of its kind, the huge success of Friday Night Live sparked a wave of similar alternative musical worship experiences in communities across North America. Four years later, Craig introduced "One Shabbat Morning" at Adat Ari El in Valley Village, California. One Shabbat Morning is a unique fusion of the ancient Cantorial style with a modern folk sensibility — an emotional and powerful prayer experience that helps reveal the magic of Shabbat. The following principles that guide One Shabbat morning are informative and enlightening for those seeking to create a similar worship experience, and come from Craig's One Shabbat Morning Songbook.

Worship services are a chance to celebrate life and confront our vulnerabilities with a community that supports us in good times and bad. Prayer is a chance to grow spiritually, a chance to come into contact with the source of our higher selves, a chance to connect with God.

American Jews know how to think, but they don't always know how to pray. To pray means to relinquish control. It means to reveal your innermost thoughts and emotions, allowing yourself to be vulnerable. Worshippers want to pray, but they don't want to go to school to learn how to do it. We need to engage them in ways that open the meaning and emotion of the prayer to them without being analytical and didactic.

Here are our responses to some common concerns:

"I can't get into prayers because I don't know Hebrew." Many (if not most) worshippers are not familiar with the prayer book and *davening* – praying. It is imperative that the texts of all songs and prayers be provided in Hebrew, transliteration, and translation. Worship is a right brain activity. Music is a right brain activity. The worship service needs to be filled with music and drama. In addition to reading texts aloud, consider chanting the text repeatedly in Hebrew or English, or presenting texts as a choral reading or dramatic presentation.

"Everything is so slow and static." The service needs to have highs and lows, fast pacing alternating with slow pacing. People need time to celebrate and to

And so rabbis and cantors alike are responding to this hunger for empowerment by offering their laity opportunities to study Hebrew, lead *t'filah*, chant from the Torah, and sing along in prayer as much as possible. Cantors are needing to think about the keys that they are singing in, and the accessibility of the melodies they select. Similarly, our seminaries are thinking about the training that our rabbinic and cantorial students are receiving to help them prepare for this new breed of congregant. In the School of Sacred Music at Hebrew Union College, guitar is now a required instrument for all cantorial students. A new required course has been added to the cantors' curriculum entitled "Understanding and Empowering the Congregational Voice."

Congregations across the denominations are seeking ways to involve the congregational voice. Some rabbis are using the formerly reserved "rabbi's sermon slot" as a time for congregational discussion. Others are engaging the congregation in *chevrutah* study (partnered discussion), to help them understand the *parasha* that is about to be read from the Torah. In many congregations, prior to the recitation of the *Mi Shebeirach* blessing, clergy are inviting congregants to say aloud the name of the loved one for whom they are requesting healing. Other congregations are reserving a time during the service where people can share their "*shehecheyanu* moments" of the past week. Congregants share aloud what they are grateful for, or what *simcha* they have just celebrated. And still, in other congregations, prior to the recitation of *Kaddish*, congregants who are commemorating a *yahrtzeit* are given the opportunity to say something about their deceased love one for whom they are reciting *Kaddish*.

How better to encourage congregational par-

---

meditate. This has to be planned consciously to work. Worshippers can and will gladly listen to "performance" pieces, but they need to be spread out during the service. Even then, don't have too many of them, and when possible choose material that has a refrain that people can sing along with. Perhaps the most significant addition to our service is the use of instruments, which has helped us add a new excitement to the service. Often, with the help of the instruments, we can dance in the middle of the service for up to 10-15 minutes.

"I don't know the melodies." Our philosophy is "Do more of less." By repeating material numerous times there is a point in the process where a congregant can begin to develop a comfort level and sing along. The Hassidic style of repeating a melody over and over releases us from the confines of rationality and allows our creative/emotional side to come into play.

"I don't know how to pray." Worshippers like to know something about the prayers, their historical content and context. Create moments in the prayer experience to teach about prayer. The learning component of the service is vital to its success, for both newcomers and veterans. We teach something new every service so there is at least one communal learning experience. For those who are interested in more intensive study, consider offering a class immediately prior to the service.

"I don't get anything out of praying." Telling a personal story describing how a prayer affects you is emotional and can help give the worshippers a model of how to approach prayer. If the leaders of the service allow themselves to be vulnerable and admit to their own difficulties with prayer, it helps the congregation to do the same. This is the first step to real prayer.

"I can't find God when I pray." Perhaps the worshipper doesn't know what they are looking for? Give worshippers an opportunity to be part of the service and they will be much more inclined to get something out of the service. We have made One Shabbat Morning percussion shakers that are distributed at each service. We also have made a point of inviting congregants to share original poems, stories, and songs in the body of the service. People love to be involved. We have developed the "journey" section of our service as an attempt to make the service more relevant and personal, inviting individuals to share a piece of their life story with the community. Other people are empowered when they hear the personal struggles and triumphs of members of their community.

"Prayer is not relevant to anything going on in my life." Develop and utilize a questionnaire that explores how your congregation is reacting to the service. After every service we solicit the feedback of our participants, evaluating their suggestions and incorporating their ideas into future services. The service becomes a balance between *keva* (fixed prayer, in time and language) and
continued on next page

ticipation than through the music? We are seeing the creation of special worship service models where congregational singing is the norm — Friday Night Live, One Shabbat Morning, Shabbat Unplugged, the Carlebach Minyan, to name just a few. Some congregations learn to expect this particular type of service as the first Shabbat of every month. Others exist weekly as an alternative *minyan*. Some are created with little in the way of spoken text: They might consist of one congregational melody followed by another congregational melody, sometimes woven together by a story or an *iyyun* offered by the rabbi. As the community together intones one prayer after another, the sense of *Kehilah K'dosha* is pervasive. People are empowered, involved, and engaged. Many speak of these Shabbat experiences as the highlight of their week.

Of course, not everyone wants to participate in this way. Some in fact find this kind of worship to be somewhat imposing and would far prefer to listen. Some are uncomfortable with the expectation of participation. They miss the more classical and traditional melodies usually sung solo by the cantor. This presents a challenge for the clergy and the lay leadership of the congregation. How do we respect the needs of all of our congregants? How do we create an inclusive community, where everyone's prayer needs can be honored? It is not so easy to accomplish. Some congregations feel that by offering a monthly menu of services that include a different style each week, all congregant's needs will be met. Others feel that they need to offer multiple *minyanim* that meet simultaneously every week, so that all needs can be addressed each Shabbat. Needless to say, the

---

ONE SHABBAT MORNING
continued from previous page

kavanah (a meaningful prayer experience).

"The service is too long." This is a common complaint with a very simple solution. Make the service shorter. Our service begins at 10:00 am, and is preceded by a class and some food to nosh on. We try to finish services no later than 12:00 pm, whereupon the entire congregation participates in a community meal.

"My kids can't sit still." One Shabbat Morning welcomes the entire family, but it is not a "family service." It is a two-hour service that requires focus and participation, which are foreign to most children under the age of nine or ten. We provide free, top-notch childcare for those who need it and strongly urge families to take advantage of the program. Toward the end of the service we invite the childcare participants back into the service for the concluding songs.

"All the tunes sound so old fashioned" or **"When I go to modern services it doesn't sound Jewish to me."** One of the primary goals of our service is to build bridges between tradition and modernity. Working closely with cantors, rabbis, artists, and congregants, our goal is to create a liturgy that bridges the past with the present, creating a model for the future.

In conclusion, attention to detail and a passionate desire to make the service work are the keys to success. Are the chairs set up? How is the room temperature and lighting? Is the sound balanced? Is there enough food? Are there greeters? Have you called people and invited them to the service? We look at each service as an opportunity to create a holy moment. While having exceptionally high expectations, we take nothing for granted. Every month, the clergy, lay and professional leaders are invited to a study session on prayer. While the meeting is often difficult to fit into our schedules, everyone in attendance agrees that it is one of the highlights of the month.

We wish you much success in this spiritual journey and look forward to hearing your feedback.

Craig Taubman first began performing at the age of fifteen when he was encouraged by a counselor at Camp Ramah in Ojai, California to take hold of a guitar and lead services. His interest in music became interwoven with his passion for Jewish history and culture. Craig's music bridges traditional Jewish themes and ancient teachings with passages and experiences of contemporary Jewish life. Synagogues, camps, youth groups, and Jewish schools across North America regularly use Craig's music, and his eleven Jewish recordings have become an integral part of the Jewish community, weaving song and spirit into the fabric of Jewish life.

staffing requirements for this kind of worship can be quite labor intensive, and for many congregations, simply prohibitive. Although the solution to this question is not yet clear, the journey to discovering this solution is an exciting challenge.

WHERE ARE WE HEADED?

We are living during a wonderful, opportune time. People finally understand the important role that music plays in our Jewish lives. It is our responsibility to seize this moment. We must listen, we must respond, we must educate, and we must lead.

The purpose of music in prayer is to deepen the prayer experience. We must take the emphasis off of the particular music that is being sung and instead shift the focus on how well it serves the prayer experience. The truth is that in order to meet the diverse needs of our praying communities, we must find an artful synthesis of the many Jewish musical styles available to us. Cantor Jack Mendelson, who serves on the faculty of the cantorial schools of both Hebrew Union College-Jewish Institute of Religion and the Jewish Theological Seminary, refers to this as "Jewish music fusion." We need to find a way to move prayerfully from *nusach* to folk music to *hazzanut*, from participatory moments to listening moments, from the majestic sounds of the choir to the communal voice of the congregation. For it is in this combination of musical styles that we will find a way to speak to everyone. The answer need not lie in everyone's being able to sing everything, but rather in everyone's being engaged and honored in the prayer experience.

With an increased emphasis on serious Jewish adult education, congregants can be taught to appreciate *hazzanut* and *nusach* and eventually to even participate in both. Our Jewish musical heritage is a rich one, and one that we surely want to keep alive. In order to do that we need to partner this genre of music alongside the more easily accessible folk melodies, allowing our congregants opportunities for engagement both through listening and through singing along. As

Cantor Ellen Dreskin teaches, if we are indeed creating sacred communities, in which one honors the traditions of all of its members, every melody of every prayer need not speak to each and every person in the same way. We just need to recognize that each person relates to prayer differently and that different melodies will serve people in different ways. As long as we know that the intent of each piece of music is about heightening the prayer, then we can trust the integrity of the selection. We can learn to appreciate the different styles, and we can weave an even richer tapestry of Jewish worship music.

RESOURCES

BOOKS AND ARTICLES

Eisenstein, Judith Kaplan. *Heritage of Music: The Music of the Jewish People*. Wyncote, PA: The Reconstructionist Press, 1990.

Hoffman, Lawrence A. *The Art of Public Prayer: Not for Clergy Only*. Woodstock, VT: Sky Light Paths Publishing, 1999.

Hoffman, Lawrence A. and Janet R. Walton, eds. *Sacred Sound and Social Change*. Notre Dame, IN: University of Notre Dame Press, 1992.

Synagogue 2000. *Itinerary for Change: Prayer*. Los Angeles, CA: Synagogue 2000, 2002.

MUSIC

Arian, Merri Lovinger. *R'fuah Sh'leimah: Songs of Jewish Healing*. Los Angeles, CA: Synagogue 2000, 2002. Songbook. Available from Transcontinental Music Publications.

———. *Nefesh: Songs for the Soul*. Los Angeles, CA: Synagogue 2000, 2002. Compact disc.

Taubman, Craig. *Friday Night Live*. Sherman Oaks, CA: Sweet Louise Productions, 1999. Compact disc and songbook. Available from A.R.E. Publishing, Inc.

———. *One Shabbat Morning*. Sherman Oaks, CA: Sweet Louise Productions, 2002. Compact disc and songbook. Available from A.R.E. Publishing, Inc.

Merri Lovinger Arian is Director of Music for Synagogue 2000, an organization that works collaboratively with synagogues of all denominations to realize the power of sacred community through a transforming process of prayer, study, and social justice. She serves on the faculty of the Hebrew Union College School of Sacred Music in New York, and teaches courses in Music Education, Conducting, Congregational Singing, and Guitar.

Merri holds a Master of Arts in Teaching, a Bachelor of Fine Arts in Music Education, and a Certificate in Music Therapy. She has written articles on the educational value of youth choirs, and published a book and tape of her own choral arrangements. Merri edited the songbook R'fuah Sh'leimah: Songs of Jewish Healing, *and recorded a CD for Synagogue 2000 entitled* Nefesh: Songs for the Soul.

CHAPTER TWENTY:
SEEKING THE SILENCE WITHIN
JEWISH MEDITATION

Nan Gefen

Over the years you've undoubtedly had experiences that were spiritual in nature. Perhaps they took place while you were reading a poem, or holding a sleeping child. Or walking in the woods, or watching the sunset. Or while you were praying.

These experiences — and more — have helped you know that something exists beyond your regular, everyday reality. This "something" is what I call "the silence within." To many of us, this state seems both familiar and mysterious. It has the quality of spaciousness, and it appears to have no boundaries.

Like a pregnant pause before a sentence, the silence within contains all possibility. It is the raw material of creation, the formlessness that exists before the concrete emerges. When we enter into this state, we have our most intense spiritual experiences and receive our most significant moments of understanding.

If you are like many people, you probably don't pay much attention to the silence within as you rush from place to place, juggling responsibilities and meeting deadlines. But you sense its existence. In the quiet moments it hovers just outside your consciousness, and you are drawn to it. It might even frighten you, the scary unknown.

All of the world's major religious traditions acknowledge the existence of the silence within. Whatever name they give it, or however they describe it, they see it as something that can be explored. Each tradition has created ways for doing this, and passes them on to succeeding generations.

Likewise, nontraditional spiritual teachers, such as those in the New Age movement, assume that transcendence of everyday life can take place. The experience of the spiritual realm, they say, does not depend on a traditional belief in God or adherence to a particular religion.

In these times of spiritual seeking, many people are turning to Jewish meditation as a pathway to the silence within. They are discovering that the practice is wise and beautiful, and that over the years it can lead to great spiritual transformation.

WHAT IS JEWISH MEDITATION?

Most simply, Jewish meditation is a spiritual practice found within the Jewish tradition.

The best way to describe it is to consider its name. The word "Jewish" is included because meditation has been — and is — a part of Judaism. Traditionally it exists alongside other aspects of Jewish observance, such as prayer and Torah study. Less traditionally, it is done alone as a spiritual practice. Jewish meditation uses images, words, and symbols that come from the Jewish tradition. The meditations themselves, and the teachings that go along with them, reflect Jewish understanding. Because of this, people who are introduced to Jewish meditation will not mistake it for any other meditative practice.

Now we move on to the "meditation" word in Jewish meditation. Meditation is a specific kind of activity that involves directing the mind. It follows a prescribed order, and it uses techniques different from ordinary thinking or daydreaming. The activity takes place during a prescribed time period, and thereby has a beginning and an end. Although the contents of Jewish meditation are unique in many ways, it joins other meditative traditions in directing the mind to the silence within.

Jewish meditation can be further described as an organic practice that has grown and changed through history. Although it is part of Judaism, it nevertheless has absorbed elements from other traditions, such as Sufism, Gnosticism, and Buddhism. The practice contains a great variety of teachings and meditations. At different times creative bursts of collective insight into the use of meditation have taken place. One, in fact, is going on right now.

WHAT IS THE RELATIONSHIP BETWEEN JEWISH MEDITATION, JEWISH MYSTICISM, AND KABBALAH?

Jewish meditation is a technique rooted in certain understandings. The main philosophical base of Jewish meditation is Jewish mysticism. This tradition has existed throughout Jewish history, and it centers on an intimate, immediate contact with the Divine. Many of the images we use for meditation and the ideas we teach come from it.

Jewish mysticism seeks to answer the basic questions of life, such as the nature of God, the meaning of creation, and the existence of good and evil. It transmits understanding through the study of mystical texts like the *Sefer Yetzirah*, which was written between the third and sixth centuries C.E., and the *Zohar*, which was written toward the end of the thirteenth century. The language of mysticism is poetic and evocative, and it opens the imagination to perceiving God in new ways.

Jewish mysticism has an experiential side. It considers meditation to be a pathway to an intense connection with the Divine. Through the centuries, mystics have taught their students the meditations they've devised, and some of them have been written down. Jewish meditation, as we know it today, draws meditations from this great treasury, as well as from other sources.

It is important to understand that Jewish mysticism has always had strong ties to traditional Judaism. The mystics of the past had rigorous Jewish practices, even though they saw the Holy Cosmos in nontraditional ways. Their spiritual experience through meditation added depth to their religious commitment rather than providing an alternative way of life.

If Jewish mysticism is the base of Jewish meditation, what about *kabbalah*? This word, which is bandied around a lot these days, often confuses beginning meditators.

Kabbalah means "to receive" in Hebrew. It refers to the mystical tradition within Judaism from the twelfth century to the present day. Like the rest of Jewish mysticism, it is directed to the experience of union with the Divine.

The *Kabbalah* can be described as a nontraditional response to spiritual concerns. God, for instance, is seen as indwelling as well as transcendent, and as both male and female. The world is perceived as ever-changing, radiant, and reflective of the Divine. All life contains sparks of holiness. These understandings differ from the traditional view of God as outside the natural world and separate from humankind.

The Jewish mystical tradition, including the *Kabbalah*, is a collection of many teachings about the structure and nature of reality. It has evolved through the centuries. We speak of it as though it is a completed point of view, but it is like a tree sending out new branches in surprising directions: Its shape is still emerging.

HOW DOES JEWISH MEDITATION COMPARE TO OTHER KINDS OF MEDITATION?

Jewish meditation aims toward exploring the silence within. In this way it is like other religious meditative traditions. All of them direct meditators to let go of their everyday concerns and ordinary patterns of thinking as they open their minds to spiritual experience.

Most religious traditions consider meditation to be an important path to personal transformation. So too does Judaism. One of the ways this takes place is through self-refinement. During meditation, our ego defenses dissolve and we become more aware of who we really are. We then can act to strengthen our positive qualities and diminish or transform those qualities that are destructive. As a result, we are able to make more of a contribution to those around us and to the world. Our inner "light" or "soul" becomes more revealed.

A further similarity between Jewish meditation and most other traditions is found in the intention to bring the meditator closer to God. In past centuries this was the reason for Jews to meditate. The meditator yearned to close the distance between the self and the Divine, and meditation was the vehicle for this to take place. Today, the emphasis on connecting to the Divine still exists, although we teach and practice meditation in ways that are not necessarily the same as those of past centuries.

Jewish meditation resembles other religious meditative traditions also in that it holds the understanding that we have a responsibility to make the world a better place. Buddhists regularly perform acts of service, and Christians are guided by the edict to "love your neighbor as yourself." Jews commit themselves to *tikkun olam* (repairing and healing the world). Meditation alone is not enough: We also must become involved in changing the world. This basic tenet of Judaism is fulfilled even more effectively when we retreat into meditation for periods of time. Within meditation, we can find the strength, the balance, and the purpose we need to continue this task.

We've discussed some of the similarities between Jewish meditation and other religious traditions. But what about relaxation meditation, that popular antidote for illness and emotional distress? There are similarities here too. Both use specific techniques to enter into a state of meditation. These techniques sometimes appear to be the same, as in meditations that focus on the breath.

The point of this type of meditation is to relax so that restoration and healing can take place. But we can't relax if our minds are whirling around. Likewise, we can't enter into the silence within if our minds are spinning out of control. We must find a way to stop the busyness. Meditation

provides this, whether the end goal is to relax or to transcend our ordinary reality.

All forms of meditation — including Jewish meditation — share a common base of techniques. But differences exist in their purposes and how they are used. In transcendental meditation, the meditator repeats a mantra again and again. The mind focuses on the sound, although it has no inherent meaning to most meditators. In Jewish meditation, the same mantra technique is sometimes used, but meditators are instructed to focus on Hebrew letters or words. The goal is for them to become "filled" with these letters or words, and to merge with them so that they enter into a deep meditative state and experience the presence of the Divine. An example is the *Sh'ma* meditation, based on the traditional *Sh'ma*, a prayer that proclaims the unity of the Divine. The words of this prayer are repeated silently, like a mantra, and the meditator is instructed to pay attention to their sound, not to their meaning. Even so, these words are undeniably Jewish and they resonate with most Jews.

The most obvious way in which Jewish meditation differs from other traditions is its Jewish context. Jewish meditation is part of Judaism, not Sufism, Buddhism, or any other religion. It developed through the centuries as a Jewish pathway to the Holy, and it was practiced by those committed to traditional religious Judaism.

Today, many non-Orthodox Jews are adopting Jewish meditation as a spiritual practice without taking on rigorous Jewish observance. They are discovering that it gives their lives spiritual meaning. Still, Jewish meditation is so strongly grounded in Judaism that they experience it as Jewish meditation rather than general meditation. Jewish meditation can be distinguished from other meditative traditions also by its content. The meditations come from the wellspring of Jewish understanding, and they include Jewish symbols, words, and images. Although some of them have themes found in other traditions, they also are located within Judaism.

But perhaps the most important difference between Jewish meditation and other traditions is how it feels to sit in a room with others who are doing this practice. The experience is not like

Buddhist or Hindu or Sufi meditation. For many of us, it feels like coming home.

WHAT ARE THE HISTORICAL ROOTS OF JEWISH MEDITATION?

Jewish meditation goes back a long way. Some scholars suggest that it was present even in the Torah, the first five books of the Bible. They note that Isaac engaged in an activity that appears to be meditative: "And Isaac went out to walk in the field in the evening" (Genesis 24:63). According to some interpretations, this experience of meditation or prayer was so intense that his presence radiated outward, causing Rebecca, his bride-to-be, to fall off her camel when she first saw him. Jacob too seems to have entered a meditative state when he isolated himself in preparation for his reunion with his brother Esau: "Jacob was left alone" (Genesis 32:25). In his solitude he wrestled with an angel — just as we sometimes struggle with our desires and fears during meditation.

Other hints of the existence of meditation can be found in the Psalms. They describe the yearning that leads to the spiritual experience that we most often associate with meditation or prayer: "My soul yearns for You, my flesh pines for You" (Psalm 63:2). They also show us the importance of becoming connected to the Divine: "I have continuously placed God before me; God is at my right hand so that I shall not falter" (Psalm 16:8).

At the time the Bible was completed, around 400 B.C.E., meditation appears to have been wide-spread. A few sources claim that over a million Israelites meditated on a regular basis, but most say that this figure is wildly exaggerated. Meditation during this period — and for many centuries thereafter — can be described as apocalyptic and visionary. People learned to focus their minds on fiery chariots, angelic hosts, wild beasts, and sometimes terrifying images of Divine majesty. Accounts of these meditations sound hallucinatory to our contemporary ears.

When the Jews were dispersed into other countries after the fall of the Second Temple in 70 C.E., many of them continued to meditate. Rabbis spoke out against this practice, however, because they feared that it would lead to abandonment of Judaism. Meditators might be tempted to try out foreign spiritual practices, and eventually they would be seduced away from the tradition of their birth.

Over time, Jewish meditation seems to have gone underground. By the Middle Ages, only small, select groups of religious men continued the practice. Most people weren't even introduced to it: The prescription held that one must be male, over forty, and married to study *kabbalah* and to meditate. This elitist control over meditation remained in effect for many centuries until the Hasidic movement began in Eastern Europe in the eighteenth century.

In the meanwhile, Jewish mysticism and Jewish meditation continued to develop through the writing and teaching of the Kabbalists. For example, Abraham Abulafia in the thirteenth century devised meditations that focused on the name of God and the pure forms of the letters of the Hebrew alphabet, and Isaac Luria in the sixteenth century transmitted a radical mystical understanding of creation that was the basis of many meditations. The insights of great teachers such as these helped to shape Jewish mysticism and meditation as we know it today.

During the centuries before the Hasidic movement, Jewish meditation consisted mainly of focusing on the letters of the Divine Name in various combinations — a practice thought to be dangerous for the uninitiated. Once Hasidism became established in Eastern Europe, however, meditation became more accessible. Rabbis in the eighteenth and nineteenth centuries brought it into widespread use by teaching that prayer could be done as a mantra. Anyone could climb the spiritual ladder through all the states of being and experience the opening of the heavens by praying in this meditative way. These rabbis also developed contemplative forms of meditation aimed at helping people increase their awareness of God's presence and refine their character traits.

In its heyday Hasidism had hundreds of thousands of adherents. But by the twentieth century it had shrunk in size and influence, and meditation was less a part of religious practice. Many Hasidic rabbis who knew how to do it died during the Holocaust.

Until recently, the existence of Jewish meditation was barely known in the United States. Mainstream American Jews historically have viewed spirituality with suspicion. As a result, synagogues and Jewish organizations have failed to support the spiritual quest, and seekers have had to look outside their own tradition to learn a meditative practice.

But this is changing. In the last two decades the word about Jewish meditation has gotten out. Aryeh Kaplan, an Orthodox rabbi, wrote several books on the subject in the 1970s and 1980s. Other publications followed that helped to break through the wall of ignorance. (See the list of publications at the end of this chapter.) Meditative texts from past centuries are now being translated and taught. Several centers of Jewish meditation exist in the United States, and undoubtedly more will be established. Meditation classes and sitting groups are proliferating, synagogues are bringing the practice into their communities, and several conferences on the practice have been convened. As more people experience Jewish meditation's power and wisdom, they are helping to spread it further within the Jewish world. After centuries of being hidden, meditation finally is beginning to be accepted as a legitimate part of American Judaism.

WHAT IS JEWISH MEDITATION LIKE TODAY?

Jewish meditation is a stream fed by three sources.

The first is the Jewish meditative tradition. Some of the meditations we teach come from past centuries, discovered within old texts or passed down orally from teacher to student.

The second source of Jewish meditation is the creative work of meditation teachers today. Using Jewish symbols and images, we are fashioning meditations that are especially meaningful for people in this postmodern era. Although these meditations are "new" in the sense that we have

no record of them being done before, they build respectfully on the contributions of teachers in the past and on the tradition of Jewish meditation.

Jewish meditation is being influenced by a third source: Buddhism. In recent decades many Jews have adopted Buddhist meditative practices. Almost a third of American Buddhists are Jewish by birth. Many of these people have found a spiritual path within Buddhism that they didn't find within Judaism, but they want to reconnect with their Jewish roots. We are pleased to introduce them to Jewish meditation. As they learn about it, they bring the knowledge and wisdom gained from Buddhism to their practices. Their insights help to shape the direction of Jewish meditation.

If you look at current teachers of Jewish meditation, you will see that we don't all teach the same material or use the same approach. This is because we come from different backgrounds. Some of us, as traditionalists, are committed to passing on meditations learned from Kabbalistic or Hasidic sources. Others blend these traditional meditations with contemporary ones. A few bring Zen or Vipassana insight meditation into the Jewish setting, and they teach Buddhist awareness practice along with other, more traditional Jewish meditations.

The differences continue: Some teachers think that Jewish meditation includes meditative singing, chanting, and movement. Others hold to a more strict definition, saying that the practice should be done by sitting and focusing in a traditional way. They consider these more expressive techniques to be meditative warm-ups, and dismiss them as not the real thing.

The different approaches have not been integrated, although efforts are being made in that direction. Meditation teachers, for instance, are discussing how to bring in elements of Buddhist practice without losing Jewish meditation's essential character. In time, there will be more clarity — although I wager there will always be various schools of thought about the nature and practice of Jewish meditation.

The variety in teaching styles resulting from this lack of agreement can confuse beginning meditators. They often ask, "What is proper Jewish meditation, anyhow?" The answer is that

HITBODEDUT: ALONE WITH GOD

Rabbi David Cooper

One of the best-known forms of Jewish meditative prayer is called *hitbodedut*. It comes from the Hebrew root *bodad* (to be isolated), and it means to seclude oneself — in essence, to be alone with God. It is a very simple technique that is also quite effective. One merely speaks out whatever happens to be on one's mind to the Creator of the universe.

It is important to be alone so that you can use your voice without worrying about others listening in. You can do the meditation at home if you feel comfortable there, but it is often recommended that one be in nature when doing *hitbodedut*. The most famous Hasidic leader who used and taught this method — Rabbi Nachman of Breslov — suggested that people should go into the woods, especially at night, to do this practice.

Many people shy away from speaking directly to God; they often feel embarrassed, unworthy, or unbelieving. The important aspect of this method is that anything becomes grist for the mill. An integral part of the *hitbodedut* practice is to speak out loud — do not merely think the thought. In kabbalistic terms, actually speaking the words carries much more emotional content than thinking the words. In Jewish mysticism, prayer needs to be articulated; the combination of sounds will reverberate throughout the universe and have more impact than thought waves.

When you feel like communing directly with the Divine, *hitbodedut* is an excellent method. Although it is often done standing or walking, you can also sit quietly to enhance the inner power of the meditation. If you are at home, please try to find a place where you will not be interrupted and where others in the house cannot hear you.

1. Begin with the basic sitting technique: relaxed, eyes closed. Try to sit fairly straight without effort. Breathe normally. Notice the rising and falling of the chest with the breath.

2. Now, find your own words to express one of the following ideas:

   Whatever is at the center of creation, whatever you call yourself, if there is any way that you can do this, please help me believe that I can really communicate with you.

   God, I am not really sure who or what you are; please help me feel your presence.

3. If you are unable to experience anything at all, you can either continue asking for help, or you can literally pretend; use your imagination, and imagine being cradled or hugged by a warm, loving entity of some type. Imagine that you are in the arms of pure love. In essence, pretend that you are talking to a loving source, speaking your heart's deepest secrets, asking for whatever you need to get an inner healing. Being held like this, close, secure, loved, let yourself speak out in your own words; let your heart flow with whatever is in it. You will discover along the way that although this process may begin as an exercise in pretending, it will ultimately become an experience of great healing — it really works! Try it.

4. When you are ready, please finish a request with something like the following:

   a. Oh, I want to be free — please help me be free.

   b. I need to feel better — please help me feel better.

   c. If only I could have peace — please help me find peace.

   Once you have completed this exercise, even though it may feel strange at first, simply notice brief memories of the experience that may arise over the next few days. Try to do this *hitbodedut* meditation at least once a week for a few months, and in between the practice sessions keep noticing how the mind occasionally turns to the memories. Eventually, barriers will begin to fall and you will most likely find greater comfort in the practice. Slowly it will bring you closer to connecting with something mysterious, which will lead to a letting go of some boundaries so that you will be able to have a sense of greater peace. This is a major practice for ultimately attaining *d'veikut*, merging with the Divine, and is highly recommended.

Rabbi David A. Cooper has been called "one of today's leading teachers of Jewish meditation." He is an active student of the world's great spiritual traditions and is the award-winning author of many books on Judaism, mystical practice, and meditation. Rabbi Cooper and his wife Shoshana lead Jewish meditation retreats nationwide, and live in the mountains of Colorado near Boulder.

no one way is "best" or "more Jewish." Each has something to offer.

In this discussion about Jewish meditation today we haven't yet mentioned a most obvious and important fact: The practice is now open to everyone. Thankfully, you no longer have to be male or traditionally observant to practice Jewish meditation.

The effects of this change are already apparent. People from all backgrounds feel welcomed into Jewish meditation. And as more women and nonobservant Jews become involved, they bring their unique perspectives and insights to the practice. They are part of the creative process, helping to develop a meditative practice that includes but extends beyond traditional concerns. Through sharing their experience, they are contributing to the shape of Jewish meditation for the future.

RESOURCES

BOOKS

Cooper, David A. *The Handbook of Jewish Meditation Practices: A Guide for Enriching the Sabbath and Other Days of Your Life*. Woodstock, VT: Jewish Lights, 2000.

Davis, Avram, ed. *Meditation from the Heart of Judaism: Today's Teachers Share Their Practices, Techniques and Faith*. Woodstock, VT: Jewish Lights, 1997.

Gefen, Nan Fink. *Discovering Jewish Meditation: Instruction and Guidance for Learning an Ancient Spiritual Practice*. Woodstock, VT: Jewish Lights, 1999.

Kaplan, Aryeh. *Jewish Meditation*. New York: Schocken, 1985.

WEB SITES

Jewish Meditation from an Authentic Source — Rabbi Yitzchak Ginsburgh
http://www.inner.org/meditate/

Reclaiming Judaism as a Spiritual Practice: Introduction to Jewish Meditation by Rabbi Goldie Milgrom
http://www.rebgoldie.com/Meditation.htm

Yehi Or — New England Jewish Meditation Center
http://www.yehior.org

Nan Gefen, Ph.D., is widely recognized as a leading teacher of Jewish meditation. She is president of Chochmat HaLev, an independent center of Jewish meditation in Berkeley, California. She teaches meditation, trains teachers, and leads workshops at the Center and elsewhere. Ms. Gefen's training in Jewish meditation has spanned two decades of study and development of her own practice, and she has been a leader in the field for the past ten years. She is the author of Discovering Jewish Meditation: Instruction and Guidance for Learning an Ancient Spiritual Practice, *as well as co-founder of* Tikkun *magazine.*

CHAPTER TWENTY-ONE: SEEKING WHOLENESS
THE JEWISH WAY OF HEALING

Rabbi Nancy Flam

When Eve W. was diagnosed with lymphoma, she sought the finest medical treatment available. But she wanted more than high-tech medicine could offer. Like millions of Americans, she supplemented her medical treatment with complementary therapy. Eve began to practice Buddhist meditation, Hindu yoga, and natural diet. Deeply committed to her Judaism, Eve was nonetheless unaware of Jewish practices for strengthening the body and spirit at times of illness.

In response to his AIDS diagnosis, David M. began seeing one specialist after another. In addition, he tried to meet his emotional challenges by working with a therapist, taking part in a twelve-step group, and staying in contact with close friends. Then, one day he saw an advertisement for a "Spiritual Support Group for HIV+ Jews." With no clear sense of what he might gain, he called the number and registered for the group.

Shoshanna A. had never been religious or Jewishly affiliated. But when she was diagnosed with metastatic breast cancer, she called the Jewish Healing Center. "I rebelled against Judaism all my life. I couldn't deal with the sexism of my brothers getting Jewish educations and fancy bar mitzvahs while I got nothing. So social activism became my religion. But now I'm sick and I'm not sure how to cope, and I wonder what I've been rejecting all these years. Maybe Judaism has something to offer me?"

Eve, David, and Shoshanna's cases are typical. In times of sickness, pain, and trouble, many Jews seek spiritual comfort and healing through non-Jewish means, such as twelve-step recovery programs, new-age communities, and mind-body institutions. For some, however, there may come a point when one turns toward the Jewish tradition and community to see what it has to offer. Such seekers can find abundant resources in Judaism, which has addressed questions of health and recovery for millennia.

BODY AND SPIRIT

Recent research in the mind-body field suggests that mind and spirit may not be as separate from the biochemistry of physical illness as we once thought: the disease process itself may be affected by psychosocial healing. Dr. David Spiegel of Stanford University found that women with metastatic breast cancer who participated in a one-year support group lived significantly longer than women who received similar medical treatment without a support group (*Healing and the Mind*, Doubleday). Being part of a meaningful community that encourages self-expression can affect the course of an illness.

In a study conducted at the Mid America Heart Institute in Kansas City, Missouri, and published in *Archives of Internal Medicine* (October 25, 1999), about 1,000 heart patients admitted to the institute's critical care unit were secretly divided into two groups. For an entire year, half were prayed for by a group of volunteers and the hospital's chaplain; the other half were not. The health of the patients was then scored according to pre-set rules by a third party who did not know which patients had been prayed for and which had not. The results: The patients who were prayed for had eleven percent fewer heart attacks, strokes and life-threatening complications.[1]

And, according to a 2002 survey of more than 31,000 adults by the National Institutes of Health, large numbers of Americans believe in a connection between the physical and the spiritual. Forty-three percent of respondents had prayed for their own health, twenty-four percent had asked others to pray for their health, and ten percent had prayed for health in a prayer group.[2]

Jewish tradition has long recognized that there is both a physical and spiritual dimension to the experience of illness. The physical assaults to the body are often plain to see, yet illness makes a host of other assaults to a person and his or her sense of self. There are the emotional assaults of dealing with fear, anger, depression, sadness, and boredom. There are social assaults as illness often displaces one from normal social roles as parent, partner, friend, or worker. And there are spiritual assaults including a sense of God's abandonment, a lack of meaning, or a feeling of cosmic injustice. While the physical pains may draw attention and care, it is crucial to be mindful of a person's spiritual pains as well.

It is important when discussing Jewish healing to recognize the difference between *curing* and *healing*. Healing is not about the alleviation of physical symptoms, but rather about drawing upon Jewish resources and the Jewish community to develop strength, courage, perspective, a sense of meaning, and the feeling of belonging both to an ancient tradition and to an active living community. While cure is not always possible, some level of healing can usually be found. A key part of Jewish healing focuses upon establishing — or, perhaps, re-establishing — a relationship between the community and those in need of healing. It should be clear that contemporary Jewish healing does not seek to replace conventional medicine, but rather to complement and supplement medical treatments and practices.

At the point when Shoshanna turned toward the Jewish community, she was not expecting to find a physical cure, but she desperately hoped for healing of the spirit. Shoshanna needed to overcome her negative association with Judaism in order to benefit from its religious wisdom. With greater hunger for spiritual nourishment, she enrolled in a seminar about Jewish views of health and illness, took part in a study group exploring Judaism and feminism, and began attending regular "Services of Healing" where Jews dealing with illness and grief prayed together for strength and comfort. At fifty years of age, she began her own journey of Jewish learning and spiritual development.

SPIRITUAL HEALING: BIKUR CHOLIM

A fundamental feature of Jewish spiritual healing is *Bikur Cholim* (visiting the sick), which responds to two of the greatest burdens of contemporary life: isolation and lack of community. At a time of illness, *Bikur Cholim* offers us the comfort of human connection and interdependence, a sense of community we so desperately need.

The *mitzvah* of *Bikur Cholim* helps fulfill the obligation to "love your neighbor as yourself," and it is required of every Jew (Maimonides, *Mishneh Torah*: Laws of Mourning 14). Like comforting mourners and performing other acts of kindness, *Bikur Cholim* brings goodness to the world (*Avot de Rabbi Natan* 39:1).

Torah teaches that one who practices *Bikur Cholim* imitates God, whose presence visited Abraham after his circumcision (Genesis *Rabbah*, 8:13). The sources teach that each of us is visited by God's presence when we are ill, which we may interpret as feeling a sense of hope, care, and protection. This is exactly what a loving visitor can inspire. The Codes teach that God's presence rests upon the head of the bed of anyone who is sick, and that we must not sit there for fear of blocking it (Maimonides, *Mishneh Torah*: Laws of Mourning 14). This suggests that the visitor must reflect and not obscure God's presence when attending to the person who is ill.

[1] William S. Harris, Ph.D., et al., "A Randomized, Controlled Trial of the Effects of Remote, Intercessory Prayer on Outcomes in Patients Admitted to the Coronary Care Unit." *Archives of Internal Medicine* 159, no.19 (October 25, 1999): 2273-2278.

[2] Patricia M. Barnes, M.A., et al., "Complementary and Alternative Medicine Use Among Adults: United States, 2002." *Advance Data From Vital and Health Statistics* 343 (May 27, 2004),

Bikur Cholim demonstrates the healing power of relationship. There are many stories in the Talmud about Rabbi Yohanan ben Zakkai, famed for his power to heal. When he heard of another rabbi who was sick, he would visit and speak with him about his suffering. After speaking, Yohanan ben Zakkai would hold out his hand, and the other rabbi would rise. One day Yohanan ben Zakkai fell ill. He was visited by Rabbi Hanina, who, after speaking to the stricken sage, held out his hand, and Yohanan ben Zakkai stood up. "Why couldn't Yohanan ben Zakkai raise himself?" the disciples asked, as he was known to be a great healer. The answer: "Because the prisoner cannot free himself from prison" (*Berachot* 5b). Here we learn that even the greatest of Jewish healers needs another person to help free himself from the prison of fear, hopelessness, and isolation.

David found his first positive adult experience of Jewish community by participating in the spiritual support group for HIV+ Jews. Having been rejected by the Jewish community during his adolescence because of being gay, David had, in turn, rejected Judaism. It was only later, in his mid-40s, emboldened by a sense that he now had "nothing to lose," that David met with other Jews for support and comfort. His experience in the spiritual support group radically changed his attitude toward Judaism, as he grew to see that in fact there was a place for him. Having looked to eastern religions for a spiritual home in his young adulthood, David was relieved to find that he "no longer had to knock on any doors: the door to Jewish tradition was open." When the group came to a close, David and two other participants joined a local Reform synagogue. The ensuing *Bikur Cholim* visits provided by synagogue members and Jewish professionals bolstered him tremendously during the difficult days of illness that lay ahead.

SPIRITUAL HEALING: PRAYER

In addition to *Bikur Cholim*, Jewish tradition teaches that we should pray for ourselves and others during a time of illness. Many modern Jews are resistant to praying in general, and especially skeptical about praying for something specific, such as good health or a cure.

One reason such prayer can be difficult is that we may not envision God in a classically Jewish way, as One who hears prayers and answers or fails to answer them. Another reason is that we often feel unjustly afflicted: when we have led ethical lives but nonetheless find ourselves struggling with disease, we may feel that God has been unfair. Instead of rejecting God, however, we might instead reject some aspects of classical Jewish theology (such as the idea that God rewards good with good), and search for a more satisfying way to think about God's ways.

Prayer allows us quiet time for reflection. Like meditation, it can be calming and relaxing, thereby allowing us access to regions of our inner selves. It can help us get in touch with our strength and faith. Prayer can also provide release and relief from anxious thoughts that exacerbate both physical and psychic pain. The mental relaxation of prayer can bring us comfort when we take the perspective that our lives are ultimately in God's hands.

In addition, when we pray in community and use traditional Jewish liturgy, we not only benefit from the company of other Jews, we find comfort in knowing that the words of the psalms and blessings have been spoken by millions of Jews past and present who, like us, yearn for healing.

The *Mi Shebeirach* prayer, traditionally recited for someone who is ill, asks God for *refuah shleima*, a complete healing, and then specifies the two dimensions of healing recognized in Jewish thought: *refuat hanefesh*, healing of the soul, spirit, or whole person, and *refuat haguf*, cure of the body. To cure the body means to wipe out the tumor, clear up the infection, or regain mobility. To heal the spirit involves creating a pathway to sensing wholeness, depth, mystery, purpose, and peace. As previously discussed, cure may occur without healing, and healing without cure. Pastoral caregivers and family members of seriously ill people know that sometimes lives and relationships are healed even when there is no possibility of physical cure: in fact, serious illness often motivates people to seek healing of the spirit.

The *Mi Shebeirach* prayer is powerful in a

number of ways. Traditionally offered in the synagogue after an *aliyah* to the Torah is completed, the assembled community hears the name of someone for whom the prayer is being said and is alerted to the fact that someone is ill. The prayer then functions partly as petition and partly as community announcement. Linking prayer to deed, some people might fulfill the *mitzvah* of *Bikur Cholim* as a result of having heard the prayer.

Further, Jewish teaching mandates that when we pray for the healing of one person, we include in our prayers all others who are ill. Therefore, at the end of the prayer, one prays for the individual who is called by name, "along with all who are ill." For the person who is ill, being included in the collective prayer can be a source of comfort. One is reminded that one is not alone, that there are many who are in pain, and that pain is indeed

MI SHEBEIRACH
Debbie Friedman

In October of 1987, four designated individuals took their places on the *bimah* and opened a huge *tallit*. All those who were in need of healing were invited to come forward to gather under the *tallit*. A mass exodus ensued and there was no one left sitting in the congregation. One hundred fifty people were huddled beneath the *tallit*. This would be the very first time I was to sing the *Mi Shebeirach* publicly.

We climbed inside each word and in between each line looking to be enveloped and comforted, acknowledging our fragility and our brokenness. We knew that we were alone and yet not alone; that we were in a community and however isolated we might have felt before this experience, we were now a part of something much greater. There were tears, there was hope, and a long silence when we finished singing the *Mi Shebeirach*.

I wrote this setting of the *Mi Shebeirach* for a friend who was celebrating her 60th birthday. She was struggling with the recent death of her husband as well as other significant difficulties in her life. I wanted and needed to write something that would speak to both the pain and the joy of this occasion. Those of us in her circle of friends were also met with various personal challenges. At that time there was no liturgical vocabulary nor were there any set rituals to help us manage such challenging times as these.

I wrote this piece when I was hearty and healthy, I wrote it for my friends. It was written from a part of me that felt great love and great compassion. At the first singing I recognized the power of these words. In the same way that reciting the *Al Cheit* on Yom Kippur helps us to acknowledge the ways in which we have missed the mark, the *Mi Shebeirach* gave us the words we needed to address our pain.

The *Mi Shebeirach* is a prayer for the individual and the community. It can be uttered amidst havoc or in calmness. It can be uttered aloud or in silence . . . in moments of joy and relief or in times of anguish and despair. There is room to be angry and still utter these words, affirming life and maintaining a connection to our ancestors who also felt anger.

In these moments of reflection, we are forced to face whatever obstacles are in the way of our living fully. While we know full well that healing of the body may not be a possibility, we know that healing of the soul has infinite possibilities. There are times when we feel like we are in the midst of a living nightmare. We cannot imagine that anything will ever look "right" again. At some point we must be willing to confront the pain, the enemy, and befriend it; that it become not only our teacher, but a teacher to all of those who are in our circle of life, our community. Jewish life was not meant for us to experience alone; not the joy and not the sorrow.

For those in need of healing, for those afraid to ask, and for the many for whom there is no one to ask, the *Mi Shebeirach* is for you. May the source of strength who blessed the ones before us, help us find the courage to make our lives a blessing, and let us say Amen.

Debbie Friedman is widely recognized as one of the most popular creators and performers of Jewish music in our time. She is a teacher who poignantly turns her concerts into deeply moving experiences of communal and personal healing. Debbie's music is performed in synagogues, schools, summer camps, and around holiday tables in Jewish homes all over the world. She has received countless awards for her pioneering role in contemporizing the language and music of faith, to broaden its appeal and to make it inclusive. With twenty recordings over the course of her nearly thirty-five year career, Debbie's music is living Judaism, music that gives voice to the soul.

an ineluctable feature of this physical creation. As the natural tendency of illness is to isolate, knowing that one is not the only one "singled out" for such hardship can in itself further spiritual healing.

Before Eve went into the hospital for surgery, she called me for counseling and support. Because she lived far away, I provided support by phone. At the end of our conversation, I asked her if she wanted to pray together. "That would be wonderful," she said. After a moment of centering silence, I offered the *Mi Shebeirach* prayer for her. When we were done, she told me that both her doctors were Jewish and asked if I would send them a copy of the *Mi Shebeirach*. After her surgery, Eve called to tell me that the operation had gone well. Immediately following the surgery, the doctors had buzzed the administrator from the operating room and requested that she bring in a copy of the *Mi Shebeirach*. Eve's two doctors then prayed on her behalf. When her husband described this final ritual of the operating room to Eve after she woke from surgery, she was deeply moved and grateful. (For more insight into the *Mi Shebeirach*, see the sidebar article by Debbie Friedman on page 178.)

OTHER JEWISH TOOLS

The Torah can be a source of healing for the spirit and psyche. Some rabbis "prescribe" sacred verses for use in mediation. For someone who is anxious about her self worth, a rabbi may recommend she sit quietly, breathe slowly, and for five minutes twice a day repeat this verse: *"Yismach Moshe b'matnat chelko;* Moses was satisfied with his portion." Or for fear, the last lines of *Adon Olam*: *"B'yado afkid ruchi, b'eit ishan, v'aira, v'im ruchi geviyati, Adonai li v'lo ira;* into God's hands I entrust my spirit, when I sleep and when I wake; and with my spirit and my body also, God is with me, I will not fear." Or for insecurity: *"Adonai karov l'chol korav, l'chol asher yikrauhu v'emet:* God is near to all who cry out to God, to all who cry out to God in truth." Or to enhance a sense of gratitude: *"Zeh ha'yom asah Adonai, nagila v'nism'cha vo;* This is the day that God has made; let us rejoice and be glad in it."

Rabbi Richard Levy of Los Angeles teaches the wisdom of writing the verse and affixing it where one will see it throughout the day: above one's desk, on the telephone key pad, on the dashboard. Meditation upon a verse of Torah, upon the *Sh'ma*, or upon Hebrew letters can calm the spirit, and bring it into communion with the Divine.

The Hasidim have historically made great use of the *niggun*, the wordless tune, which has become part of many healing services. By repeating a wordless tune over and over again, or one with nonsense syllables (like "Yai bai bai"), one can begin to still the mind and open the heart. Nonsense syllables are especially helpful, occupying the linear language-making part of our brains so that it is easier to let go of thoughts as they arise. The nonsense syllables function as a mantra whose message is that our being is greater than our thinking. (For more on chanting as a healing modality, see the sidebar article by Rabbi Shefa Gold on page 180.)

The psalms have been our primary devotional literature of healing. The rabbis have prescribed different lists of ten, eighteen, and thirty-six psalms to be recited at times of illness. These sacred verses invite the person reading them to identify with the psalmist in his pain and longing. Psalms of healing take the reader through a cycle of bewilderment, anguish, complaint, and renewed hope and faith. (For more on psalms and healing, see the sidebar article by Rabbi Rachel Cowan on page 181.)

Jewish tradition also offers active modes of spiritual healing. When the experience of illness compromises our sense of power, we need to feel that we are contributing to the good of the world by acts of *tzedakah* and *g'milut chasadim* (kindness). For the Jew, *tikun olam* (repair of the world) and *tikun hanefesh* (repair of the soul) are inseparable.

Taking part in Jewish communal life breaks the isolation that often accompanies illness. The mandate *"al tifrosh min hatzibur,* do not separate yourself from the community," is never more important than at a time of illness. Of course, this means that Jewish institutions must be especially responsive to the particular needs of Jews who are ill.

Eve, David, and Shoshanna are testimony to Judaism's richness and importance in helping bolster the spirit. Eve recovered beautifully, and now volunteers as a lay counselor with others who are struggling with cancer. Prior to David's death, he expressed enormous gratitude for the connection and warmth he felt from the Jewish community. Shoshanna continues to participate in healing services, has joined a synagogue, and participates in a women's Torah study group. In preparing for her own passing, she is guided by the wisdom of Jewish tradition. In a recent conversation, Shoshanna expressed her regret for not having actively brought up her children as Jews, adding: "I think it's not such a bad lesson to leave them with, after all, to see that their mother

CHANTING AS A HEALING MODALITY
Rabbi Shefa Gold

Chanting, the melodic repetition of a sacred phrase, is a way of transforming words of liturgy into doorways. They become entrances into expanded states of consciousness. From those expanded states, we can have access to the fullness of our power to bless and to heal, both ourselves and others. Rabbi Abraham Joshua Heschel says, "It is only after we kindle a light in the words that we are able to behold the riches they contain." We kindle a light in the words through careful and loving attention to breath, intention, meaning, sound, melody, harmony, tone, rhythm, and through the will to repeat a phrase long enough that a shift in consciousness can occur. We use chanting to open the center of the spirit and body within us, allowing the sounds to move through, transforming our small selves into radiating transmitters of God's love. Energy that is generated in the chant can then be focused and refined for healing.

The difference between chanting and singing is crucial. Chanting is primarily a meditative process. It requires an inward focus on the one hand, and a willingness to serve the group, on the other. This is especially important in the context of a prayer service. It is important to gradually connect one's solitary meditative practice with formalized communal prayer, so that the spiritual benefit from one can inform the other. By opening the heart, we find within ourselves more to give the group. And by becoming a servant to the group, we are given access to the deeper realms of our own hearts.

When the sound of the chant has ended, the most subtle, transformative, and powerful part of the experience can begin. By entering into the silence, we can receive both the Divine influx and the gifts that bubble up from the soul. The silence after the chant is a completely different yet complementary practice to the chant itself, allowing us to focus attention on the breath moving gently in and out. In the silence, the chanter has a new awareness, knowing that a heightened attention is necessary in order to enter through whatever doors have been opened by the power of the chant.

In Kabbalah we learn that there are four worlds: the physical world of action; the emotional world of expression, feeling, and creativity; the intellectual world of knowing; and the spiritual world of Being and connection. The chant becomes a healing force when all four worlds within the chanter are engaged. The chant vibrates through the body, opening up and enlivening the physical world. The emotions are reawakened through the building of intention. The world of knowing is revitalized through learning about the content and context of the sacred phrase. And the spiritual world is activated as our sense of separateness dissolves and we open up to the One through expanded states of consciousness. Through the practice of chant we can engage all our disparate parts at once, and become the vehicle for God's healing power.

Rabbi Shefa Gold is a leader in ALEPH: Alliance for Jewish Renewal and is the director of C-DEEP, The Center for Devotional, Energy and Ecstatic Practice in Jemez Springs, New Mexico. She received her ordination both from the Reconstructionist Rabbinical College and from Rabbi Zalman Schachter-Shalomi. Shefa composes and performs spiritual music, has produced nine albums, and her liturgies have been published in several new prayerbooks. She teaches workshops and retreats on the theory and art of chanting, devotional healing, spiritual community building, and meditation. Shefa combines her grounding in Judaism with a background in Buddhist, Christian, Islamic, and Native American spiritual traditions to make her uniquely qualified as a spiritual bridge celebrating the shared path of devotion.

found her own authentic way to Judaism in her fifties. Maybe they'll follow my example and find their own authentic Jewish paths as well."

RESOURCES

Arian, Merri Lovinger, ed. *R'fuah Sh'leimah: Songs of Jewish Healing.* New York: Synagogue 2000, 2002.

Moyers, Bill. *Healing and the Mind.* New York: Doubleday, 1993.

ON PSALMS AND HEALING
Rabbi Rachel Cowan

When my husband Paul was sitting in the hospital radiation room, deadly rays destroying his bone marrow and the leukemia cells hiding within, I read him psalms through the two-way intercom. He was terribly frightened. So was I. Alternating with the psalms I played him songs of the civil rights movement.

The civil rights songs were the voices of people of faith who risked their lives, secure in the belief that God would care for them. They brought Paul memories of the times in the Mississippi Delta when he too had been brave and overcame the fear of death. The psalms were a different kind of poetry, speaking to him in the echoes of the ancient language of his people. Somewhere back in biblical times, a psalmist had been terrified, and had found hope and strength from calling out to God.

After Paul died I found the Book of Psalms my greatest source of consolation. These poems are the most personal pieces of writing in the whole Bible. Amongst the 150 poems, I could find a psalm to reflect every mood. Reading them, I felt as if a friend were speaking personally to me — across 3000 years of human experience.

In Psalm 88, the writer protests to God:

Why Adonai, do You reject me, do You hide Your face from me?

When I felt alone — walking on a beach, or coming back to my empty apartment — I would sing out as loudly as I could, in my off-key voice *"Min ha metzar, karati yah"* — from the depths I called to God. At the time, all I could do was call. I could not hear an answer. Over time, it began to seem to me as if the calling out was in itself a kind of answer. The words no longer vanished into thin air, nor crashed against a stone wall. I felt better from calling. I felt heard. Then phrases from other psalms began to lodge in my imagination:

Psalm 42 reflects the swings of mood that I would so often feel:

Why so downcast my soul, why disquieted within me? Have hope in God; I will yet praise You, my ever-present help, my God.

And Psalm 30:

Adonai, I cried out and You healed me. Sing to Adonai all you faithful, Acclaiming Your holiness. Your anger lasts a moment; Your love is for a lifetime. Tears may linger for a night, but joy comes with the dawn.

But for me, the most extraordinary psalm of healing is the beloved Psalm 23. Like the others, it is written in the first person. It can both speak to deep pain, and provide hope. At Paul's funeral I was wrapped in the cantor's song — paradoxically devastated by the acknowledgment of loss which the psalm has come to mark, and yet comforted deeply by the words: *"Yea though I walk through the valley of death I will fear no harm, for thou art with me. Thy rod and thy staff, they comfort me."* Somehow, unbearable as Paul's death was, I would get through the pain. I would walk; I would experience goodness and mercy.

Perhaps the aspects of the psalms I love most — beyond the beauty of their words and images, beyond the lift my heart experiences when the congregation sings them together — is that they remain today a spiritual mirror. They still reflect back the joy and sorrow, the despair and yearning which Jews have known in their own hearts for thousands and thousands of years.

Rabbi Rachel Cowan is Director of The Institute for Jewish Spirituality in Northampton, MA, an organization that fosters growth and transformation of the Jewish soul through contemplative study, discussion and practice. She previously served as Director of the Jewish Life Program at the Nathan Cummings Foundation in New York. Rabbi Cowan received her rabbinic ordination from Hebrew Union College-Jewish Institute of Religion in 1989, and is a sought-after teacher, writer, and speaker.

Rabbi Nancy Flam is a pioneer in the field of Jewish healing. Having co-founded the Jewish Healing Center in 1991, she then directed the Jewish Community Healing Program of Ruach Ami: Bay Area Jewish Healing Center in San Francisco. She was Founding Director of the Institute for Jewish Spirituality, a retreat-based learning program for Jewish leaders, and now serves as its Co-Director of Programs. She has served as a consultant for Synagogue 2000 and the National Center for Jewish Healing.

Rabbi Flam earned her B.A. degree in Religion (Phi Beta Kappa, Summa cum Laude) from Dartmouth College in 1982, her M.A. degree in Hebrew Literature from the Hebrew Union College-Jewish Institute of Religion in 1986, and was ordained in 1989. She was trained in Clinical Pastoral Education (C.P.E.) at Lennox Hill Hospital, and has served as volunteer chaplain at Memorial Sloan Kettering Cancer Center and the Long Island College Hospital. She lectures widely on the topic of Judaism and Healing, and has written on the issue for numerous publications. Rabbi Flam lives in Northampton, Massachusetts with her husband and two children.

GLOSSARY

Aggadah – Ethical and moral teachings or stories and legends; sections of the Talmud and *midrashim* containing such

Ahavat Olam – morning prayer prior to the *Sh'ma* which denotes God's love of the people Israel

Ahavah Rabbah – evening prayer, with the same themes as *Ahavat Olam*

Al Cheit – confessional prayer recited in each *Amidah* of Yom Kippur

Aleinu – central prayer of the concluding part of the service

Aliyah (Aliyot, pl.) – honor of being called up to recite the Torah blessings

Amidah – core of the daily worship service

Ana B'cho'ach – Kabbalistic prayer

Aron HaKodesh – Ark of the Covenant

Ashamnu – confessional prayer

Ashkenazic – Jews of German or Central or East European ancestry

Ashrei – Psalm 145

Atarah – decorative neckband for the *tallit*

Aufruf – *aliyah* given a bridegroom prior to his wedding; blessing given to a couple prior to their wedding

Avneit – Torah belt or binder

Avodah – sacrificial service in the Temple and the special ritual for the Day of Atonement; contemporary usage: worship

Avot – the first blessing of the *Amidah*

Eitz Chayim (Atzei Chayim, pl.) – literally, tree of life; refers to the wooden roller(s) to which a Torah scroll is attached

Ba'al Korei – one who reads the Torah

Bar'chu – call to worship

Bar Mitzvah – literally, son of commandment; from the age of thirteen onward, one who is responsible for observing the commandments

Bat Mitzvah – literally, daughter of the commandment (see Bar Mitzvah)

Beit HaMikdash – the First or Second Temple in Jerusalem in biblical times

Beit Knesset (Batei Knesset, pl.) – synagogue(s)

Bimah – the raised platform for the Torah reading, located at the front or in the center of the sanctuary

B'reishit – first book of the Torah, Genesis

Birkat HaMazon – blessings after eating

Birchot HaShachar – the Morning Blessings

Brachah (Brachot, pl.) – blessing(s)

Brit Milah – circumcision, entering a son on his eighth day into the Covenant of Abraham

Chanukah – eight day festival celebrating the victory of the Maccabees

Chidur Mitzvah – to beautify ritual objects

Chilul HaShem – desecration of the Name (of God)

Chupah – wedding canopy

D'var Torah (Drash, Drashah, Drashot) – words of commentary, delivered in conjunction with the reading of the Torah portion

Duchen – to recite the priestly blessing as a *Kohen* from the *bimah*

Emet Ve'emunah – the prayer which comes after the *Sh'ma* in the evening service

Emet V'yatziv – the prayer which comes after the *Sh'ma* in the morning service

Erev Shabbat – Sabbath eve

Gabbai (Gabbaim, pl.) – functionary responsible for logistics in synagogue

Gematria – interpretations of a text based on numerical values of Hebrew letters

G'milut Chasidim – deeds of loving-kindness

G'vurot – second blessing of the *Amidah*, refers to God's greatness

Great Assembly – institution of the Second Temple period; was responsible for transmitting the oral tradition and made important contributions to the liturgy

Haftarah – reading from the Prophets or Writings, done in addition to the Torah reading

Haggadah – the book of the Passover *Seder* service

Hakafah (Hakafot, pl.) – the carrying of the Torah in a circuit around the synagogue

Halachah – Jewish law; sections of the Talmud or codes containing such

Hallel – psalms of praise recited on special occasions

Hasidism (Hasid, Hasidim, Hasidic) – religious movement founded in the eighteenth century; emphasizing joy in prayer

Hashkiveinu – second blessing after the *Sh'ma* in the evening service

Havdalah – ceremony to conclude the Sabbath and festivals

Hazzan (Hazzanim, pl. Hazzanut) – cantor(s), chanting

Hoshanna Rabbah – the seventh day of the feast of Sukkot

Kabbalah – Jewish mysticism

Kabbalat Shabbat – psalms and the *L'cha Dodi* which begin the Sabbath eve service

Kaddish – prayer praising God used in a variety of ways in Jewish liturgy

Karaites – Jewish sect (eighth century C.E.) which denied the authority of the Talmud

Kavanah – intention, devotion, concentration, or spontaneity of prayer

K'dushah – third paragraph of the morning *Amidah*, responsive litany recalling the angels praise of God

Keva – the fixed content and/or recitation of prayer

Kiddush – the blessing recited over wine

Kipah (Kipot, pl.) – head covering

Kohen (Kohanim, p.l.) – priest; descendant(s) of the tribe of Levi through Aaron

Kohen Gadol – High Priest

Kol Nidrei – part of the Yom Kippur liturgy, a declaration proclaiming all vows and obligations as null and void

Kotel – the western retaining wall of the Temple mount, built by Herod (first century B.C.E.)

Kriat HaTorah – the Torah service and reading

L'cha Dodi – liturgical poem, part of *Kabbalat Shabbat*

Levi (Levi'im, pl.) – descendant(s) of the tribe of Levi through Moses, assistants to the *Kohanim*

Ma'ariv – the evening service

Ma'ariv Aravim – prayer before the *Sh'ma* in the evening service, praises God for bringing on the evening

Machzor – cycle of prayers; originally used in place of *siddur*, but came to refer to the Rosh HaShanah and Yom Kippur prayerbook

Machzor Vitri – the prayerbook from the French community of Vitri, eleventh century

Mechitzah – a partition in the synagogue separating the men and women

M'eel – mantel, cloth cover of the Torah

Mezuzah – a handwritten parchment containing the first two paragraphs of the *Sh'ma*; placed in a case, it is affixed to the doorposts of Jewish homes

Mi Chamocha – two verses from the Song of the Sea describing Israel's redemption from Egypt

Midrash (Midrashim, pl.) – rabbinic writings which explain, explore, explicate the biblical text; stories, anecdotes, and allegories

Minchah – afternoon worship service

Minyan – a minimum of ten men required for a traditional prayer service

Mi Shebeirach – prayer asking God's blessing, often for the sick

Mishnah – codification of Jewish law, first part of the Talmud

Mitzvah (mitzvot, pl.) – commandment(s)

Mohel – individual trained to perform ritual circumcision

Motza'ay Shabbat – Saturday evening after Shabbat

Musaf – additional service for Shabbat and festivals

Ne'ilah – final service of Yom Kippur

Parashah (Parashiyot, pl.) – weekly Torah portion

Pirke Avot – Chapters, Sayings, or Ethics of the Fathers; a tractate of the Mishnah

Piyyut (Piyyutim, pl.) – *siddur* poetry

P'sukei d'Zimrah – literally, passages of song; psalms which introduce the morning service

Re'tzei – first of the final three *brachot* of the *Amidah*

Retzu'ah – the *tefillin* strap

Rimonim – finials which decorate the *atzei chayim*

Rosh HaShanah – Jewish New Year

Sandak – individual who holds the baby during the circumcision

Sanhedrin – assembly of Jewish elders which was the political, judicial, and religious authority during the Roman period

Sefer Torah (Sifrei Torah, pl.) – Torah Scroll(s)

Sephardic – pertaining to Jews whose ancestors came from Spain, Portugal, the Netherlands, the Balkans, and Mediterranean countries

Shabbat – Sabbath

Shabbat Kiddush – blessing over the wine on the Sabbath

Shacharit – morning service

Shaliach Tzibur – generic term for the person who leads the worship service

Shalom Rav – final blessing of the evening *Amidah*

Sh'ma Uvirchoteha – *Sh'ma* and its blessings

Sh'monah Esrei – the Eighteen Benedictions; *Amidah*; *Tefilah*

Shiva – initial seven day mourning period after burial of the deceased

Sh'lom Bayit – peace in the family

Shochet – ritual slaughterer

Shofar – ram's horn

Shomer Shabbat (Shomrei Shabbat, pl.) – one who is scrupulous in observing Shabbat

Siddur (Siddurim, pl.) – prayer book

Sim Shalom – final blessing of the morning *Amidah*

S'michah – rabbinical ordination

Tachanun – penitential prayers which are part of the weekday liturgy

Tallit (Tallitot, pl.) – prayer shawl

Talmud – Mishnah and Gemarah; compendia of Jewish law, legend, life, written in Palestine (first-fifth centuries C.E.) and Babylonia (first-sixth centuries C.E.)

Tanach – the Hebrew Bible; from an acronym for its three sections Torah, *Nevi'im* (Prophets), and *Ketuvim* (Writings)

Tefilah – prayer; the *Amidah;* the *Sh'monah Esrei*

Tefillin – phylacteries; two small leather boxes containing the *Sh'ma*, one strapped to the upper arm and the other for the forehead

Torah – Five Books of Moses in scroll form

Tzitzit – the fringes on the four corners of a prayer shawl

V'ahavta – the first paragraph of the *Sh'ma*

Yahrzeit – anniversary of a death

Yamim Nora'im – literally, the Days of Awe; Rosh HaShanah and Yom Kippur

Yetzer HaRa – the evil inclination

Yetzer HaTov – the good inclination

Yizkor – memorial service held on Pesach, Shavuot, Yom Kippur, and Sukkot

Yom HaAtzma'ut – Israel Independence Day

Yom Kippur – Day of Atonement

Yom Yerushalayim – day commemorating the reunification of Jerusalem

Yotzer Or – morning prayer which focuses on God's role as the creator of light

Zechut Avot – merit of the Fathers

Zohar – Kabbalistic work which is a commentary on the Torah and other books of the Bible

APPENDIX A

PRODUCED AND DIRECTED BY JOEL LURIE GRISHAVER

Connie: Welcome back. My name is Connie Kaufman. I am a tenth grader in the confirmation class at Temple Brit Kodesh and this is "God Talk." Tonight's topic is Jewish Mysticism and we are very lucky to have three very special guests with us. First, we have Rabbi Simeon bar Yochai, one of the Judean scholars of the second century who is reputed to be the author of that major mystical work — the Zohar. Rabbi Simeon, we are glad that you could join us tonight.

Rabbi Simeon: Thank you Connie. I don't go out very often, but I am really glad to be able to join you.

Connie: Our second guest is Isaac Luria, the great mystical scholar of the sixteenth century. Rabbi Luria was born in Jerusalem, studied in Egypt, and then taught in the holy city of Safed. Rabbi Luria, thank you for coming.

ABOUT THE AUTHOR

Joel Lurie Grishaver is the author of *Sh'ma is for Real* and other innovative materials.

The Ari: Thanks, Connie, but most people call me the Ari.

Connie: Doesn't Ari mean lion?

The Ari: Yes it does, but people used to call me the Ashkenazic Rabbi Isaac. If you take the first letter of each word, you come out with Ari.

Connie: Thank you, Rabbi Isaac, it's nice to have you hear. Our third guest is Rabbi Israel Baal Shem Tov, the rounder of chasidic Judaism. Rabbi Israel, would you tell us about your name?

The Besht: Connie, I assume that you don't want to know about the name Israel, which God gave Jacob when he wrestled with the angel, but about my title as *Baal Shem*. *Baal Shem* means a person who knows or is master of the Name; that is, God's secret name. As a *Baal Shem*, I used my knowledge of the Name to help people, so they called me the Baal Shem Tov, the Master of the Good Name. But usually we shorten that to the Besht.

Connie: If you used this name to work special favors for people, didn't that make you a magician? Is Jewish mysticism just a Jewish kind of magic?

The Besht: Not at all, Connie. Each of us is really trying to get to know God. To reach a kind of unity with God where we can understand the highest truths. None of us is trying to do it for ourselves, but because we believe by doing so we make the world a better place.

Connie: I'm not sure I understand how it works.

The Ari: Let me help you. A scientist spends a long time studying and trying to solve problems. When a scientist finds an answer that no one before has ever found, he or she can use that information to help all people, even if no one else can understand the scientist's work. We are like that; we are looking into the secrets of the world and creation by coming to understand the Creator.

Connie: I sort of understand, but how

is this different from sorcery or witch-craft?

Rabbi Simeon: What all of us are trying to do is bring the Messiah and bring the world and all people to their redemption. We are not trying to change things or break the patterns of nature, but rather we are trying to help humanity reach its highest potential — just like it teaches in the Torah.

Connie: I'm still not sure I understand, but let's try to explore this question from another angle. Could each of you tell us about one mystical experience you have had?

Rabbi Simeon: Once the Romans wanted to put me and my son Rabbi Eleazer to death. We hid in a cave for twelve years. God caused a well to spring forth and a carob tree to grow to give us sustenance. For twelve years, we did nothing but pray and study Torah. We never left the cave. When Elijah the prophet told us that it was safe, we came out and saw people plowing fields and sowing seeds. I got very angry because they were engaged in the work of this world when they could have been studying, preparing for the eternal life. Then God got mad at me and sent me back into the cave saying: "Have you emerged to destroy my world?" We spent another year in the cave and came out to find a man preparing for Shabbat by carrying two bundles of myrtle and a sweet-smelling herb which smelled like it had come from the Garden of Eden. At that moment, we understood the real meaning of all this.

Connie: I'm not sure I understand.

Rabbi Simeon: In my day, Jewish mystics talked about things like the chariot, the palace, and the throne. Each of these metaphors represented the levels that brought you near to God. The chariot took you from earth to heaven. Then you had to enter God's palace, and work your way room by room towards the throne room. Once you made it to the throne room, you had to work your way up step by step, curtain by curtain, till you were near God's Presence. Do you understand?

Connie: Not really.

Rabbi Simeon: We have to move step by step, insight by insight, secret by secret towards God. When my son and I came out of the cave for the second time, we suddenly understood that you don't have to leave this world in order to reach God, but rather you move through these steps by total understanding of this life. That is what that sweet herb taught us.

Connie: So you're saying that really understanding life is reaching God.

Rabbi Simeon: Yes, that is part of it.

Connie: Rabbi Isaac, how about your story?

The Ari: When I was eight years old, my father died, and my mother and I moved to Egypt so my uncle could help with my education. In a few years, I had learned all that the sages in Egypt could teach me, so I went to a distant region of the Nile and began spending time alone in study and meditation. Every night, when I fell asleep, my soul left my body and was guided by Metatron, one of the divine angels, to the academies of Rabbi Eliezer, or Rabbi Akiba, or Rabbi Simeon bar Yochai, and in this way I learned the secrets of the universe.

Connie: Rabbi Isaac, can you reveal any of these secrets?

The Ari: Connie, part of it I can explain to you. You've got to imagine that the world is full of divine sparks — sparks of God, sparks of truth and good hidden in everyone and everything. Our job is to find these sparks and free them. If we can find the good, the beauty, the holiness in everyone and everything and unify all of them, then we bring the world to the kind of peace and justice God wanted for it. We have to learn how to find and hold these special sparks. Those were the secrets I was learning.

Connie: So our job is to find and gather these holy moments. Rabbi Israel, perhaps you have a story for us?

The Besht: Certainly. Every time I take

a walk through the woods or in a field, I have a mystical experience. Just living is a mystical experience. I remember one Friday night we had a minyan of my students at our house. In our celebration of Shabbat we all began to dance in a circle. My wife opened the kitchen door and saw us dancing in a circle of fire. The power of friendship, our love for one another, and the power of our celebration was that strong. Now friendship, that is real mystical power. Does that help you understand?

Connie: You mean that simple things can be profound.

The Besht: Exactly. We can find God and come to understand life with song and dance, with celebration, with love and friendship. By loving people, we learn how to love God. It doesn't always take laws and rules and study. As we become the best people we can be, we make the world a better place. That is mysticism.

Connie: We have heard a lot about dreams and caves, sparks and castles, and the experiences all of you have had with God. We have only a few minutes left. Do you think you could give our readers some practical suggestions about how to find God?

The Besht: Celebrate life, like yourself, and find the specialness of everything God created.

The Ari: Jews aren't mystics by themselves. Find some friends and share your insights. Help each other. Collect your sparks together.

Rabbi Simeon: Find a teacher from whom you can learn, one who can teach you both by example and knowledge. The Jewish mystical tradition is very deep, and there are lots of steps to understand, some of which you can find on your own, but much of which takes a guide.

Connie: Thank you, gentlemen; we are out of time. You have left us with a lot to think about . . .

BIBLIOGRAPHY

SIDDURIM

Abrams, Judith Z. *Selichot: A Family Service.* Rockville, MD: Kar-Ben Copies, Inc., 1990.

Abrams, Judith Z. and Paul J. Citrin, eds. *Gates of Repentance for Young People.* New York: Central Conference of American Rabbis, 2002.

Birnbaum, Philip, ed. *Daily Prayer Book: Ha-Siddur Ha-Shalem.* New York: Hebrew Publishing Company, 2002.

Cahan, Leonard, ed. *Siddur Sim Shalom for Shabbat and Festivals.* Rev. ed. New York: The Rabbinical Assembly, 1998.

Gates of Awe: Holy Day Prayers for Very Young Children. New York: Central Conference of American Rabbis, 1991.

Gates of Prayer for Young People: Services for Shabbat and Weekdays. New York: Central Conference of American Rabbis, 1997.

Gates of Wonder: A Prayerbook for Very Young Children. New York: Central Conference of American Rabbis, 1990.

Greenberg, Sidney and D. Levine, eds. *Mahzor Hadash: The New Mahzor for Rosh Hashanah and Yom Kippur.* Bridgeport, CT: The Prayer Book Press, 1978.

———. *Likrat Shabbat: Worship, Study, and Song for Sabbath and Festival Services and for the Home.* Bridgeport, CT: The Prayer Book Press, 1973.

———. *Siddur Hadash: Worship, Study, and Song for Sabbath and Festival Mornings.* Bridgeport, CT: The Prayer Book Press, 1992.

Hertz, Joseph H. *The Authorised Daily Prayer Book,* Revised Edition. New York: Bloch Publishing Company, 1975.

Hirsch, Samson Raphael, trans. *The Hirsch Siddur.* New York: Feldheim Publishers, 1982.

Kol Haneshamah: Shabbat Eve. Wyncote, PA: The Reconstructionist Press, 1989.

Levy, Richard N., ed. *On Wings of Awe: A Mahzor for Rosh Hashanah and Yom Kippur.* Washington, DC: B'nai B'rith Hillel Foundations, 1985.

———. *On Wings of Light: The Hillel Siddur for Kabbalat Shabbat and Shabbat Evening.* Washington, DC: Hillel: The Foundation for Jewish Campus Life, 2000.

Prager, Marcia. *A Siddur for Shabbat Morning.* N.p., n.d. Also available is a *siddur* for Friday night. Available from ALEPH: Alliance for Jewish Renewal, http://www.aleph.org.

Scherman, Nosson and Meir Zlotowitz, eds. *The Complete Artscroll Siddur.* Brooklyn, NY: Mesorah Publications, Ltd., 1989.

Siegel, Daniel, ed. *Siddur Kol Koreh.* N.P., n.d. Available from ALEPH: Alliance for Jewish Renewal, http://www.aleph.org.

———. *Siddur Kol Koreh Resource Companion.* N.P., n.d. Available from ALEPH: Alliance for Jewish Renewal, http://www.aleph.org.

Stern, Chaim, ed. *Gates of Prayer for Shabbat & Weekdays: A Gender-Inclusive Edition.* New York: Central Conference of American Rabbis, 2000.

———. *Gates of Prayer: The New Union Prayerbook for Weekdays, Sabbaths and Festivals.* New York: Central Conference of American Rabbis, 1996.

———. *Gates of Repentance: The New Union Prayerbook for the Days of Awe – Gender Inclusive Edition.* New York: Central Conference of American Rabbis, 1999.

Stern, Chaim, comp. and trans. *Paths of Faith: The New Jewish Prayer Book for Synagogue and Home.* New York: S.P.I Books, 2003.

Teutsch, David A., ed. *Kol Haneshamah: Shabbat Vehagim.* Elkins Park, PA: The Reconstructionist Press, 2002.

Wolfe-Blank, David. *Meta Siddur: Recipes for Jewish Renewal.* N.P., n.d. Available from ALEPH: Alliance for Jewish Renewal, http://www.aleph.org.

Zaslow, David, ed. *Ivdu Et Hashem B'Simcha: Serve the Holy One with Joy!* N.p., n.d. Available from ALEPH: Alliance for Jewish Renewal, http://www.aleph.org.

JEWISH PRAYER

The following books provide a comprehensive overview of Jewish prayer and are recommended for the teacher.

Cohen, Jeffrey. *Blessed Are You: A Comprehensive Guide to Jewish Prayer.* Northvale, NJ: Jason Aronson, Inc., 1993.

Donin, Hayim Halevy. *To Pray as a Jew: A Guide to the Prayer Book and the Synagogue Service.* New York: Basic Books, 1980.

Elbogen, Ismar. *Jewish Liturgy: A Comprehensive History.* Philadelphia, PA: The Jewish Publication Society of America/The Jewish Theological Seminary of America, 1993.

Garfiel, Evelyn. *Service of the Heart: A Guide to the Jewish Prayer Book.* Northvale, NJ: Jason Aronson Inc., 1999.

Hammer, Reuven. *Entering Jewish Prayer: A Guide to Personal Devotion and the Worship Service.* New York: Schocken Books, 1994.

Harlow, Jules. *Pray Tell: A Hadassah Guide to Jewish Prayer.* Woodstock, VT: Jewish Lights Publishing, 2003.

Idelsohn, Abraham Z. *Jewish Liturgy and Its Development.* New York: Dover Publications, Inc., 1995.

Jacobson, B.S. *The Weekday Siddur: An Exposition and Analysis of Its Structure, Contents, Language and Ideas.* Tel Aviv: Sinai Publishing, 1978.

Millgram, Abraham. *Jewish Worship.* Philadelphia, PA: The Jewish Publication Society of America, 1971.

Nulman, Macy. *The Encyclopedia of Jewish Prayer: Ashkenazic and Sephardic Rites.* Northvale, NJ: Jason Aronson Inc., 1995.

Steinsaltz, Adin. *A Guide to Jewish Prayer.* New York: Schocken Books, 2000.

OTHER RESOURCES

Adler, David A. *A Children's Treasury of Chassidic Tales,* adapted from S.Y. Zevin's *A Treasury of Chassidic Tales.* Brooklyn, NY: Mesorah Publications, Ltd., 1983.

Alexy, Trudi. *The Mezuzah in the Madonna's Foot: Marranos and Other Secret Jews — A Woman Discovers Her Spiritual Heritage.* San Francisco, CA: Harper SanFrancisco, 1994.

Berman, Melanie. *Parts of the Synagogue: A Primary Instant Lesson.* Los Angeles, CA: Torah Aura Productions, 1988.

Bialik, Hayim Nahman and Yehoshua Hana Ravnitzky, eds. *The Book of Legends: Sefer Ha-Aggadah.* New York: Schocken Books, 1992.

Bokser, Ben Zion. *The Siddur: The Prayerbook.* Springfield, NJ: Behrman House Inc., 1983.

Brichto, Mira Pollak. *The God Around Us: A Child's Garden of Prayer, Revised Edition.* New York: UAHC Press, 1999.

Bronstein, Herbert, ed. *A Passover Haggadah: The New Union Haggadah.* New York: Central Conference of American Rabbis, 1974.

Brooten, Bernadette J. *Women Leaders in the Ancient Synagogue: Inscriptional Evidence and Background Issues.* Brown Judaica Studies 36. Chico, CA: Scholars Press, 1982.

Building Jewish Life: Synagogue (Activity Book). Los Angeles, CA: Torah Aura Productions, 1991.

Buber, Martin and Olga Marx. *Tales of the Hasidim, Vol. 2: Later Masters.* New York: Randon House, 1961.

Cohen, Arthur A. and Paul Mendes-Flohr, eds. *Contemporary Jewish Religious Thought.* New York: Free Press, 1988.

Coles, Robert. *The Spiritual Life of Children.* Boston, MA: Houghton Mifflin, 1990.

Cooper, David A. Cooper, David A. *The Handbook of Jewish Meditation Practices: A Guide for Enriching the Sabbath and Other Days of Your Life.* Woodstock, VT: Jewish Lights, 2000.

————. *God Is a Verb: Kabbalah and the Practice of Mystical Judaism.* New York: Riverhead Books, 1997.

Davis, Avram, ed. *Meditation from the Heart of Judaism: Today's Teachers Share Their Practices, Techniques and Faith.* Woodstock, VT: Jewish Lights, 1997.

Davis, Eli and Elise Davis. *Hats and Caps of the Jews.* Jerusalem: Massada Ltd. Publishers, 1983.

de Breffny, Brian. *The Synagogue.* New York: Macmillan Publishing Co., Inc., 1978.

de Saint-Cheron, Philippe-Michael and Elie Wiesel. *Evil & Exile.* Notre Dame, IN: University of Notre Dame Press, 1990.

Earthworks Group. *50 Simple Things You Can Do To Save the Earth*. Second edition. Berkeley, CA: Bathroom Reader Press, 1995.

Edwards, Michelle. *Blessed Are You*. New York: Lothrop, Lee & Shepard Books, 1993.

Eglash, Joel , ed. *The Complete Shireinu: 350 Fully Notated Jewish Songs*. New York: Transcontinental Music Publications, 2001.

Eilberg-Schwartz, Howard. *People of the Body: Jews and Judaism from an Embodied Perspective*. Albany, NY: State University of New York Press, 1992.

Eisenstein, Ira, et al. A Minyan of Opinions of "Kingship" as a Metaphor of Prayer. *Reconstructionism Today*. Autumn, 1993: 11-15.

Eisenstein, Judith Kaplan. *Heritage of Music: The Music of the Jewish People*. Wyncote, PA: The Reconstructionist Press, 1990.

Encyclopaedia Judaica. Jerusalem: Keter Publishing House Jerusalem Ltd., 1972.

Falk, Marcia. *The Book of Blessings*. Boston, MA: Beacon Press, 1999.

Feuer, Rabbi Avrohom Chaim. *Shemoneh Esrei: The Amidah/The Eighteen Blessings*. Brooklyn, NY: Mesorah Publications, Ltd., 1990.

Gackenbach, Dick. *Harry and the Terrible Whatzit*. Boston, MA: Houghton Mifflin Company, 1984.

Gamoran, Hillel. *The Jewish Law Review Vol. II: The Mishnah's Laws of Lost and Found*. Los Angeles, CA: Torah Aura Productions, 1991.

Gates of Song: Music for Shabbat. New York: Transcontinental Music Publications, 1987.

Gates of the House: The New Union Prayerbook. New York: Central Conference of American Rabbis, 1977.

Gefen, Nan Fink. *Discovering Jewish Meditation: Instruction and Guidance for Learning an Ancient Spiritual Practice*. Woodstock, VT: Jewish Lights, 1999.

Gerber, Jane S. *Jews of Spain: A History of the Sephardic Experience*. New York: Free Press, 1994.

Gillman, Neil. *Sacred Fragments: Recovering Theology for the Modern Jew*. Philadelphia: Jewish Publication Society, 1990.

Ginzburg, Louis, ed. *The Legends of the Jews*. Philadelphia, PA: Jewish Publication Society of America, 2002.

Gold, August and Matthew J. Perlman. *Where Does God Live?* Woodstock, VT: Skylight Paths Publishing, 2001.

Gold, Yeshara. *Hurry, Friday's a Short Day: One Boy's Erev Shabbat in Jerusalem's Old City*. Brooklyn, NY: Mesorah Publications, Ltd., 1986.

Goodman, Robert. *Teaching Jewish Holidays: History, Values, and Activities*. Denver, CO: ARE Publishing, Inc., 1997.

Goodman, Roberta Louis and Sherry H. Blumberg, eds. *Teaching about God and Spirituality*. Denver, CO: A.R.E. Publishing, Inc., 2002.

Gordis, Daniel. *Becoming A Jewish Parent: How To Explore Spirituality And Tradition With Your Children*. New York: Harmony Books, 1999.

Greene, Jacqueline Dembar. *Butchers and Bakers, Rabbis and Kings*. Rockville, MD: Kar-Ben Copies, Inc., 1984.

Greenspan, Jay Seth. *Hebrew Calligraphy: A Step-by-Step Guide*. New York: Schocken Books, 1981.

Grishaver, Joel Lurie. *And You Shall Be a Blessing: An Unfolding of the Six Words that Begin Every Brakhah*. Northvale, NJ: Jason Aronson Inc., 1993.

————. *19 Out of 18: The All New Shema Is for Real Curriculum*. Los Angeles, CA: Torah Aura Productions, 1991.

Grishaver, Joel Lurie and Scott Bolton. *Think Prophets*. Instant Lessons. Los Angeles, CA: Torah Aura Productions, 2000.

Groner, Judye, and Madeline Wikler. *Thank You God!* Rockville, MD: KarBen Copies, 1993.

Guide to the Treasures of the Temple Exhibition. Jerusalem: The Temple Institute, n.d.

Hample, Stuart and Eric Marshall, eds. *Children's Letters To God: The New Collection*. New York: Workman Publishing, 1991.

Handelman, Maxine Segal. *Jewish Every Day: The Complete Handbook for Early Childhood Teachers*. Denver, CO: A.R.E. Publishing, Inc. 2000.

Hirsh, Marilyn. *The Rabbi and the Twenty-nine Witches*. New York: Scholastic Book Services, 1976.

Hoban, Russell. *Bedtime for Frances*. New York: Harper Trophy, 1995.

Hoffman, Lawrence A., ed. *Gates of Understanding 2: Appreciating the Days of Awe*. New York: Central Conference of American Rabbis, 1984.

Hoffman, Lawrence A. *The Art of Public Prayer: Not for Clergy Only*. Woodstock, VT: Sky Light Paths Publishing, 1999.

———. *My People's Prayer Book: Traditional Prayers, Modern Commentaries. Volume 1 — The Sh'ma and Its Blessings*. Woodstock, VT: Jewish Lights Publishing, 1997.

———. *My People's Prayer Book: Traditional Prayers, Modern Commentaries. Volume 2 —The Amidah*. Woodstock, VT: Jewish Lights Publishing, 1998.

———. *My People's Prayer Book: Traditional Prayers, Modern Commentaries. Volume 3 — P'sukei D'zimrah (Morning Psalms)*. Woodstock, VT: Jewish Lights Publishing, 1999.

———. *My People's Prayer Book: Traditional Prayers, Modern Commentaries. Volume 4 — Seder K'riat Hatorah (The Torah Service)*. Woodstock, VT: Jewish Lights Publishing, 2000.

———. *My People's Prayer Book: Traditional Prayers, Modern Commentaries. Volume 5 — Birkhot Hashachar (Morning Blessings)*. Woodstock, VT: Jewish Lights Publishing, 2001.

———. *My People's Prayer Book: Traditional Prayers, Modern Commentaries. Volume 6 — Tachanun and Concluding Prayers*. Woodstock, VT: Jewish Lights Publishing, 2002.

———. *My People's Prayer Book: Traditional Prayers, Modern Commentaries. Volume 7 — Shabbat at Home*. Woodstock, VT: Jewish Lights Publishing, 2003.

———. *The Way into Jewish Prayer*. Woodstock, VT: Jewish Lights Publishing, 2000.

Hoffman, Lawrence A. and Janet R. Walton, eds. *Sacred Sound and Social Change*. Notre Dame, IN: University of Notre Dame Press, 1992.

Isaacs, Ron H., and Kerry M. Olitzky. *A Jewish Mourner's Handbook*. Hoboken, NJ: Ktav Publishing House, Inc., 1991.

Jacobs, Louis. *The Book of Jewish Belief*. New York: Behrman House, Inc., 1984.

———. *Hasidic Prayer*. New York: Schocken Books, 1987.

Kadden, Barbara Binder and Bruce Kadden. *Teaching Mitzvot: Concepts, Values, and Activities*. Revised Edition. Denver, CO: A.R.E. Publishing, Inc., 2003.

Kadushin, Max. *The Rabbinic Mind*. New York: Bloch Publishing Company, 1972.

Kanof, Abram. *Jewish Ceremonial Art and Religious Observance*. New York: Harry N. Abrams, Inc., n.d.

Kaplan, Aryeh. *Jewish Meditation*. New York: Schocken, 1985.

Karkowsky, Nancy. *Grandma's Soup*. Rockville, MD: Kar-Ben Copies, Inc., 1989.

Kerdeman, Deborah and Lawrence Kushner. *The Invisible Chariot: An Introduction to Kabbalah and Jewish Spirituality*. Denver, CO: A.R.E. Publishing, Inc, 1986.

Kolatch, Alfred J. *This Is the Torah*. Middle Village, NY: Jonathan David Publishers, Inc., 1994.

———. *Who's Who in the Talmud*. Middle Village, NY: Jonathan David Publishers, Inc., 1964.

Kops, Simon. *Fast, Clean and Cheap or EVERYTHING the Jewish teacher (or parent) needs to know about ART*. Los Angeles, CA: Torah Aura Productions, 1989.

Kushner, Harold S. *When Bad Things Happen to Good People*. New York: Avon, 2001.

———. *When Children Ask About God: A Guide for Parents Who Don't Always Have All the Answers*. New York: Schocken Books, 1995.

Kushner, Lawrence and Karen Kushner. *Because Nothing Looks Like God*. Woodstock, VT: Jewish Lights Publishing, 2000.

Lamm, Maurice. *The Jewish Way in Death and Mourning*. Revised and Expanded Edition. New York: Jonathan David Publishers, 2000.

Laytner, Anson. *Arguing with God: A Jewish Tradition*. Northvale, NJ: Jason Aronson Inc., 1998.

Leibowitz, Nehama. *Studies in Devarim: Deuteronomy*. Jerusalem: The World Zionist Organization, 1980.

Liss-Levinson, Nechama. *When a Grandparent Dies: A Kid's Own Remembering Workbook for Dealing With Shiva and the Year Beyond*. Woodstock, VT: Jewish Lights Publishing, 1995.

Loeb, Sorel Goldberg and Barbara Binder Kadden. *Teaching Torah: A Treasury of Insights and Activities*. Denver, CO: ARE Publishing, Inc., 1997.

Magnus, Joann. *An Artist You Don't Have To Be! A Jewish Arts and Crafts Book*. New York: UAHC Press, 1990.

Maimonides, Moses. *The Commandments, vol. 1*. New York: Soncino Press, 1967.

Mayer, Mercer. *There's a Nightmare in My Closet*. New York: Dial Publishing, 1968.

Montefiore, C.G. and H. Loewe. *A Rabbinic Anthology*. New York: Schocken Books, 1987.

Motzkin, Linda. *Aleph Isn't Tough: An Introduction to Hebrew for Adults*. New York: UAHC Press, 2000.

Moyers, Bill. *Healing and the Mind*. New York: Doubleday, 1993.

Musikant, Ellen and Sue Grass. *Judaism Through Children's Books: A Resource for Teachers and Parents*. Denver, CO: ARE Publishing, Inc., 2001.

Newman, Shirley. *An Introduction to Kings, Later Prophets and Writings*. West Orange, NJ: Behrman House, Inc., 1981.

Oberman, Sheldon. *The Always Prayer Shawl*. Honesdale, PA: Boyds Mills Press, 1994.

Olitzky, Kerry M. *Jewish Paths Toward Healing and Wholeness*. Woodstock, VT: Jewish Lights Publishing, 2000.

Olitzky, Kerry and Ronald H. Isaacs. *The Second How-To Handbook of Jewish Living*. Jersey City, NJ: KTAV Publishing House Inc., 1996.

Person, Hara. *The Mitzvah of Healing: An Anthology of Essays, Jewish Texts, Personal Stories, Meditations and Rituals*. New York: UAHC Press, 2003.

Petuchowski, Jakob J. *Prayerbook Reform in Europe: The Liturgy of European Liberal and Reform Judaism*. New York: The World Union for Progressive Judaism, Ltd., 1968.

———. *Understanding Jewish Prayer*. New York: Ktav Publishing House, Inc. 1972.

Pinkwater, Daniel. *Bare-Knuckled Rituals: A Look at How Jewish Ceremonies Speak to Us*. Instant Lesson. Los Angeles, CA: Torah Aura Productions, 1989.

Plaskow, Judith. *Standing Again at Sinai: Judaism From a Feminist Perspective*. San Francisco, CA: Harper-Collins Publishers, 1990.

Plaut, W. Gunther, ed. *The Torah: A Modern Commentary*. New York: UAHC Press, 1981.

Polish, Daniel F. *Bringing the Psalms to Life: How to Understand and Use the Book of Psalms*. Woodstock, VT: Jewish Lights Publishing, 2000.

———. *Keeping Faith with the Psalms: Deepen Your Relationship with God Using the Book of Psalms*. Woodstock, VT: Jewish Lights Publishing, 2003.

Portnoy, Mindy Avra. *Ima on the Bimah: My Mommy Is a Rabbi*. Rockville, MD: Kar-Ben Copies, Inc., 1986.

Prager, Marcia. *The Path of Blessing: Experiencing the Energy and Abundance of the Divine*. New York: Bell Tower, 1998.

Prusan, Peretz. *A Guide to Hebrew Lettering*. New York: UAHC Press, 1981.

Ray, Eric. *Sofer: The Story of a Torah Scroll*. Los Angeles, CA: Torah Aura Productions, 1986.

Reif, Stefan C. *Judaism and Hebrew Prayer: New Perspectives on Jewish Liturgical History*. Cambridge, England: Cambridge University Press, 1995.

Reiss, Fred. *The Standard Guide to the Jewish and Civil Calendars*. West Orange, NJ: Behrman House, Inc., 1986.

Rose, Or. *God in All Moments: Mystical and Practical Spiritual Wisdom from Hasidic Masters*. Woodstock, VT: Jewish Lights Publishing, 2003.

Rosenblum, Richard. *The Old Synagogue*. Philadelphia, PA: The Jewish Publication Society of America, 1989.

Rose, Shirley. *Let's Discover the Bible*. Set 2. Springfield, NJ: Behrman House Inc., 1997.

Rosenzweig, Franz. *The Star of Redemption*. Boston, MA: Beacon Press, 1972.

Rosman, Moshe. *Founder of Hasidism: A Quest for the Historical Ba'al Shem Tov*. Berkeley, CA: The University of California Press, 1996.

Rossel, Seymour. *A Child's Bible Book 2: Lessons from the Prophets and Writings*. Springfield, NJ: Behrman House Inc., 1989.

Rossoff, Donald. *The Perfect Prayer*. New York: URJ Press, 2003.

Rowe, Alan. *The Well Dressed Torah: A Primary Instant Lesson*. Los Angeles, CA: Torah Aura Productions, 1986.

Saltzman, Shulamit. "Movement of Prayer." In *The Second Jewish Catalog*, compiled and edited by Sharon Strassfeld and Michael Strassfeld. Philadelphia, PA: The Jewish Publication Society of America, 1976.

Sasso, Sandy Eisenberg. *Cain and Abel: Finding the Fruits of Peace*. Woodstock, VT: Jewish Lights Publishing, 2001.

———. *God's Paintbrush*. Woodstock, VT: Jewish Lights Publishing, 1992.

———. *God Said Amen.* Woodstock, VT: Jewish Lights Publishing, 2000.

———. *In God's Name.* Woodstock, VT: Jewish Lights Publishing, 1994.

———. *What is God's Name?* Woodstock, VT: Jewish Lights Publishing, 1999.

Schachter-Shalomi, Zalman. *Paradigm Shift.* Northvale, NJ: Jason Aronson, 1993.

———. *Wrapped in a Holy Flame: Tales and Teachings of the Hasidic Masters.* San Francisco, CA: Jossey-Bass, 2003.

Schechter, Solomon. *Aspects of Rabbinic Theology: With a New Introduction by Neil Gillman, Including the Original Preface of 1909 and the Introduction by Louis Finkelstein.* Woodstock, VT: Jewish Lights Publishing, 1999.

Schwartz, Amy. *Mrs. Moskowitz and the Shabbat Candlesticks.* Philadelphia, PA: The Jewish Publication Society of America, 1983.

Schwartz, Howard. *Elijah's Violin and Other Jewish Fairy Tales.* San Francisco, CA: Harper & Row, 1983.

Sher, Nina Streisand and Margaret Feldman. *100+ Jewish Art Projects for Children.* Denver, CO: ARE Publishing, Inc., 1996.

Shuart, Adele. *Signs in Judaism: A Resource Book for the Jewish Deaf Community.* New York: Bloch Publishing Company, 1986.

Sh'ma: a Journal of Jewish Responsibility. 22/436 September 4, 1992.

Siegel, Adam and Ruby G. Strauss. *Let's Discover the Synagogue.* Springfield, NJ: Behrman House, Inc., 1997.

Siegel, Richard; Michael Strassfeld; and Sharon Strassfeld, eds. *The First Jewish Catalog.* Philadelphia, PA: The Jewish Publication Society of America, 1973.

Silver, Cherie Ellowitz. *Pass the Torah, Please: Jewish Leaders from Mattathias to Saadia.* Denver, CO: A.R.E. Publishing, Inc., 1990.

Spector, Shmuel, ed. *The Encyclopedia of Jewish Life Before and During the Holocaust.* Washington Square, NY: New York University Press, 2001.

Steinberg, Milton. *Basic Judaism.* New York: Harcourt Brace Jovanovich, 1975.

Steinbock, Steven E. *The Gift of Wisdom: The Books of Prophets and Writings.* New York: UAHC Press, 2001.

Stern, Chaim, ed. *On the Doorposts of Your House: Prayers and Ceremonies for the Jewish Home.* New York: CCAR Press, 1994.

Strassfeld, Sharon and Michael Strassfeld, eds. *The Second Jewish Catalog.* Philadelphia, PA: The Jewish Publication Society of America, 1976.

Syme, Daniel B. *The Jewish Home: A Guide for Jewish Living.* New York: UAHC Press, 1988.

Syme, Deborah Shayne. *Partners.* New York: UAHC Press, 1990.

Synagogue 2000. *Itinerary for Change: Prayer.* Los Angeles, CA: Synagogue 2000, 2002.

Tallit: An Instant Lesson. Los Angeles, CA: Torah Aura Productions, 1986.

The Talmud: The Steinsaltz Edition, Vol. 1: Tractate Bava Metzia, Part 1. New York: Random House, 1989.

Techner, David and Judith Hirt-Manheimer. *A Candle for Grandpa.* New York: UAHC Press, 1993.

Thompson, Marlena C. and Susan Van Dusen. *Let's Discover God.* Springfield, NJ: Behrman House, Inc., 1988.

Twersky, Isadore, ed. *A Maimonides Reader.* New York: Behrman House, Inc., 1989.

Umansky, Ellen M. and Dianne Ashton, eds. *Four Centuries of Jewish Women's Spirituality: A Sourcebook.* Boston, MA: Beacon Press, 1992.

Ungerleider-Mayerson, Joy. *Jewish Folk Art from Biblical Days to Modern Times.* New York: Summit Books, 1986.

Van Dusen, Susan and Marc Berkson. *The Synagogue: House of the Jewish People.* Springfield, NJ: Behrman House, Inc., 1999.

Viorst, Judith. *The Tenth Good Thing about Barney.* New York: Atheneum Books, 1971.

Waddell, Martin. *Can't You Sleep Little Bear?* Cambridge, MA: Candlewick Press, 1992.

Weber, Vicki L. and Scott E. Blumenthal. *Let's Discover Shabbat.* Springfield, NJ: Behrman House, Inc., 2004.

Weiner, Shohama Harris and Jonathan Omer-Man, eds. *Worlds of Jewish Prayer: A Festschrift in Honor of Rabbi Zalman M. Schachter-Shalomi.* Northvale, NJ: Jason Aronson, 1993.

Wiesel, Elie, and Albert H. Friedlander. *The Six Days of Destruction: Meditations toward Hope.* New York: Paulist Press, 1988.

Wigoder, Geoffrey, ed. *Jewish Art and Civilization.* Fribourg, Switzerland: Chartwell Books, Inc., 1972.

Wigoder, Geoffrey. *The Story of the Synagogue: A Diaspora Museum Book.* San Francisco, CA: Harper & Row, 1986.

Wolfson, Ron. *A Time to Mourn, A Time to Comfort: A Guide to Jewish Bereavement and Comfort.* Woodstock, VT: Jewish Lights Publishing, 1996.

Wolpe, David J. *Teaching Your Children About God: A Modern Jewish Approach.* New York: Henry Holt and Company, 1993.

Zwerin, Raymond A. and Audrey Friedman Marcus. *Shabbat Can Be.* New York: UAHC Press, 1979.

STUDENT TEXTS AND ADDITIONAL RESOURCES

Berman, Melanie. *Building Jewish Life: Prayers and Blessings.* Los Angeles, CA: Torah Aura Productions, 1991.

Building Jewish Life: Rosh Ha-Shanah Mahzor. Los Angeles, CA: Torah Aura Productions, 1988.

Building Jewish Life: Synagogue Activity Book. Los Angeles, CA: Torah Aura Productions, 1991.

Building Jewish Life: Yom Kippur Mahzor. Los Angeles, CA: Torah Aura Productions, 1988.

Ehrlich, Carl S. and Michal Shekel. *Exploring the Prayer Book II (Reform).* Hoboken, NJ: Ktav Publishing House, Inc., 1986.

———. *Understanding the Siddur II (Conservative).* Hoboken, NJ: Ktav Publishing House, Inc., 1986.

Fields, Harvey J. *B'chol L'vavcha.* Revised edition. New York: UAHC Press, 2001.

A Gateway To Prayer: The Shabbat Morning Service Book I: The Shema and the Amidah. Springfield, NJ: Behrman House, Inc., 1989.

A Gateway To Prayer: The Shabbat Morning Service Book II: The Torah Service and Concluding Prayers. Springfield, NJ: Behrman House, Inc., 1989.

Grishaver, Joel Lurie. *Shema Is for Real: A Book on Prayers & Other Tangents.* Los Angeles, CA: Torah Aura Productions, 1993.

———. *Basic Berakhot.* Los Angeles, CA: Torah Aura Productions, 1988.

———. *Building Jewish Life: The Siddur Commentary.* Los Angeles, CA: Torah Aura Productions, 1992.

———. *19 Out of 18: The All New Shema is for Real Curriculum.* Los Angeles, CA: Torah Aura Productions, 1991.

———. *Shema & Company.* Los Angeles, CA: Torah Aura Productions, 1989.

Harlow, Jules, ed. *Companion Siddur.* Conservative Edition. Springfield, NJ: Behrman House, Inc., 1993.

———. *The High Holy Days Mahzor: A Prayer Service for Young Children and Their Families.* Springfield, NJ: Behrman House, Inc., 1990.

———. *The Shabbat Morning Service Book 1: The Shema & Its Blessings.* Springfield, NJ: Behrman House, Inc., 1985.

———. *The Shabbat Morning Service Book 2: The Shabbat Amidah.* Springfield, NJ: Behrman House, Inc., 1986.

———. *The Shabbat Morning Service Book 3: The Torah Service & Selected Additional Prayers.* Springfield, NJ: Behrman House, Inc., 1987.

Karp, Laura. *Student's Encounter Book for When a Jew Prays.* Springfield, NJ: Behrman House Inc., 1975.

Kaye, Terry. *Hineni 1: The New Hebrew Through Prayer.* Springfield, NJ: Behrman House, Inc., 2004.

———. *Hineni 2: The New Hebrew Through Prayer.* Springfield, NJ: Behrman House, Inc., 2004.

———. *Hineni 3: The New Hebrew Through Prayer.* Springfield, NJ: Behrman House, Inc., 2004.

Maiben, Dina and Hillary Zana. *Z'man L'Tefilah: The Time for Prayer Program Book 1: B'rachot.* Denver, CO: A.R.E. Publishing, 1998.

———. *Z'man L'Tefilah: The Time for Prayer Program Book 2: Sh'ma.* Denver, CO: A.R.E. Publishing, 1998.

———. *Z'man L'Tefilah: The Time for Prayer Program Book 3: Amidah.* Denver, CO: A.R.E. Publishing, 1999.

———. *Z'man L'Tefilah: The Time for Prayer Program Book 4: Torah.* Denver, CO: A.R.E. Publishing, 2000.

Miller, Deborah Uchill. *My Siddur: A Prayer Readiness Book.* Springfield, NJ: Behrman House, Inc., 1984.

Moskowitz, Nachama Skolnik. *A Bridge to Prayer: The Jewish Worship Workbook Volume One: God, Prayer, and the Shema.* New York: UAHC Press, 1988.

———. *A Bridge to Prayer: The Jewish Worship Workbook Volume Two: The Amidah, Torah Service, and Concluding Prayers.* New York: UAHC Press, 1989.

———. *A Teacher's Guide to A Bridge to Prayer: The Jewish Worship Workbook Volumes One-Two.* New York: UAHC Press, 1989.

Raphael, Chaim. *Kabbalat Shabbat: The Sabbath Evening Service.* Springfield, NJ: Behrman House, Inc., 1985.

Rossel, Seymour. *When a Jew Prays.* Springfield, NJ: Behrman House, Inc., 1973.

Rowe, Debi M. *Introduction to the Siddur Vol. 1: The Brakhah System.* Los Angeles, CA: Torah Aura Productions, 1990.

———. *Introduction to the Siddur Vol. 2: The Shema & Its Blessings.* Los Angeles, CA: Torah Aura Productions, 1991.

———. *Introduction to the Siddur Vol. 3: The Amidah, The Torah Service & Concluding Prayers.* Los Angeles, CA: Torah Aura Productions, 1992.

The Shabbat Morning Service Book 2: The Shabbat Amidah. Springfield, NJ: Behrman House, Inc., 1986.

Siegel, Seymour and David Bamberger. *Teaching Guide for When a Jew Prays.* Springfield, NJ: Behrman House, Inc., 1973.

Stern, Chaim, ed. *Companion Siddur.* Reform Edition. Springfield, NJ: Behrman House, Inc., 1993.

Stern, Shirley. *Exploring the Prayer Book I.* (Reform). Hoboken, NJ: Ktav Publishing House, Inc., 1983.

———. *Understanding The Siddur I.* (Conservative). Hoboken, NJ: Ktav Publishing House, Inc., 1984.

Tallit: An Instant Lesson. Los Angeles, CA: Torah Aura Productions, 1986.

Weisser, Michael. *My Synagogue.* Springfield, NJ: Behrman House, Inc., 1984.

Zimmerman, Sheldon. *The Family Prayerbook. Volume 3: Shabbat.* New York: Rossel Books, Inc., 1992.

AUDIOVISUAL

20 Israeli Folk Dances for Young Children, Part A. Adi Sulkin-Vardit Publications. Audiocassette.

Arian, Merri Lovinger. *R'fuah Sh'leimah: Songs of Jewish Healing.* Los Angeles, CA: Synagogue 2000, 2002. Songbook. Available from Transcontinental Music Publications.

———. *Nefesh: Songs for the Soul.* Los Angeles, CA: Synagogue 2000, 2002. Compact disc.

Beged Kefet. *Beged Kefet: The First Album!* Livingston, NJ: Beged Kefet, 1987. Compact disc or audiocassette. Available from Sounds Write Productions, Inc.

Benson, Bruce. *The Jazz Service.* Oakland, CA: Bensongs, 1986. Compact disc and audiocassette. Available from Sounds Write Productions, Inc.

———. *Ki Sarita.* Oakland, CA: Bensongs. Compact disc and audiocassete. Available from Sounds Write Productions, Inc.

Black, Rabbi Joe. *Aleph Bet Boogie.* Albuquerque, NM: Lanitunes Music, 1991. Compact disc. Available from A.R.E. Publishing, Inc.

Celebrate With Us: Shabbat, Chanukah, Passover. San Diego, CA: Jewish Family Productions, 2003. Two compact disc set. Available from A.R.E. Publishing, Inc.

The Complete NFTY Recordings: 1972-1989. New York: Transcontinental Music Publications, 2003. Five compact disc set. Available from Transcontinental Music Publications.

The Corridor: Death. Teaneck, NJ: Ergo Media Inc., 1989. Videocassette, 25 minutes, not rated.

Fiddler on the Roof. RCA Cassette #OK-1005; CD #RCDI-7060.

For Out of Zion. Teaneck, NJ: Ergo Media Inc., 1973. Videocassette, 15 minutes, not rated.

Friedman, Debbie. *And You Shall Be a Blessing.* San Diego, CA: Sounds Write Productions, Inc., 1989. Compact disc. Available from A.R.E. Publishing, Inc.

———. *Debbie Friedman Live at the Del.* San Diego, CA: Sounds Write Productions, Inc., 1990. Compact disc. Available from A.R.E. Publishing, Inc.

———. *In The Beginning.* San Diego, CA: Sounds Write Productions, Inc., 1994. Three compact disc set. Available from A.R.E. Publishing, Inc.

———. *Shirim Al Galgalim: Songs on Wheels*. San Diego, CA: Sounds Write Productions, Inc., 1995. Compact disc. Available from A.R.E. Publishing, Inc.

———. *The World of Your Dreams*. San Diego, CA: Sounds Write Productions, Inc., 1993. Compact disc and songbook. Available from A.R.E. Publishing, Inc.

Glaser, Sam. *A Day In The Life*. Los Angeles, CA: Glaser Musicworks, 1994. Compact disc. Available from A.R.E. Publishing, Inc.

———. *The Bridge*. Los Angeles, CA: Glaser Musicworks, 2002. Compact disc. Available from A.R.E. Publishing, Inc.

———. *Presence*. Los Angeles, CA: Glaser Musicworks, 2003. Compact disc. Available from A.R.E. Publishing, Inc.

Hirschhorn, Linda. *Gather Round: Songs of Celebration and Renewal*. Berkeley, CA: Oyster Albums, 1989. Compact disc, audiocassette, and songbook. Available from Sounds Write Productions, Inc.

Israeli Folkdances. Israel Yakovee. Audiocassette.

Klepper, Jeff and Jeff Salkin. *Bible People Songs*. Denver, CO: A.R.E. Publishing, Inc., 1981. Audiocassette/songbook set. Available from A.R.E. Publishing, Inc.

Klepper, Jeffrey and Susan Nanus. Especially Jewish Symbols. Denver, CO: A.R.E. Publishing, Inc., 1977. Audiocassette/songbook set.

Kol B'Seder. *Snapshots: The Best of Kol B'Seder Vol. 1*. West Roxbury, MA: Kol B'Seder, 2004. Compact disc. Available from A.R.E. Publishing, Inc.

———. *Songs for Growin'*. New York: Transcontinental Music Publications, 2001 Compact disc and songbook. Available from A.R.E. Publishing, Inc.

Mah Tovu. *Days of Wonder, Nights of Peace*. Springfield, NJ: Behrman House, Inc., 2001. Compact disc and activity booklet

———. *Only This*. Denver, CO: Mah Tovu, 1996. Compact disc. Available from A.R.E. Publishing, Inc.

———. *Turn It*. Denver, CO: Mah Tovu, 2001. Compact disc. Available from A.R.E. Publishing, Inc.

Paley, Cindy. *Shabbat Shalom*. Sherman Oaks, CA: Cindy Paley Aboody, 1989. Compact disc and audiocassette/songbook set. Available from Sounds Write Productions, Inc.

———. *A Singing Seder*. Sherman Oaks, CA: Cindy Paley Aboody. Compact disc. Available from Sounds Write Productions, Inc.

Parashah: Chanting Your Torah and Haftarah Portion. New York: Transcontinental Music Publications. Audiocassettes. Available from Transcontinental Music Publications.

Poisson, Jeremy. *Hineni 1 Interactive CD*. Springfield, NJ: Behrman House, Inc., 2004.

Preparing for Your Bar Mitzvah/Bat Mitzvah. Seattle, WA: Mitzvah-Vision. Instructional videotapes. Available from MitzvahVision.

Raiders of the Lost Ark. 1981, 115 minutes, rated PG. DVD or videocassette. Available from video stores.

Recht, Rick. *Shabbat Alive*. St. Louis, MO: Vibe Room Records/Banana Head Publishing, 2001. Compact disc. Available from A.R.E. Publishing, Inc.

Richards, Stephen, ed. *Manginot: 201 Songs for Jewish Schools*. New York: Transcontinental Music Publications, 1992.

Ruach 5761: new Jewish tunes. New York: Transcontinental Music Publications, 2003. Compact disc and songbook.

Ruach 5763: new Jewish tunes. New York: Transcontinental Music Publications, 2003. Compact disc and songbook.

Schachet-Briskin, Wally. *The Cantor Wally Songbook*. Northridge, CA: Six Point Productions, 1997. Available at www.cantorwally.com.

Shalom of Safed. Teaneck, NJ: Ergo Media Inc., 1969. Videocassette, 30 minutes, not rated.

Shir Hadash. *And You Shall Teach Your Children*. Vancouver, BC: Shir Hadash, 1990. Compact disc and audiocassette. Available from Sounds Write Productions, Inc.

———. *Or Shalom*. Vancouver, BC: Shir Hadash, 1987. Compact disc and audiocassette. Available from Sounds Write Productions, Inc.

Shir L'Yom Chadash: A Song for a New Day. San Francisco, CA: UAHC Camp Institutes for Living Judaism Camp Newman, 1999. Compact disc. Available from Sounds Write Productions, Inc.

Shir Mi-libeinu: A Song From Our Heart. San Francisco, CA: UAHC Camp Institutes for Living

Judaism Camp Swig, 1984. Compact disc. Available from Sounds Write Productions, Inc.

Silver, Julie. *From Strength to Strength*. Newton Highlands, MA: A Silver Girl Production, 1993. Compact disc. Available from A.R.E. Publishing, Inc.

Simon, Jon. *New Traditions*. Bethesda, MD: Silver Lining Records, 1988. Compact disc. Available from Sounds Write Productions, Inc.

———. *New Traditions 2*. Bethesda, MD: Silver Lining Records. Compact disc. Available from Sounds Write Productions, Inc.

Sounds of Creation/Sounds of Freedom. San Diego, CA: Sounds Write Productions, Inc., 1991. Compact disc and/or songbook. Available from A.R.E. Publishing, Inc.

Stanislow, Sunita. *City of Gold*. Minneapolis, MN: Maxemilian Productions, 1997. Compact disc. Available from http://www.musicmax.com.

Symphony No. 3 *Kaddish* by Leonard Bernstein. Israel Philharmonic Orchestra. Deutsche Grammophon. Compact Disc #423582-2-GH.

Taubman, Craig. *The Best of the Rest*. Los Angeles, CA: Craig 'n Company, 2003. Compact disc and songbook. Available from A.R.E. Publishing, Inc.

———. *Friday Night Live*. Sherman Oaks, CA: Sweet Louise Productions, 1999. Compact disc and songbook. Available from A.R.E. Publishing, Inc.

———. *One Shabbat Morning*. Sherman Oaks, CA: Sweet Louise Productions, 2002. Compact disc and songbook. Available from A.R.E. Publishing, Inc.

Tiferet, Hanna. *I Am My Prayer: The Hanna Tiferet Songbook*. Boston, MA: Hanna Tiferet, n.d. Available from http://www.hannatiferet.com.

Tov Lanu Lashir: It is Good for Us to Sing. San Francisco, CA: UAHC Camp Institutes for Living Judaism Camp Swig, 1975. Compact disc. Available from Sounds Write Productions, Inc.

Trop Trainer. Key West, FL: Kinnor Software. Available from www.kinnor.com.

Wrapped: The How and Why of Tallit and Tefillin. Teaneck, NJ: Ergo Media Inc., 2001. Videocassette, 31 minutes, not rated. Available in traditional and egalitarian versions.

AUDIOVISUAL DISTRIBUTORS

Adi Sulkin-Vardit
3 Pilichovsky St.
Ramat Aviv, Israel 69341

A.R.E. Publishing, Inc.
6708 E. 47th Avenue Drive
Denver, CO 80216-3409
(800) 346-7779
FAX (303) 322-7400
http://www.arepublish.com

Behrman House, Inc.
11 Edison Place
Springfield, NJ 07081
(800) 221-2755
FAX (973) 379-7280
http://www.behrmanhouse.com

Ergo Media Inc.
P.O. Box 2037
Teaneck, NJ 07666-1437
(201) 692-0404
http://www.jewishvideo.com

Kinnor Software
1415 Alberta Street
Key West, FL 33040
(305) 293-8801
FAX (305) 293-8803
http://www.kinnor.com

Maxemilian Productions
www.musicmax.com

MitzvahVision
2214 Crescent Drive
Seattle, WA 98112
chermer@pipeline.com

Wally Schachet-Briskin
4718 Lemona Avenue
Sherman Oaks, CA 91403-2008
(818) 995-5778
FAX (818) 995-1975
http://www.cantorwally.com

Hanna Tiferet Siegel
FAX (617) 363-0371
http://www.hannatiferet.com
HannaTiferet@verizon.net

Sounds Write Productions, Inc.
6685 Norman Lane
San Diego, CA 92120
(800) 9-SOUND-9
FAX (619) 697-6124
http://www.soundswrite.com

Transcontinental Music Publications
633 Third Avenue
New York, NY 10017
(800) 455-5223
FAX (212) 650-4109
http://www.transcontinentalmusic.com

Israel Yakovee
Woodland Hills, CA
(818) 340-7654
iyakovee@yahoo.com

OTHER TITLES IN THE A.R.E. TEACHING SERIES

Each title in this ever-expanding series features useful background and concepts, laws and traditions, ceremonies and observances specific to their topic. Hundreds of imaginative activities for all grade levels, for family education, for assemblies, and for all-school projects make each volume indispensable. These books are the ultimate reference library for Jewish teachers!

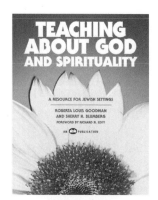

TEACHING ABOUT GOD AND SPIRITUALITY

by Roberta Louis Goodman and Sherry H. Blumberg

The ultimate source book on . . . the Ultimate

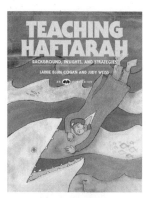

TEACHING HAFTARAH

by Lainie Blum Cogan and Judy Weiss

An essential companion volume to Teaching Torah

TEACHING JEWISH HOLIDAYS

by Robert Goodman

The consummate encyclopedia of holiday activities

TEACHING JEWISH LIFE CYCLE

by Barbara Binder Kadden and Bruce Kadden

Celebrate Jewish life!

TEACHING JEWISH VIRTUES

by Susan Freeman

Mastering middot and becoming a mensch . . .

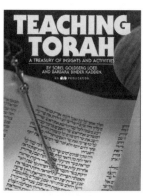

TEACHING MITZVOT

by Barbara Binder Kadden and Bruce Kadden

An exceptional guide to learning and teaching about mitzvot – newly revised!

TEACHING TORAH

by Sorel Goldberg Loeb and Barbara Binder Kadden

A teacher's bible for teaching the Five Books of Moses

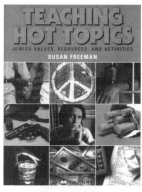

TEACHING HOT TOPICS

by Susan Freeman

Comprehensive and informative — fascinating texts and engaging activities bring complex issues to life

Available from:

A.R.E. Publishing, Inc. ◆ 6708 E. 47th Avenue Drive ◆ Denver, Colorado 80216-3409
Toll-free (800) 346-7779 ◆ In Colorado (303) 322-7400 ◆ FAX (303) 322-7407
E-mail: orders@arepublish.com ◆ On the Web at www.arepublish.com